An A to Z of
Sporting Collectibles

Pitch Publishing Ltd
A2 Yeoman Gate
Yeoman Way
Durrington
BN13 3QZ

Email: info@pitchpublishing.co.uk
Web: www.pitchpublishing.co.uk

First published by Pitch Publishing 2021
Text © 2020 Carl A. Wilkes

1

Carl A. Wilkes has asserted his right in accordance with the Copyright, Designs and Patents Act 1988 to be identified as the author of this work.

All rights reserved. No part of this publication may be reproduced, stored in a retrieval system, or transmitted in any form or by any means, electronic, mechanical, photocopying, recording or otherwise, without the prior permission in writing of the publisher and the copyright owners, or as expressly permitted by law, or under terms agreed with the appropriate reprographics rights organization. Enquiries concerning reproduction outside the terms stated here should be sent to the publishers at the UK address printed on this page.

The publisher makes no representation, express or implied, with regard to the accuracy of the information contained in this book and cannot accept any legal responsibility for any errors or omissions that may be made.

A CIP catalogue record for this book is available from the British Library.

13-digit ISBN: 9781785316739
Design and typesetting by Olner Pro Sport Media - www.olnerpsm.co.uk
Printed by Replika Press, India.

An A to Z of
Sporting Collectibles
Priceless Cigarette Cards and
Sought-after Sports Stickers

CARL WILKES

Acknowledgements

Dedicated to Joss

In 2016, a holiday with Joss led to the writing of this and the previous tome. It's fair to say that without her neither book would be. Reams of notes & photos which had been collected during the previous decades would have become no more than lost data on failed floppy discs, corrupted CDs & bit-decayed hard drives.

Paper books and paper photos will last longer than electronic storage of the same!

Thanks to all the buyers of the previous book: you made this one possible.

Dearest thanks to Potter, a buzz to Bee, Graham & Jayne
Special thanks to James Cotton, the curator of vintagefootballers.com
Jim Donnelly, the curator of *The Unofficial Liverpool Football Club Museum*
Roger Pashby, the curator of *1920s Heaven* and other blogs on cards
& especially to Alan Jenkins for *Football Cartophilic Info Exchange*.

Thank you very much to Matthew Stevens
Dan Castledine and Florian Rosenlehner
Martin Horton and Nik Yeomans.

Particular thanks to The Lioness.

Thanks to all of the contributors on this writer's social media soccer cards channels.

Thanks to Jane and Paul at Pitch Publishing for wanting to publish the book
Thanks to Duncan, Matt & Ciaran at Olner Pro-Sport Design, for its beauty.

In memoriam

Football-mad uncles Saddler *Berk* Wilkes & Villain Sam Harvey of Aldridge CC
Nan & Elsie Wilkes for the first cards & stickers

&
the cats.

Carl Wilkes

Introduction

Nicki Lauda rookie, 1974

James Hunt on a French card from 1978

Sports cards are both attractive collectibles and great investments. In the last three decades soaring values for rare sports cards have outperformed gold, house prices and the stock market. A soccer card which changed hands for just $75 in 1999 sold for $75,000 in 2020. Baseball cards which cost $,3000 in 1987 have since resold for $3 million! The very same cards had cost less than a penny each to buy when they were new. That's an investment beyond the wildest of dreams. It's also an investment in something beautiful.

This book illustrates and evaluates sporting trade cards and sports trading cards of yesteryear, from golf to tennis, athletics to cricket, rugby to soccer; from equestrian events to motor car racing and many more sports besides. It highlights which cards will probably be the next winners; the next cards to skyrocket in value. In pointing readers towards vintage sports cards which remain, by and large, available and affordable it serves as an invaluable guide to tomorrow's treasures.

This writer has a track record of spotting the right sports cards. Since the 1990s, card collectors have been buying recommended cards and profiting from them. All of the cards this writer has reviewed favourably have gone up in value – bar none! Collectors from as far afield as Wales and West Virginia have benefitted from recommendations made in his journal, *Football Card Collector Magazine*, and in his previous book, *An A-Z of Football Collectibles, Priceless Cigarette Cards and Sought-after Stickers*.

In these pages, readers will be introduced to specialist auction houses, such as Loddon and Tim Davidson, and to trustworthy sellers of rare cards, like Martin Horton. Readers will learn where to buy, for less, and how to sell, for more. Further, readers will become acquainted with the art of rookie-card alchemy. In recent years, the earliest cards of famous sports stars have netted card miners a fortune. The mining of rookie cards is an art rather than hard work. How to turn leaden cards into golden rookies will be revealed. Moreover, non-rookie rare cards are an unrealised resource. They remain undervalued. This book shows where to find tomorrow's treasures.

Sports cards were first published in Great Britain. The earliest cards were made in England, at the end of the 1870s, and the first stickers to show sports stars were made in Scotland, in 1914. Such cards and stickers are now produced all around the world. Some of them sell for millions! Yesterday's parental advice such as, *'don't waste your money on stickers'*, or, *'put your pocket money in a piggybank; don't waste it on bubblegum cards'*, was well meant but staid thinking. Recent sales, enormous prices and champagne-quaffing profit takers have proven naysayers to be wrong.

By 1880, the earliest sports cards were already in circulation, having been produced by match-ticket printers, such as Williamson of Aston. They were given away as promotional gifts with products like soap; and by merchants such as milliners and boot makers. Hoteliers bought bespoke cards and distributed them to attract guests for high tea. Football match results would be telegraphed in to hotel tea rooms which were crammed full of eager supporters awaiting news of their sporting wagers. The cards were also used as badges to show the wearer's allegiance. An article in a Leeds newspaper, from 1884, refers to a crowd at a match wearing *football cards* of team favourites and star players in their hatbands. Other cards were made as buttonhole badges, with a stem to slip through apertures in clothing fabric. They showed club colours and famous players.

During the early–1880s sports cards came to be sold in surprise packets, inside sealed envelopes, much like today's stickers. By the end of the decade they were also packaged with tobacco, used as decorative supports to stiffen paper packets so that cigarettes should remain unbroken. Later on, they were given with chocolate and comics, with foodstuffs and other merchandise.

When sealed packets of trading cards first appeared, in the early–1880s, they introduced a thrill to buying and collecting. With a sealed packet the buyer knew not which cards were inside. Hope and risk made sealed packets fun and they remain driving factors behind such purchases. The hope of finding star players and favourite teams balances the risk of getting the

1920s Italian trade card

same cards over again. Spare cards become currency in acquiring wanted cards from friends – swaps. Sealing cards in surprise packets was smart marketing.

Packets of sports cards were first made by John Baines, a Bradford-based merchant well ahead of his time. Baines sold packets of sports cards 80 years before Panini! Though the Italian firm is these days credited, wrongly, with inventing packets of football cards they were, in fact, made in Bradford as early as 1884. Producers around the world continue to sell such packets of cards and stickers today so Baines started a multi-billion dollar industry which has lasted 150 years.

The printers of the nineteenth century could not have imagined what they were starting when they published the world's first sports cards. They were made not only by John Baines but also by Sharpe of Bradford, Richardson's of Leeds and Ormerod Brothers of Rochdale, to name but a trio of his earliest rivals. Some of the cards made by these firms have breached the five-figure mark and one or two are set to go higher still!

Historically, long before the internet and some decades before television, trade cards were the industrial world's pocket encyclopaedia. They covered just about every subject, including every sport, and they came to be collected and saved as a pictorial reference source. Homes would keep a box full of old cards for the facts and images found on them. Family forebears passed them on, as heirlooms, to beneficiaries by whom more cards were added. Millions of households around the world came to possess a collection of family scrapbooks bulging with small picture cards collected by previous generations. Unlike the internet, however, whose search results are at the mercy of very powerful interest groups by whom enormous influence is brought to bear on what search engines do and do not reveal, not to mention the order in which results are shown, the subjects seen on cards are not easily filtered away to suit commerce or prevailing political mores and social trends. It's not possible to *edit* the past when it comes to vintage ephemera, such as trade cards. This is one of the reasons old cards are sought by archives, reference libraries and museums worldwide, not to mention myriad collectors. Moreover, old trade cards and rare vintage stickers, unlike *fiat* money and newly made cards and stickers, cannot be reprinted at will; and they do not devalue like paper money does. Due to their innate scarcity, values for rare vintage cards have been on an upwards curve for decades.

Like trade cards, trading cards have been around for a long time. Trade cards are cards given by a trade, a type of business, to advertise products. On the other hand, trading cards are primarily sold as gaming cards to collect and to play with; to swap with friends and to fight over; and, above all, to encourage further sales to complete collections. Like trade cards, trading cards may well show a brand name, or advertise a trade, but advertising is not their *raison d'être*. Their reason for being is to encourage buyers to buy more of them. It was not just children who fought over the cards. Newspaper articles from the 1880s reveal disputes between rival sellers of packets of football cards; retailers taking each other to court!

Vintage sports cards are tomorrow's treasures yet there are relatively few such cards available. Once they are gone they rarely return to the market, with the exception of cards which have been *mined* and *flipped*. That is, cards which were bought at low prices, repackaged, then remarketed aggressively at inflated prices. This is called card flipping and it usually involves something known as *slabbing*, which is the sealing of a card in a soft plastic bag within an almost indestructible, sealed plastic box. Some collectors don't seem to mind

7-times world champion billiards star Joyce Gardner, 1935

INTRODUCTION

Puskás on a West German gum card by Heuinerle, 1960

but others hate the oily-waste material plastic which entombs cards forever. Either way, it's become part of cards culture thanks to plastics-industry marketing and cold-eyed business from a cabal of baseball card *couturiers*. These days, there are often more buyers than there are rare cards so there is a huge demand, even for cards you can no longer touch! In fact, one firm in USA does not want its buyers to possess their cards at all. It keeps them in a vault even after buyers pay thousands for them. Well, it's actually a lock-up storage facility but vault sounds better. The clever business encourages buyers to be satisfied with seeing their cards remotely, online. Well, it takes all types!

New buyers may not know how or where best to search for and buy rare cards. This book will help. Some collectors buy from auctions after bidding against other bidders to secure a card, while others join networks of collectors. Some buyers prefer to deal directly with one reputable seller; others rummage through stalls at antique markets and collectors shops. The recommended sellers section in this book is not to be missed.

In 2020, two particularly rare soccer cards, made in 1958, sold in auction for around $250,000 each. Both auction results were emblematic of rookie-card alchemy, which readers will learn in this book. The cards had cost their sellers only a tiny fraction of the amount they sold for. In the 1990s few people had known of or wanted such cards. Less still had been willing to pay more than $100 for them. Today it's all different with the top sellers applying rookie-card alchemy and netting themselves a fortune. With the help of this book, the reader will be able to do similar *magic*, by finding today's low-cost cards of yore and by preparing them for greatness, and great returns.

Just a few years ago, rare soccer cards were where most of the cards in this book find themselves now: affordable and available. Only two decades ago the rarest basketball cards were not costly but a basketball card of LeBron James recently sold for about $2 million! In 2020, it was the turn of soccer cards to rise dramatically in value.

Had you bought a Pelé card by Bremer Kaffee or Alifabolaget, in the year 2000, you would have probably paid less than $100 for each card. Although the Bremer cards were next to impossible to find, it was possible; and you certainly could have found examples of the Alifabolaget card with relative ease. Today, the same cards are impossible to come by and each example in very good condition or better may net you $100,000.

Like the 1952 Topps Gum card of Mickey Mantle, which was worth $3,000 in the 1980s, and is now worth $3 million, rare soccer cards are on a similarly steep curve skywards. Since the time of the first book, *An A-Z of Football Collectibles, Priceless Cigarette Cards and Sought-after Stickers*, in 2019, cards which were quite easily available have quickly become hard or impossible to find. For example, just two years before the book was printed a buyer could find an internet auction full of affordable 1960s Italian cards of world greats, for very little money. It's no longer so. In just five years the everyday has become exotic, and often quite costly.

The values of cards of other sports, as introduced in this book, remain available and affordable at the time of printing but they may soon follow soccer, baseball and basketball cards into the profit stratosphere. Readers must remember that most of the other sports cards featured in this book, excepting American sports and cards with golf subjects, are presently valued at roughly where vintage soccer cards were valued two decades ago. Athletics cards, tennis cards, rugby cards and cricket cards, etc have been slowly rising in value but a surge in prices may happen at any time. All it takes is a handful of new collectors. Within no time the few surplus cards presently available will be snapped up. The resulting paucity of available cards will inevitably drive values higher. Some of the cards may eventually become as scarce as the most desirable cards in soccer and baseball.

It is important for the reader to understand that nothing in this book is meant as financial advice. Although the value of antique cards has risen for as long as anyone can remember a buyer may lose money by buying badly, especially when buying contemporary cards. If you feel a card is very rare and it's affordable you may want to take a risk but if you are unsure about what you are doing, especially if you cannot afford to spend the household's budget on a long shot, think twice! Be very wary of paying a lot for anything made since 1990. Cards made before 1970 are safer bets, and those from before 1960 are safer still.

The chapters and appendices in this book will guide readers around present prices and the availability of thousands of rare sports cards. Towards the end of the book, the Soccer Cards Rarity Scale is the world's first guide to the scarcity of vintage soccer cards. The appendices in this book will inform readers on rookie-card alchemy and specific soccer cards, such as the *real* Beckham rookie cards.

CASA DA MOEDA DO BRASIL

Ordem nº 754.494   Nº 079400

AN A TO Z OF **SPORTING COLLECTIBLES**

Angling on cigarette and non-tobacco trade cards

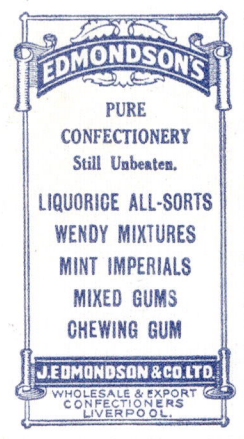

Edmondson's *Popular Sports*

Liam Devlin *Irish Fishing* card

A damp towpath alongside a canal somewhere near the south Staffordshire Doomsday Book settlement of Pelsall was where this writer had his first piscatorial experience, and, not least, where he netted his first fishing trade cards. The rod was cast during Christmastide 1982. On St Stephen's Day, following a hearty luncheon of turkey pie and white wine – only the second of the two days in the year when alcohol was permitted to be served at home – newly gifted tackle was freed of its Yuletide wrapping paper, and a family group traipsed out into the grey daylight, towards the rich fishing grounds of a nearby canal. Surely this would trump going to swampy ponds, in summertime, with day-glow coloured nylon nets shouldered on bamboo sticks. It was, after all, grown-up fishing. With a brother, carrying his new rod, fresh tackle and lively, squirming maggots; aside an uncle who wore an oversized winter overcoat, and mocked Wenceslas with cheery but dry wit, the trio stepped out. They carried folding summer-weather deckchairs, rainy-weather brollies and a scrumptious hamper of mince pies which Santa could have sold his soul for. The stage was set for a farce. Well, it followed that the pastry provisions were consumed long before there were any important bites. The live bait showed more activity than the waters of the cut. Were the fish hibernating? Meanwhile, the frozen family was quiet and still. A sprinkling of snow fell in the ever-dimming light. The grim cheer and rapidly diminishing expectations of line action were good reasons to head home, albeit empty-handed, for the compensation of colourfully wrapped chocolates dispensed from a pair of huge, round tins; confections once typical for that time of year – when such chocolates tasted of creamy goodness, not of artificial flavours and chemicals. So, with eventide came a pre-arranged, maternally chauffeured automobile to collect the wearisome party of three. The untested tackle was stowed and the party boarded for departure as a wise-cracking wag approached. The Irish-accented man had been keeping an eye on the sorry state of affairs from his lock-keeper's cottage, nearby. Maybe he sensed the lack of appreciation in hearing out his joke, so he curtailed a yarn about apprentice anglers reeling in nothing but tin cans and offered something by way of compensation for the lack of fish and out of goodwill for the entertainment he'd had watching. A booklet on fishing, he promised, would reward serious study. His gift turned out to be an album of trade cards, showing fish and bait. So, there was a catch that day, of a sort. It was titled Irish Fishing. An album full of trade cards made by a sweets manufacturer called Liam Devlin. The lock-keeper said he'd collated it and looked after it for over 20 years. It was a welcome consolation present.

Readers from the British Isles may remember similar trade cards, for example,

Liam Devlin *Irish Fishing* card

Liam Devlin *Irish Fishing* card

Wills *Playing Card* cigarette card

Wills *Sporting Girls* card

Allen's Fruit Drops *National Flags & National Sports* card

those issued by Brooke Bond tea, like Freshwater Fish, in 1960. Tea-trade cards were given one at a time with loose tea. Two or three cards were included in a carton of tea bags. This writer's household only ever had loose tea so it took an age to collect anything. Even with the help of enthusiastic aunts, and a kindly grandmother, collections of cards were rarely completed.

Irish Fishing, the gift from the lock-keeper, was complete. It's a superb series of cards. Though the images show only basic line drawings of fish, bait and fishermen, barely coloured by a trio of tones, the artwork is attractive. The cards also feature some top angling locations. Today, they are not easy to find, and if they come up for sale they may seem expensive. They are rare, if they remain in an unused state, free of glue or damage to the back.

In the 1970s, Brooke Bond released The Sea Our Other World. It was more contemporary in style than the firm's earlier collection, and far more so than Devlin's cards. It was also an exciting series to collect, with Jacques Cousteau diving amidst exotic fish, underwater perils and submerged treasures. Alas, though it was a beautiful collection, neither it nor most other tea cards became worth much as investments. Tea merchants issued their cards in very high numbers and tea collections were collated all over the country. So, unlike scarcer foreign-issues by Brooke Bond, domestic issues by the same firm are worth very little. In fact, you could wallpaper your house in such cards and still find enough spare cards to offer your neighbour the same, dubious décor, and all for very little cost. Typhoo tea is another matter. Very often Typhoo cards – at least those cards marketed before the 1970s – are worth much more than Brooke Bond cards. Fish subjects are to be found in Typhoo's 1918 series, Conundrums; and in its Aesop's Fables series, from 1924.

A brand of sweet cigarettes made by Barratt & Co., of Wood Green, in London, followed Brooke Bond's 1960 lead when, in 1962, its

AN A TO Z OF **SPORTING COLLECTIBLES** 15

ANGLING ON CIGARETTE AND NON-TOBACCO TRADE CARDS

Phillips Sporting Series

MacRobertson's Sports

confections of candy sticks included a single Fish & Bait card. They look very similar to tea cards, and the influence of one brand on the other is apparent. The Barratt cards are worth a little more than the Brooke Bond cards, typically costing around 50p each. By contrast, the Brooke Bond cards have been seen to sell at just 50p for the entire set!

Collectors of earlier generations would have been more accustomed to cards given with tins of tobacco, and in packets of cigarettes, than with sweets or with tea but there were exceptions. Cadbury's was more than 50 years ahead of Barratt's angling cards, and well ahead of tobacco cards, when it issued one of the earliest British series devoted solely to angling. The chocolatier's Fish & Bait cards were available from as early as 1909! Thus, it was a year ahead of Wills tobacco's 1910 collection of the same name, and Churchman's use of the same images, in 1914.

There are earlier cards which bear scenes of an angling interest. The 1890s playing card cigarette cards series, by Wills, is one such issue. Card #36, with the 6 of diamonds, inset, shows a trio of anglers, and the witty inscription: a band of hope. Be prepared to pay over £20 if you want this card.

There are 50 angling-related cards in Wills's 1914-issue, Fish & Bait. They cost a little less than the same images used on the 1914 cards, by Churchman. Nowadays, such colourful cards, issued by both these tobacconists, may be acquired easily and inexpensively. The Wills cards can be had for as little as £1 each, and you'll pay only a little more for those by Churchman. However, it is the scarcity of the Cadbury's series, from 1909, that takes the prize in any rarity stakes. Not only are its six, large cards very different to those issued by the tobacconists, so too are its values. You may have to pay £200 for the set of half a dozen Cadbury cards. A second issue by Cadbury, from 1910, called simply Fish will also be costly to acquire. Its cards may command £20 each, or more, though they are rarely seen for sale, and a set of 12 may be all but impossible to acquire.

Wills tobacco had included a flirty flasher in its *Sporting Girls* cards of 1913. The cheeky image owes more to what-the-butler-saw mutoscope loops than to angling reels but the solitary card is an attractive addition to

Cadbury's British Marvels

Helios Jams, a Spanish trade card from the 1970s

Ogden's ABC of Sport card

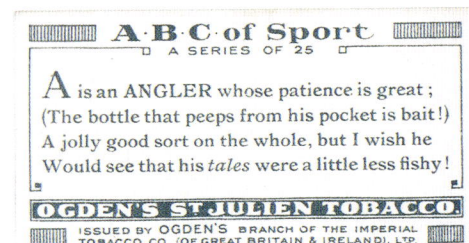

Formaggino Bebe, an Italian trade card from the 1950s

Player's *Country Sports* card

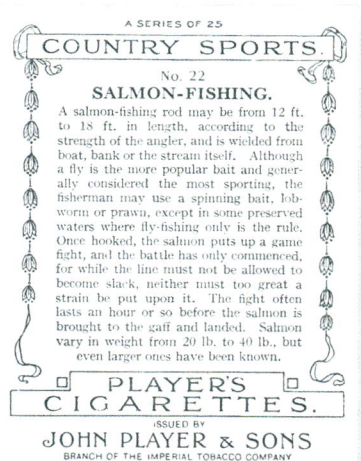

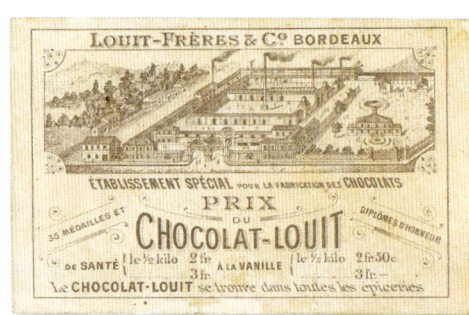

A French trade card by Joseph Milliat

French trade card from circa 1890

any angling collection. An earlier collection by Phillips tobacco, the *Sporting Series* of 1910, had similarly included a singular image of angling. Such cards may be had for around £20 each.

MacRobertson's *Sports* series, issued around 1917, includes two fishing-related cards: salmon fishing, at card #1; and, fishing at card #18. This series is very rare and the cards may cost more than £20 each.

William Ruddell tobacco was distributed with one *Rod and Gun* card in each packet. The 1924 blood-sports series is very hard to find, these days. Occasionally single cards come to market, for which you will have to pay over £20 each. The year 1924 also saw Imperial Tobacco, of Canada, reissue the Wills 1910 and Churchman 1914 cards. Today, such cards are worth around £2 each.

During the second and third decades of the twentieth century, Edmondson's produced three very attractive sports cards series. Anglers will want the Edmondson card from the later series, *Popular Sports*, issued in 1930. It's one of the most difficult angling cards to find anywhere in the world. Thankfully this unnumbered fishing card is not as costly as its fellow, a golf card, from the same series which sells for up to £200! Around £100 may be just about enough to reel it in.

The cheeky image owes more to what-the-butler-saw mutoscope loops than to angling.

ANGLING ON CIGARETTE AND NON-TOBACCO TRADE CARDS

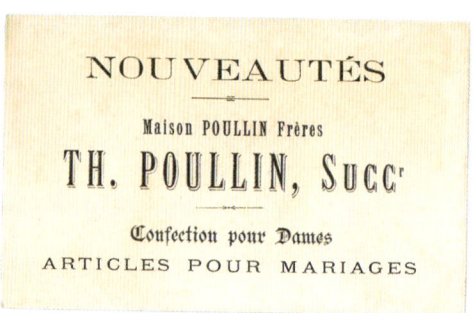

French trade card from circa 1910

French trade card from circa 1900

In 1927 Ogden tobacco published a colourful and humorous series, called *ABC of Sport*, in which the first card, the *A-is-for-angling* card, represents fishing. It's worth seeking out and can usually be had for around £5. It's similar in theme and wit to the more costly cards issued during the previous years, namely *Sports & Pastimes* by Copes, itself based upon the illustration & rhyme cards issued by Coudens, in 1924: *Sports Alphabet*. The sets include cartoons of sports, drawn by Frank Reynolds and John Hassall, wittily versed by Roland Carse. The Angling card goes thus: *"The angler delights to go splashing about in a stream, in pursuance of sport; with a hopeful surmise that a fish will soon rise, while he passes the time manufacturing lies as to weight, and to quantity caught"*. Priceless – and damned rare! It'll cost you well over £50, if you ever find it. The similar Copes card is more easily secured, and at around £10, it's less costly too. The pair is worth more than one without the other. The two cards, together, ought to be insured for at least £100.

Player's cigarettes issued a bloody series of images, in *Country Sports*, which came out in 1930. Aside from bullies with guns massacring harmless animals and cute critters, there are several calmer and kinder pursuits featured, including the rod and line subjects, which range from salmon fishing to coarse angling. A word on pricing: do not pay more than £2 for an original card; and if you buy a reprint, pay no more than £5 for the entire set of 25 cards, because modern reprints exist in the thousands!

Cadbury's put on the waders again, for *British Marvels*, a series of stickers issued in the 1930s. Series 2 includes angling. It's rare, and most will have been long-since glued down, but a sticker in decent condition ought not cost the angling collector more than £30.

French trade card from circa 1910

French trade card from circa 1900

18 AN A TO Z OF **SPORTING COLLECTIBLES**

French trade card from circa 1900

French trade card from circa 1930

Allen's of Australia accredited angling with New Zealand. In 1930, Allen's Q-T Fruit Drops came with a *Kiwi* angler at card #14, in its *National Flags & National Sports* series. £20 ought to be enough to secure this scarce item.

Carreras's Canadian issue, *Sportsman Guide – Fly Fishing*, from 1950, is one of the final series of tobacco cards to feature angling. After the war cigarette cards had diminished and all but disappeared by the 1960s. Interests such as angling moved to non-tobacco trade cards.

Arguably the most attractive trade cards featuring angling are those issued in Gaul. Since before 1900 images of fish and fishers have graced French trade cards. Women anglers, as well as fishermen, adorn cards as varied as those by Botot toothpaste, and Crochard et Fils, a manufacturer of shoes. Yet more female fisher folk are found on trade cards by chocolatiers Poullin Freres, and a rival firm called Felix Potin.

Cards by producers such as Joseph Milliat and the aforementioned brands are among the most attractive known. Further afield, both Italian and Spanish trade cards also employed fish and anglers, as a sales ploy, to tempt customers to purchase cheeses, chocolates and chewing tobacco. A fabled praying fish, based upon the little fish of Aesop's tales, is used on cards by many manufacturers, notably Formaggino Bebe, the Italian cheesewright. Further, look out also for Badshaw Teas's 1971 series *Fish & Bait*, and Helios's 1970s jam-jar sports cards, to name but two of many series out there.

As an afterword on fish, and fish on trade cards, this writer's imaginative affair with the undersea world went unappreciated by a certain teacher invigilating an exam. The O-level still-life demanded that a mackerel be drawn. Most children had brought in smelly lumps of frozen fish, grey-silver shiny flesh, to draw. Not Wilkes.

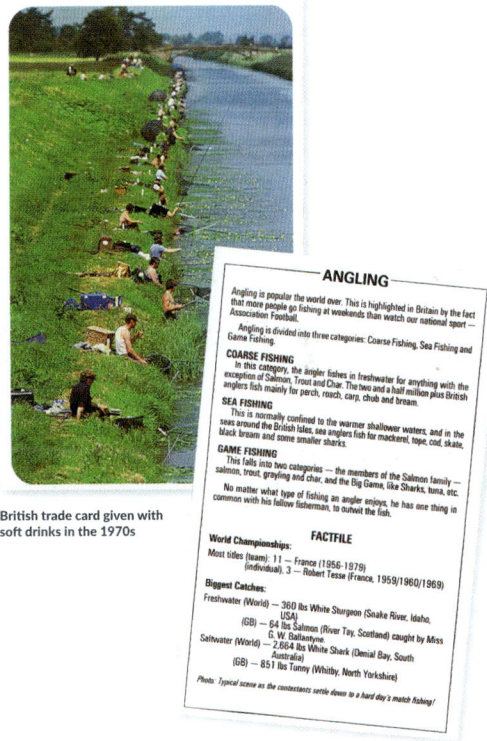

British trade card given with soft drinks in the 1970s

French trade card from circa 1910

Arguably the most attractive trade cards featuring angling are those issued in Gaul.

AIRE LIBRE

REVISTA
DE
DEPORTES

50 cts

His was a tea card showing a mackerel. Such a still life, of a still life, was considered much too creative and the card was confiscated. A hasty trip to the local fishmonger was arranged. The result was a greenish-hued fish which was anything but mackerel. The shop had long-since sold out of its silvery shoal. The fishmonger had assured the buyer it would be OK, and no one would see the difference. It was not so. The examination started. As usual, with all exams, silence was enforced with the threat of expulsion. Thus, silence reigned until it was broken by the invigilating pottery teacher, Miss Davies, guffawing and uttering loudly, "Wilkes, your fish looks dead!" She was serious. There was no detectible irony. The room was awash with dead fish! She was, thereafter, removed and replaced by a less irksome member of school staff, a man who knew how to keep silence, if not the occasional smile. Thus, the inadmissible trade card triumphed, in the end. Had it not been for that, the green-gilled 'dead' mackerel-substitute fish would not have helped secure an A-grade.

French trade card from circa 1930

Silence reigned until it was broken by the invigilating pottery teacher, Miss Davies, guffawing and uttering loudly, "Wilkes, your fish looks dead!" She was serious. There was no detectible irony. The room was awash with dead fish!

Couden's *Sports Alphabet* card

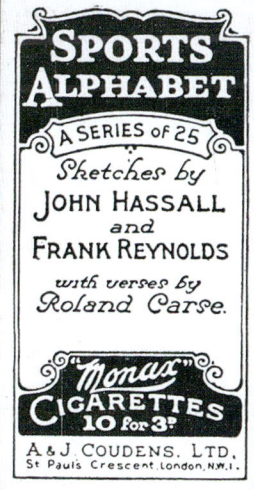

French trade card from circa 1900

Archery on cigarette and non-tobacco trade cards

French trade card for cigarette papers, circa 1890

ernie the Bolt, the crossbow-archer from Golden Shot, a classic television game show where contestants aimed high for low-brow prizes, was the friendly face of archery – for most people the only face of archery – in the 1970s. During that time, and earlier eras, archery was little more than a junior affectation enjoyed by kids sporting balsa bows in street games known as *Cowboys and Indians*. As a means of medieval murder, archery was portrayed on TV, in adaptations the like of Robert Louis Stevenson's *The Black Arrow*, not to mention the many versions of Robin Hood. Archery, as a competitive sport, was unknown in most British neighbourhoods of the 1970s but newly issued gum cards of fantasy archers were treasured. As well as Disney's *Robin Hood* fox, and his merry zoomorphic men, the *hot* stickers of the time included the swashbuckling *Sandokan* pirates; bow-wielding Japanese warriors, in *The Water Margin*; and the legendary, far-eastern folktale archer known as *Monkey*. It was thanks, once again, largely to the TV that such cards existed. Yet, two Europe-wide collections of Olympic Games cards and stickers, by Panini, which showed real archers, missed the British audience. Panini's *Mexico 70* football collection had been a costly venture into British territory, with trade tariffs in the way the firm needed a subsidiary British company to distribute its wares. Thanks to import taxes and other legal issues, before the UK was admitted to the EEC (which became the EU), British kids missed out on the real thing, three times over between 1972 and 1976. No wonder archery, as a sport, was barely known in the UK.

The lack of widespread archery activity in the UK is also down to the sport being a relatively costly pastime. Archery requires expensive equipment and sizeable land on which to shoot, needing up to 200 yards for clout archery, and 100 yards for target archery. The land acreage of a wealthy estate is ideal, but not that of a typical suburban family, with a small garden and next-door neighbours the other side of the fence, their kids and pet dog in an inflatable paddling pool just a few feet from your arrows. So, a junior bow with wooden arrows, and rubber suckers, was about all most people saw in suburbia, in 1975. Real archery was something this writer first encountered when a pair of previously harmless-looking teenage classmates professed that they were toxophilites! However did two swots from Shenstone come to possess weapons with fibre-optic, guaranteed-kill sights? The amazons bragged of their countryside homes, with gardens long enough for archery practice – without tears. Aiming noses airily, they took questions unquivered and passionately defended their pastime, distributing little cards around the class, which advertised their highbrow archery club. The pointed piece of ephemera remains in this writer's collection, today.

A dearth in archery cards had followed the decline of the tobacco card, after the 1930s. It was only reversed when archery was readmitted to the Olympic Games, in 1972. Panini, the Italian sticker king, celebrated said reprise of the bow & arrow with attractive cards in both its Olympic Games collections from that year: *Olympia* and *München 72*.

Previously, in the British Isles, archery had been illustrated on cards since Edwardian times. Though there'd been Victorian-era archery cards issued in Continental Europe, the earliest known British card is from Mitchell's *Prize Crop*

French trade card from chocolates, circa 1900

French trade card from chocolates, circa 1900

Spanish trade card, circa 1925

Sports series, from 1907, showing targets and a waistcoat-and-suited gentleman, in a cap, aiming a six-foot bow. The very same image was also used on a plethora of other, often very rare cards, by the likes of Hudden, by Miranda, and by Goodbody cigarettes, to name but three, though the least costly card is that by Mitchell, which may sell for around £10.

Archery subjects may also be found on cigarette cards by Wills, of Bristol. Apart from those included in various sporting series, archery is known among the *Lucky Charms*, of 1923. John Player tobacco issued Arms & Armour, in 1909, which also includes an archery card. Similar cards are also to be found in United Services's *Ancient Warriors*; Dobie & Son's *Weapons of All Ages*, from 1924; Mills's *Warriors Through the Ages*; and, Edwards, Ringer & Bigg's *Sports & Games in Many Lands*.

Sporting archery is somewhat less well reflected than historical archery, on British trade cards. Though archery was included in an attractive series called *Comicartoons of Sport*, by James Illingworth, in 1927; and also in *Optical Illusions* by Drapkin, in 1926, there is relatively little else in British tobacco history for the archery aficionado. Thankfully, the producers of non-tobacco trade cards, especially abroad, treated it as a favourite subject.

Perhaps the most attractive non-tobacco trade cards featuring the bow are those made by French firms in the latter years of the nineteenth century, and at the very start of the twentieth century. Among better known names on trade cards, Au Bon Marché, Chocolate Favarger, Chocolat Moreau, Papier Goudron, Cosmydor Eau de Toilette, and Trébucien Café all produced beautiful chromo lithographic cards of archery.

Spanish cards issued by Juan Vidal Segura, called *Todos Los Deportes* (meaning, all sports), included *Tiro Al Arco* (archery). In later years, Fher, the Spanish sticker king of the 1950s and 1960s, published a series of stickers, many of which show archery, from Robin Hood, the film with Burt Lancaster starring as the man in lincoln green. Torras, a chocolatier, issued *Escala en Oceania*, in 1966; and Bimbo published *El Libro de las Adivinanzas*, in 1973, in both of which archery is to be found. Spanish gum cards by Keisa, in 1974, and trade cards by Helios jams, in more recent times, maintained the Iberian fascination with archery.

In Italy, it was not just Panini at work. Rival firms, like Mira and Edis, included pan-sports stars and themes, such as archery, in their collections. Edis's *La Vera Storia del West* being but one example. While Panini issued archery stickers in *Campioni dello Sport 1973-74*, and in *Sports Vedettes*, in 1974, archery was also used in Edis's *Olimpiadi Montreal 76* collection. Though rare, archery cards like these are often very affordable. Try Italian eBay, using Italian words to seek archery stickers – it's easy on a translator – or see, under the archery tab, a quiver of rare images at www.footballsoccercards.com.

French trade card from chocolates, circa 1890

Belgian trade card, circa 1950

ARCHERY ON CIGARETTE AND NON-TOBACCO TRADE CARDS

Other countries also celebrated the bow and arrow on trade cards. In the 1960s, Belgian Cote d'Or ('*Le Bon Chocolate Belge*') included archery in a series of dual-language, large format sports cards, called *Folklore Belge*. In the Soviet Union, in the 1970s and 1980s, pocket-size calendar cards often featured archers. In Portugal, there are pan-sport stickers from various Olympic Games collections, showing bow & arrow. German tobacco cards of the 1930s, notably Greiling cards, included a wide range of such cards, too.

The British, while not having many tobacco-trade cards to seek, had plenty of non-tobacco trade cards to choose from. Edmondson's confectioners, of Liverpool, produced some very attractive, now very rare, sports cards, notably *Sports & Pastimes*, in 1912, *Popular Sports*, in 1930, and *Humourous Sporting Scenes*, issued at some point betwixt the other two.

Anglo American Gum, a British firm from Halifax, in England, included archery on one of its paper gum inserts in a 1950s series called *Sports Parade*. Insert number 44 features two world champion archers, Deutgen of Sweden, and Kurkowsk from Poland. A&BC Gum's *Civil War News* includes a card titled, *Deadly Arrows*; Anglo Confectionery's *Tarzan* gum cards from 1966 included archery, and so on.

Belgian trade card, circa 1950

Mentioned here are but a few. This introduction to archery on trade cards has but limited space and merely intends to give an introduction to, and an outline of the subject. The archery enthusiast, in cards, is both fortunate and unfortunate, in that there are, as yet, few competitive collectors for such cards, and prices remain relatively low but, conversely, there are no known series devoted to the sport. Further, the few cards and stickers extant may often be difficult to find. So, if you see a ready-made archery cards collection for sale, snap it up! It may well have taken its owner many years to compile, and it will save you much searching. Prices for archery cards can only go one way, up, because they are starting from such a low base. Most British tobacco cards cost less than £3 each, and many of the more attractive foreign trade cards may be found for less than £20 each.

French trade card, circa 1930

Belgian trade card, circa 1890

French trade card, circa 1930

Spanish trading cards packet, circa 1950

ATHLETICS: TRACK AND FIELD DISCIPLINES ON TRADE CARDS

in plastic is rooted in a business idea born in the 1990s, sprinkled with the banking adage of taking someone else's livelihood, and making money off it. It goes like this: to market a card better (to make more money from collectors) seal it in two sets of plastic, then add a 'card quality' grade, and sell it at an inflated price. No matter how valuable rare postage stamps are – and some stamps have sold for over $10 million each – they don't get slabbed. Neither do postcards, nor does bullion. So, cards don't need to be slabbed either. Avoid slabs, if you can, and you'll save money. The money you save you can spend on more slab-free cards.

Boomer Gum, in Spain, issued a series of waxy paper gum inserts in the early 1980s, called *Boomer Chicle Olimpico*. This attractive and unusual series includes Dick Fosbury and Bob Beamon, as well the usual legendary inclusions: Owens, Nurmi and Zatopek. If you can find them expect to pay over £10 each.

Boys' Magazine, a British comic, issued *Sportsmen*, a series of 'real photographic' cards, in 1922. Such things were new-fangled developments back then. Harold Abrahams, of *Chariots of Fire* fame, found his way into this series, as did other well-known runners of yore. The cards may be found for as little as £2 to £5 each.

Bravour tobacco cards, from Hitler's Germany, include some world-famous stars, though they tend to be Nordic and blond, rather than black. It's a rather nationalistic, Germans-for-Germany series of rarities. For a fairer selection of world stars see Germany's Muratti tobacco cards from 1934.

British Automatic weighing machines issued weight cards called *Speed*, in 1949. The machines were typically found in Woolworth, or outside high street chemists. The customer would stand on the scales, insert a penny, and out popped a colourful card of a famous athlete, plane, rocket, ship or a fast-paced animal, with a recorded weight in stones printed on the rear.

Brooke Bond tea included *Olympic Greats* cards with teabags and loose tea, in 1979. These cards were produced in copious numbers and are easy to obtain for very little. Almost worthless glued down they must be obtained loose, in near-mint new condition to be worth anything at all.

Bruguera's *Ases del Deporte Mundial*, with Daley Thompson and Steve Ovett, are stickers that were issued in Spain, circa 1983. They came in sheets of six, to cut and stick. If you find an unused, uncut sheet it may be worth £30. Cut single stickers of stars are worth £2 to £5.

Bulgaria tobacco, a German cigarettes issuer of the Weimer years, issued an immensely large series, in 1932, called *Sport-Photos*. It includes over 90 track and field stars, including two cards showing Eddie Tolan.

Cadet sweets, of Slough in England, issued cards and decal transfers in the 1950s and 1960s. Its 1956 *Record Holders of the World* cards feature various famous runners, and can be collected quite inexpensively, unlike the firm's 1956 series of decals, which is far rarer. The decals include athletes, as well as drivers, golfers and other sportsmen. It's an immensely difficult series to find, let alone piece together, because most of the delicate transfers ended up on skin, as make-believe tattoos; or were transferred to school exercise books, or any other surface at hand, so, the decals are mostly long lost to the ravages of time. The fun but ill-chosen modes of use and storage, by children in the 1950s, have served to

German tobacco cards of GB gold medallist Tommy Hampson, from 1932

French trade card, circa 1900

French trade card, circa 1910

Spanish trade card, circa 1920

Spanish trade card, circa 1925

French trade card, circa 1920

French trade card, circa 1910

French trade card, circa 1930

French trade card, circa 1950

ensure the values of unused transfers are often enormous. Some may be worth £200 or more!

Cafes Gilbert, of France, issued a sporting series of cards in the late 1930s. It includes various, very attractive scenes from track & field. The cards are rare but not too costly. To see these cards, and more like them, go to the athletics section at www.footballsoccercards.com

Carreras issued a series of *Turf Sportsmen* tobacco cards in 1948, of which some show track & field athletes. The cards are what are known as packet issues. The cards were designed to be cut from the slider within the cigarette packet. Uncut cards, on intact sliders, may cost between £10 and £20 each but cut cards can be found for as little as £1.

Casanova's Sport-Album of *Leichathletick* was issued in 1926. The Casanova trademark, a dog smoking a cigarette, is more impressive than the cards, which feature a strictly Germanic order of finely honed Aryan flesh. Some of the athletes came to survive their *Volkssturm* duties in the defence of Berlin, as middle-aged men, 20 years later. The unluckier ones were blown to smithereens at Stalingrad and Kursk.

Champion comic issued *Famous British Record Holders*, in 1922, a series of photographic cards of sportsmen, which included some track & field stars. Due to the large number made, and the wide distribution of these cards, they can still be found for as little as £2 each.

A decade later, Champion gave away small folders of sports cards, which contained concertina-like, fold-out selections of several sportsmen. Those called *Champions Of The Empire*, and *Sporting Marvels In All Sorts Of Sports* include track & field. Some collectors have cut these joined-cards selections down to singles, so if you find an uncut folder, with all its images intact, it's worth quite a bit, especially those with famous American athletes, and footballers. The one with track and field stars is one of the more economical, and may be bought for as little as £10.

Churchman cigarettes issued cards called *Sporting Celebrities*, in 1931, and *Kings of Speed*, in 1939. The former series showed illustrations of sports stars, in which there are a handful of athletes. The latter series covered everything from steam trains to sportsmen, and there are also a handful of track & field stars to seek out, including Nurmi and Owens. The same firm had also published a series of sports caricatures, in 1928, called, *Men of the Moment in Sport*, which also included track and field athletes. Thankfully, for the collector of athletics cards, these cost a lot less than the three-figure prices paid for golfers, from the same series.

Clevedon Confectionery, a Blackpool-based firm, is best remembered for its sports caricatures on cards it sold with candy cigarettes. A triumvirate of pan-sports series are known, as well as three series devoted solely to football. From 1960 there is *International Sporting Stars*; and from 1961, *The Story of the Olympics*. By 1963 *Sporting Memories* had completed the trio. Of the many athletes featuring in the three, Jesse Owens is one of the most sought-after cards, at #21 in *Sporting Memories*. Whether you will be able to find such cards is another matter. They are ever rarer and up in price. Owens may cost £50.

AN A TO Z OF **SPORTING COLLECTIBLES** 33

ATHLETICS: TRACK AND FIELD DISCIPLINES ON TRADE CARDS

 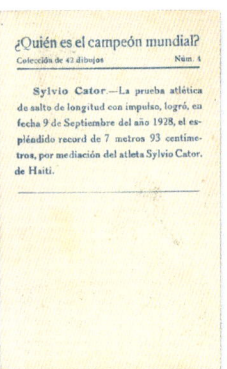   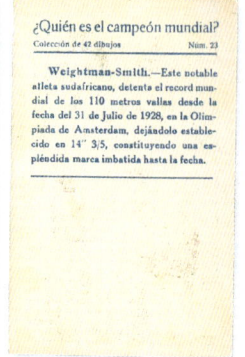

Spanish cards from the Olympic Games 1928 of Haitian footballer & silver medallist long jumper Silvio Cator

Spanish cards from the Olympic Games 1928 of Anthony 'Nick' Winter the Aussie triple jumper

Spanish cards from the Olympic Games 1928 of Springbok decathlete George Weightman Smith

Cloetta, of Sweden, issued a series of sports cards around 1933, in which are to be found many athletes, including world-famous stars of track & field. The cards are rare but do not tend to cost more than £5 or £10 each, if and when they come up for sale. Cloetta cards are typical of a genre of Swedish brands that includes Alfa, Mazetti and Marabou, all of whom issued various series of sports cards in the 1930s.

Comet Sweets, of Slough in England, issued packet-issue cards, to be cut out from boxes of sweets, called *Olympic Achievements*, in 1959. The yellow-framed cards show illustrations in red, and have plain backs. They are very rare, and quite valuable, selling for up to £10 cut, and over £20 if uncut, on a still-intact box of sweet cigarettes. The firm's follow-up issue, with the same series title, was of standard fare: regular cards, similar to those made by Barratt. A later series, *Record Holders of the World*, was issued in 1962. It includes a dozen record-holding athletes.

The Co-operative Wholesale Society issued athletics cards as early as 1906. They'll cost you a small fortune, if you can find them, today. Of the 50 cards, half a dozen feature athletics events, illustrated in colour. The very pretty cards are identified by the letters CWS on the rear. Expect to pay £25 to £50 each.

Copcards, as they are known, were issued by local police forces during the 1980s. The various series of *Copcards* are best known for footballers but some issues show famous track & field athletes. Depending on the star, not to mention the police force, the cards may be worth over £5 each.

Cope Brothers issued *Sports & Pastimes* cards, in 1925. The colourful, witty cards feature a single track & field scene, the high jump, amidst sports both known and less known. Some of the less usual sports include Indian-club swinging, kite flying, nine-pin bowling, and, surely the laziest of all sports: going for picnics in the countryside! Inexpensive for their age and quality, these cards may sometimes be acquired for as little as £10 each.

A Coudens cigarette card ought to be in every collection. *Coudens's Sports Alphabet* cards, from 1924, include chirpy rhymes and witty illustrations of sporting moments. These poetic, attractive and unusual cards will make you smile. The designs were also used on the Cope Brothers *Sports & Pastimes* cards, of 1925. Cope's cards are more colourful but Coudens cards are far rarer! Having both cards of one sport, a pair of high jumpers, in this case, will weigh in at around £50 the pair.

Credilivro, of Portugal, issued *Moscovo 80*, a collection of 266 stickers with blank backs, which are often wrongly assigned to a firm called Gnomo Credicultura. The Credilivro stickers include an image of Steve Ovett. If you can find them expect to pay £20 each for unused examples of the top stars.

Daddies Sauce bottles came with a card collar, in 1980. The unfurled collar revealed three *Olympic Greats* cards, to cut out. The series consisted of 18 cards, of which half a dozen showed athletes, from Lasse Viren to Mary Peters. The uncut collars are worth much more than cut cards. The easiest and least costly way to obtain the series is to buy an album, complete with 18 cut-out and glued-in stickers, at around £5, though this will never be worth as much as loose, un-glued, un-cut cards.

Devlin of Dublin issued *Right or Wrong* cards, in 1963, with its sweet cigarettes. The series of 48 illustrated trade cards includes a handful of track & field events. They are rare so they may be costly. Expect to pay at least £10 each card.

Disgra (Fher), the soccer stars sticker kings issued *Atletas Tokio 1964*, in Spain. It includes stickers of athletics greats from Jim Thorpe to Wilma Rudolph, including Jesse Owens. Unused examples may sell for £10 each.

Donaldson's *Sports Favourites* were all the rage in post-war Glasgow. The cards showed colourful illustrations of footballers, cricketers, boxers and

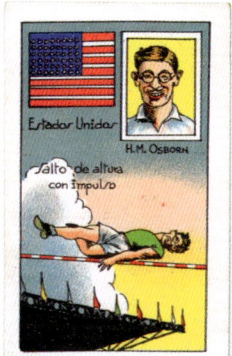 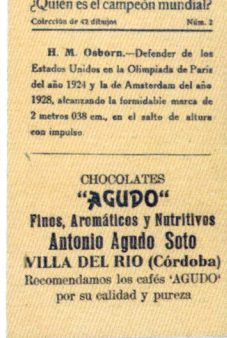 

Spanish cards from the Olympic Games 1928 of Harold Osborn, the USA high jump gold medallist

Spanish cards from the Olympic Games 1928 of Gold medal marathon runner Ahmed El Ouafi of Algeria

Children would buy them to separate the cards to swap and collect, thus, staple holes found in such cards are as issued.

34 AN A TO Z OF **SPORTING COLLECTIBLES**

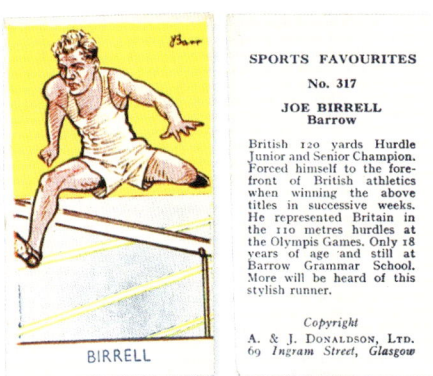
Scottish cards from 1948 by Donaldson and by Kiddy's Favourites

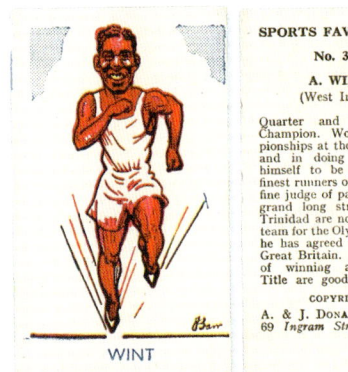
Scottish cards from 1948 by Donaldson and by Kiddy's Favourites

Scottish cards from 1948 by Donaldson and by Kiddy's Favourites

other athletes. Donald Robertson, the marathon runner, features alongside a handful of other track & field stars of the time. The cards were issued stapled together in 'booklets' of five or six cards each. Children would buy them to separate the cards to swap and collect, thus, staple holes found in such cards are as issued. Some of the athletics cards from the collection are very rare and may exceed £10 each but, when compared to the prices paid for football cards by the same issuer, which may top £100, track & field cards seem like a good deal at one tenth the cost.

Donat Dupont from France issued cards called *Indiana-Sport*, in the 1930s. The cards feature a wealth of sporting heroes and well-known sports events, including many athletes too. Expect to pay over £20 for each track & field card, if you ever see such rarities on the market, that is. Other sports cards in this series have sold for over £100 each!

Duisberger margarine issued a series of cards called *Olympia 1952*. The series consists of both monotone photos of stars of the day, and colourful cards which represent competing nations, from USA to New Zealand. Prices tend to be around £5.

Duplo's *Olympia '84* series of 30 stickers includes a permed Steve Cram and the loveable triple jumper Willie Banks. For a modern-times issue, this collection is quite hard to find, and prices are on the rise. Typically sellers ask £5 each card.

Dutton's Beers issued a series of cards in 1981, in which British sprinter Donna Hartley features alongside snooker players, cricketers and footballers. Easily available, the dozen cards can be had for £1 a piece.

Echo Verlag's 1968 series of summer Olympic Games stickers includes Dick Fosbury and Tommie Smith. The series is very similar to the Swiss stickers made by Poly, and similar marques, in the same era. Expect to pay over £10 for unused stickers of famous names.

Edis, of Italy, made *Olimpiadi Montreal 76* for the Olympic Games, in 1976. The stickers include world legends from track & field's past, and athletes contemporary in the 1970s, stars such as Don Quarrie and Brendan Foster. Unused stickers are worth from £2 to £20 for better-known names.

Erdal Kwak was a German producer of the 1920s. It published beautiful cards for which few collectors seem to care. Thus, the value of these attractive cards remains startlingly low. Even 100 years later Erdal Kwak cards can be had for just £1 each.

Esso printed a series of colourful cards in 1972, including stars of track & field, called *The Olympics*. The collection includes legends like Jim Thorpe, as well as contemporary stars. Prices are on the rise. Expect to pay £5 or more.

Folgore, of Italy, produced a 1960s series of stickers called *Chronology of the World*, in which an atypical subject is to be found: Jess Owens! It's the set-breaker. Many sports card collectors and dealers have sought it, pushing near-mint examples towards £50 each.

Franck Coffee, of Germany, produced various sports series in the 1920s and 1930s, from Weimar issues, like *Olympia 1928*, to Nazi issues, like *Olympia 1936*. These series are replete with famous names in athletics, yet they may be a little too Teutonic for some tastes. They are quite rare and costly, so expect to pay over £10 each.

Gallaher Tobacco's sports series, *British Champions of 1923*, includes cards of *Chariots of Fire* legends Harold Abrahams and Eric Liddle. It's a beautiful little gem of a collection, which can

Bob Beamon on an Italian sticker by Edis from 1974

AN A TO Z OF **SPORTING COLLECTIBLES** 35

ATHLETICS: TRACK AND FIELD DISCIPLINES ON TRADE CARDS

often be had, in its entirety, for only £75. Not bad, considering single cards sell from £1 to £20 each, depending on the subject.

Gallaher's Park Drive series of *Champions*, from 1934, are colourful cards. They come with two fronts: with or without the name of the star featured. An octet of athletes is to be found in both variants of this series, from the marathon runner Sam Ferris to Donald Finlay, the sprint hurdler. Two years later Gallaher made *Sporting Personalities*, which included *Chariots of Fire* runner Harold Abrahams. His card will often sell for a premium price but most others are inexpensive, at only £1 each.

In 1938, Gallaher published *Island Sporting Celebrities*, which includes runners at card numbers #1 and #26. The first card may cost double the going rate of the other one simply because of end-number collectors, by whom the first and last cards in a set are collected. It takes all types!

Gartmann cards were made in Germany from the dawn of the twentieth century until the 1930s. Athletics stars and events are featured across various Gartmann series. The cards are eminently affordable, and boast some of the most attractive designs on trade cards of the period. They come recommended for beauty and value for money.

Giornalino was an Italian magazine for children and young teenagers. In the past it regularly issued free cards, which were fastened into the publication in sheets, to tear apart, to glue into dedicated albums which were also given with the journal. Most cards became separated to singles then got glued down, somewhere; or they were lost or damaged, as is the case with most trade cards which have youngsters as their target market. It's rare to find complete sheets of cards, as issued, but they are worth seeking. Giornalino has been issuing its colourful cards since the 1970s. During the 1980s and 1990s the magazine issued Olympic Games athletes, including cards of Olympic greats, like Jesse Owens. In complete sheets these are quite valuable.

Golden Wonder crisps included plastic-wrapped cards of athletes in its 1979 series, *All Stars*. Donna Hartley, Sonia Lannaman and Brendan Foster feature. The cards are easy to find, to this day, and worth very little but if they retain their clear plastic, outer wrappers they'll be worth a premium, maybe £5 each.

Goodies made candy cigarettes in the early 1970s. As well as a series of cards about the football World Cup, Goodies produced a series of 24 *Olympics* cards, in 1972. The two dozen Olympic images may cost £100, these days. Many collectors have bought only the cards with the great names, like Jesse Owens and Emil Zatopek, which is why complete sets are now hard to find, and relatively expensive for a 1970s series.

Goodwin's *Games & Sports* cards of 1889 included such subjects as 'foot race' and 'putting the shot', as well as the more typically recognised events of track & field. The cards were issued in USA and, if in top condition, they are coveted and paid highly for. Individual cards may cost way over £100 each.

Gregoire, a French food brand, included a series of stickers called *Sport et Dance* with its biscuits, in 1957. The issue contains many images of athletics. Such cards typically sell for below £5 each.

Greiling was a German cigarette manufacturer. In the 1920s the firm issued copious amounts of cards, including cards of athletics stars. Its 1934 series, *Rekord Im Sport*, devoted a quarter of its run to athletics cards, with over 80 to seek. They're mostly Teutonic but some notable world stars of track & field are also included. Prices may top £20 for better known stars.

Heuko, of West Germany, produced a series of stickers in 1952 for the Olympic Games, called *Olympic 1952*. Though heavily weighted towards national athletes it did include track & field legends like Owens and Zatopek. Further, Yvette Williams, Marjorie Jackson and the Jamaican men's 400m relay team are also featured. Prices start at around £5.

Heinerle, of West Germany, with the cooperation of Keystone, issued its first athletics gum cards in 1960 – not 1958, as has been claimed. The firm issued more cards featuring athletics in 1961. A white border makes the latter issues easy to spot. Some of the images from the second series were reissued, in 1962, by a vending machine gun cards issuer called Lutter. The later cards are a little taller and their backs show titles which are not found on the 1961 Heinerle cards.

Hellas, of Scandinavia, produced cards bearing the Jenkki legend. Cards with such a marque ought to be treated with care, as they can be very valuable. A series by this firm, called *Olympos*, is now one of the rarest sports series known, and you'll pay over £100 for some of its cards.

Herba's 1964 series, *Olympische Sport*, was issued in sheets of nine or ten stickers each. This collection is easily available but is often found complete, with all the stickers glued into the commercially available albums. Like so, it's of little worth. Finding the stickers in uncut sheets, as new, is another matter, and as such it's worth rather more!

Japanese gold medallist long jumper Chuhei Nambu on a German card

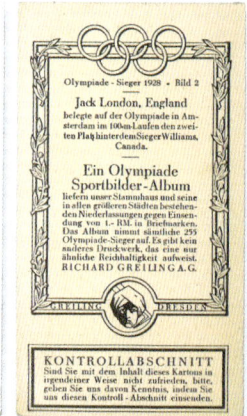

1928 Olympics silver & bronze medallist Jack London, on a German card

USA triple-gold medallist Wilma Rudolph on a card by Lutter from 1962

Old Calabar cards are often modern copies like this one

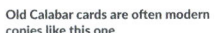
French trade card, circa 1950

Roger Bannister, world record breaker on a West German gum card

Hill, a London tobacconist, issued a series called *Sports*, in 1936; and a second called *Celebrities of Sport*, in 1939. The former series of monotones includes half a dozen athletes, while the latter, a series of coloured cigarette cards, features several more. All of the cards can usually be acquired inexpensively, for only a couple of pounds each.

Hitschler issued Bergmann-related images with its gum, which was sold in West Germany, in 1970. The small, paper gum inserts are as fragile as they are rare. As well as scenes from the history of athletics and its events, stars like Mary Rand, of Great Britain, feature alongside enduring legends, like Nurmi, and pop stars like Marc Bolan of T-Rex!

Hocus Focus, of West Germany, issued small gum cards of sportsmen, in the late 1950s. As well as footballers like Puskás, the record-breaking runner, Roger Banister makes an appearance. Puskás will cost football collectors a small fortune but Bannister is more affordable, at around only £10.

Hoyer, of Germany, issued a very attractive series of athletics cards in the late 1920s. The series, called *Sport*, includes half a dozen beautiful track & field images. Prices start at £5.

Huntley & Palmers biscuits issued sports cards as far back as the 1890s, including scenes from track and field. These have been reprinted so be careful not to pay too high a price for recently made cards. Originals may cost £50 each, or more.

Ilsa's various *Sportovcu* collections come from Czechoslavakia. The trio of known collections includes a range of world-famous sportsmen. Issued between 1933 and 1935, cards from each of the three series are rare and often pricey. Beware of modern copies, many of which have been erroneously graded as authentic by American slabbers. English language backs are a warning! People in Bohemia and Moravia, not to mention other north-eastern regions of the former Austro-Hungarian Empire, did not speak English, in the 1930s. No cards producer in Bratislava or Brno would have dreamed of using American-English terminology on their cards. Genuine cards may cost as much as £100 each. Forgeries are worthless. Avoid cards whose numbers are without serifs.

Jostella margarine, a post-war German firm, issued the stunning *Olympic & World Records in Athletics* series, in 1950. The colourful cards include a raft of track & field legends, including Owens, Nurmi and Zatopek. Prices start at around £5 each.

Kemmel chocolates, of France, issued two series of *Les Vedettes Sportives*, during the 1930s. The sepia-toned picture cards feature well-known names of sport, as well as French favourites of the time. Prices start at £10 and may exceed £50 for bigger stars.

Kiddy's Favourites were made in Glasgow, in the late 1940s. The firm issued cards stapled together in small booklets. The young buyer would separate the cards thenceforth play with, collect or swap them. Kiddy's Favourites are best known as football cards though a series of *Popular Olympics* was also issued. It includes a card of *Chariots of Fire* runner, Eric Liddell, and one of Jesse Owens too. Prices for such cards may exceed £20 each.

Knorr, the foods manufacturer, produced *Siege-Rekord-Sensationen*, in 1954. This series of black-&-white paper stickers includes Blankers-Koen, Zatopek & other great athletes. Prices range from £2 to £5.

In the early 1950s a German firm called Kosmos tobacco gifted its Roxy cigarettes smokers a series of cards, called *Olympische Spiele Helsinki 1952*. It includes a surprising array of stars yet values are low due to enormous production and a surfeit of unsold stock.

Kraft foods commemorated Queen Elizabeth's quarter-century reign with a series co-produced by The Co-operative Society. The *Silver Jubilee Athletics Collection* includes British stars of the past, from Chris Chataway to Mary Peters, though

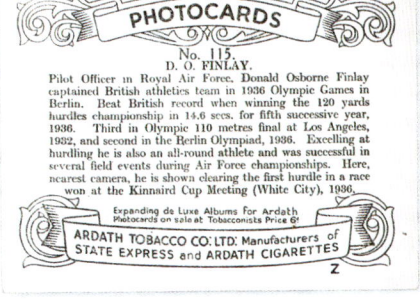
An Ardath tobacco *Photocard* from the 1930s

Beware of modern copies, many of which have been erroneously graded as authentic by American slabbers.

AN A TO Z OF **SPORTING COLLECTIBLES** 37

ABRAHAMS
1924 100 METRES **1924** 4 X 100 METRES RELAY

ALLAN WELLS
1980 100 METRES
1980 200 METRES

Abrahams breaks the tape to win the gold medal at the Paris Games in 1924.

BORN 1899, BEDFORD.
DIED 1978, ENFIELD, MIDDLESEX.

As the first European to win an Olympic sprint title, Harold Abrahams holds a unique place in history. In Paris in 1924, he won the Olympic 100 metres and his friendly rivalry with Eric Liddell, the 400 metres champion, provided the theme for the award winning film Chariots of Fire.

In addition to being the world's greatest sprinter, Abrahams was also a champion long jumper. He won the British title twice and in 1924 set an English record which stood for 32 years. After a leg injury ended his career in 1925 he became a distinguished journalist and commentator.

BORN 1952, EDINBURGH.

Allan Wells, in a photo finish, won the 1980 Olympic 100 metres title by the narrowest margin in history. In Moscow, Wells was given the same electronic time as pre-race favourite, Silvio Leonard of Cuba, but the judges gave the verdict to the Scotsman. Wells was involved in another desperately close finish in the 200 metres but this time the decision went against him and he failed by inches to win a second gold medal. An exceptionally powerful physique enabled Wells to remain a top sprinter for many years but he never improved on his performance at Moscow in 1980.

Allan Wells

Allan Wells, Scotland's greatest sprinter.

ATLETICA

661 - GROSSI MIGI
anni 23, nato a Milano, 400 m. piani

662 - TOSI GIUSEPPE
anni 34, nato a Borgo Ticino, lancio del disco

663 - CONSOLINI ADOLFO
anni 33, nato a Verona, ex campione del mondo lancio del disco

664 - SIDDI TONINO
anni 27, nato a Cagliari, 400 m. piani

665 - BAL...
anni 28, na...

666 - ROSSI MARISA
80 metri ostacoli

667 - PIERUCCI SILVANA
salto in alto e in lungo

668 - GABRIC CALVESI G.
lancio del disco

669 - FRANCO ELDA
100 metri piani

670

671 - SIVI LAURA
100 metri piani

572 - BORA MICAELA
80 metri ostacoli

673 - CRESPI BOZZANO
lancio del giavellotto

674 - CORDIALE GENTILE E.
campione italiana lancio del disco

ATHLETICS: TRACK AND FIELD DISCIPLINES ON TRADE CARDS

Bilder Olympiade 1928 pan-sport cards were issued by a Dresden-based cigarettes manufacturer called Salem. Of three series of cards issued only the second and third contain athletes of track & field, of which there are many, from as far afield as Japan, featuring less-well remembered names, like Ethel Calderwood, as well as legends like Nurmi. They are not too costly, and cards can be had for £2 or £3 each.

Shredded Wheat, the breakfast cereal, once issued cards with a decidedly stomach-turning look. *Kevin Keegan's Keep Fit With The Stars*, a series from 1978, had garish, road-pizza designs that brought on an a decidedly unsettled feeling. The questionable talent of the illustrator of such cards went unnoticed by many in the era of brown flock wallpaper and pretty much dull-everything else, too. Brendan Foster's card shows him running in what appears to be scatological trails of waste. Pay little!

Shredded Wheat gave away a more sober series in 1984. The *Champions of Sport* cards were sponsored by well-known British boxer, Henry Cooper. Gone were the splatter designs of 1978. The newer cards feature Steve Cram, Daley Thompson, and other sports stars of the permed hairdo. Values are low: less than £1 each.

Spalding's *Champion* cards of 1926, from USA, include around two dozen track & field athletes. These very rare cards may cost you over £100 each but that's nothing compared to other champs in this series, which start at £1,000 each, rising sharply for the baseball and golf stars.

Smith's *Champions of Sport*, from 1902, came in two types: with red backs, and with blue backs. If you can find them you'll probably have to pay over £100 per card to acquire the walkers and runners included. Compared to money paid for other sportsmen, these are low prices! Beware of recent reprints which are worth nothing.

Sweetule candy tobacco included Junior Service *Famous Sports Records* cards, in 1957. At least four world-famous athletes are included, such as Roger Bannister. They can be found at about £2 each card.

Topps, the gum producer, issued *Magic Photos*, in 1948. The tiny, monotone picture cards are a shadow of the firm's later, magnificent output, but they are much sought after today. The huge series includes a sub-series called *Track & Field Champions*, which comprises 17 cards. Values are upwards of £5 each.

Top Trumps have been produced by various makers over the years, from Dubreq to Waddington. During their heyday the cards games giants issued at least two athletics games: *Olympic 80 Field & Track*, a set including Sonia Lannaman, Steve Ovett, Ed Moses and Greta Weitz; and, *Olympic All-Time Greats*, featuring legends of the past. Complete sets can be bought for around £20 a box.

Trumpf Chocolates, of West Germany, issued a series of monotone stickers, *Durch Alle Welt*, in the 1950s. Alongside footballers, there is a smattering of athletes. Trumpf cards are very rare and have been seen to sell for as much as £75 each.

Typhoo tea's *Great Achievements* cards, of 1962, include Roger Banister. It's an easy card to find and ought to cost no more than £1.

Vallardi, of Italy, teamed up with a petrol giant, Fina, to issue a series of *Supercampioni* in the late 1980s. The stickers include an odd mix of Italian stars, like Alberto Cova, and world legends like Ed Moses and Ben Johnson. These are rare by the standard of modern stickers, and may cost some pounds each, for bigger names.

Our Heroes was a collection produced by a firm called Venorlandus, and TV's *World of Sport* show, in 1979. The cards find athletes like Geoff

Steve Cram on a card issued with Shredded Wheat, 1984

The title card from a deck of Top Trumps game cards

USA gold medallist discus thrower Al Oerter on a Spanish gum insert

Roger Bannister on an Irish gum insert by Chix, 1950s

Capes, the *Superstars* TV show celebrity shot putter, alongside middle-distance runner, Steve Ovett, to name two of the greats. They can be found in small format and also in super-postcard size. Prices have tumbled from double figures to low singles, since a massive supply of overstocked, unsold cards was found, quite recently.

Weetabix produced a series of colourful *World of Sport Quiz Pic* cards, which it gave away in boxes of breakfast cereals, in 1986. The series was named after a TV show, so, rather than celebrating global sports as its name may suggest, it featured solely British sporting heroes, like Steve Ovett and Mary Peters. Modern day cereal cards like these are not costly to acquire. Many were made. Prices are likely to be less than £1 each.

Wills cigarettes issued a very attractive *Sports of All Nations* series of cards, in 1901. The cards show national flags and ascribe certain sports to particular countries. Wills, in its infinite wisdom, decided that running was ostensibly a British sport. That's nationalism for you! Prices for such cards are around £5.

Wills included runners in its *British Sporting Personalities*, a series of monotone photographic cigarette cards, issued in 1937, which are worth very little, even today.

Younger's beers issued *Tartan Sporting Greats*, in 1989. The series of world-famous sports stars includes footballers, cricketers, rugby players and athletes. The track and field quintet has Daley Thompson, Seb Coe, Steve Ovett, Carl Lewis and Ed Moses. A set is worth but a few pounds.

British gold medallist 50km walker, Tommy Green on a German tobacco card

> *Our Heroes* was a collection produced by a firm called Venorlandus, and TV's *World of Sport Show*, in 1979. The cards find athletes like Geoff Capes, the *Superstars* TV show celebrity shot putter, alongside middle-distance runner, Steve Ovett, to name two of the greats.

Olympic medallist Tom Evenson mounting the steeplechase hurdle, a German card

French trade cards from the 1930s

AN A TO Z OF **SPORTING COLLECTIBLES** 45

AVIATION: AN INTRODUCTION TO THE SPORT OF FLYING ON CARDS

Early French cards have all sorts of fantastical flying scenes. The cards were made by diverse trades, such as confectionery and herbal remedy apothecaries. While cards of the interwar decades failed to stem the whacky flights of fancy dreamed up by earlier fabricants, the realism seen on the cards from a 1930s food producer, Jean Donat Dupont, of Lille, is quite majestic. The firm's series of *Indiana-Sport* cards include many aviators and their machines. For buyers, value for money is very high because prices for such rarities remain relatively low, well below £20 each – for now. The design quality is excellent and the number extant is of single digits.

In the 1920s Spanish pharmacies gave away very colourful trade cards called *¿Quién es el Campeón Mundial?* They show flying machines like the Graf Zeppelin, with its creator, Doktor Eckener; and the winner of the Schneider Trophy for seaplane racing, the British sports pilot Augustus Orlebar. This Brit won the award three times yet was barely mentioned on British cards of the time. This Spanish series is one of the most beautiful to behold, and just as rare. The wealth of sports stars included has some very famous athletes of the day. Prices often remain very reasonable, around £20 each card.

Spain regularly issued trade cards with a gaming element. Thus, alongside the heroes of sport were the four suits – owing more to Tarot cards than traditional playing cards – of swords, coins, cups and batons (or wands). The famous flyers often featured in such collections regularly include Charles Lindbergh. French, Belgian and American issuers were just as keen to include Lindbergh, and collections of this legendary flyer have since been built around the world. He was included on a card made by the food multinational, Heinz. It issued two collections of *Famous Aviator Pictures*, which came with cereals. The Heinz Lindbergh card may sell for more than £100, if it's in top condition. Most cards featuring the legendary airman may generate similar, premium prices.

Aviation legends were honoured in Italy by inclusion in both general interest series and in flying-dedicated collections of trade cards. Italian air aces featured on cards issued as far back as the 1920s. Such cards were typically given with chocolates. The cards tended to be small, photographic monotones, so it can be quite difficult to see what's what, and who is who. Yet, more colourful air aces appeared as caricatures on cards during the latter years of the 1930s.

By the 1950s, Lavazza coffee dedicated a series of cards to *L'Aviazione*. During the same

French trade card, 1930s

French trade card, 1910s

French trade card, 1900s

> **This Spanish series is one of the most beautiful to behold, and just as rare.**

French trade card, 1910s

French trade card, 1910s

French trade card, 1900s

decade Lampo, one of the first Italian issuers of stickers, published two collections: almost 400 stickers called the *Storia Completa dell Aviazione (Complete Story of Aviation)*, which includes a score of heroic flying legends; and, a shorter collection, *Aviazione d'Oggi (Aviation Today)*, which also includes aviation heroes.

Across the Atlantic, the American Tobacco Company had celebrated aviators on large-size cards which it gave with its Mecca and Hassan cigarettes. The *Series of Champion Athletes* includes the flyers Ralph Johnstone and Charles Hamilton. A further collection of 25 cards was dedicated solely to airborne sportsmen, called *The Aviators*, in 1911. It's a stunning collection of cards, and well worth looking out for. You may have to pay over £50 for such cards in very good condition but you'll get them for less than £10 if you'll accept cards with faults. They are beautiful, no matter what state of preservation they are in.

American strip cards were born in the 1920s. Such cards have nothing to do with people removing their clothes in burlesque shows. The generic term for the cards comes from the format in which they were sold. A sheet of cards would be trimmed down, strip by strip, each strip having a number of different sports stars.

French trade card, 1910s

French trade card, 1910s

This brief introduction can only but touch upon the subject of sports flying on cards. Buyers interested in acquiring such cards ought to seek out so-called *general interest* collections, such as were issued by most tobacco merchants in the 1900s. Flyers may often be found in such multi-themed collections. In fact, famous flying names like Lindberg, Amelia Earhart, Wilbur Wright, Amy Johnson, and even the Red Baron are very often featured in them

AN A TO Z OF **SPORTING COLLECTIBLES** 49

BRILLIANT BIRD-M

Left:
C. W. A. SCOTT.
Record-breaking flight from England to Australia. Took only eight days, twenty hours.

Right:
SIR ALAN COBHAM.
Has flown from England to Australia and back; and England to South Africa and back.

French trade card, 1910s

Some stores would sell a strip of stars for a cent. The buyer would usually cut the strip to single cards. Typically strip card designs were drawn and executed by amateur artists. Notwithstanding the probability that enormous quantities were once issued, 100 years ago, some of the cards can be incredibly rare, these days. Strip cards typically showed images of famous baseball players and boxers, though some included aviators. Today, though such cards are hard to find they are often under-valued, so they are usually good investments. Whether the price for strip cards stayed low because collectors did not like the idiosyncratic artwork, or because many collectors do not know of such cards, and do not seek them, it's hard to say. What's noticeable is that smart buyers – very often the leading sports card dealers – are always buying strip cards, and very often at bargain basement prices. It's a fair bet that such cards are set to go skyward in value.

This brief introduction can only but touch upon the subject of sports flying on cards. Buyers interested in acquiring such cards ought to seek out so-called *general interest* collections, such as were issued by most tobacco merchants in the 1900s. Flyers may often be found in such multi-themed collections. In fact, famous flying names like Lindberg, Amelia Earhart, Wilbur Wright, Amy Johnson, and even the Red Baron are very often featured in them. One example of such is by the Gutermann firm, in Belgium. It issued a dual-language series of cards known as famous personalities, in the 1920s, in which Wilbur Wright features. You can seek such rarities on the many European auctions websites and you may see many more, under the aviation tab at www.footballsoccercards.com.

French trade card, 1900s

Top Sellers Panini-licensed sticker from 1974

Boxing: pugilism on trade cards

The first boxing card this writer possessed had arrived in the wake of the first colour TV coming to the street. It was a big day, not just for the new TV. The reason for the upgrade from black & white, to colour, was the Muhammad Ali fight, a Monday nighter, which had been billed as *The Fight of the Century*. It was one of the first fights to be broadcast around the world. This writer's mother loved to watch boxing – perhaps a little too often, and with too much glee – though she disdained TV wrestling (because of the feminine leotards, she said). So, she had organised a TV upgrade, from black & white to colour, and she'd invited family and friends round to see it. Neighbours came too. A home full of adults watched the spatter of bright-red blood drip on to beige canvas while they chowed-down on cheese-and-pineapple cocktail sticks. The bruised American fighters went all the way to pink wines from Portugal.

Growing up in the suburbs at the edge of a metropolitan sprawl meant almost perpetual ennui, not least for the adults. Swinging or colour TV seemed to be the binary choice. So, it was colour TV. Houses up and down the street were having new, colour TVs. In those days a man called a service engineer brought newly manufactured British TVs directly to the home. Also known as TV-repair men, they fitted new TVs, and removed old ones. That was before big business had cottoned on to the con of shadow work. *Shadow work* is when you work for nothing, for someone else, typically for someone who has a lot more money than you have. Petrol suppliers, flat-pack furniture makers, post offices and supermarket chains all benefit from this kind of work without pay. Getting the customer to do the pumping, the lumping, the delivering and the fixing (even the scanning, nowadays) saves multinationals millions in paying people to have jobs doing what people in the past were paid to do.

Few people bought TVs back then. Like houses, TVs were less costly to rent than to buy. There was no year-on-year financial yoke, repairs were free (when and if things went wrong), someone brought the goods to your home and installed them for you, and there were fewer debt traps than today. Upgrading TV sets for bigger, brown cabinets with colour tubes was the norm. Sometimes, the TV delivery men would give gifts to the children of the home: items of distraction so he could fiddle away with wires, valves and tubes, unmolested by curious kids. Thus, the TV firms, namely Granada TV Rental, Radio Rentals, and Vision Hire issued colourful trade cards, badges and other attractive merchandise, which featured cartoon characters, television personalities – when personalities were known to a nation and not only to a niche – and even sports stars, the likes of which you could see if your parents rented a new, more expensive TV. Such promotional trade cards given by these firms are now extremely rare and quite valuable items, much like the boxing card of Ali versus Foreman, given by Granada TV Rentals.

Aside from the cards given by Granada TV Rentals, the first boxing cards to land in this writer's hands were the super-size colour images of Ali and Joe Frazier, from a pop-culture series called *Superstars* issued by Top Sellers, in 1975. The large stickers were actually produced by Panini, behind the sales front of its British agent, Thorpe & Porter, whose sales imprint Top Sellers was responsible for horror magazines, sports cards and soft porn magazines. Though the

Italian trade card of Bugs Bunny, 1930s

Spanish trade card of Felix the Cat, 1920s

French trade card of cats boxing, 1920s

Spanish sticker of Max Baer by Bruguera, circa 1940

Spanish trade card with cut-out moving figures, 1920s

Spanish trade card, 1930s

legend on the stickers suggests a firm called STIG were behind the printing, the Italian variations of the very same stickers clearly show Panini's logo.

After a clearout of boxing cards, in 2003, the Ali and Frazier stickers sold for over £100 each! Joe Bugner also features in the same collection. All have since been reacquired. The regret which often follows getting rid of rare collectibles – they only get rarer and usually costlier – was moderated, in this case, by finding the same items again, and for a lot less, in a mixed lot bought from a general auction.

Boxing fell off the junior radar after the 1975 series of *Superstars*. It was not until Panini revived children's interest in the sport, in 1982, with stickers of Larry Holmes, Marvin Hagler and Alan Minter, in its own *Superstars* collection, that boxing stickers were once again collected in the British Isles. Panini reprised and renamed the pan-sport collection as *Supersport*, in 1986, which includes stickers of Frank Bruno and Mike Tyson. The firm revisited *Supersport*, in 1987, with a new collection of stars. Its sticker of Mike Tyson, from 1986, will set you back over £100 if you want one in near-mint condition. It is numbered #153 but there's also a metallic sticker of Tyson, twinned with Marvin Hagler, at #109. So-called card flippers are known to price these, once easily available, stickers at many hundreds each! Flippers buy low then try to re-sell quickly, at a much higher price, many times higher than the price they paid. Internet auctions are full of flippers hoping to attract naïve buyers with more cash than sense. Be patient. You'll probably get both of these rarities for a lot less than £100 each, in time. Remember, Panini 1980s stickers were not made in small numbers. Sooner or later, there'll be one with your number on it.

Boxing stickers from the latter half of the twentieth century have their roots in rarer and far more beautiful cards from far back. Pugilistic images have enticed card collectors since the 1880s, when the raw charm of boxing was first seen on cards. The earliest cards, which are from America, were issued with tobacco. Thence, further afield, such cards were also included with British cigarettes, and with many types of European confectionery.

It is believed that Lorillard's *Prizefighters* cards, issued in 1887, first brought bare knuckle fighters to the American smoker's eye. These days you may have to pay well over £150 for a single card, in any kind of condition, though some cards, those of the most sought-after boxers, will cost a lot more than that!

Allen & Ginter's boxing cards, of 1888, called *The World's Champions (series 1&2)*, are a little easier to find, and perhaps more beautiful than the Lorillard cards. *Caveat emptor*: these have been reprinted, so don't pay much for reprints. They'll probably never make for a good investment, so £1 for a reprinted card is top dollar! For the originals you'll pay more than £100 each. Ever rarer and usually always up in price, an original is almost always a better investment than any reprint. Look out for the one, solitary boxing card in a mixed sports series called *World's Dudes*, also by Allen & Ginter. *The Dude* from *The Big Lebowski* would, no doubt, have been included were that series to have been contemporary.

In the British Isles Ogden's *Guinea Gold*, and Ogden's Tabs-brand cigarettes issued pictorial cards of boxers around 1900. Notable is a series called *Heroes Of The Ring*. Such cards are as hard to find as the earlier American cards but they'll cost a lot less, starting at around only £5 each card. Prices will rise steeply for rarer, and more

BOXING: PUGILISM ON TRADE CARDS

Rocky, on a Spanish trade card from the 1980s

Topps Bazooka Joe gum insert, 1960s

French trade card, 1920s

Spanish gaming card of Georges Carpentier, 1920s

French trade card, 1890s

French trade card, 1920s

popular names, like John L. Sullivan. Expect to pay £100 for suchlike.

Some of the most impressive boxing cards were issued by children's comics, like *Boys' Friend* and *Boys' Cinema*. A superb, sepia-toned picture of Jack Dempsey was presented with the latter, in 1920. As such, it is the earliest British *rookie* card of this legendary boxer, beating rivals, like *Champion*, *Sports Fun* and *Boy's Magazine*, whose cards of this legend of the ring were released two years later. Expect to pay many hundreds, if you can find it. Note: it's rarer than any of the 1919 cards from USA, including the Underwood & Underwood *rookie*.

For full-colour cards the Yanks win hands down. Cards issued by the American Tobacco Company, namely *Pugilistic Subjects*, of 1908, and *Champion Pugilists*, from 1910, show boxers in splendid colours on larger-than-usual cards for the time. Typically, duller cards were issued in the British Isles, at this time. The British monotone photographic cards are also smaller, being half the scale of the more colourful American issues. However, some are now highly valued, widely sought and avidly collected, notwithstanding their lack of hue.

British cigarette cards of notable boxers were issued by Ogden's, in 1908 and 1909. The *Pugilists & Wrestlers* series of cards was issued in two parts. Of the 75 cards, in all, 25 were issued in 1914, and a further 50 came out in 1915. They can be acquired inexpensively due to the high volume of sets published. These days, in America, card flippers tend to buy such cards cheaply, usually from sellers in Great Britain. Then, the flippers seal said cards in plastic slabs, grade them, and try to re-sell them for ten times the price they paid. With a little patience these colourful cards, showing head and shoulders water colours, will come along free of plastic sealed slabs, at prices which are very much more affordable than £30. Starting at around only £3 each, patient buyers will save over £25 on each card they buy loose, ungraded and free of plastic.

Wills Scissors-brand cigarettes drafted pugilists from the British Empire's armed forces into a collection which it issued just before World War One. The fusilier fist fighters and bombardier boxers made up the *British Army Boxers Series*. Alas, the propaganda call-to-arms series is dull. It's also maudlin, for the monotone photos of strong men from the ranks include, no doubt, many chaps for whom slaughter on the Somme awaited; if not mangled-body mutilation elsewhere in the muddy fields of the so-called Great War. The cards may be bought for around £3 each.

Wills issued a second series of pugilists in the same year, again with its Scissors brand of tobacco. The full-colour cards are without a series title but they show illustrations of famous boxers in action. Known to cards buyers and sellers simply as *Boxers*, the colourful images guarantee more liquidity for your money than the *British Army Boxers*, that is, they'll be easier to re-sell if the need arises. You'll pay around £5 for very good condition cards.

Though less colourful, a series of cigarette cards issued by Cope Brothers, in 1915, shows full-length photographic studies of famous boxers in posed action, and, like Wills beforehand, it includes military service personnel: amateur boxers in their service uniforms. The monotone cards are

  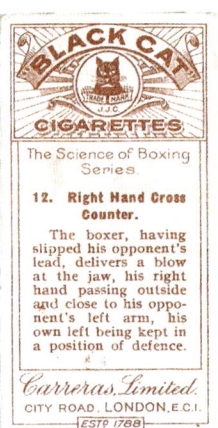  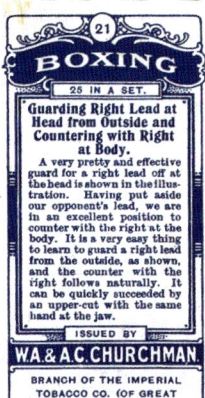 

Carreras cigarette card, 1914 **A reissue by Churchman of a card from 1914 by Ogden's** **Carreras cigarette card, 1914**

French trade card, 1900s **French trade card, 1900s**

rarer than the earlier series by Ogden's, and you'll be paying higher prices for famous names, but many numbers from this series of 126 cards can be found for less than £5 each.

Carreras's Black Cat cigarettes opted for *The Science of Boxing*, with images of boxing techniques, rather than for boxing stars, for its colourful-curtains cards, in 1914. Every card shows a pair of chaps slugging it out in front of a fine selection of haberdashery! The designer avoided what would have been a dour series of images by adding colourful stage curtains, in blues, greens, yellows, purples, browns, and other hues. A set of these cards can be had for relatively little, around £2 each. As well as learning how to defend yourself, you'll get a colour-test guide for your next drapes.

Ogden's followed Carreras's lead, with an instructional series on how to hit out and survive in a fight, with 25 cards, simply called *Boxing*, issued in 1914. The cards, which show a pair of sparring partners ducking and punching, pale in comparison to the more colourful Black Cat issue by Carreras. Pay around £2 per card.

Ogden's came out fighting with a second series of boxing cards, in 1915. The firm had gone back to basics. The cards were very similar in style to those from the 1908 collection, *Pugilists & Wrestlers*. The later issue sits well, twinned with the earlier collection. The 1915 *Boxing* cards number 50 hitters, with no wrestlers. Pay up to £6 for cards in top condition.

After World War One aggressive subjects were the last thing to be found on cards. For some years boxing remained, by and large, a subject only to be found on cigarette cards of the past. So it remained until a younger generation, free from the horrific memories of fighting, celebrated new-generation boxing headlines with newly printed commemorative cards, issued by comics, in the British Isles; and on strip cards, in America.

Strip cards of sports personalities were sold by the strip, hence the name. Strip cards are often found with uneven trimming. Unlike the amateurish designs seen on some strip cards, British comic cards of the same decade, the 1920s, were usually made from real photographs.

AN A TO Z OF **SPORTING COLLECTIBLES** 55

AN A TO Z OF **SPORTING COLLECTIBLES**

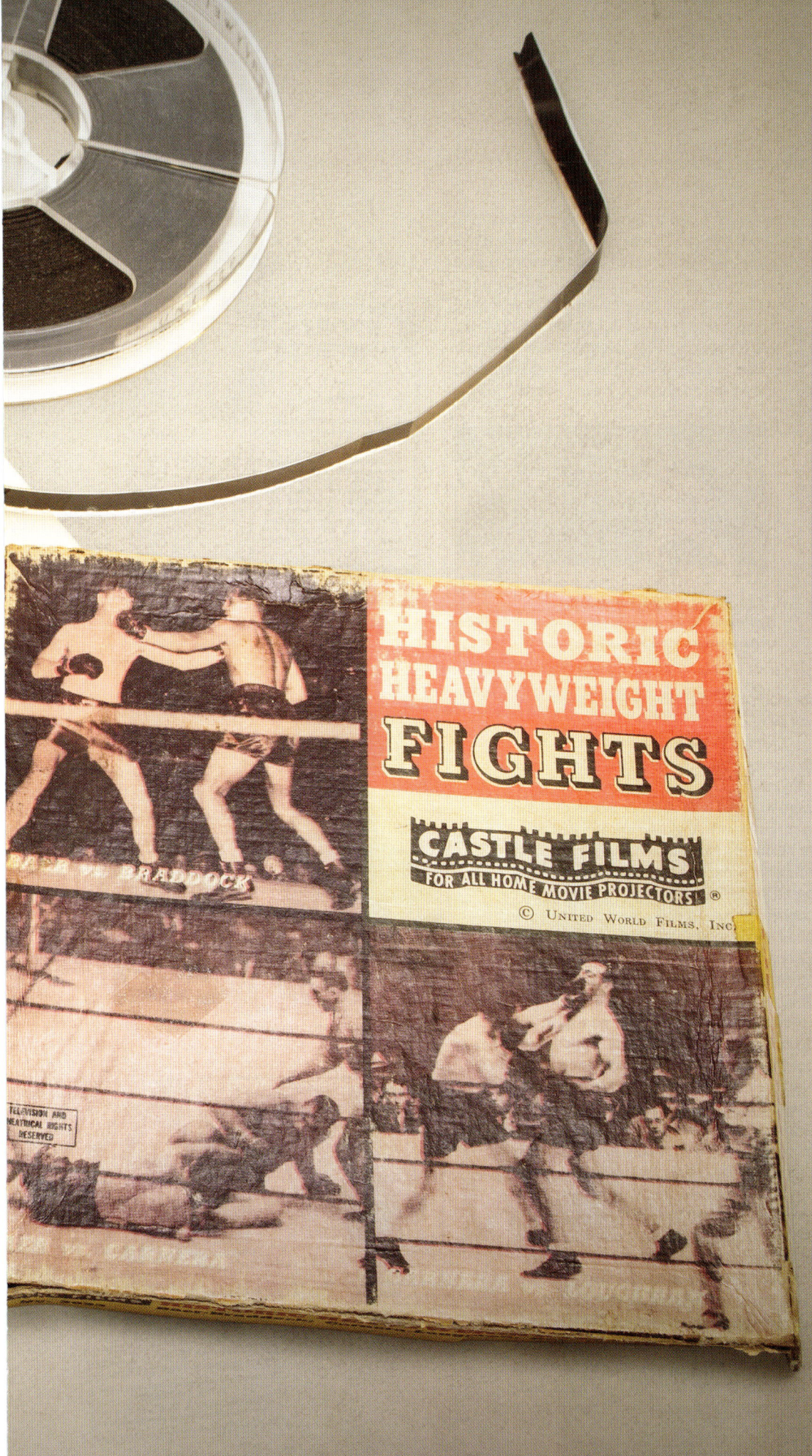

seemingly endless variations to find. The Joe Louis card is highly prized and can be found in different print matrix finishes, so, a complete collection of all the Joe Louis cards, of all the known varieties, could be almost beyond price. Not that the cards are worth more than gold. It's just this: the rarest cards of yesteryear cannot easily be found, for any money – not even for gold!

Cummings & Son followed Donaldson's *Sport Favourites* with an attractive and stylish, red-&-black-coloured series of *Famous Fighters Swop Cards*, in 1949. Like the Donaldson series before it each card shows a caricature of a famous fighter. Today, most Cummings cards can be found for as little as £2 each but you may be surprised to see American slabbers offering them – sealed in plastic – for one hundred times this cost. If you only want one card, as an example, the treasured Joe Louis card can be had, with some patience, for as little as £20. Full sets of 50 cards may come up for sale at specialist cards auctions for less than £100.

Kiddy's Favourites are another example of post-war trading cards from Scotland. Between 1947 and 1952 the Glaswegian firm issued various series of caricatures of sportsmen. Most were footballers but 50 *Popular Boxers* were also printed. The firm's step into the ring, in 1950, produced a set of attractive, if not comical cards which can be found for as little as £1 each. Sports card specialists may ask far more, especially

AN A TO Z OF **SPORTING COLLECTIBLES** '63

Cricket: an introduction to cricketing on trade cards

  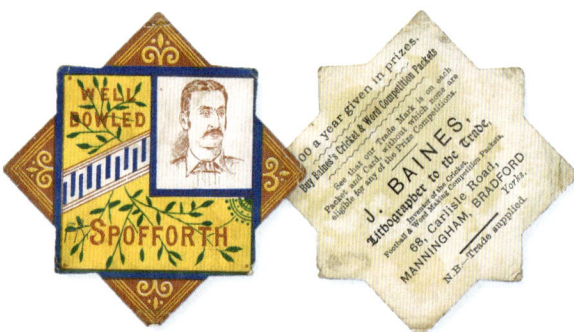 

Victorian paper scraps of a cricket match & cricketers, 1880s

Australian demon bowler Fred Spofforth, an early Baines card, 1882

Frank Sugg, Lancashire CCC & Derby County legend, 1887 card

This writer's uncle played for Aldridge cricket club. He said it was some compensation for not playing for Aston Villa. His trial at Villa Park had been cut short by National Service in the Royal Engineers. Cricket welcomed him back to civilian life, in 1950. He played the summer game for four decades, from first-team glory to fun in the seniors. Uncle Sam, who was first acknowledged in *An A-Z of Football Cards, Priceless Cigarette Cards and Sought-after Soccer Stickers*, treated his nephews and their sister with fortnightly trips to lands of make-believe. While winters were spent in the cold stands at Villa Park, where he worked, warmer weather weekends were whiled away at the cricket club, where he played.

In the 1970s, the club had two pavilions and a building which served as a scoreboard. The older, abandoned pavilion was said to be haunted, if not graced by cricketers past. Was it a gust of wind, or the sight of a *Bosie* googly which lifted those shutters fleetingly? The phantom facade of the pavilion beckoned curious children to the wrong side of the cricket ground. There was a certain air about it, and hairs would stand on end when entering the cobwebbed changing rooms. Hand-hewn elm planks groaned when walked upon, and the silence spoke of the sadness of things. A breeze made the blinds on otherwise sleepy windows blink. Wind rattled the two-tiered bleachers on the porch. The squeaky seating occasioned to lisp an icy '*six!*' at spectacular strikes. After a while the chill warmed to a youngster's curiosity and the pavilion's poltergeists occasionally gifted children rare finds, such as long-lost cigarette cards of once-great cricketers, falling from dusty lampshades which swayed below still ceilings for no apparent reason.

The newly built club house incorporated a younger pavilion. What it lacked in elegance it made up for in amenities, with squash courts and a hockey pitch. Along with two cricket fields and a golf course it was quite some club, for a small village. On one flank, the club was bordered by a small wood of deciduous trees which, for children who'd clambered the branches, afforded views of all the action, and more. From high up, when cricketers were at tea and all was quiet, an untimely, and unlikely slap of leather – not to mention the sigh of willow – could be overheard emanating from curtained windows at the nearby rectory, a ball's throw from the wicket. The slaps and sighs bemused one and all. Junior *swallows and amazons* barely comprehend what *sport* had been played out in the vicar's sacristy but Paul McDonald's books, like *Kiss Me Softly Amy Turtle*, are a comical exposé of such kinky rites in the conservative wards of Walsall's boroughs.

When not scaling trees, whiling away sunny Saturdays in a shady den below the elevated score box was an ideal distraction for young teenagers. Being thus ensconced, at the far side of the wicket, adventurously away from the reality of mountains of school homework was

Special Souvenir. Presented with "The Captain" Magazine, August, 1912.

THE SOUTH AFRICAN CRICKETERS, 1912.

idyllic. The odd kerfuffle at the crease made for the occasional distraction – there was a ground-level aperture which served as a spyglass in the grass – and it really was the perfect summer hideaway, a place where one could concentrate on comics, cards and other distractions. One such matter was the movement of Mrs Robinson. The attractive woman lounged low in a form-describing, fabric deckchair while she kicked her sling-back, high-heeled sandals ever higher, crossing and re-crossing her long legs from her sedentary position. It was as if she meant to distract the wicketkeeper at his bails. Fair play!

In the 1970s cricket cards had been in short supply, partly due to the sport's momentary dip into the realm of the unfashionable, at least in the eyes of youngsters. Packets of sweet cigarettes made by Bassett had been the confection of choice for children wanting cricket cards but the firm's hiatus meant seven years had passed between the second series of *Gold Flake Sportsmen*, in 1971, and two, newer series of cricketers which came out in the latter part the decade. Again, after those years, the cricket card drought resumed, and worsened, until the arrival of Panini's seminal *Cricket 83* sticker series, and its dedicated album.

Earlier on, during the 1950s and the 1960s, cricket cards had been issued in Great Britain with gum, with sweets, and with comics. During most years there was a set to be collected but by the end of the 1960s things were dour. Soccer stars stickers and footballer gum cards were the thing, and traditional summer sports, like cricket, had to compete with Olympic Games collections, and also with summertime football collections, for the World Cups. The production of cricket cards was in the doldrums. How different it was from the early years of the twentieth century and Victoriana!

The oldest known cricket cards are trading cards which hark back to the first years of the 1880s. They were issued by Baines Litho, a printer based in Manningham. The cards have a coat of arms to the rear, showing a cricketer and a rugby footballer. There will be much more on these rarities, and their values, in a little while.

The earliest British tobacco-trade cards to show cricketers were issued with Wills cigarettes, in 1896. The most sought-after cards from the series are those of W.G. Grace and Charles Burgess Fry, which are worth some hundreds each. Fry was also a well-known England international soccer player, and a star with Corinthian and Southampton football club.

Yearly, from the *fin de siècle* until shortly after World War Two, at least one new set of cricket cards was produced by someone, somewhere. Typically the cards were made by tobacco merchants, or published with journals, or given with sweets. Then, in the 1950s, it all slowed down quite dramatically. The post-war death of cigarette cards was, to all extents and purposes, the end of the yearly series of cricket cards. Newer producers, like the firms which made bubble gum, issued all but two sets of cricket

cards over 20 years, notably in 1959, and again in 1961. Confectioners like Barratt of Wood Green produced a couple of collections too, but without the incessant production of cigarette cards very lean times were upon collectors of cricket cards. Even the once proud, golden-age comics were folding, and closing down. Both *Skipper* and *Boys' Magazine* had disappeared. Also gone were *Pals* and *Boys' Realm*. All had regularly issued cricket cards during the years before the war.

Yet it had all started so well, in the 1880s, and it was not only in Great Britain where such cards were made. They were issued in South Africa, Australia and New Zealand, too. Cricket trade and trading cards were also published in unlikely places such as USA, France and Belgium – and these exotic types are some of the most beautiful cricket cards known.

The rarest cards include those that were given with the Tally-Ho brand of cigarettes, issued by the National Cigarette Company of Australia, in 1897; and cards by MacDonald tobacco, issued in Great Britain between 1900 and 1902. An example from the Antipodean series, in any kind of condition, will set you back many hundreds of pounds, while the rarer still, Glaswegian tobacco cards by MacDonald, of cricket teams, may cost more than £1,000 each! There are two series of MacDonald cards known: colour cards from 1900, and monotone cards from around 1902. Only one coloured card has been seen: Yorkshire CCC. The Headingly-based club was also featured in the later black-&-white series of which there are 12 cricket team cards. The phenomenally rare cards are known with two brand names: *Tontine* and *Winning Team*. Of the dozen cricket teams, ten show English county teams while the reaming pair features Australia and England. Were one of these cards to come to auction, in 2021, it should undoubtedly cost a four figure fee.

Approaching the subject of cricket cards in a book like this, an introduction to sports cards in general, would test the best of editors. The task of collating the most interesting, the rarest and most unusual cricket cards, between these covers, is a game of limited overs. Still, this book does what no other has done: it presents colour images of cards previously unpublished, and lists some of the rarest cricket cards known.

American & British Gum is what collectors once thought A&BC stood for. It's nothing to do with American. The initials are actually those of the founders' surnames. The group of British friends had dreamed up the idea in the 1940s. Messrs Aynsz, Braun and two Coakley brothers incorporated a limited company, registered in Great Britain, in the name of A&BC Chewing Gum Limited. The company allied with an eccentric home-based chemist, Oscar Janser, in issuing artificially created chewing gum. The gum was similar to American chewing gum but had no need of the American ingredients;

AN A TO Z OF **SPORTING COLLECTIBLES**

yet fully appreciated for their rarity or value. In fact, they remain shockingly undervalued. In USA $3 million was paid for one of over 50 known exemplars of a certain baseball player cigarette card. It's probable that no Baines card exists in a double-figures quantity! Most Baines cards have a global 'population' of but one or two exemplars.

Baines soccer cards have recently been seen to sell for up to and over £500 each. Cricket cards by Baines are far rarer than the firm's soccer cards! It's only a matter of time, maybe just a few years more, until a Baines cricket card exceeds £1,000.

The 20 known cricketers on cards which bear the marque of Baker & Co., issued in 1902, are the same score of faces featured in similar series issued by Charlesworth & Austen, Faulkner, Rutter and other manufacturers. The *Cricketers Series* collection was a collection shared by many different merchants, each of whom added their name and advertising legends. The cards are also known without sponsors, with plain backs. Whichever marque they bear these cards are rare, and individual examples may cost you three-figures each card.

Barratt was, once upon a time, the United Kingdom's best-known manufacturer of candy cigarette cards. The firm's first cricket cards were issued circa 1923. The unbranded photographic cards of cricketers, and other sportsmen, were produced by a London printer called Hills & Lacey. The collection revived a Victorian-era tradition whereby a printer would produce cards with blank backs for other firms to customise with their own brands or marques. These cards, with their plain-backs, marked a sea change for the confectionery trade. The 1923 cricket

Amongst earlier cards, alongside the cricket balls, Baines also printed shield-shaped and other fancy, die-cut cards (fans, diamonds, ovals, squares, clubs, etc.) Showing famous players on the cards helped sell the designs by the million! Not many of the earliest types remain extant. In fact, the relatively few early Baines cards known exist in quantities of as few as one or two of each design, and no more. It has been noted, in old newspapers and other archival sources, that while millions of cards were sold, and hundreds of thousands of different designs were employed, few of the cards were spared from World War Two's old paper pulping war effort.

Baines cards, and similar-looking cards by the firm's erstwhile competitors (Sharpe, Briggs, Ormerod, Richardson, etc.), are of the rarest genres of sporting ephemera but they are not

AN A TO Z OF **SPORTING COLLECTIBLES** 71

CRICKET: AN INTRODUCTION TO CRICKETING ON TRADE CARDS

Tarrab Brand Rock card by Barrett, without the Hill & Lacy imprint, 1925

Player's tobacco card, 1913

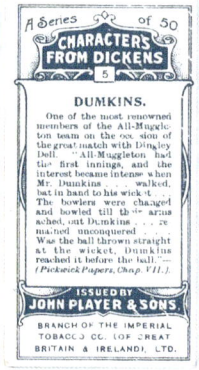

Tarrab Brand Rock card by Barratt with a Hill & Lacy imprint, 1924

Bunsen Confectionery card, 1922

in the 1930s, a decade that almost defies the existence of very rare and valuable tobacco cards. It's worth remembering that non-tobacco trade cards from the 1930s are often much scarcer, and can be much more valuable than tobacco issues from that time. Given the choice always opt for sports cards given with candy cigarettes, or comic-issue cards over cigarette cards of the 1930s, for value.

A non-sports collection in which to find cricketers is that of Carreras's *Popular Personalities*, a series of oval-shaped cards from 1935. Values are around £1 each.

After World War Two Carreras was one of the few tobacconists to continue issuing cards, though they were not cigarette cards in the classic sense. Carreras started printing the cigarette card on the cigarette box itself, on the packaging. It was meant to be cut out. Cards of this type are known as packet issues. Unlike earlier packet issues, from the 1930s, by Phillips, where the card was printed on the outside of the box, Carreras hid the design inside. It was printed on the internal slider, the part of the confection that raised and lowered the cigarettes. In this case, at the moment of purchase, the buyer would not know which sportsman he or she would find, unlike the earlier Phillips packets.

In 1949 Carreras included a selection of cricketers in its mixed *Sports* series of slider-design packet issues; and, a year later, it went all the way with 50 different cricketers in a series dedicated to the sport.

Carr's of Carlisle made savoury snacks. In 1967 the firm issued a very attractive series of trade cards, which it named *Water Biscuits Sports*. The collection of 40 colourful cards includes 20 cricketers. These days the cards sell for over £10 each.

Champion was a 1920s British comic. Like its rivals, *Adventure* and *Boys' Magazine*, it issued trade cards to attract readers. *Sporting Champions*, of 1922, included seven monochrome cricketers. These can be found for as little as £1 each. Champion followed this series with *Famous Test Match Cricketers*, which were issued in tandem with its sister-publication, *Triumph*. The 32 cards are worth around £2 each. However, a seller can expect to multiply this price by a very large factor if a card is paired with an original comic, with the particular issue with which the card was given. Prices of well over £100 have been seen for such rare combinations, partly because of the cross-over to the comics market, and partly because the comics themselves are now much rarer than the cards. The hardier and easier to store, small cards have lasted the test of time. Most comics were pulped, in the war, or else have failed to survive in any number. You'll find 100 of each card before you find a single copy of the comic with which it came. The card is often featured on the front of the comic. So, it makes for a great pairing.

Champion Test Match Record Breakers was one of eight miniature folders of sports cards, issued in 1935. To be collected into a *Portfolio Of Sport* booklet, the miniature folder contains a concertina of seven cricketers. Other folders in the series include boxers, racers, footballers, etc. This particular folder includes Don Bradman and it may cost well over £50 if it's free from glue damage – most were glued into the *Portfolio*. The *Portfolio Of Sport* was so successful that *Champion* soon issued a second, similar collection called *The Champion Sports Wallet*. The value for uncut folders from either collection is around £50 but cut single images, taken from the folders, are worth a fraction of this. Many sellers have foolishly cut up folders to sell single images. In such a case don't pay more than £1 for their butchered items. The value is in uncut folders, not in scissored singles.

Champion issued some of the world's earliest albums of sports cards, one of which is called *Sportsmen of the World*, from 1934. Its 32 sports cards were given weekly, in strips of four. An uncut quad of cards is worth between £50 and £100, depending on the players included. Individual cut cards sell for a lot less than £5 each. The complete album is not rare, as most cards were cut, stuck down and kept. It can be

Between 1924 and 1928 about 80 cricketers were thus issued. The backs of the cards show one of four different adverts for Barratt confectionery. All four types of back were printed at the same time, as partial sheets of uncut cards have proved.

Sports Fun Photo Stamps, uncut sheet as issued, 1922

Pattreiouex tobacco card, 1931

From 1938, a radioactive card by Bocnal tobacco!

Stollwerck chocolates card from Germany, 1910

found for less than £50. There are four cricketers in the collection. Don Bradman features on one of the strips.

Chums comic issued photographic cricket cards of teams, in 1922, and players a year later. The score of players from 1923 are relatively easily available and cost as little as £2. Five teams are known: Yorkshire, Nottinghamshire, Surrey, Lancashire and Middlesex and, if you are patient, you may find prices just as low.

Churchman cigarettes included a beautiful series of 25 *Famous Cricket Colours* with its smokes, in 1925. It's *the* Churchman cricket set to have. The cards show caps and emblems, in full colour. The designs were taken from a pull-out free gift, a lithographic poster which was given with a certain boys' comic, issued earlier in the century. The cards are quite easily available for as little as £2 each, condition being all; and a set of cards in average, or good condition can be had for less than £50.

During 1936, Churchman tobacco issued a set of 50 colourful *Cricketers* with its cigarettes, one per packet. The vignette-style design of the portraits of rather swotty-&-spotty-looking sportsmen seems like a throwback to earlier types of tobacco cards. The rather conservative nature of the artwork on these portraits is one of the drawbacks to this collection. It does not stand out, lacking something in identity, and the cards are not very rare, no matter what sellers may state on their sales. Millions were printed so don't pay more than £50 for the set, at the very highest, and only for the finest condition cards. The stockpiles of 1930s cigarette cards waiting to come to market would surprise many a collector! A set of these cards in average condition could probably be had for as little as £10. Remember,

AN A TO Z OF **SPORTING COLLECTIBLES** 79

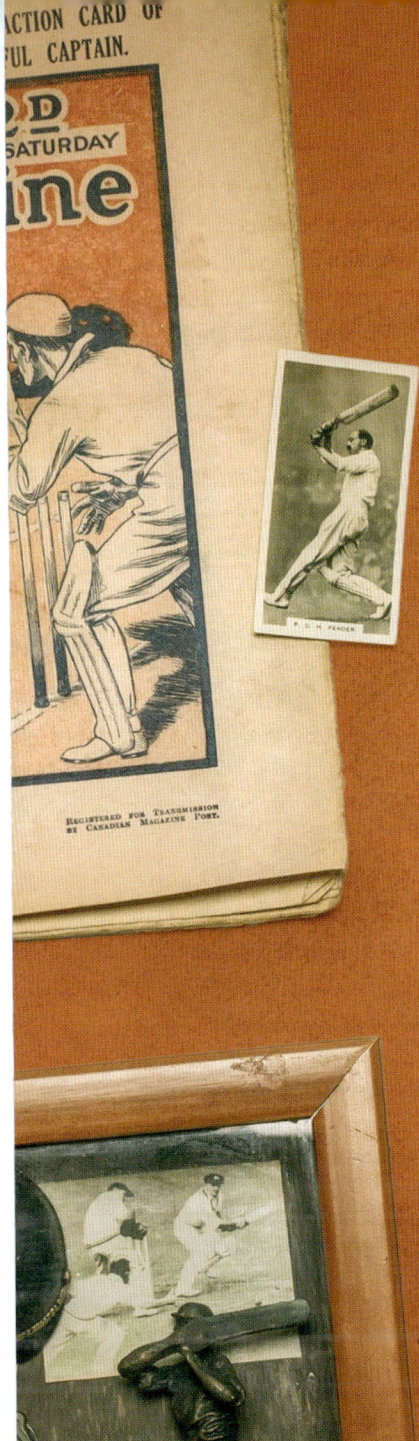

THE LEAGUE OF YOUNG ATHLETES!

THE BOYS' REALM
of Sport & Adventure.
1D

KING CRICKET!
By Charles Hamilton.

Lagden is clean bowled for a duck's egg.

EVERY SATURDAY—ONE PENNY.   [SATURDAY, APRIL 27, 1907.

No. 256.   VOL. V.]

CRICKET: AN INTRODUCTION TO CRICKETING ON TRADE CARDS

A folding card given with candy tobacco, by Barratt & Co, 1932

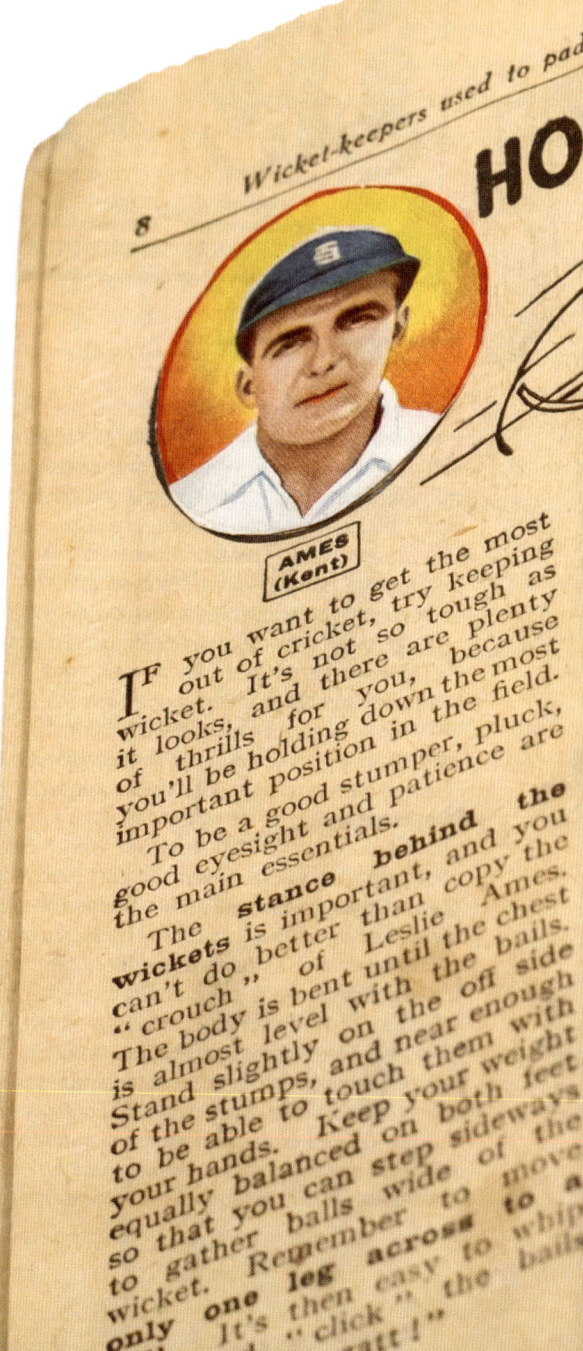

Series. A score of cricketers are included, with such greats as Charles Burgess Fry among them. It's an affordable set of highly attractive cards. Values for most cards start at as little as £2.

In 1926, the Irish firm went all in with cricket, producing a series of 100 *Famous Cricketers* cards, of which most feature photography capturing full-on action shots, albeit frozen into rather dull monotones. Oddly, there are one or two portraits in the set which seem like they are from a different series. Don't pay too much! Some sellers ask for £5 each for singles. It's possible to buy a set of 100 for less than £150. So, these cards are not rare and patience will reward the careful buyer. Fairer sellers offer single cards for about £2 each.

Gallaher went on to issue various series of *Champions* and *Sporting Personalities* throughout the 1920s and 1930s, in which cricketers are to be found. Most cards are easily available and cost as little as £1 each.

Goodwin's Old Judge brand issued cricket cards in the late 1880s. The American cards include legends like Grace and Blackham, and they may cost you a small fortune, should you be lucky enough to find an original. You probably won't. Such very rare cards were long thought to be the first cricket cards but it is not so! Goodwin was not the first. Baines of Manningham, in England, was first. It produced earlier cricket cards, including a Blackham and a Grace card, in the early 1880s. Goodwin Graces and Blackhams have sold for £2,000 each. Imagine what a Baines would make? Baines are rarer.

Hignett's *Prominent Cricketers of 1938* is the very same series as that issued by Ogden's, in the same year. The latter cards cost a lot less.

Hill issued a series of 28 *Famous Cricketers*, in 1912. The cards come in two types, with fronts in blue, and with fronts in brown. Note: there are two cards numbered #1. One shows Rhodes, the other Douglas; one being blue, the other brown. It's the same for card #13, which has the pair of players sharing that number too. Needless to say these cards have become the most difficult odds to acquire, thanks to collectors seeking the foursome as a pair of differently coloured twins. Hill reused the *Famous Cricketers* title for a series of 40 cards, in 1923. The later, sepia-toned cards can be found for £1 each but the 1912 issues may cost you 50 times the price! The bright blue cards seem to be the rarest.

With its Sunripe brand, in 1925, Hill included photographic portraits on large-format cigarette cards, called *Famous Cricketers*, which it followed with *Caricatures of Famous Cricketers*, one year later. The later cards were available in both large and small formats. The three types can be had for as little as £1 per card.

Kinnear's *Handicap* cricket cards were issued in 1899. They have since been reproduced, allowing collectors to have cheap copies of otherwise expensive cards. Copies will never repay the money you spend so don't pay too much. A set of 15 reprints can be had for less than £5. By contrast an original card in very good condition may top £100! Note: similarly rare cricket cards by the Victorian issuer Marcus may be found with Kinnear overprints to the rear.

Richard Lloyd's *Bondman* cards state: *£150 Must Be Won!* The 25 cards in the series are also known as *Names of Famous Cricketers* puzzle cards. Issued in 1930, the conundrums are almost too difficult to solve, nowadays, being names of mostly long-forgotten sportsmen, but the cards are attractive in their own right. Most have been

...eir shirts with straw.

'S ZATT!

No Byes!

The secret of safe catching [is] simple. Keep the hands [c]lose together, the fingers [p]ointing groundwards, not out[w]ards or the ball may hit the [t]ips and give you a nasty injury. [K]eep that secret fresh, and the [f]ast bowling will have no terrors [f]or you. Some keepers like [t]o tie a **piece of steak** across [t]he palm of each hand for fast [b]owling, and it certainly takes [t]he sting off any thunder[b]olt.

Good wicket keepers rarely [u]se the pads to stop the ball, [b]ut if you have to do it, try [a]nd **hit the wickets off the [r]ebound**. It's a trick that's [often] stumped a batsman.

One more hint. When the [b]all is thrown in from the field, [a]lways get behind the wickets [s]o that they are **between [you] and the fielder** throwing [the] ball.

The distance between the wickets is 22 yards.

- HOW TO STAND BEHIND THE WICKETS
- USING THE PADS TO HIT THE WICKETS WITH THE REBOUND
- FAST BALLS WON'T PASS YOU IF YOUR HANDS TAKE THEM LIKE THIS
- PROTECT YOUR PA[LM] WITH A LUMP OF [STEAK]
- ONLY ONE LEG MOVES
- AT A TIME [THE] WICKETS [ARE] BETWEEN [YOU AND] THE [FIELDER]

CRICKET: AN INTRODUCTION TO CRICKETING ON TRADE CARDS

written on, so cards without answers are worth more, at around £5 each.

Marcus cricket cards from 1895 are desirable and valuable. The cards were issued with the firm's Handicap brand of cigarettes, and though they share a name with a brand made by Kinnear, the Marcus cards are very different. The unusually narrow cards show beautiful, coloured illustrations. The artwork is unusual, tending towards a slight caricature of the featured cricketer. On the other hand, the Kinnear cards are broader and show black-and-white photographic portraits. The Marcus cards are known with and without Kinnear overprints. Likely prices per card are in the many hundreds! If you get one, keep it! You may never find another. These cards are always upwards in value.

Millhoff cigarettes issued a pair of cricket series, in 1928, each consisting of 27 *Famous 'Test' Cricketers* [sic], one series being larger than the other, a standard cigarette card size and a broader type. The brand name, De Reszke, is prominently displayed on the rear of the cards. The larger cards are worth up to £5 each while the smaller size cards sell for about half that. There are typographic differences between the two sets. The same producer included some cricketers in its later series, called *In The Public Eye*, in 1930.

Amidst a host of footballers Murray & Sons included 20 cricketers in its cigarette cards *Series H*, in 1912. The black borders on the cards are all too easily chipped and otherwise defaced, so values are often influenced by condition. Cards of famous players will attract higher prices and cards with perfect black borders will demand premiums. Buyers should beware of a process of improving the look of such cards, known as *tipping in*, whereby black is added to a damaged border. It may not be noticed at first glance. Look carefully, as a card may look better than it really is!

Ogden's cricket cards range from rare Victorian masterpieces to overly abundant art deco classics. The earliest, from around 1895, show women cricketers in playful poses. The cards owe a certain something to keyhole thrills, and *what the butler saw* … and rather less to the sport of cricket. Putting pretty damsels on tobacco cards, whether dressed or not, was found to be effective in the promotion of cigarette sales. Later in the 1890s Ogdens replaced the wanton waifs with sober images of gentlemen in sporting colours, or Sunday *best*, in a set of 36 cards which has come to be known as the 'green gravure' *Cricketers & Sportsmen* series. Some of the images were used again on Ogden's *Guinea Gold* sports cards issued by 1900. The green gravure cards will cost more than £100 each. The *Guinea Gold* cards are generally easier to find, though there are rare and expensive varieties known and they may also top £100 in price.

From 1900 onwards, Ogden's issued various, so-called *General Interest* series of cards which, upon initial glance, look quite similar. Several different series include sports and sporting personalities alongside other subjects. The first of the so-called general interest series was styled after *Guinea Gold* cards. They have plain backs and show the Ogden's Cigarettes legend, to the front of the card, with a wafting-shaped, smoky tail emanating from the second letter g. The cards no longer show the *Guinea Gold* inscription but they are eminently similar. Grace is included and his card's value is worth over £100. Note: there are many different Ogden cards of Grace from this short period. 1899–1904. There are two among the *Guinea Gold*-style cards (the cards with cursive lettering legends to the front) and at least three to be found among the various series of Ogden's *Tabs* cards, from circa 1901 to around 1904. So, look out for Grace on a card with the legend, *Guinea Gold*; and another on a card with *Ogden's Cigarettes* (without *Guinea Gold*) in cursive lettering. These are two of the oldest black-card types.

Ogden's followed the change of monarch with a change in style, and the introduction of *Tabs*-brand cards, in 1901. These are many and varied but most are easier to identify than the earlier *Guinea Gold* types, because most *Tabs* cards have numbers or series titles. Yet, there is also an unnumbered series, simply known as *General Interest*; and there are other, letter-identified *General Interest* series, too, such as *General Interest A Series* (there's a Grace card therein), and *General Interest D Series* (wherein there is another, different Grace card). The values for Ogden's *Tabs* cards vary widely, and sometimes wildly. Some dealers think they can add value to a card by having it sealed in a toxic block of plastic which was made of oil waste products. Don't fall for it! A rare card does not need a 'grader' to slab it for eternity, nor that slabber's uncertain knowledge. Graders are typically from a new-cards, non-cricket

Australian matchbox label, 1940s

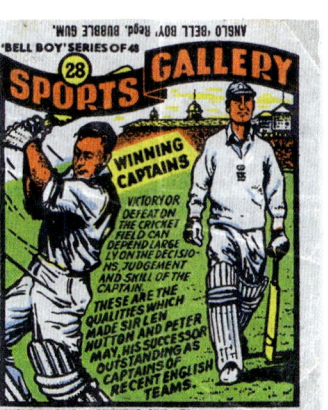

Anglo-American Gum Bell-Boy Sports Gallery insert, 1957

1930s German tobacco card by Lloyd

South African tobacco card, 1939

Peter May on a transfer decal by Cadet Sweets, 1956

Bill Edrich on a transfer decal by Barratt, 1949

Denis Compton on a cadet Sweets card, 1956

background and, thus, have little or no expertise in the sport, let alone in old cricket cards from the British Commonwealth.

Ogden returned to cricket in later times, notably in 1926, and in 1938, with further series each consisting of 50 cards. These series are easy to find, values remain low and the cards are eminently affordable.

Pattreiouex cigarettes included cricket in many of its card collections, though the best known series are the early ones. In 1922 both its Casket and Critic brands of fags included cards from a series numbered up to 96. There are, actually, only 84 different cricketers included. For reasons lost in time, the firm used some of the same sportsmen twice, giving each of a dozen reprised stars different numbers. Look out for card 84 which is known to have two different players. In 1925, the firm issued a second series devoted solely to cricket, which included 75 different cricketers.

Phillips is a name that's been around since the earliest cigarette cards. Godfrey Phillips & Sons issued sports cards as early as the 1890s. Its so-called General Interest series of cards, issued in 1896, includes a pair of cricketers, one of which is Grace. The worth of these cards is somewhere over and above £150 each card but if you have Grace, in excellent condition, you may be looking at £1,000.

Phillips featured 17 cricketers in its next sports cards series, in 1900, which was inscribed simply Guinea Gold – just like the name of the Ogden's brand. The footballing cricketer C. B. Fry is included herein, and his card was seen to sell for £200, in an internet sale, in 2020.

Apart from an odd card in the Sporting Series of 1910, Phillips issued no more cricket cards for a decade, until the 1920s, when it manufactured a fabulous series of so-called cricket silks. Silk cigarette cards had been a new-fangled type of tobacco promotion. Manufacturers found that silks appealed to women as well as to men, and many a quilt was stitched from the small rectangles of woven or printed fabric given with cigarettes between 1914 and 1921. The 17 known silks in the BDV Cigarettes County Cricket Badges series are stunning, and every collector ought to have at least one type in his or her collection.

Pinnace cards were first issued by Phillips in 1919 (footballers) but the first cricket subjects date only to 1922. Phillips's Pinnace cricket cards come in three sizes, none of which are standard or typical, when compared to classic cigarette cards. As well as very small-size cards there are also medium-size cards (similar in dimension to classic gum cards of the 1960s), and large cards (a little like postcards, in size). There are around 200 cards in each size, with many variations to the fronts. The photos, the lettering and the numbering are often different, card to card. It's advisable to take cards which seem to be the same and lay them side by side to check for subtle variations. Values for the small cards start at around £1 each but rise significantly for rarer types and sought-after cricketers. Buyers can expect to pay a lot more for medium-size and larger cards.

In 1924 Phillips issued more photographic images, about 225 cards in all, in a collection called Series of Cricketers. This series consists of more or less standard-size cards in the classic

South African team on a Pattreiouex card, 1936

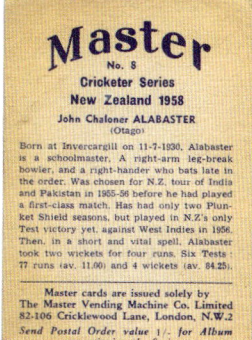

New Zealand cricketers by Master Vending Gum, 1958

AN A TO Z OF **SPORTING COLLECTIBLES** 87

CRICKET: AN INTRODUCTION TO CRICKETING ON TRADE CARDS

Donaldson *Sports Favourites* card, 1948

Radio Fun cricketer trade card, 1950s

cigarette card dimension. Today, the cards can be found for as little as £2 each. Cricket remained Phillips's sport of choice and by 1926 another series, called *Famous Cricketers*, was also being collected by its smokers. Values for the 1926 series remain low, and its cards are affordable at around £1.50 each.

Phillips continued issuing cricket cards throughout the 1930s: *Personalities of Today* (1932), *Australian Sporting Celebrities* (1933), *Who's Who in Australian Sport* (1933), *In The Public Eye* (1935), *Spot The Winner* (1937), and *Test Cricketers 1932–33*. Most of these cards may be obtained very inexpensively, often for as little as £1 a card.

Phillips produced a notable series of beautiful cards as part of its packaging, in 1932. The packet hull cut-out cards came with BDV Sport Cigarettes. The initials stand for a tobacco leaf called Boyd Dibrell Virginia. The cigarettes were sold in both paper and card packaging. So, BDV packet issues include footballers, boxers, jockeys, tennis players and other notable sports stars of the time. There are also plenty of variations between the cards. Certain images are slightly larger than others, some have thinner frame lines, others have wider frame lines; some have duller printing, others are brighter and more colourful. One year to another, different photographs were used. The captions also differ, by name and in punctuation. Cards that remain uncut, on a fold-out paper packet, or on a card slider, or on a complete box of cigarettes, are worth far more than cut cards. The trim of cut cards affects values. Wider borders generally mean higher prices. Though prices for some cards start low, at about £5 each, rarer examples and uncut boxes may push them over £100, for the most sought-after cards. Over 50 different cricketers are known but with variations, you may be collecting double that number! Previously unrecorded types keep showing up and estimates of the total number of different varieties are often rendered obsolete as soon as they are updated.

Following World War Two, Phillips returned to the production of packet-issue cards, that is, cards to cut out. It issued so-called *Sports Slides* – a slider was part of the box of cigarettes – and packets that showed a sports star on the hull. Four different series of *Cricketers* and *Sportsmen* (which included cricketers) were issued between 1948, 1951, 1953 and 1954. Cut cards are worth between £1 and £10 each, while uncut packets start at £25 and may exceed £50 for those featuring notable players. The 1953 and 1954 collections are the most valuable. The hardest to obtain, by some measure, is the 1954 collection. Its prices may exceed those mentioned here, especially for an entire, uncut packet of the 1954 Denis Compton. Note: there are three different Denis Compton cards to be found between the four series. Likewise there is a trio of different Len Hutton cards, though he did not feature in the 1954 series.

Player's cigarettes issued four large sets of cricket cards – 50 cards each – with cigarettes in 1926, 1930, 1934 and in 1938. Due to the very high number of cards printed by John Player it's possible to find excellent condition cards for very little money. These sets, *Cricketers Caricatures by Rip*, from 1926, and the three series of *Cricketers*, from the 1930s, are eminently affordable and attractive, colourful cards. Yet, perhaps the most appealing of Player's cricket cards were those issued in earlier series of mixed subjects, in collections of so-called general interest or other themes, such as *Characters from Dickens* (numbered to 25, issued in 1912; numbered to 50, reissued in 1923), in which there are a pair of cricket cards; and *Everyday Phrases* (1901), in which the *So Sorry I Was Out* card features an amusing

Uncut strip of weighing scales cards by British Automatic, 1955

Bimbo Spanish sticker, 1973

Bassett sweet cigarettes card, 1979

cricketing illustration. Player's cards from before World War One are much rarer and more valuable than most from afterwards. As such, the firm's earlier and less usual cricket cards may cost as much as £20 each, whereas the 1930s issues will cost but £5 for 50 cards! For sets that are glued down into albums, there is little worth.

Smith's cigarettes were sold with so-called *Champions of Sport* cards, in around 1902. The series is known with both red backs and with blue backs but the cards with blue backs are actually of a different series altogether. It includes different cricketers! In the series with red backs there are four cricketers among the 50 cards. The foursome come inscribed with various marques, and it's possible to have four of each player, each with different backs. The brands include Glasgow Mixture, Trilby, Harvest Moon and Morning Gallop. Conversely, in the series with blue backs there are 29 cricketers! However, unlike the series in red, the blue cards only have one type of back to each player. Both issues are of rarity and value, and more than £150 is often paid for the cricketers in the collections – if and when such cards come up for sale. However, the four red cards and one blue card of W.G. Grace may exceed this figure. Note: the series with blue backs has been reprinted, so be careful you are not buying copies when you want originals. The recent, low-value reprints are worth almost nothing and the cards will probably be worth less after buying them unless you spend very little – thousands of sets have been printed – so don't expect to improve your money by buying reprints.

Smith's published a series devoted to cricket, in 1912, which includes 70 players. It is called, simply, *Cricketers*. The cards numbered 51 to 70 are actually from a second series and bear the title, *2nd Series Cricketers*. The 70 cards display 12 different brand names on their backs, including *Kashan*, *Auld Brig*, *Pinewood*, *Orchestra*, etc. Values for the cards depend very much on condition, as with all cards, but especially so in the case of cards with black borders, like these. Black borders may have been 'improved' by unscrupulous sellers, or previous owners, so look carefully at the cards before spending a lot of money. Typically, very good condition cards sell for around £10 each but excellent condition examples may exceed that by some way. All-time greats in top condition may do better still.

Sniders & Abrahams, in Australia, is best known for Australian football cards but during the early years of the twentieth century it issued men in cricket whites. The so-called *Australian Team Cricketers* series of 15 cards, from 1905, is made up of lilac-tinted monotone portraits of players, which may sell for up to £50 each, if they are in excellent condition. Yet more colourful cards were produced for the rarer *Cricketers in Action* series, which bears the brand name Milo and was issued in 1906. Such cards command prices over £50 each. A third cricket-related series, called *Cricket Terms*, dates to around the same time. It comprises comical sketches and prices of around £40 each may be paid for cards in very good condition.

Clive Lloyd on a folding card given with Shredded Wheat, 1976

The rather conservative nature of the artwork on these portraits is one of the drawbacks to this collection. It does not stand out, lacking something in identity, and the cards are not very rare, no matter what sellers may state on their sales.

Ice cream card, 1974

Champion Chewing Gum's *Sports Champions* is but one collection produced by Sweetacres, an Australian gum cards issuer best known for cricket cards. Though there are cricketers in the *Sports Champions* series, which dates to around 1932, many cricket cards will be found in the firm's other collections, such as the cards with the Minties marque. Other cards come without marques but show colourful caricatures of cricketers. Prices start at £5 each but famous names will attract much higher figures.

Taddy tobacco issued around 240 *County Cricketers* on cigarette cards, in 1908. This was quite a leap from the 15 *South African Team* cricket cards in Taddy's earlier series, in 1907. The *County Cricketers* represent 16 different English counties and the rarest cards have been seen to top £100 in auction, whereas the South African cards tend to sell for up to £50. There is a Taddy card of W.G. Grace. His card, in excellent condition, may cost hundreds of pounds. Recently, Taddy cards have been reissued. Modern day reprints are worthless as investments so don't spend more then £10 for an entire run of all 16 counties, all 240 cards. That sounds like a lot of cards for very little but modern reprints are just money-spinners for the printers by whom 1,000s of sets of cards may have been printed. More may be printed at will, so there is no limit and no rarity factor in spurious, so-called *limited editions*. Buy them for reference, if you must, but spend money on them and you will probably lose in the short, the medium and the long terms.

Wills, of Bristol in England, is the last entry in this short, alphabetical-list summary of the biggest tobacco issuers of cricket cards. Wills was one of the first firms to issue cricket cards, as far back as 1896, when it issued 50 *Cricketers*, a series in which one of the all-time great footballers and cricketers, Charles Burgess Fry, is to be found. It's Fry's veritable 'rookie' card and this earliest-known card of said all-round sports star is worth some hundreds of pounds! The other cricketers in this very fine series are worth around £80 each – that's for cards in very good condition. Lesser condition cards fall dramatically in value.

Wills printed a second series of *Cricketers* in 1901. The 50 newer cards are easily distinguished from those of 1896. They have a two-line inscription to the top of the front of the card, which has WILLS's, in mostly upper-case lettering, set above the word Cigarettes, with a capital C. There is a small dot below the final, raised letter in WILLS's. The first 25 cards each have two types: one with a partly cloudy background – known as vignette cards – and one with a plain white background. The latter 25 cards are known only with plain, white backgrounds. Values for cards in excellent condition are around £20 each but average-condition cards may be had for as little as a £5! Beware of reprints. Look closely at the cards before buying. Reprints are like new cars: the moment you buy them they become worth less than what you paid. They are 'good investments' only for the printer, just as purchases of new cars are only good bets for the car retailer and the car maker.

Wills produced a glorious series of sports cards in 1901, which it called *Sports of All Nations*. It was issued with both Capstan Navy Cut cigarettes and with Westward-Ho cigarettes. The 50 cards include a trio of colourful cricketing themes alongside a flag known as the Royal Standard of the United Kingdom. Such cards may sell for £10 each if their condition is superb.

Wills returned to a series devoted to cricket with a third set of 50 cards in 1908. These *Cricketers* may be identified by their blue backs, and the firm's single-line, upper case inscription on the front of the card. Exemplars from this series are quite easy to obtain and values rarely exceed £5 each.

Whilst Wills was busy issuing the above-named collections to smokers in the British Isles, its overseas branches were producing other, very attractive series of cricket cards, notably those in Australia. One collection of special note dates from 1903. It was given with Wills's Capstan brand and is called *Australian and English Cricketers*. The cards are rare beauties and can sometimes be found for less money than similar, less attractive and easier-to-find British issues.

For more images of rare and exotic cricket cards see the cricket tab on the website www.footballsoccercards.com

Tell Your Pals to Get

THE CHAMPION 2d
The Tip-Top Story Weekly

Free Real Photos of Famous Sporting Champions GIVEN Every Week!

THE CHAMPION is the Biggest, Brightest, and Best of All Adventure Story and Hobby Papers. Great New Serials Now Starting!

Don't Forget the Name—

THE CHAMPION

The Paper with the "Personal Touch"!
EVERY MONDAY - 2d.

PICTURE GALLERY
—OF—
FAMOUS SPORTSMEN

This Album is the Property of
G. E. HOPE,
KNUTSFORD.

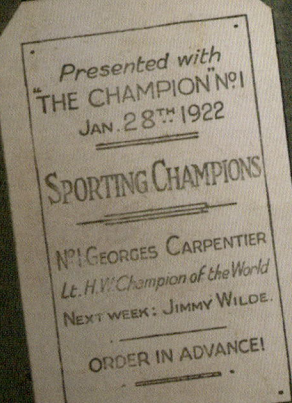

Presented with "THE CHAMPION" No. 1
JAN. 28TH 1922
SPORTING CHAMPIONS
No. 1 GEORGES CARPENTIER
Lt. H.W. Champion of the World
NEXT WEEK: JIMMY WILDE
ORDER IN ADVANCE!

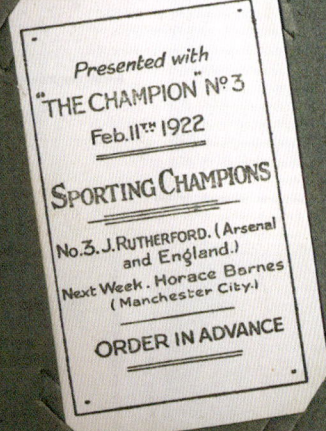

Presented with "THE CHAMPION" No. 3
Feb. 11TH 1922
SPORTING CHAMPIONS
No. 3 J. RUTHERFORD. (Arsenal and England.)
Next Week: Horace Barnes (Manchester City.)
ORDER IN ADVANCE

Presented with "THE CHAMPION" No. 2
Feb. 4th 1922.
SPORTING CHAMPIONS

Presented with "THE CHAMPION" No. 4
Feb. 18TH 1922
SPORTING CHAMPIONS
HORACE BARNES

JESSE PENNINGTON (West Bromwich Albion)

STEVE DONOGHUE

B. CARSLAKE

Golf: an introduction to golf on trade cards

Golf cards are among the most eagerly collected trade cards in the world. Golfing subjects command some of the highest prices paid for any type of card. The fancy socks & caps brigade is known for being a monied band, with cash to splash, and some people put the ever-higher prices paid for golf cards down to this factor. However, values for golf cards are also high because such cards have been collected for longer than most other genres of sporting trade card, and the market is well developed. Books on golf cards, price guides for golfing ephemera, and catalogues for collecting golf trade cards and postcards have been in print for decades. Yet, there are many golf cards which remain elusive to even the keenest collector. The cards illustrated in this section of the book include very rare types, some of which will be unknown to readers. One such card had arrived in the post, one summer morning over 40 years ago.

There was a wooded copse on the western boundary of Aldridge golf course. It was a favourite spot, an ideal den; perfect for whiling away school holidays. One summer morning it became impossible to enjoy the privacy promised by the woods. Upon settling down to open the newly delivered package of collectibles (a comic, some gum cards and badges sent by a pen pal, in Italy, in exchange for similar British-made items) the sound of others was detected. A pair of Conservative & Unionist Club officials – two *big* ducks in the very small pond that was the Aldridge village – had veered off the golf course, entered the spinney and started going at *it* between ash and elder, three oaks thither. They were known for such *off-piste* activity. They'd once been snapped *in flagrante* on a tomb in the nearby church graveyard! Though the verger with the camera had bemoaned their brevity, the vicar had offered up a blessing.

The golfing councillors – you'd have called her a *Sloane Ranger*; him a *stooge* – had ended up within an acorn's throw. They'd been following wayward balls towards the next hole when, instead of walking by, as expected, they turned towards the trees. Traipsing into the woods, in the direction of yours truly, they tripped over each other, stumbling into the undergrowth. Clubs and clothes were discarded and frolicking in the ferns ensued. Within a few moments the frantic activity ceased. A pair of wood pigeons let fly, above. Silence followed. Then other voices could be heard. More people were approaching.

The lovers' abandoned golf trolleys were discovered by an advancing duo of elderly but spritely gentlemen. Anxious dressing was quietly completed and the red-faced couple collected themselves before parading from the copse, each holding aloft their trophies: a pair of *retrieved* golf balls. He sliced his, and it seemed the sporting thing was to follow him into the rough, with mine," scoffed the *Sloane Ranger*. One of the gentlemen retorted approvingly, "Well, don't *cher* know?" His pal chortled, adding, "Faulkner's

Oriental art deco *Golf Girl* **cigarette cards from China, 1920s**

THE GOLFER'S GAME.

The solution to each question is a Golfing term.

Question.   Answer.

1—A River.

2—Pre-historic Weapons.

3—To Carve a Joint.   Course

4—When two are exactly alike. Slice

5—Where you find the 19th Hole. Double

6—Carried Home after a good day's Sport. Clubhouse

7—Where tea is always to be found. Bag

8—A two-coloured silk.   Caddie

9—A Saucer.   Club

10—To smooth a Kitten.

11—In the Children's Playground. Swing

12—One who takes second place.

13—Every Country has its own.

14—Not a Square.

15—A Description sometimes given to Country Folk.

16—A Coal Hole on a Ship.

17—To value a thing.   Prize

18—A Hobgoblin.

19—One under Bogey.   Eagle Birdie

20—Chauffeur.   Driver

21—A Clannish Coterie.

22—Must be replaced.   Divot

23—In front.   Fore

24—A Bird of Prey.   Eagle

The "DAINTY" SERIES—No. G669.   Copyright.   Printed in England.

GOLF: AN INTRODUCTION TO GOLF ON TRADE CARDS

British cigarette card, 1927

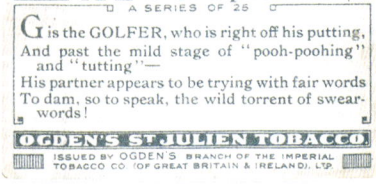

German cigarette card, 1920s

French decal transfers, 1910s

French trade card, 1930s

Woolett, etc., will typically cost more than cards with generic golf scenes.

So, the earliest golf cards issued by Baines will have this legend on the rear: *Gold Medal Golf and Military Cards*. Remember, most Baines golf cards are not from this Victorian-epoch issue. Most are from later on, sometimes much later on. A host of these later-issue cards have been wrongly graded by well-known slabbers, in USA, as 1897. In fact, most of the graded golf cards this writer has seen are incorrectly graded. It's amazing that so many people pay for such a service, if it can be called a service! Edwardian era golf cards have, simply, *Gold Medal Football Cards* on the backs. These are from 1901 to 1909. After John Baines's death in 1909, it would be another decade before the third type of golf cards appeared, those with the Oak Lane address on the back.

Barratt & Company, of London, issued sports cards with confectionery, between the 1920s and the 1970s. Most cards were of soccer stars and cricketers, so golfers rarely featured. 1927 was different. In that year a series of cards called *Leaders of Sport* appeared with Barratt's wares. The elegant series of 48 cards includes five golfers, one of which is Abe Mitchell. This card is the known set-breaker. If you have Abe you may stand a chance of getting the others, in time. If not, don't expect to find him. His card is feverishly sought. It's extremely rare and valuable. A top condition card of Mitchell may fetch over £1,000!

Golf made a return to Barratt's cards in 1959. *The Giants of Sport* cards are generally worth about £5 each but Dai Rees and Peter Thompson may fetch more. They are typically harder to find than most other cards in the series.

Barratt issued golf cards for a third time, between 1970 and 1971, in a pair of very similar, back-to-back series. Most collectors don't realise the *Goldflake Famous Sportsmen* title was given to two, distinct series of cards. That's because Barratt simply continued one collection, from 1970, into the next, in 1971, removing certain sports stars and replacing them with new faces. The changes went unannounced. The golfer Peter Thompson appeared at card #22, in 1970, but by 1971 he had been replaced by the boxer Joe Bugner. Jack Nicklaus, at #6; Gary Player, at #11; and Tony Jacklin, at #27 all appear in both collections.

A further variation in these cards is also known. One type comes with the legend *Printed in England* while another is without the inscription. Prices are ever higher for these cards. In autumn 2016, a collection of 50 cards, advertised wrongly as a set (they were a mix of cards from both sets) sold for $1,920 in an American auction. Three of the golf cards cost around £10 each. Thompson is the rarest of the four and often sells for more.

Bell's *Scottish Clan Series* cards, of 1903, include two tartans which also feature golf accoutrements. They are numbers #6 and #13. Both cards may also be found with Stephen Mitchell & Son backs. The latter are worth more, around £30 each card. The Bell cards typically sell for £20 each.

Berlyn's Burline Mixture tobacco came with 25 cards called *The Golfers' Blend*, in 1910. The cards are worth a small fortune! Were a set ever to appear on the market it should exceed £5,000. Single cards may sell for £100 even in the poorest of condition. The designs used were also produced in a larger format, in the style of postcards, for which eye-watering prices have been paid. A set of 25 postcard-size Berlyn trade cards may exceed £25,000! Buyers beware: reprints exist. Bewlay's

  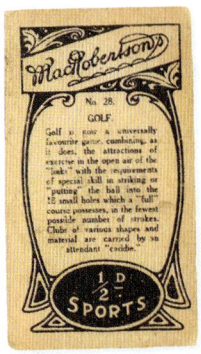   

Village Maid and MacRobertson cards, 1917   British cigarette cards, 1914

 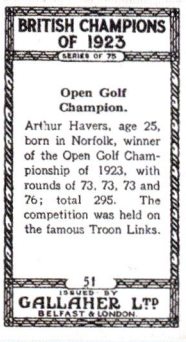  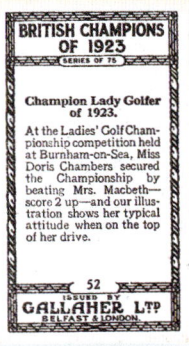  

British cigarette card, 1924   British cigarette card, 1924   British cigarette card, 1925

Flor de Dindigul humourous cigar cards, issued in 1909, include one golfing subject. It shows a young caddie smoking one of the firm's cigars whilst his master swings a club high. Prices are around £500 for an original!

Bocnal's 1938 issue is radioactive. No joke! The golf card is coloured in a ghastly-green hue. It's a glow-in-the-dark card. It comes from a set of radioluminescent cards called *Luminous Silhouettes*. It may be as deleterious to health as it is distracting to the eye. Though radium's half-life is comparatively short, when compared to better known isotopes, there remain at least 15 centuries of emissions still to eradiate from such cards! If you are willing to risk having the green golf card in your home it may be found for less than £20.

Boguslavsky's Turf Cigarettes came with *Sports Records*, in 1925. The series includes two golf cards: one men's golf, the other women's golf. They are easily available and ought to cost less than £5 each.

Brinkman Lloyd cigarettes, issued in Germany, in the 1930s, are known for showing animals in comic capers with sporting equipment. There are a handful of golf-interest cards, with chimps and dogs driving and putting. They'll cost over £10 each.

British & American Tobacco (BAT) reissued cards originally published by American Tobacco, in the series called *Champion Athletes and Prize Fighters*. The half a dozen golf cards in the BAT collection are numbered, unlike the earlier cards, but they are otherwise similarly hard to find, and they'll cost over £100 each, in any kind of condition.

In 1913 BAT issued a series of cards which were also distributed by Wills. Unlike those by Wills the *Sporting Girls* cards by BAT have plain backs. The card with the golfing theme will typically cost around £30. Similarly, BAT also reissued the Wills series called *Sports of the World*, in 1917. The same series is also known on cards by other manufacturers, like Village Maid, and there's a monotone take on it too, by a firm called MacRobertson.

Golf subjects also appear in various non-sports series by BAT. Look out for the golf cards in *Cinema Stars*, of 1924; *Period Costumes*, of 1929; and *Do You Know*, of 1931. Golf subjects tend to outperform other types of cards, in values, and often make for so-called set-breakers – those cards which are hardest to get to complete any particular collection. Prices for BAT cards go stratospheric when it comes to American golfers of fame and fortune, like Bobby Jones. The 1927 series, *Who's Who in Sport*, typically sells for £1 each card, but the Jones card will fetch a figure at least 100-times higher. See also: Lambert & Butler, for the same series of cards with a different marque on the back.

Bucktrout was one of many smaller tobacconists which co-sponsored the reissue, in 1926, of a bloody series of cards from 1912. *Sports & Pastimes* contain scenes showing the hunting of elephants for ivory; the sadistic sticking of pigs; brutal baiting of bears, and kangaroo killing for fun. Amidst such bloody scenes there are one or two images which retain an air of civility, including a golfing card. This particular golf subject is known with various, different backs. The co-sponsors of the reissue were many. As well as Bucktrout, Miranda, Taddy, Almond, Collins, Edmondson, Evershed, Goodbody, Hudden, Redford, Sandorides and Sword are but some of their names. There is also a card with a

AN A TO Z OF SPORTING COLLECTIBLES   113

plain back, which was issued by Teofani. Sale prices depend on the particular card. Some are far rarer than others. Taddy originals, from 1912, tend to sell for over £50 each but certain reissues, from 1926, may even exceed that price, upwards of £200.

Bulgaria tobacco, based in Germany, issued *Sport-Photos* during the early years of the 1930s. The golfing subjects include Walter Hagen. The Hagen card will sell for over £100, though most of the others cost as little as £5.

Carreras combined cigarette cards with playing cards, in 1925, creating a series called *Happy Families*. This game is the distant relative of Top Trumps. The 1925 collection includes two cards with a golfing theme. Values remain low, 100 years later, and the cards may be had for less than £5 each.

Carreras introduced an attractive card design in 1935. The oval-shaped cards were the first to have been seen since cards by Richardson, of Leeds, and W. N. Sharpe, of Bradford, in the 1880s and 1890s. The oval-shaped *Popular Personalities* include a selection of sporting stars

Harry Vardon

1870-1937, who formed with Taylor and Braid one of the famous "Triumvirate", won the Open Championship six times between 1896 and 1914, and the American and German titles once each, among his sixty-two first-class tournament successes.

GOLF: AN INTRODUCTION TO GOLF ON TRADE CARDS

> **Carreras was one of few tobacco merchants which continued to issue cards after World War Two. The firm printed cut-out cards, which are known as packet issues, inside the cigarette box itself.**

amidst which there is a pair of golfers. Such cards were widely saved, so availability is easy and prices remain affordable. Most can be found for as little as £1 each.

Carreras was one of few tobacco merchants which continued to issue cards after World War Two. The firm printed cut-out cards, which are known as packet issues, inside the cigarette box itself. Unlike the 1930s packet issues developed by a rival firm, Phillips, Carreras hid their cards from sight. A smoker had to buy a packet of cigarettes before seeing the hidden card, which was printed on to the slider. In 1949, these *Sports Series* cards came in two formats: packets of 10 cigarettes, with a single image; and packets of 20 cigarettes, with a pair of sportsmen, side by side. Cut cards are easily found and values are low, at around £1 each, but uncut slides command higher prices. Single slides, intact, with all borders, sell for around £10 each, while uncut doubles are worth over £20.

Over the four years in which Cavanders cigarettes came with the *Homeland Series* of cards, 1924 to 1928, the firm reissued variations of the very same card, over and again. There are, for example, two different golf course scenes known on card #11. One card shows a solitary golfer, and this card is much rarer, and worth a lot more than the card of the same number showing a group of golfers. Both versions of card #11 are known in regular-size formats. There is also a larger than standard-size card available. Cards with different colours abound. So, it's possible to have a handful of the same card each of which are coloured differently. Be prepared to pay £20 for the card with the solitary golfer. The other one, with the group of golfers, may be had for as little as £1.

The Churchman's tobacco series called *Sporting Trophies*, issued in 1927, comes in two sizes. The smaller series of cards includes a trio of golf subjects. The larger series, of just 12 cards, includes a pair. You'll find the British Open and the British Amateur trophies in both series, but the Walker Cup only features in the set of smaller cards. The small cards cost little. The larger cards are much costlier, and far scarcer. Whereas a set of small cards may be had for as little as £50, albeit for cards below very good condition, the larger ones will cost quadruple this figure, for similarly average condition cards. For top condition large cards expect to pay £50 each.

In 1927, Churchman cigarettes came with three different series of cards, all of which are called *Famous Golfers*. The least costly series, of 50 cards, is of regular cigarette card dimensions. The others are larger cards and both consist of 12 cards each. The larger cards will cost you more for just a dozen cards than you'll pay for all 50 of the smaller types. The three collections contain a plethora of well-known golfing faces. The small cards numbered #27 and #33 are

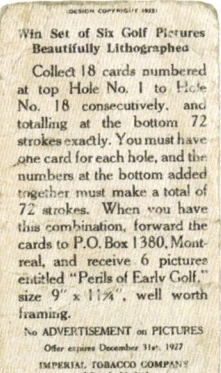
Canadian cigarette card, 1926

French trade card, 1920s

British cigarette card, 1931

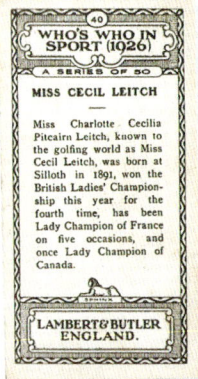
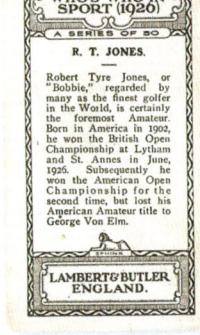

British cigarette card, 1927

the set-breakers: Bobby Jones and Tom Morris, respectively. For card #27 you may see asking prices of over £100. Card #33 will usually be around half that price. The two sets of larger cards bear the legends: *Series of 12*, and *2nd Series of 12*. Walter Hagen, Bobby Jones and Harry Vardon feature in the first, and are worth over £150 each; while Tom Morris tops the values league in the second, again at around £150. These prices are for very good condition cards. Cards in excellent or better condition may cost much more than this!

Churchman repeated the pattern for *Men of the Moment* in Sport, in 1928. There were three series: 50 small cards and two sets of 12 cards each. There are ten golf cards in the smaller series. Two golfers are included in each of the larger-size sets. The small Bobby Jones card is presently worth around £50 (prices have fallen in recent years, due to large stocks of this card being released unto the market following the liquidation of a major London cards dealer's stock) while the large version of the same will cost at least double that price. Likewise, the large card of Walter Hagen, from *Men of the Moment in Sport, 2nd Series of 12* will also cost over £100.

Churchman's *Prominent Golfers* cards, from 1931, also came in small and large formats. The better known the golfer is, the higher the price will be. So, Bobby Jones will cost at least £50 for a small card and £100 for a larger one; Gene Sarazen's small card is worth around £25 (he was not included in the larger series); and Walter Hagen will cost you £30 for small and around £100 for a large one. Prices are based on cards in very good condition. You'll pay more for better.

Churchman's *Sporting Celebrities* cards, also from 1931, include seven golfers, one of whom is Walter Hagen. His card may cost you £50. Most of the other cards in the series can be had for less than £5 each.

Churchman cigarettes published a very unusual series of cards, in 1934. The collection of 58 cards is called *Can You Beat Bogey at St. Andrews?* There are actually 54 numbered cards and four *Joker* cards. The jokers are the most valuable cards in the set, and may cost over £100 each. Some cards were overprinted in red, with an 'exchangeable' legend on the back, so there are those varieties to look out for, too. A set of the cheapest variations of the basic 54 cards, with at least one joker, will probably cost you over £200. There are different values for the regular cards, which come with different 'golfers'. Cards showing *Mr. Tiger* are worth £5, or more, each card, whereas those with *Mr. Everyman* are worth only £1 or £2 each. It's a fascinating and quite beautiful series but one to keep you frustrated, if not poor, for trying to complete the set.

Churchman issued two, very similar series, both of which are called *3 Jovial Golfers*. There is a 36-card set, which is worth about £150; and a 73-card set, which may cost over £500! The latter includes a rare *joker* card, which is valued around £150.

Willards Chocolates golf cards, 1925

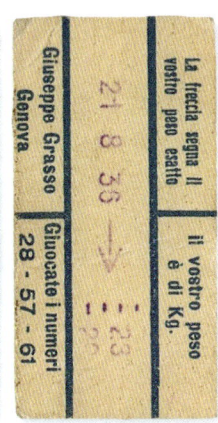

Italian weighing scales card, 1936

GOLF: AN INTRODUCTION TO GOLF ON TRADE CARDS

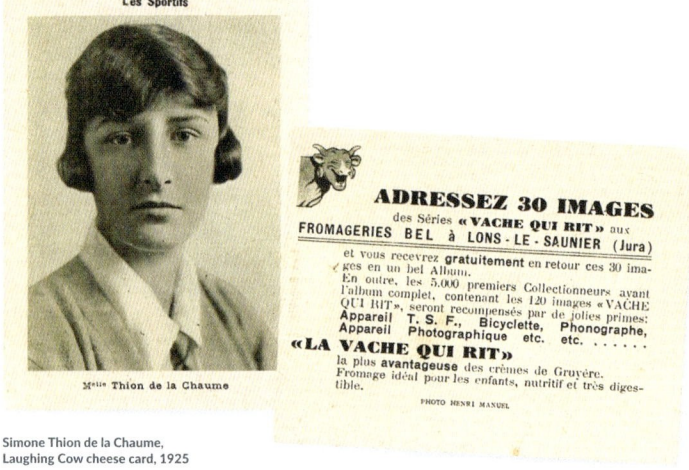

Spanish trade card, 1920s

Simone Thion de la Chaume, Laughing Cow cheese card, 1925

British cigarette card, 1928

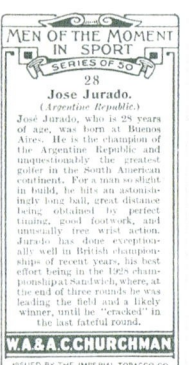

Walter Hagen, German tobacco card, 1930s

Clarke's Turkish cigarettes came with a dozen humorous *Golf Terms* cards, in 1912. The cards still induce a laugh, though not when you are paying for them. They'll often cost well over £100 each! Perhaps the most sought after card is *Dead on the Green with his Second*, which shows a dying golfer, bloodied after a duel with pistols, being cared for by his friend, while the victor bolts away, at some speed, in a horse-drawn carriage. Faulkner issued a similar series of cards, one year later. Faulkner's cards are less costly and very slightly less attractive, in terms of design, but the humour is as sharp. Together they make for an exceptional pair of collections of evergreen golfing silliness. Beware of reprints!

Clay & Bock, a Cuban tobacconist, issued a huge series of cards called *Sports*, with the Susini brand of smokes, around 1926. One of the cards shows a golfer and is worth around £75. It's a tougher one to find than its price suggests.

Cope Brothers tobacco was sold with cards called *Cope's Golfers*, in 1900. They are one of the best-loved sets of golfing cards on the market. Beware of worthless reprints which have appeared in recent years. Whereas originals, in very good condition, are worth about £60 each, and some golfers fetch much more than that, reprints are worth almost nothing. Confusing the two could be costly.

In 1923, Cope's Kenilworth brand of smokes were sold with cards called *Golf Strokes*. Most of the 32 cards sell for around £5 each but those featuring Harry Vardon are pricier, at up to £15 each, so the entire Vardon sub-set range will cost you around £150 if you want all ten.

Cope's included a solitary golf cartoon in *Sports & Pastimes*, in 1925. The same image can also be found on a much rarer golf card issued by Couden's, in *Sport's Alphabet*, from 1924. Whereas the Cope's golf card may sell for up to £30 – it's the so-called set-breaker for *Sports & Pastimes* – it's easily outsold by the rarer Couden's golf card, which sells for up to triple that price.

John Cotton, an Edinburgh-based tobacconist, issued various series of *Movie Golf Shots*, as component pages to create a flicker-book of 50 cards. The cards have photographs on both sides. Thus, each of the three different series, issued in 1937, 1938 and 1939, have two 'movies' each. All shots are demonstrated by the same golfer, Archie Compston, from such delicacies as *putting* to the all-out *full drive*. Individual cards sell for around £5 each.

One of the most desirable collections of golf cards in the world, and one of the most elegant editions ever made, is a Chinese-issued series from the 1920s. Dah Tung Nan's brand of Golf Cigarettes came with 20 different so-called *Golfing Girl* cards. The design is art deco, through and through. The series is the Clarice Cliff of cigarette cards. The scenes on the cards are often suggestive, as well as stylish. There's more than golf and 1920s design to be found in this very rare edition. Golf course shenanigans, under yellow skies, contrast well with the other delicate,

 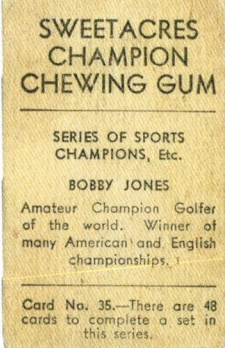  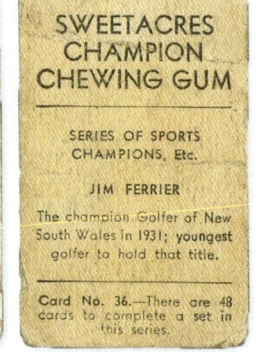

Bobby Jones and Jim Ferrier, Australian gum cards

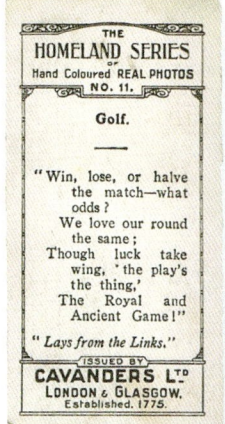

British cigarette card, 1924

almost fragrant hues and the imagery evokes delicately-charged erotica. For example, one card shows a slavish male caddie crouching, assuming a happily servile position, below the gaze of the dominant woman golfer. He delicately sets her tee, yet his hand might well be caressing her ankle. She pushes a knee into his back. He smiles. She tilts her head to the sun as she sweeps back her hair. She blushes lightly. Another card shows a pair of lady golfers standing almost cheek to cheek – posterior cheeks – back to back, one of whom bends over and seems to push her buttocks into her immovable companion. Another playful scene shows a golfing maiden with legs akimbo: she's half into a bunker, half out, grappling the delicate task of coaxing her ball out of the rut. Many of the cards show a quietly precocious boy. He's the set's narrator, sometimes gazing directly, at the viewer, with a knowing look.

The cards are highlighted with stylishly stripped-back oriental motifs, the juxtaposition of which, set against the pale-coloured figures, amidst angular landscapes, makes this set stand out from the rest. These are extremely rare cards as well as being some of the most beautiful. They come in two sizes and four series: regular and larger than standard size, and with four types of backs: brown Chinese lettering, on small cards; green Chinese lettering on larger cards; a factory scene, in green, on larger cards; and there's also a larger-sized back which shows a golfing woman, in green, and a packet of *The Golf* cigarettes.

Cards from all four series, in very good condition or better, may sell for around £500 each because they are more than just sports cards, these are art deco classics.

After World War Two, A. J. Donaldson, a Glaswegian firm, successfully issued hundreds of thousands of trading cards. The firm's early issues were sold stapled together in small booklets. Each booklet of *Sports Favourites* was designed to be to ripped asunder, played with, swapped and collected. Later issues, in the 1950s, were die-cut cards which came in sealed paper packets. Donaldson was also known for producing 'scraps', much like the Victorian chromo-lithographic scrapbook fare that was all the rage in earlier times.

The 1949 golf cards are numbered in the 300 range, of the 500 cards issued in Donaldson's *Sports Favourites* series. Today, the values of some of the naïvely drawn images are surprisingly high. Though the golfers are not the costliest Donaldson cards (*Golden Series* footballers often sell at more than £100 each) their prices are ever higher. Expect to pay £25 each card.

Drapkin tobacco issued *Sporting Celebrities in Action*, in 1930. The cards are notorious for often being overpriced by slabbers. Slabbers are sellers who 'flip' cards. They buy cheaply, usually by buying complete sets or collections, then they pick out select cards and inflate their worth by putting them inside a sealed plastic wedge, then adding a high price. Alas, plastic slabs may be useful for hiding forgeries, as the modern copies

 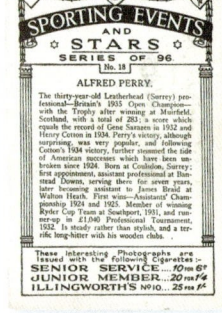

British cigarette card, 1935

British cigarette card, rare red overprint variety, 1936

AN A TO Z OF **SPORTING COLLECTIBLES** 119

of the 1930s Ilsa confectionery cards prove – many slabbed Ilsa sportsmen are actually modern reprints! Meanwhile, the 1930s Drapkin cards, with their monotone photographs of famous sports stars, have become steadily rarer and costlier. A top condition Bobby Jones card may now cost many £100s, whereas even an average Walter Hagen will sell for close to £100! The old-fashioned cigarette cards price guides still value such sought-after cards at just £3 each. Which price is right only sales on the open market will prove, but it's probably somewhere in the middle. Most Drapkin cards, even those with athletes whose golden aura has been diminished with time, sell for around £5 each. Bigger names, especially those in tennis, golf and soccer, ought to be valued somewhere between £20 and £50 each.

Faulkner's 1901 series, *Golf Terms*, are worth around £100 each card, if they are in top condition. The comical scenes and jokes are very often found to have resonance today. Collectors for whom such Edwardian sillies have appeal may like to know that Faulkner's sister series, *Cricket Terms*, also contains a card with a golfing theme. It's called *Leg Hit* and shows a golfer clutching his shin, hopping around in pain. With that card it makes 13, in all, to collect. The cards have plain backs. They are not usually as expensive to buy as the similar but finer cards by Clarke tobacco, but the Faulkner cards in top condition may sell for £80 each.

Gallaher included a golfing card amongst the *Latest Actresses*, in 1909. Unlike most of the cards in the series, which struggle to sell, even at £5 each, the golfing actress, Marie Studholme, remains attractive to contemporary buyers, much though she adorns a costly card. Around £50 is the price you're likely to have to pay for either variety of this card: one is known in sepia brown, the other in black & white.

Gallaher's *Sports Series* includes ten golf subjects. Most cards in the set of 100 are relatively affordable; at around £5 each, but the golfers will cost double this price.

You'd hardly know a slaughter was afoot by the cards Gallaher came out with in the middle of World War One. The firm's Park Drive brand packed *Kute Kiddies* [sic], a series drawn by diverse children's artists. It contains one golfing subject which is worth around £15.

Gallaher's *British Champions* of 1923 came to the public eye in 1924. The yellow-framed, colourful cards are not only attractive, they are inexpensive. If you enjoy sports collectibles then those factors alone are good reasons to collect this series. Golf specialists will also enjoy the boon of chasing the collection's four scarcest cards, the golfers, each of whom is worth around £10. Most of the other cards can be had for less than £2 each.

Look out for the golf-ball card in *The Reason Why*, a series of 100 cards issued by Gallaher, in 1924. The card is #70. It ought to cost little.

Gallaher returned to the theme of pan-sport champions, in 1934 and 1935, with two collections of 48: *A Series of 48 Champions* and *2nd Series of 48 Champions*. Both sets remain affordable. They contain a host of world-famous names including a trio of golfers in the earlier collection and a pair in the latter. You'll be able to find most of them for less than £2 each.

Gallaher's final golf card of the 1930s is one which was featured in a collection shared between many different brands. *Our Countryside* cards may be found with various brand names, including Peter Jackson, Senior Service by Pattreiouex, Illingworth, Gallaher, and others. The 1938 series includes a card (#37) which shows a highland scene from a golfing tour in Scotland. For most varieties of this card £1 is about right but some brands are harder to find than others, and costlier. In some cases it may be more economical to buy a full set of cards, to remove the card you want, then to resell the rest.

Hignett tobacco issued the same series of images found on Ogden's *Champions of 1936* cards. While the Ogden's cards are much more affordable – in fact you may be able to buy the entire Ogden's set for the price you'll pay for

British cigarette card, 1935

British cigarette card, 1931

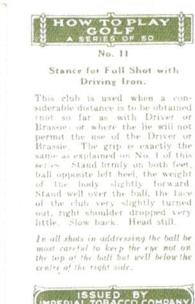

Canadian cigarette card, 1935

British cigarette card, 1927

 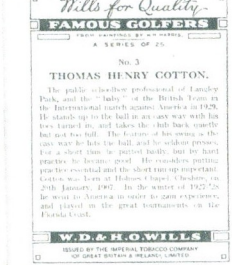 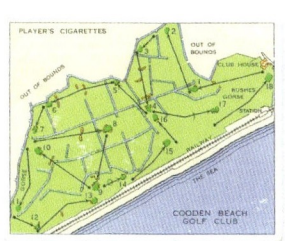 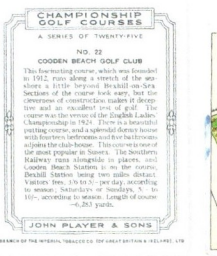 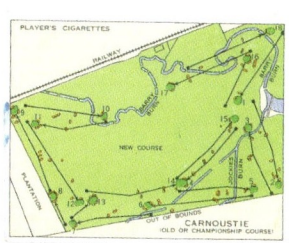 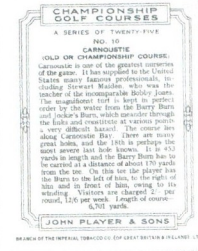

British cigarette card, 1930   British cigarette cards, 1936

 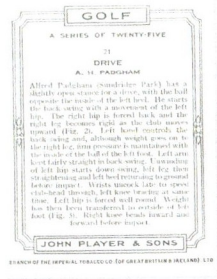  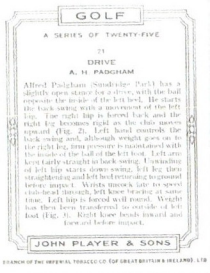

British cigarette cards, 1939   OXO trade card, 1928

just one of the Hignett golfers – those with the Hignett logos will give the golf completist a challenge.

Hill's *Celebrities of Sport* includes a pair of golf cards. The 1939 set may be bought for around £50, complete, and single cards can be found for around £2 each. These cards are available with two backs: one has a Gold Flake Honeydew logo; the other mentions it was *Issued by R.J. Hill*. The former are rarer and a little costlier.

Hudden was one of the brands (along with Bucktrout, Goodbody, Sword, etc.) to imprint its marque on the backs of a series of reissued Taddy *Sports & Pastimes* cards, in the 1920s. Hudden is mentioned here, in its own right, as it's one of the rarest types. The golf card has been known to sell for over £100. Most of the other cards show scenes of cruelty to animals and are ever downwards in value as most people have moved on from such barbarity. Their prices tumble year on year whereas the golf card holds its value.

Illingworth included a terrific golfing sketch in the highly attractive *Comicartoons of Sport* series, in 1927. The collection is one of silhouetted silliness and each sport covered in this very desirable issue comes with a free snigger but a sense of humour is required. Prices of over £20 for the golf card are about right. It's one of the set-breakers.

Lambert & Butler issued cigarette cards which had also been given with other brands. Such marques were controlled by British & American Tobacco (BAT). These cards, if they don't bear the Lambert & Butler marque, make no mention of firm or brand. In 1927 cards called *Who's Who In Sport (1926)* [sic] appeared. They are known with and without trademarks as the series which followed, in 1928: *The World of Sport*. There are golf cards in both collections. So, the same golf card may be found with and without the logo of Lambert & Butler. Slabbers are known to seek out the golf cards, making it hard to complete such sets. However, you don't need to buy their expensive, slabbed cards to complete your set, or to acquire the golfers you need. If you have patience, and you can wait a while, it may be less costly to buy a set of these cards from a public auction, or from a specialist cartophilic sale. You'll get the rare cards, like Bobby Jones (#2 in the 1926 series), and the rest of the cards for less than some sellers ask for Jones alone!

MacNaughton Jenkins, a Dublin-based limited company, issued an encyclopaedic series of cards about rubber – that is, the utilitarian uses of the now kinky fashion material. Card #49 of a 50-card set is dedicated thus: *For The Golfer*. Some years ago such cards could be found for a few pounds each but slabbers have followed the money trail, putting what was a £5 card into plastic and asking £150 for the courtesy! A set has been known to come to market every now and then. Look out for that, and in so doing you'll probably get all 50 cards for the same price as some sellers charge for a single card in a slab.

In 1914, Marsuma Virginia cigarettes were issued with the so-called *Famous Golfers & Their*

> **Lambert & Butler issued cigarette cards which had also been given with other brands. Such marques were controlled by British & American Tobacco (BAT). These cards, if they don't bear the Lambert & Butler marques, make no mention of firm or brand.**

"OLD TROOPER"

"THE DRINK"

122 AN A TO Z OF **SPORTING COLLECTIBLES**

BEN HOGAN NEW GOLF KING
July 10, 1953

"TRUE SCOT"

Barratt sweet cigarettes card, 1961

French sticker, 1980

Phonecard, 1990s

French trade card, 1890s

from 1905, also by Wills: the so-called *Sketches in Black & White* woman golfer. Wills stayed with women for *Sports of the World*, in 1917. Values for all three of these women golfer cards are over £20.

Wills published a series called *Golfing*, in 1924. Each card shows a famous golf course. These cards may be found for as little as £2 each, if quality is not a prerequisite. For a set of 25 cards in the best possible form the cost will rise to over £100.

Famous Golfers, a set of 25 cards issued by Wills in 1930, tends to be a favourite with all, even with non-golfing sportspeople. The slick artworks are easy on the eye. The cards show the fashionable gear seen on the greens of the interwar years, from argyle socks to plus fours! The rendering of the golfers is redolent of work by two well-known painters, both of whom are named Lynch: J. H. Lynch, the artist responsible for *Tina* and other mid-century women, like the *Gypsy Girl*; and Brent Lynch, the Jack Vettriano-like painter responsible for *Cigar Bar* and *Evening Lounge*. If you like your art not to demand answers to uncomfortable questions, then these reassuringly conservative compositions may be for you. The cards are usually priced around £10 but those of Hagen and Vardon will cost significantly more, unless you buy a full set. In this case you may spend less than £200 for the lot. Full sets appear at this price, from time to time.

Wills included odd golf cards in various general interest, mixed themes collections which it issued throughout the inter-war decades. Such collections include two distinct series of *Homeland Events*, from 1927 and 1932; and a collection called *British Sports Personalities*, from 1937. The cards are rather dull, being monotone photos, but they are not costly, and may be had for as little as £1 each.

A handful of golf scenes are included in a comical series of cigarette cards, from the 1930s, called Henry. The collection of capers was issued with Kensitas, a brand by Wix cigarettes. Golf also finds its way on to Kensitas's *Says Jenkyn* cards, also known as *Jenkynisms*, in which a reassuringly calm butler decants anecdotes or whispers things like, "*Your golf score, Sir*". Such autonomous sensory meridian responses, otherwise known as ASMR, were *softly, so softly* ahead of their time. The cards are easy to find and cost little so don't pay more than £1 per *Jenkyn*, or *Henry*.

Wix tobacco's *Bridge Favors and Place-Cards* [sic] were issued with Kensitas cigarettes in 1937. For cigarette cards these rare collectibles are most unusual, and highly attractive. The four golf cards in the series are among the rarest and may cost more than £50 each.

In 1992, Worthington beers reissued six cards from a pre-war series by Churchman, called *Prominent Golfers*. The six are quite scarce, for cards made in modern times. The sub-set sextet generally cost less than £30.

This introduction to golf cards is all too brief due to space constraints. For more in-depth reading on golf cards please see the bibliography. Moreover, to see rare golf cards for sale please see the golf section under 'other sports' at www.footballsoccercards.com

John Allen trade card, 1996

Coudens cigarette card, 1924

Bocnal luminous cigarette card, 1928

Gymnastics: gymnasium sports on trade cards

French trade card, 1900s

French trade card, 1900s

French trade card, 1900s

Gymnastic exercises at school were the bane of many a child's life. Masochistic mistiming above pommels, and ripped groin muscles from ungainly splits feature highly in recounted mishaps among old school friends. However, ungainly charges into wooden horses are child's play in the light of injuries sustained from gasp-inducing slips off the high beam, and rapid, burning descents down ill-charmed ropes. Yet, it could all have been far worse, as the gymnasium scene in James Herbert's *The Fog* made bloodily clear. That particular book closed more gyms than any virus.

Miss Fisher, a junior school all-round teacher had made gym a very welcome distraction. Her deft and delightful gymnastic movements had charmed students. She looked like a Scandinavian javelin thrower, or a Germanic long-distance runner. She played all sports well and she taught academic subjects with a flourish. She nurtured envy in other teachers. One winter's day, circa 1976, when the school boiler had broken and the gymnasium was colder than Siberia, she took gym to the classroom. With the aid of a collection of antique cigarette cards, which she passed around for the students to study, she delivered an unorthodox lesson on ropes and bars. The cards showed gymnasium scenes and keep-fit exercises. It was fun: exercising while sitting down. A class such as this was ahead of its time! Passing colourful cards around proved more fun than freezing in the gym. Blessed were that cougar's cubs, not least for the cards. It seemed to lead to a spike in collecting among the students.

Around that time, Olga Korbut and her generation's ribbon-waving waifs managed to inflame revaluations of gymnastics. Fortunately, cards and stickers came to capture, for eternity, photographic stills of the Soviet starlet and her sylph-like compatriots. It was the era of black-&-white, or grainy colour TV, long before the pause and record playback of VHS, let alone catch-up

TV's watch on demand services. In 1976 if you blinked you missed it. Panini soothed a little the lack of playback.

The Italians leapt from having presented conservative images of gymnasts, throughout two of their 1972 collections, *Olympia* and *München 72*, to showing colourful full-frontals in *Sports Vedettes* and in *Montreal 76*. Panini's glamourous presentation of gymnastics attracted new collectors and new followers of the sport. The scantily-clad bodies in acrobatic action, or *Kama Sutra* contortions, were not explicit, nevertheless such images encouraged young imaginations to work on joining up dots that weren't necessarily there.

Olga Korbut's first sticker came in Panini's pan-sport collection *Campioni dello Sport 1973-74*. The very same image of the *Slinky* spring-like Soviet also came to be used, in the same season, on a gum card issued in Spain. Such rookie stickers and cards are more valuable, nowadays, than solid silver Britannia coins! Similarly, an unused Nadia Comăneci sticker from Panini's *Montreal 76* is worth more than a solid silver dollar. There are two versions of this collection: the standard pan-European language version and a Serbo-Croat variant. Expect to pay over £100 for an unused Comăneci sticker from Yugoslavia. The standard version sells for more than £50, if unused.

Reeling back to the first decade of sports cards, Duke's *Gymnastic Exercises* was a naughtier collection than any of Panini's stickers. The 1887 cards include images of women in all sorts of compromising positions – at least for those with puritan sensibilities. Some lasses straddle devices with hoops and handles, while others hang akimbo from sloping ladders. They roll on their backs; they play with giant balls; legs apart their feet trace the air like burlesque dancers from the Moulin Rouge. Such cards are something to behold! There are some downright bizarre exercises, such as hanging by the toes during which the woman seems to impersonate a bat. Saucier-still images include saddle vaulting, especially the so-called outside hand vault. Values start around £20 for fair condition cards and rise accordingly. You may see prices of over £150 for the naughtier cards if condition is of the best order.

A swinger is included in Allen & Ginter's *The World's Champions*, and also in *Second Series of the World's Champions*. These swingers of 1888 have little in common with those who played risqué games behind pampas grass in the 1980s. It's all about the risky activity of throwing a heavy weight, at speed, around one's head. Bruised elbows and cracked crania aside, the once-popular gymnastic sport of swinging has swung low in popularity. The cards from the second series are available in two sizes. For cards in top condition, buyers should expect to pay over £100.

There's a swinger known amidst the myriad subjects shown on Baines cards. The British card is from some time between 1910 and 1920 (the Oak Lane address, on the back, dates it so) and shows a demure portrait of a certain 'Miss Bell'. Her vignette is framed against a gymnasium array of clubs, still rings and dumbbells, in which a gentleman in a leotard swings his clubs aloft. Prices for such Baines cards are similarly of three figures.

The 1907 Sniders & Abrahams series, *How to Keep Fit*, includes a chap strutting about in the lower half of what appears to be a French Foreign Legionnaire's kit – with a summertime cut. His low-slung waistline is adorned with a red sash. It feels like the cards were meant to appeal to a very particular clientele. Today, the cards are worth around £3 each. A few years later a firm called Drapin would take the design a few masculine steps further.

In 1910, the exclusive Singleton & Cole brand of smokes came with *The Wallace-Jones Keep Fit System*. The cards show a colourfully dressed gentleman doing floor and air exercises. The design traces his movements with dotted lines. Thus, the exercises may be fully followed and copied by the viewer. In recent years Edwardian keep-fit systems have lost a lot of their pull but these elegant cards have lost none of their charm. The cards may be acquired for around £5 if condition is not too important. In top form they may sell for over £10 each.

Drapkin's 1912 Crayol-brand series, *How to Keep Fit*, is an affordable one. The cards can be had for around £3 each. The images show two gents, one moustached and one clean-shaven.

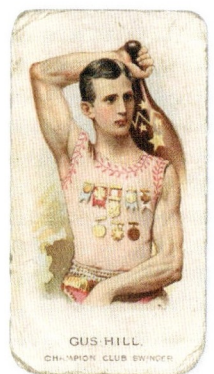

American tobacco card by Allen & Ginter, 1888

French trade card, 1900s

Olga Korbut on a Panini sticker, 1976

French trade card, 1890s

115. CABA

109. GIMNASIA

117. LUDMILLA TOURISC

French trade card, 1930s

Italian chocolates card by yFerrero, 1950s

Italian metal token cards, 1930

Motor sports: MotoGP, Formula 1 and other petrol-head pictures on trade cards

In days of yore, the publisher of *Football Card Collector Magazine* (*FCCM*) would arrive at ephemera fairs, and cards conventions, on a Blackbird. That's a CBR-X 1100, in biker lingo. Cards fairs were commonplace 30 years ago.

They were often held in giant halls, sometimes on the scale of Wembley National Exhibition Centre, other times in town halls. Fairs would be full of tables where dozens of vendors sold millions of trade cards to countless collectors, each cramming around a stall to steal a glance, or make an offer. People queued around the block, since early in the morning, for such events. One vendor would moan, *"Still collecting sports trade cards, young man? You know, most adults prefer cigarette cards. Now, let me show you some Poultry cards made by John Player ..."*

How times change. Nowadays, sports cards are the foundation of any business in cards. One of the most undervalued genres of antique sports cards is that of motorsport. This writer's first such stickers had come two decades earlier. They showed motocross rather than MotoGP, and customised buggies rather than F1 motor cars. They'd been made by a firm synonymous with soccer stickers: Fuentes, Kantor & Shipton, otherwise known as FKS, if not by ruder variants of the three initials. The firm had a hand in more than sport, as drinkers in Soho's Coach & Horses pub knew all too well. They referred to FKS as *Fucking & Kids Stuff*! An altogether shorter, blunter and even ruder five-letter nickname was bestowed on FKS by sex workers based near the firm's Wardour Street office. FKS was located in Soho because it was a merchant of smut, as well as sports stickers. These days, Soho has long-since been sanitised but in the 1970s, and during the first years of the 1980s, it was seedy, and a little dangerous, yet always interesting. FKS was based between collectibles shops, kinky bookshops, pimps and strip shows. The collectibles, along with the girls, the non-stop ecstatic dancing and erotic cabaret, are long gone. So too is FKS.

In its time FKS issued all sorts of stickers, from soccer to rugby; from record breakers to science fiction. The stickers were sold in paper envelopes, and eventually in hermetically sealed packets, available for a few pennies from newsagents – shops where newspapers were once bought. Newsagents? Newspapers? These days such things are almost as anachronistic as card fairs. Yet, just three decades ago every village had a newsagent, towns had dozens, and cities had hundreds of them – and cards fairs, too!

During the 1970s FKS published various motor sports sticker collections, including *The Wonderful World of Motorcycles*, in 1974; *Motor Cycles*, in 1976; and *Grand Prix*, in 1977. It was the era of J. G. Ballard's book, *Crash*, and the real thing was often on TV, where track races could suddenly flare up into fiery deaths. A season would not go by without some fatality or serious injury and, frankly, Formula One was exciting then, not least for James Hunt and Nicki Lauda. There's something stupefying about seeing a ball of flame engulf a crew during a pit lane refuelling. It's not quite the same with MotoGP. Whereas watching Barry Sheene flying down the track, gambolling off kerb stones, fracturing and breaking bones in the process was teeth-on-edge torture, and evoked nothing but compassion; a calamitous car crash was epic and awe-inspiring. Nikki Lauda's burned-off ear, his miracle recovery, and his erstwhile victory over death was as mythic as Jim Clarke's roadside cremation in the charnel capsule of his overturned car. Not that FKS reproduced such grizzly scenes.

Before FKS, images of motorcycles on British-made trade cards had been a regular feature since the *Motor Cycle Series*, of 1914. The rather

Wallet for sports cards given with Champion comic, 1930s

Packet for motor car stickers from Spain, 1950s

 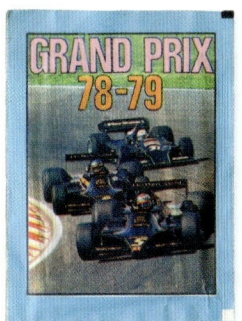 

Booklet of decal transfers by Philmar, 1930s

FKS packet of F1 stickers, 1978

Cars had appeared on tobacco earlier than motorbikes. During the Edwardian epoch Lambert & Butler cigarettes were sold with sedate images, called *Motors*.

sober cards were sponsored by a number of businesses with whose marques they are known, including Hobson of Huddersfield, Golds of Birmingham, Taylor Wood of Newcastle, etc. Some of these cards are very rare and prices of over £20 are typical.

Cars had appeared on tobacco cards earlier than motorbikes. During the Edwardian epoch Lambert & Butler cigarettes were sold with sedate images, called *Motors*. Though pretty they weren't racers. British producers would develop the theme and come to publish a wide range of motor sports cards in the remaining years of the twentieth century but it was the foreign firms which made the most attractive racing car cards; from quite early on, too.

Racing drivers have been commemorated on Italian cards since the 1920s. In Italy speed is king! Doing things at speed – drinking coffee in one shot, chattering manically, driving rapidly – is so much a part of Italian culture that, until recently, those who drove within the speed limit were mocked as inept! Italian car drivers, whose reckless probation on scooters probably taught them a thing or two about dodging things, have certainly developed skills akin to those of good motorcycle riders. Unlike Great Britain, there is almost no road rage in Italy. Killings on the tarmac occur, mostly, due to sudden braking: the dire need to come to an immediate standstill whilst doing 160kph. The Italian driver will hang on to your rear fender, waiting to overtake, even if you yourself are exceeding the speed limit. There is no velocity you can sustain at which he or she will not feel the need to pass you by. As they overtake their claxons are sounded in gratitude – for letting them pass. Italians themselves know they are a little road crazy and this comes in for humourous treatment on their own trade cards. Nannina's 1940s *Tecni-Color* [sic] cards are illustrated with panache. Comically drawn car crashes show silly scenes of smashed-in heads, above which stars spin, and windscreen ejections of unwanted chattering passengers by drivers who aim to hit trees.

Road-speed sports cards were cherished by Italian children almost as much as the chocolates with which they were given. Drivers like Ascari, Chiron, Maserati, Varzi and other legendary names of the jazz age were regularly featured. The firm of Zaini was especially prodigious with stars of MotoGP, cards of whom it included with its confectionery throughout the interwar years, and beyond.

Some of the most attractive and rarest Italian racing cards are the colourful, small metal cards of drivers and riders which were made by Gettone Italia, around 1930. Having created a new fad – metal cards – other firms followed. Metal discs made by Dea also include famous racing drivers. Today, Gettone Italia and Dea cards sell for over £50 each, if they come to market.

Venturini brothers of Verona issued tremendous, coloured caricatures of 1930s road racing, and MotoGP heroes. VAV, the initialism by which the firm is better known, survived the war and issued road sports cards anew, in the 1950s. VAV is one of the most collected names in Italy.

Like VAV, Zaini also continued making chocolates and issuing cards into the 1950s. One such series includes caricatures of famous drivers and riders, including Umberto Masetti, illustrated in futurist-style brushstrokes.

An Italian marque called Bomba-Americana made tattoo-style transfer decals, which it issued in the 1950s. Once the decal had been removed with water, children were left with sports stars printed on the other side. This encouraged collectors to retain the advertising part of the decal, the part with the firm's name, the

MOTOR SPORTS: MOTOGP, FORMULA 1 AND OTHER PETROL-HEAD PICTURES ON TRADE CARDS

otherwise disposable backing paper. Such clever marketing has hardly been tried since: a sticker's backing paper as a secondary collectible. Imagine the last 40 years of Panini and other peel-off sticker backing papers not going into landfill sites; millions of pieces of paper collected instead of being cast aside.

Ferrero chocolates issued sports cards throughout the 1940s and 1950s. Some were traditional cards, showing motorcycle racers and car drivers, while others were made in homage to the metal discs of the 1930s, so fondly recalled in Italy. Geoffrey Duke, the British MotoGP legend, was celebrated by Ferrero. The firm included the six-times world champion on at least two series of its metallic *Gettone Sportive*. The colourful metal discs were issued in two editions. One shows Duke in a racing helmet, with goggles; the other without headgear. Both are very rare and you may need to pay towards £50 for an example in fine form.

In the 1960s, new publishers like Mira, Edis and Panini took on the established name of Lampo in releasing concurrent motor racing collections. The struggle between such brands would go on for two decades. By the 1980s Panini had triumphed and would dominate thereafter. Yet, some of the cards made by the other firms are superb. Look out for Edis's *Auto e Moto* cards. The illustrated portraits of drivers are very attractive. They include such track legends as Bruce McLaren, Mike Hailwood, Stirling Moss, John Surtees and Graham Hill.

The defining pan-sport collections of the age were the different editions of *Campioni dello Sport*, issued by Panini. Anglo-American and British Commonwealth stars were widely celebrated in this series, issued between 1966 and 1973. Each year Panini made the design of the cards different so the collections are easy to distinguish. From the first, in 1966, until the last, in 1973, they featured well-known greats, the likes of Jack Brabham, Geoffrey Duke, Jackie Stewart and Hugh Anderson. The first edition, from 1966, includes cards with a plain, white border. Later issues employed colourful frames and other fancy design features. In 1967 the colour was green; a year later the cards had yellow-and-red bases; blue frames came in, for 1969; then all-yellow frames in 1970. The last collection of the type, in 1973, reverted to a simpler, black-&-white frame. Mario Andretti and Emerson Fittipaldi feature in many of the editions, and these days prices paid for them have exceeded £100 each! By 1974 Panini rebranded the collection as *Sport Vedettes*. Niki Lauda and Carlos Reutemann were among the racers to feature in the upgrade. The Niki Lauda sticker, if it remains unused (with backing paper) and in excellent condition has been seen to sell for around £100!

Italy continued to honour English-speaking racers throughout the 1970s. The Turin-based printer Ediraf, later a subsidiary of Panini, included Kelvin Carruthers, the Australian world champion, in a series called *Moto*. Rival issuer Imperia did similarly in *Auto Moto*, and in 1974 Panini followed suit with *Moto 2000*, then *Super Moto* one year later. Phil Read features in both Panini collections, and Kenny Roberts, Jack Findlay and Charles Mortimer are included in the later issue.

Lampo's EuroFlash imprint competed with Panini, into the 1980s. Its *Moto Sprint Flash* stickers took on the Modena giant's *F1 Grand Prix* collections. Alas, such editions, from the 1980s and later, are outside the scope of this book. That said, it's worth mentioning the definitive rookie of Ayrton Senna, which was made in 1984, by Panini. It's a beauty and well worth seeking out. It's a clear plastic card showing Senna in Toleman-Hart team colours. It's quite a rarity! Prices have

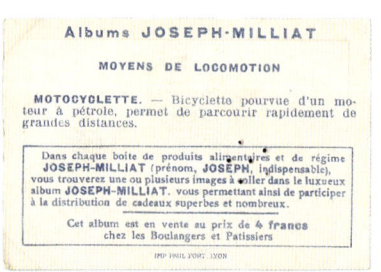

French trade card, 1930s

Ice cream cards, 1974

Italian trade card, 1930s

Italian chocolates card, 1930s

MacRobertson's trade card from Australia, 1917

> **In the 1960s, new publishers like Mira, Edis and Panini took on the established name of Lampo in releasing concurrent motor racing collections, in competition.**

140 AN A TO Z OF **SPORTING COLLECTIBLES**

 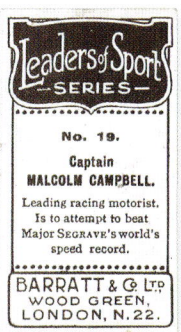  

Italian trade cards of Louis Chiron, left 1930s and right 1940s

Sir Malcom Campbell on a Barratt card, 1927; and on a French trade card, 1920s

Fangio on a booklet card by Vecchi (Lampo), 1953

Caricatures of Campari and Varzi on pre-war Italian trade cards

Ascari on Italian trade cards from the 1940s

Carlo Felice Trossi and Peter Whitehead, for Ferrari, on Italian trade cards from the 1930s and 1940s

been seen to top £200 for it and its companion card showing Senna in the car.

The best coffees in Italy are often those served at motorway service stations. A solitary barista will make half a dozen different coffees at once, in less time than it takes a team of three drive-thru coffee attendants, in other lands, to make a single cup. Autogrill is not only one of the best-known restaurants on the Italian *autostrade*, where you are guaranteed an excellent coffee quickly, it is also known for its sports cards. Autogrill issued a series called *Concorso a Premi Super Raccolta Figurine G. P. "Formula 1" 1978* [sic]. The collection includes Hunt & Lauda, as well as Cheever, Andretti and a score of other famous drivers. Ever rarer, prices are going up. Expect to pay £50 for James Hunt.

Outside Italy some of the brightest images of early racers are to be found on Spanish cards. One such series, issued in the 1920s by Amatller chocolates, shows dandy racing drivers and their mechanic co-drivers, posing together in their cockpits. Equally stunning Spanish cards also hail from the 1920s. One collection is called *¿Quién es el campeón mundial?* [sic]. The beautifully illustrated series comprises 42 colourful sketches of sporting action, with inset portraits of world champion stars. The collection is well worth seeking out. So are the sporting tarot-card games, once made in Iberia. Henry Seagrave, the first Brit to win a grand prix in F1, is celebrated in such an edition, known as the *Cine Manual* series. Scarce Spanish cards like these will cost you £30 each, or more, if you are lucky enough to find them.

Later Spanish collections of motor racing cards, issued after the Civil War, may be acquired for a lot less than the cards of the jazz age. Notable examples from the 1950s are those by Fher (the founders of FKS), which published *Automovilismo*; and Batanga, which issued *Ases del Volante*. In the 1970s, Bruguera's Bimbo created *El Mundo del Automovil* (these stickers include famous drivers of the 1970s, such as Jochen Mass). Earlier in the same decade, Xibeca Damm beer had issued *Bolidos Competiçion* cards which feature famous F1 cars and their drivers; and Panini's earliest incarnation in Spain, as Vulcano, resulted in a collection of motor sports stickers called *Moto 2000* – issued 26 years early, in 1974. Vulcano's *Moto 2000* was, of course, the Italian collection of the same name with Spanish-language backing papers. To Panini collectors the Iberian types are worth ten times the regular price paid for Italian editions.

A gigantic collection of cards, issued by Quelcom in 1979, brought post-fascist sticker-centric Spain into gum cards territory. The Topps-like cards feature James Hunt and a host of other famous drivers, as well as hundreds of other sports stars. The Quelcom cards come in two formats, one larger than the other, so you

No. 4 . . . . A. FRAZER NASH.
Specially drawn for "The Autocar" by Frank Leah.

Printed by The Cornwall Press Ltd., Paris Garden, London, S.E.1.

. . . C. M. HARVEY.
for "The Autocar" by Frank Leah

Supplement to *The Autocar*

FAMOUS RACING MOTORISTS

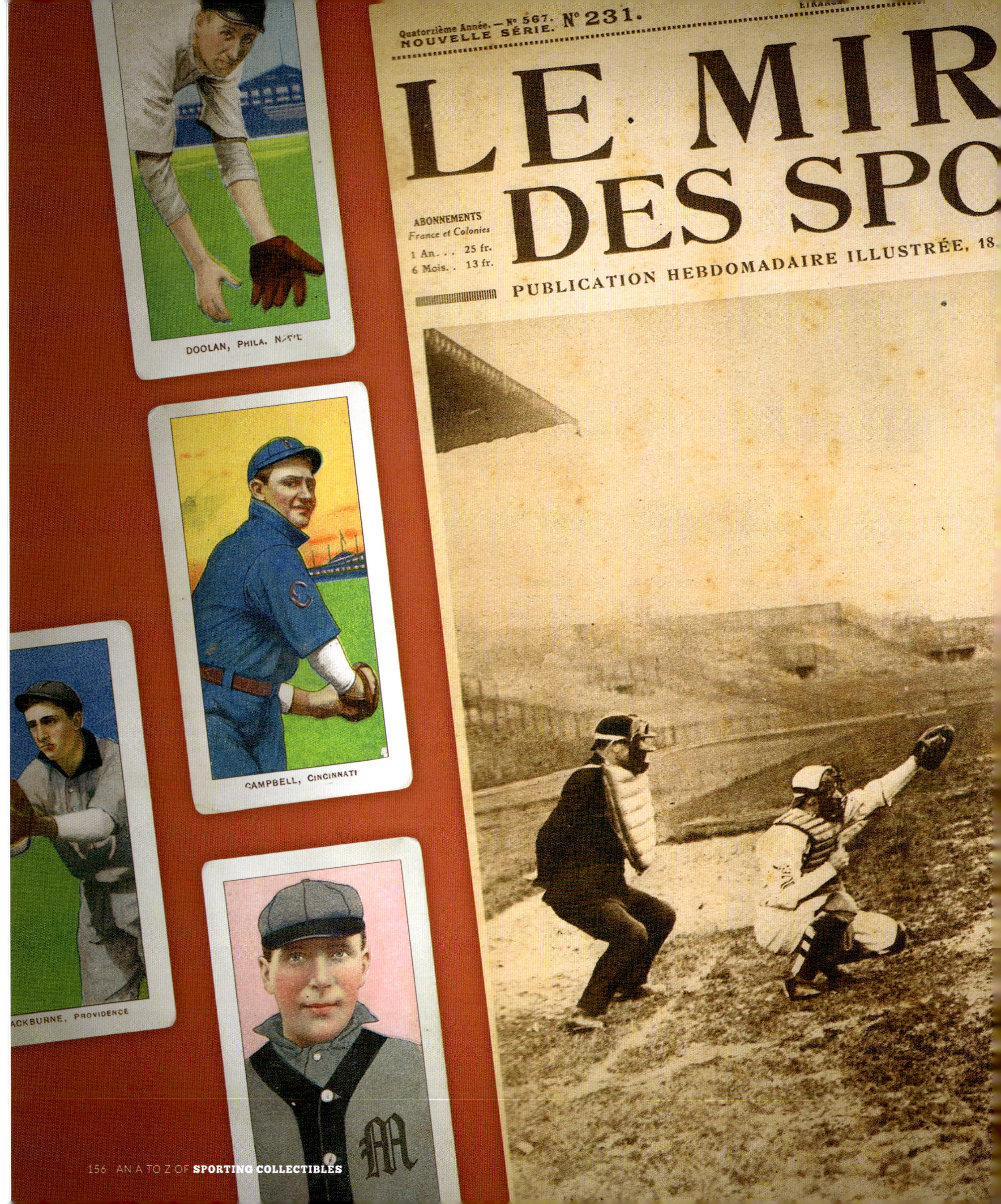

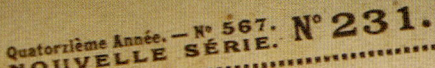

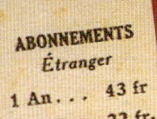

WARHOP, N.Y. AMER.

CROSS, INDIANAPOLIS

THIELMAN, LOUISVILLE

SUMMERS, DETROIT

CRAVATH, MINNEAPOLIS

AN A TO Z OF **SPORTING COLLECTIBLES** 157

Copies also show the names of stars and of teams, some of which are curiously printed in English. Why would Czech cards, issued in Prague and Bratislava, distributed in Bohemia, Slovakia and Moravia, have English language? It was not spoken there. The forger made the cards for buyers in USA!

Gridiron

As with the other New World sports, there are dedicated price guides for gridiron, or American Football, such as *Football Card Price Guide*, by Beckett, a tome which lists mostly modern-times cards. Like other sports from North America buyers in USA and Canada may have missed out on more obscure cards of their sport: those issued in Europe, and elsewhere. Here's a selection of obscure gridiron cards to seek out.

Amatller 1926 Spanish cards called *Artistas de Cine* includes Harold Lloyd as *The Freshman*
Baines of Manningham 1900 *American Football*
Bimbo 1972 *La Vuelta al Mundo*
Bimbo 1973 *El Libro de las Adivinanzas*
Churchman 1929 *Sports and Games in Many Lands*
Edito Service 1978 *Sportscaster*
Jacques Superchocolat 1968 *Sports Insolite Ongewone Sporter*
Lampo 1963 *Enciplopedia Sportiva*
Orthi 1920s Spanish-issue cinema stars and sport playing cards
Ridleys 1953 *Believe it or not*
Rollan 1957 *FBI*
Rozan & Chien Qui Saute 1950s *Sports d'Hiver*
Sharpe's of Bradford 1890s *American Sports*

American Football on a British cigarette card, 1929

Gridiron on an Italian sticker, 1960s

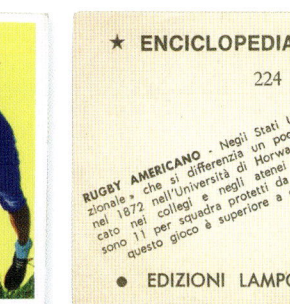

Spanish gaming card, 1920s

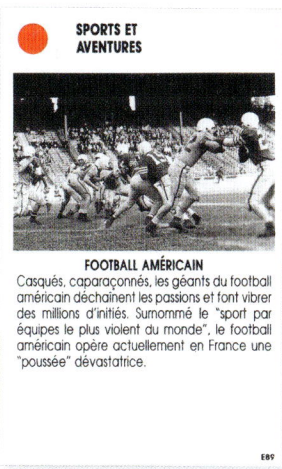
French trade card, 1980s

French trade card, 1960s

Spanish trade card, 1970s

French trade card, 1980s

Spanish trade card, 1970s

Rugby: an introduction to rugby football on trade cards

Halifax rugby Baines card, 1885   **Wakefield rugby Baines card, 1886**   **Armley rugby card by Richardson, 1870s**

The earliest rugby cards are arguably the most beautiful sports cards ever made. The creativity employed by artisan card manufacturers of the Victorian epoch; their clever designs, not to mention artistry in advertising, and the ever-changing formats of collections humbles most modern stickers. Nowadays, multinationals produce commercial images of sporting stars by the billion. Their glossy façade hides a sad truth behind such mass-produced paper: stickers made by multinationals have no soul. Unlike stickers of regular sports stars of 50 years ago today's sticky pictures of quaffed millionaires are product vehicles as much as they are sports stickers. Their primary purpose is to place kit advertising and corporate brand names into minds. Today's sports cards are tainted by this quiet infiltration of commerce over sport. Youngsters, today, may not realise what they are taking in, subconsciously, when they open a packet of next year's *Buy-Me Because I'm New & Better* stickers. Unlike slick, new stickers, whose investment worth is minimal, if anything, antique and vintage ephemera such as Baines rugby cards are priceless. Older cards are probably also a lot healthier for the mind, and spirit.

As long ago as 1880, colourful shield-shaped cards showed rugby forwards; oval-shapes came with portraits of famous full-backs, and star-shaped cards featured flying half-backs. Such cards brought a gasp to children opening packets of ever-new, always fascinating designs. Cards might be cut in the shapes of playing card suits: die-cut hearts, clubs, diamonds and spades. The next year, something different: octagonal shapes, triangles or even cards designed in the shape of rugby balls! Constant change and innovation helped make the collecting of early cards a fascinating pastime. The inclusion of the world's earliest famous footballers, and escalating prices for such cards, nowadays, makes for quite an investment, as well as a fascinating pastime.

Almost a century later, in the 1970s, toiling in the mud on wet winter days was one thing. Bully boys charging at you with the intent of doing injury was quite another. The attention of mean teachers was worse still. Evading the glare of sadistically charged glances from the sports staff and avoiding the unwelcome toe of their oversize boots, whose kicks in the pants added insult to injury, was the proverbial *straw*. These things were all *back-breaker* incentives to sidestep rugby

Millinery card for Rochdale Hornets by Holt The Hatter, printed by Ormerod Brothers, 1880s

competing armies of collectors. Rugger collectors and collectors of a soccer club's history are two. Football badge collectors are a third.

Until recently, few football badge collectors, also known as football falerists, realised that the oldest football badges were actually made of card. In the 1880s, W.N. Sharpe, a firm of lithographers in Bradford, created flower-shaped cards for fitting into buttonholes, in clothing. These cards had long stems, made of cardboard. They'd sit in a lapel buttonhole, so, on match days a supporter could proudly display his or her favourite player, and their club's colours. Just as Sharpe's floral cards adorned suits and jackets, Baines's hat-band club colours cards crowned trilby hats, and other headgear. Rugby matches

166 AN A TO Z OF **SPORTING COLLECTIBLES**

of the time would have witnessed attendees wearing such cards, and no doubt younger spectators traded suchlike, outside the grounds.

Due to their unusual shapes delicate corners were easily damaged. No wonder so few of these beautiful sports cards have survived the last 150 years. The cards were played with – as they were meant to be – in games which included throwing the cards against walls to see which bounced back best; and *spoofing*, which was a guessing game involving cards being palmed and traded; won and lost from hand to hand. Such games resulted in irreparable damage to cards, but the games were fondly loved. They also garnered many cards for skilful players. The aim of one of the wall games, depending on local rules, was to throw cards at a solid structure from a certain distance. The card landing furthest from the wall (or nearest to it) was classed as the winning card. That card's owner was victor. He or she gathered up all the other cards which were forfeited by the game's losers.

It's almost certain that the earliest sports trade cards in the world are rugby football cards, and they were issued by around 1880. The earliest soccer and cricket cards were issued later in the same decade. Other sports, including gymnastics and baseball, were published by American tobacco-trade issuers from 1887, onwards. Only the French did it earlier. Chromolithographic sports cards were issued in France as early as the 1870s.

The identity of the very first rugby football card, and the very earliest sports card, may never be known for sure, though some collectors speculate it was a card made by Richardson, a printer based in Leeds, in northern England. Until recently, many believed the accolade belonged to John Baines of Manningham, but it may well be that Petty & Sons, of Leeds, or Ormerod Brothers of Rochdale, were the first. Then again, the Wellington Hotel, in St Helens, and the Swinton Brewery are two examples of smaller businesses which produced their own rugby football cards as early as the 1870s. Such cards outdate those by the bigger names.

The earliest rugby cards are not only some of the most beautiful sports cards, such cards are some of the rarest. They also remain, for the time being, massively undervalued. This is partly because their rarity is not fully appreciated. A similar card, of a similar age, should sell for over $100,000, maybe even over $1 million, were it baseball and were it American. It's not that rugby has fewer followers than baseball, nor fewer collectors. Rugby is a worldwide sport, played on six continents. It's just that the North American market for sports cards is more developed. It is 20 years ahead of the British and European markets. Moreover, soccer certainly has many more devotees and collectors than baseball, yet the earliest and rarest soccer cards also remain undervalued. The $3 million baseball cigarette card of Honus Wager is but one of at least 50 extant copies of that card, albeit it's the best

RUGBY: AN INTRODUCTION TO RUGBY FOOTBALL ON TRADE CARDS

French trade card to cut, stand up and play, 1930s

German tobacco cards, 1930s

Italian chocolates trade card, 1930s

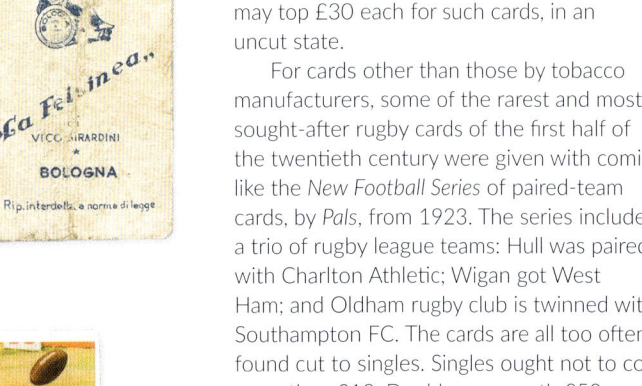
Spanish sticker, 1960s

the nature of the original confection. Phillips's Sports Cigarettes *Sportsmen* include Frank Whitcombe, of Wales; Len Aston of St Helens; and Cecil Mountford of New Zealand. Prices may top £30 each for such cards, in an uncut state.

For cards other than those by tobacco manufacturers, some of the rarest and most sought-after rugby cards of the first half of the twentieth century were given with comics, like the *New Football Series* of paired-team cards, by *Pals*, from 1923. The series includes a trio of rugby league teams: Hull was paired with Charlton Athletic; Wigan got West Ham; and Oldham rugby club is twinned with Southampton FC. The cards are all too often found cut to singles. Singles ought not to cost more than £10. Doubles are worth £50.

Barratt & Company, the London-based issuer of sweet cigarettes, published various editions of sports cards during the 1920s. The different issues have, thanks to wrongful information published elsewhere, been wrongly classified as one, unified series, known as *Footballers, Football Clubs and Cricketers*. This careless generalisation is partly down to last century's obsolete and often erroneous research. The edition is actually made up of three or four different series, issued over a four-year period. Amidst the many soccer players and cricketers are one or two rugby players, which are very hard to find. They include Jim Sullivan, the Welsh rugby player who played for the club known today as Wigan Warriors.

Barratt's edition of *Famous Footballers*, which came out for the 1935/36 season, was something different. Unlike the 1920s cards, which had photos of players without descriptions, the 1935 series included a potted biography of each player. It heralded the generic design for cards which would come to be known as gum cards, later in the century. The 100 cards in the 1935 collection include players from New Zealand's All Blacks. These numberless footballer cards, printed in black (unlike later, similar editions in sepia) start at around £25 each for association footballers, but the All Blacks are notoriously scarce and may cost well over £50 each card.

Barratt's sweet cigarettes returned to rugby, albeit briefly, after a hiatus of almost 40 years, in a series called *Goldflake Famous Sportsmen*, issued in 1970 (and reissued in 1971 with slight changes). The series included Bob Hillier, of Blackheath and England; and his national-side teammate Buddy Rogers. Patient buyers may find the cards for as little as £1 each.

A&BC Gum included a solitary rugby player in its set of 120 *All Sport* picture bubble gum

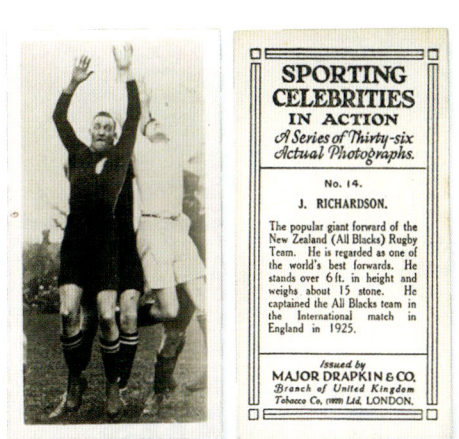
All Blacks action on a British cigarette card, 1930

Wakefield Trinity player on a card by Barratt, 1926

All Blacks player on a card by Barratt, 1935

cards, in 1954: Jackie Kyle, the Irish captain. For some reason the British gum cards giant stayed away from rugby after this series. However, its British Commonwealth rival, Chewing Gum Products of New Zealand, published an attractive series of cards, called *Famous Rugby Players 1966-1968*.

Generally there are many more rugby trade cards issued in Commonwealth countries like South Africa, Australia and New Zealand, than in the United Kingdom. Alas, they fall outside the scope of this brief introduction to rare rugby cards, but eager collectors may find them on eBay websites of the British Commonwealth, such as ebay.com.au

The imagery chosen to illustrate this section of the book has been selected, largely, because of the rarity of Victorian and Edwardian die-cut cards from the British Isles, and the similar scarcity of French trade cards of antiquity.

British cigarette cards, especially of the inter-war era, are quite easy to find and their images are accessible elsewhere, such as online auction and collector websites. A glance at such resources will show you most if not all of them. For rare rugby cards, and more images of cards you may never see elsewhere, see under the rugby tab at www.footballsoccercards.com

Legendary Welsh player JPR Williams on a *Sportscaster* card, 1978

   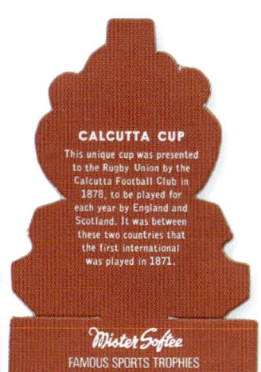
Ice cream cards, 1974

SNOOKER: AN INTRODUCTION TO BILLIARDS AND SNOOKER ON TRADE CARDS

Aussie Willie Lindrum on a South African tobacco card, 1939

Maryann McConnell, Quadriga *Snooker Kings* sticker, 1984

Mandy Fisher, Quadriga *Snooker Kings* sticker, 1984

Alex 'Hurricane' Higgins, Quadriga *Snooker Kings* sticker, 1984

Jimmy 'Whirlwind' White, Quadriga *Snooker Kings* sticker, 1984

then it's fair to expect its price to be over £50.

Also in 1933, in Australia, Sweetacres Champion-brand chewing gum was given with cards inscribed *Series of Sports Champions, Etc* [sic]. The large series of sports cards includes champion 'billiardists'.

In 1955 Blue Band margarine launched *40 Sporten en Spelen in Woord en Beeld (40 Sports and Games in Words and Pictures)*. The 150 paper stickers include two billiards stickers, which are as interesting to fashion designers and clothing historians, as they are to sports card collectors. The players wear stylish black leather jackets. With their blond short-back-and-sides haircuts, it seems that the billiards-playing *look* of the day was influenced by military and police clothing from the time of the Third Reich! The stickers tend to cost little when they come to the market and you'll find them for as little as £1 each.

John Allen issued a card of the legendary Joe Davis, in 1996, as part of a series called *Underwood's Sportsmen*. The images had been not been seen on cards until then. They are based on caricatures created by the illustrator George Underwood. Before it could be sold, most of the stock was destroyed in an accident, thus, sets of these cards are very hard to come by and the Joe Davis card is elusive. Expect to pay at least £10 for it. For a full set of all 50 cards there is no market price because there is no recorded sale.

Quadriga's *Snooker Kings*, from 1984, came out at the peak of British TV interest in the game. Had Quadriga started this way, with a very popular theme, the firm may well have survived longer than a couple of years. As a swansong to almost 20 years of FKS stickers, the pretty collection, featuring stars from Alex 'Hurricane' Higgins to Jimmy 'Whirlwind' White, was a memorable one. These days, most surviving examples are found glued down. Unused stickers are rare but they often peel away from their backing papers due to a defect in the glue. That said, values are increasing, partly due to the collectability of Quadriga, the firm which succeeded Fuentes, Kantor and Shipton. Expect to pay prices over £10 for stickers of the bigger-name stars.

In 1987, Panini also tuned into the popularity of snooker. Its British Isles issue of the generic *Supersport* collection included 15 snooker stickers, with Dennis Taylor, Alex Higgins, Jimmy White, etc. Prices for unused stickers are low, for most of the players, though big names may attract higher prices. Beware sellers on the internet whose stickers are 'recuperated'. This is obfuscating parlance for stickers which have been removed from an album, using acetone thinners. Such stickers have no backing paper and they are all but worthless, being useful only as space fillers.

More rare billiards and snooker cards may be seen under the snooker tab at www.footballsoccercards.com

Soccer: an introduction to *The Soccer Cards Rarity Scale* at the end of this book

St Mirren versus Notts County on a Spanish trade card, 1923

Dumbarton on a Sharpe's *Play Up Football* Card, 1880s

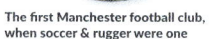
The first Manchester football club, when soccer & rugger were one

One of many lost teams of yesteryear, Imperial Rovers

In the previous book, the essential guide to soccer cards, association football cards are covered comprehensively. *An A-Z of Football Collectibles: Priceless Cigarette Cards and Sought-After Soccer Stickers*, published by Pitch Publishing, has 300 pages and 2,000 images devoted entirely to football trading cards, stickers, tobacco-trade cards and non-tobacco trade cards of football from around the world, from the 1880s to the 1980s. During the first book's preparation some things slipped through the net. They are included in this tome, at the end of this book, featured in the first comprehensive guide to worldwide soccer cards and their rarity, in *The Soccer Cards Rarity Scale*.

Notwithstanding the fact that the world has changed dramatically since the first book, in the 2020s soccer card collecting is more popular than ever. Despite recent economic stresses and the pandemic, values for antique and vintage soccer cards have gone up, sometimes wildly. In many cases, prices have risen by more than 100% in little over one year. Antique and vintage cards are not only growing in popularity, they are rapidly escalating in value. There are two reasons for this: firstly, it's partly thanks to the previous book which brought many new collectors to the hobby; and, secondly, experienced collectors have snapped up a lot of what was available since that book was published. Collectors are realising that older soccer cards are not only excellent value-store assets but that they are also safer bets, both in the medium and long term, than the risks associated with paying a lot of money for recently made stickers.

Recent public and postal auctions of football gum cards have seen higher prices, frantic bidding, and much higher participation by collectors than previously. Auction hammer prices in 2020 have exceeded all expectations. One notable case is the recent sale of 15 Taddy tobacco cards, of Southampton FC players, which made £1,700. The auctioneer had estimated the cards would sell for only £100. A score of bidding collectors were happy to prove him wrong. It transpired that the top bidder resold the cards for a price exceeding the auction hammer price!

Offers made for rare cards in other sales have also seen significant betterment. One example, seen on a well-known auction website, was the sale of a 1979 Maradona sticker, made by Panini. It sold for almost US$3,000. This price is 60 times higher than it would have been just two years earlier!

A Pelé card by Alifabolaget, made in Sweden in 1958, of which over 60 exemplars are known (of which one or two more are discovered yearly) sold for $43,000 in spring. Then, another made $75,000 before summer was done. A mere season later, another Alifabolaget Pelé card made $290,000! Hard though it may be to comprehend, for many British and European collectors, these were not the only hundred-thousand dollar prices paid for Pelé cards! In autumn 2020 a Bremer Kaffee card from West Germany, also from 1958, showing Pelé and the victorious Brazilians was offered for $195,000. The seller seemed to have taken an offer, off the auction platform, because he withdrew his card from sale after just a few hours. Within days a similar Bremer card of Pelé, but a specimen with a much lower grade, was offered for $95,000. Rare cards are surely up!

The present book, as readers will have noticed, is an introduction to a selection of other, popular sports on trade cards. Many of the antique and vintage pan-sport cards available are, for now, where soccer cards once found themselves to be: affordable and on an upwards curve in value. At the end of the 1990s, in the UK, even the rarest Pelé could be had for less

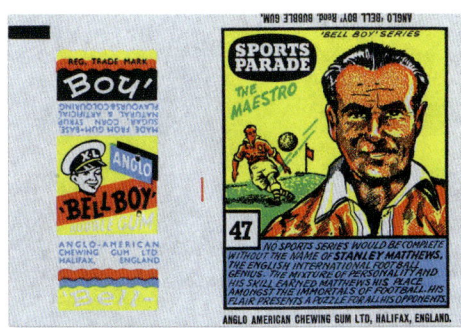
Bell Boy gum insert *proof* of Stanley Matthews, 1959

Lovell's confectionery card, 1910

Three very rare cards from 1905 by Cohen Weenen, including Joe Bache

Buxton Guild, an early soccer team card by Sharpe

Master Vending gum card of Pelé, from Italy, 1959

The rookie card for England striker Allan Clarke by FKS, 1967

than £100. The rarest soccer cards were all affordable, back then, and most scarce cards could be had for less than £20! Now, in the early 2020s, many other sports cards find themselves where soccer cards were, in that mythic realm known as the field of bargains. Perchance, they won't stay there for long.

These days, aside from the occasional undervalued Baines card, it's almost too late to find very rare antique soccer cards at prices less than £100. The few Baines bargains which remain at prices below that figure will soon be snapped up. However, if you are choosy, you can make sound investments when buying rare cards of other sports. One example is the 1959 Anglo-American Bell Boy *Sports Parade* collection of waxy paper gum inserts, which includes Stanley Matthews. Unlike most issues, some gum inserts escaped being folded, wrapped and sold with gum. They are known as *proofs* because they remain, technically, unused. They are far rarer than the typically worn and battered examples, sold with gum, which occasionally come to market. The proofs were issued in virginal condition. To keep them flat, and clean, they were stapled into card folders. The staples were punched into a plain border between the *Sports Parade* design itself,

and a sample wrapper. So, the staple holes do not damage the actual designs. The proofs also bear a factory-made fold between the two parts. It's the only such indentation and does not interfere with the artwork on either the design or the wrapper part. The folders were used as salesmen's gimmicks and were later given as redemption prizes. It seems that few were redeemed because only a handful has come to light, in over 60 years.

In 2013, a small selection of such proofs found their way to market. They were bought for the very fine sum of £20 – at the time it was considered a good price for the seller! In 2015, they were resold for more than double, at around £50 each. In 2020 they were auctioned anew. While the golfers, boxers and tennis players fetched prices over £200 each, most of the others, including hockey, track & field athletics and gridiron, made around £100. The Stanley Matthews proof sold for around £150.

No matter which sport it is, cards are up in price. Recent comparisons of top-selling sports cards to the Stanley Gibbons index of rare stamps, and a similar one for rare coins, show cards outperforming both, not just over the last ten years but also over 30 years! If it's of a

certain vintage, especially if it's antique, a sports card no longer needs to be baseball or soccer to sell well.

The Soccer Cards Rarity Scale, at the end of this book, serves not only to list and evaluate 1,000s of rare series of football cards; it is also a chance to correct a few errors in the first book. The 1958 A&BC Gum *Footballer* cards were first issued with black backs. Then, later in 1958 and early in 1959, they were reprinted. Both types of reprint have blue backs but if you lay examples of each blue-back reprint side by side you'll notice differences in the photos. This is because one reissue used slightly larger images than the other. It's quite a task to complete either of the reissued collections. So, the cards with black typeface on the rear are commoner, but some of them are now breaking into three figures for a single card! The blue-back cards are far rarer, and many collectors avidly seek various examples of such cards, so prices are climbing higher and higher, year on year. One of the blue-back Bobby Charlton cards was seen to sell for £400 in 2020.

Certain nuggets of information went AWOL from the previous book, such as the names of the three families whose initials came to be synonymous with British-made sports stickers

SOCCER: AN INTRODUCTION TO *THE SOCCER CARDS RARITY INDEX* AT THE END OF THIS BOOK

Alan Ball on a tobacco card made in the Canary Islands, 1966

Hammers on early chocolates cards by Packer, 1910

Billy Meredith Clarke's tobacco card, 1901

Billy Liddell & Peter McParland, very rare packet-issue cards by Soiree cigarettes

between 1967 and 1982. In London's erstwhile sex quarter, Soho, FKS was rudely acronymed by business rivals and neighbours. The alliterative quality of the firm's initials, FKS, led to it being known as *FucKS*, or more creatively as *Fucking and Kids Stuff*, at least to drinkers in nearby pubs like The Blue Posts, The Intrepid Fox and The Coach & Horses. Fuentes, Kantor & Shipton were the names behind millions, if not billions, of *Soccer Stars* and others sports stickers by FKS. So, finally, the mystery behind the '*apply adhesive above this line*' riddle is no more. Collectors once anxious to know what FKS stood for, and who made the stickers with the anonymous gluing instructions, now know it was the Spanish brothers Fuentes and a pair of Brits: Kantor and Shipton. The Fuentes brothers headed the family firm, Fher, which controlled FKS. Fher was short for *Fuentes Hermanos*, which translates into English as the Fuentes Brothers. Fuentes, Kantor & Shipton it is! (Thanks to Nik Yeomans for his invaluable input with FKS stickers).

Like its rival, Thorpe & Porter, whose imprint Top Sellers also came to be based in Soho, FKS was involved in the sale of smut for seniors, as well as sports pictures for juniors. While Top Sellers distributed gore-and-erotica fanzines, and top-shelf soft-core sex publications, such as the cult-classic *Cinema Blue*, FKS dealt with less bloody erotica, specialising in the distribution of soft-core pornography, alongside the evergreen *Soccer Stars* stickers. What a decade the 1970s was!

Until 2020, soccer card collecting had been a field that was impenetrable to many collectors. Now, thanks to *An A-Z of Football Collectibles, Priceless Cigarette Cards and Sought-After Soccer Stickers*, anyone and everyone can see what it's all about; which cards are rare and which types of cards and stickers to collect, or to invest in.

The previous book looked in depth at soccer cards made in Great Britain, from the 1880s until the 1980s, as well as introducing myriad foreign collections, made by issuers from around the globe. Cards made after 1990 were not included because most cards and stickers made since 1990 are not only very common, some are high risk, especially if you pay a lot of money for them.

The first book shared information that was once esoteric because everyone benefits from the dissemination of knowledge. When knowledge is cornered by a few, it may be used to manipulate markets to the benefit of a cabal at the expense of the many; just like in financial markets, oil markets and the in the world of media, not forgetting the servants of all three, the politicians. In vintage soccer cards such manipulation is very low, if it exists at all. However, within the world of contemporary soccer cards and stickers, especially those made since the 1990s, malign influence may run deep.

Soccer cards represent the biggest sport in the world, yet many soccer cards continue to remain under-priced in contrast to other sports such as baseball and basketball. Compared to those sports, whose cards have sold for $millions, antique and vintage soccer cards are still great buys, with a bright financial future.

The recent sale of a 1952 Topps Gum card of baseball legend Mickey Mantle, for nearly $3 million, only emphasised the gap in the market

182 AN A TO Z OF **SPORTING COLLECTIBLES**

Pelé Italian gum card by EDI, 1962

The rookie card of Bobby Moore, from spring 1962 by Quaker Oats

Pre-league fixture cards for Blackpool & South Shore. One mentions Newton Heath!

Pelé cards and other vintage soccer cards stand at the crossroads. Such cards are breaking price boundaries and some are due to break into seven figures before long.

between the cards of the New World and those of the Old World. Did you know that only 30 years earlier you could have had the very same Mantle card for just $3,000? So, it went up from three grand to three million, in just thirty years!

Considering that there are around 1,000 of the $million-dollar Mantle cards in circulation, and that there are only a handful of known examples of, say, the 1958 Bremer Kaffee Pelé cards in circulation, you'd be forgiven for thinking those cards would also sell for such money. They probably will, sooner rather than later. Right now, Pelé cards and other vintage soccer cards stand at such a crossroads. To cut up a William Burroughs *cut up*, rare soccer cards *are here to go*!

The British Isles has a much smaller population than USA, as do all European countries. Fewer cards were produced in Britain and Ireland than in USA. Not only were fewer cards made, cards culture in the British Isles, being what it was, resulted in fewer cards being carefully preserved. By the 1970s the North American cards market was already some decades ahead. While children in USA knew their gum cards were likely to accrue value, if the cards were well cared for, their British and Irish cousins still played street games with theirs. Relatively few British-made cards from before 1970 remain in top-grade condition, which is why you'll now see £100s being paid for certain 1950s and 1960s cards, and that's not only for cards of Charlton, Moore and Greaves. Only a few years ago these would have cost as little as £1 each!

An American friend in California, a collector of rare sports cards, recently wrote, "Soccer *is bigger than our baseball, hockey, gridiron and basketball put together.*" He's right. Worldwide, soccer enjoys a following consisting of almost a billion people, and a significant number of them collect soccer ephemera. Naturally, then, the area of biggest growth in sports cards is in soccer cards, however, prospective buyers should be aware that prices for rare such cards will rise sharply and go even higher than they are now.

Pelé is not immortal. Imagine what's going to happen to the prices of Pelé cards when the great player passes away. It's not just Pelé, either. At the moment, there are some really great-value soccer card buys out there. Did you know that only a few dozen Soirée packet-issue *Famous Footballer* tobacco cards are known to exist? For most Soirée *Famous Footballers* there are fewer than five of each card known to be in circulation. Baines cards are rarer still. Baines and other Victorian sports cards are known to have worldwide populations of only two or three cards extant for each known design. They are not getting any easier to find. In fact, many 1880s and 1890s British-made Baines cards have worldwide card populations of only a single exemplar! Imagine the cost of a baseball card with just one known example in the whole world. So, most Baines cards are a bargain, frankly. Once prices rise for these there will be no easy way to afford any of them, ever again.

Recent price explosions include the autumn-1962 Bobby Moore *Bazooka Footballer* card, by A&BC Gum, though it's not his rookie – you'll need the Quaker Oats card for that (it came out some months earlier). Another card which has rocketed in value is the 1964 Liverpool checklist card, also by A&BC Gum. Another is the 1958 Colinville Gum miniature of Jimmy Greaves (there's one of Bobby Charlton too). The aforementioned Soirée cigarette cards have sold for over £500 each, in 2020; and the 1965 George Best by Reddish Maid, a quiet rookie which most collectors won't have noticed, has gone from £50 to £200 inside a year. It's actually far rarer than his first Barratt card. Just a few years ago, all of these cards could be had for less than £20 each, most for less than £10. By the time of the North American World Cup they may be over £500.

Other British cards which have recently enjoyed a renaissance in collectability, and escalating prices, include the very rare Barratt cards of the 1920s. Few people have realised how very rare such cards really are. For every 1,000 tobacco cards made in the 1920s you will find but a single Barratt card. Photographic cards of footballers, they came with Tarrab Rock and other candy treats such as Barratt's sweet cigarettes, should out-price most gum cards because only one or two of each Barratt 1920s card remain extant and, at least for now, prices are still double-digit affordable. Some of the Barratt cards of the 1920s, may well already be *extinct*. A previously unrecorded card from the series turned up in 2015. That's after almost 100 years of collectors recording the edition. Maybe some cards are lost forever and will never show up again.

Clevedon Confectionery, a Blackpool-based business known for issuing trade cards with candy cigarettes in the 1950s and 1960s, is also seeing a boom in collectability. Though the

SOCCER: AN INTRODUCTION TO *THE SOCCER CARDS RARITY INDEX* AT THE END OF THIS BOOK

firm's caricature cards remain available, for the most part, the rarest cards issued by Clevedon are the two editions of *Football Club Managers*, which are available in mauve, and also with light-blue backgrounds. Bucking the availability trend of the firm's earlier caricatures are the cards in the *Sporting Memories* series, from 1962. Cards from this edition were changing hands for just £5 a few years ago. These days you'd be able to sell some of them for over £100 each!

So, what are contemporary cards and stickers really worth? At the end of the 1990s this writer's eyes were opened and he divested himself of all his post-1990 cards. The change of mind came during a visit to the home of a cards producer, the maker of some of the slickest and glossiest football cards of modern times. He'd made limited edition cards with metallic lettering, with laser-cut motifs, with all the add-on attractions needed to successfully market new cards. His collections arrived in the shops and sold out in no time. His cards became hard to get and ever costlier to acquire. Meanwhile, unbeknown to collectors, at his house, he had a garage full of *ex-series* cards of the very same collections which were supposedly sold out. The ruse of making *ex-series* extras is a legal loophole in limited edition publishing. It allows producers to make more than they claim to have made. An *ex-series* card does not have to be mentioned in a manifest, nor in other sworn declarations such as a *limited edition of 500*. There may exist another 500 cards, which are just the same as the cards in the official limited edition release, but as long as they are classed as *ex-series* they are legal and may eventually be sold as such. As well as his own cards, the aforementioned publisher had accrued hundreds of unopened cartons of Panini cards and stickers. He had international stock from Germany, Portugal and Italy; from France and Spain, and even from Greece. So, no matter how rare someone tells you their rookie of Cristiano Ronaldo is, remember that somewhere there may be a garage full of them, and similar material made since 1990. One day it may flood the market and crash the values of cards and stickers made since the 1990s. So, contemporary material ought to be treated as low-cost collectibles which may never yield returns on original purchase prices. For serious investments you have to look at vintage and antique cards. It's hard to go wrong with Victorian and Edwardian ephemera.

The Soccer Cards Price Rarity Scale, at the end of this book, is included to make evaluating

Barratt sweet cigarettes card, 1928

Barratt sweet cigarettes card, 1926

Baines cards, circa 1900

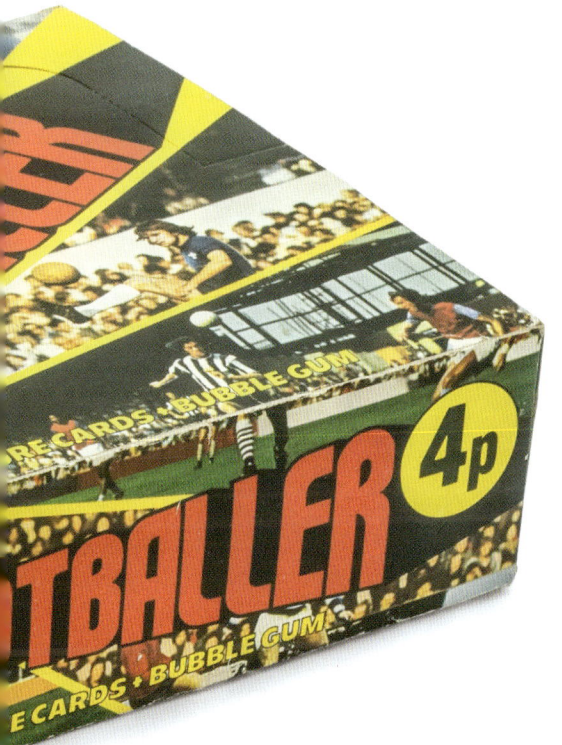

the Oliveira & Benassi *Balas Equipe* stickers of 1958, and so on. As well as listing thousands of manufacturers, their cards and certain stars, with rarity weight for rookies and Hall of Fame stars, *The Soccer Cards Rarity Scale* includes many types of foreign-made football card, along with just about all British-made association football cards and stickers from the 1880s until 1980.

One question remains. How many rare, unknown cards are still to be rediscovered? It seems every year is celebrated with at least one unearthed card treasure, long-since lost, not known about by collectors and unlisted on contemporary records. It's not surprising that cards keep appearing. It would only be surprising if they stopped appearing. Before the 1980s cards were issued primarily as playthings. No one really cared whether they were collected and few adults bothered with them. After being in favour for a while, for games or for swapping, cards were discarded, lost and destroyed.

Until the 1970s, cards were being issued by all and sundry. A legion of manufacturers could make their own football cards and reissue them season after season. Alas, that would be illegal, today. Such cards, the ones which were put away and saved, are the very cards which are now selling for big money. Today, licences and multinationals have curtailed such issues. Nowadays a couple of trans-national giant corporations benefit from a controlling the issue of sports cards worldwide, to suit themselves. There are few surprises with new cards.

Recently discovered cards, seen and recorded for the first since the 1930s, are the colourful transfers from the 1932/33 football season known as red-star decals. They first came to light a few years ago when a pad of 11 sheets was discovered in boxes of old junk in a derelict shop. Most of the 11 sheets were separated into single stamps and sold to collectors. Only a handful of intact sheets remain. One complete sheet sold for £1,000, in 2018. Just two years later another

British cigarette card of Walter Tull, 1912

British cigarette card from 1912 by Brigham

rarity easy. It's the first of its kind. In the past there were tobacco card price guides that blandly listed sundry subjects on tobacco cards, from school ties to flowers; from butterflies to famous actresses of the stage in times gone by. Those books did not service sports cards at all well. *The Soccer Cards Rarity Scale* includes cards not mentioned in the first book, like the Idamar stickers of 1963, the Holandeza issues of 1966, the Quelcom cards of 1979 and the Broadbent cards of the 1880s; through to Webcosa's Dubble Bubble *Footballer Caricatures*, of 1960; the German-issue Bremer Kaffee cards of Pelé and Yashin; the Fleece Hotel fixture cards of 1888;

AN A TO Z OF **SPORTING COLLECTIBLES** 187

Rookie card of Pelé by Bremer, 1958

Rookie card of Yashin by Bremer, 1958

Philmar decal transfers uncut sheet, 1946

Holy Head *Football Rock* card, 1920s

Rookie card of Pelé versus Jack Kelsey of Wales, 1958

complete sheet sold for £7,000, and a single Stanley Matthews made four figures! Rare cards are certainly up. For more information on these issues see page 230 in *An A-Z of Football Collectibles: Priceless Cigarette Cards and Sought-After Soccer Stickers*.

There was another, noteworthy rediscovery, in recent years, of a brand called Holy Heads. The Holy Heads *Football Rock* soccer club colours cards, which probably date to the 1920s, was *the* find of 2017. No one had recorded the Holy Heads cards beforehand. That's almost 100 years in which the cards had languished, all but forgotten about, lost from the record. So, it's quite a regular thing, the rediscovery of long-lost cards.

The images chosen for this section include some very rare tobacco cards not included in the previous book. You'll find their values in *The Soccer Cards Rarity Scale* at the back of this book. You'll find more rare cards at www.footballsoccercards.com

SWIMMING: AN INTRODUCTION TO AQUATICS ON TRADE CARDS

in pan-sport cards during the 1960s and 1970s. Mira's 1960s collection, *Tuttosport Campionissimi*, includes cards of swimmers; and Edis's *Olimpiadi 76* includes a sticker of David Wilkie, the British medallist.

Before Edis and Mira there was Nannina, in the 1940s, whose *Tecni-Color* [sic] cards were issued in folders, to be cut, swapped and collected. Many swimmers were included in its 1947 series of cards, including the American star Esther Williams. Uncut sheets or booklets are worth small fortunes; while cut, single cards fetch around £10 each.

Panini pooled swimmers and issued them in various all-sports collections called *Campioni dello Sport*, most years between 1966 and 1973. Well-known swimmers are to be found each of the collections. The cards bore different graphic designs and colours from one year to the next, so different editions are easy to distinguish from one another. The 1966 cards have a white border and show just a name and a number to the front but later series added colourful frames, in green, then in yellow, then blue, and so on. Along with a cohort of Italians there are internationals, like Mike Wenden, the Australian medallist; and world-record holder Mark Spitz, and gold-medal winner Catie Ball, both from USA.

In 1974 Panini rebranded its pan-sport collections, calling the new edition *Sport Vedettes*. It's in this series where collectors will find another Panini sticker of David Wilkie, the International Swimming Hall-of-Fame Scot. It would be two years until Wilkie won gold and silver medals in Montreal, in 1976, so his inclusion here makes for quite a rookie!

The illustrations chosen for this section of the book have been selected to show rarely seen cards. Other, better known and more easily available cards may be seen elsewhere, including below the swimming tab at www.footballsoccercards.com

West German-made card by Bergmann, 1972

German tobacco card, 1936

Water polo on a French trade card, 1930s

German tobacco card, 1920s

Tarzan & gold medallist swimmer Johnny Weismuller, 1930s

German trade card, 1930s

French trade card, 1930s

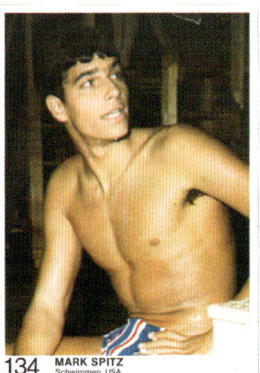
Mark Spitz the gold medallist on a West German card, 1972

Treizième Année.— N° 504. N° 163.   Le Numéro : 50 Centimes.   Jeudi 16 Août 1923.
NOUVELLE SÉRIE.   ÉTRANGER : 65 Cent.

LE MIROIR DES SPORTS

ABONNEMENTS
France et Colonies
1 An . . . 25 fr.
6 Mois. 13 fr.

ABONNEMENTS
Étranger
1 An . . . 43 fr
6 Mois. 22 fr

PUBLICATION HEBDOMADAIRE ILLUSTRÉE, 18, RUE D'ENGHIEN, PARIS

L'ITALIEN TIRABOSCHI TRAVERSE LA MANCHE A LA NAGE, BATTANT TOUS LES RECORDS

Enrico Tiraboschi, Italien résidant en Argentine, a réussi à franchir le détroit du Pas de Calais en 16 h. 23'. Parti du cap Gris-Nez samedi à 20 h. 10, il atteignit la plage de Douvres dimanche à 12 h. 33. Tiraboschi, qui a déjà fait des tentatives infructueuses en 1921 et 1922, est le quatrième qui ait réussi le difficile exploit de joindre les deux pays à la nage. Mais son temps est inférieur de cinq heures à celui de Webb, jusqu'alors recordman de la traversée. Tiraboschi est un athlète d'une résistance extraordinaire, qui nage sans lunettes et ne cesse jamais de sourire. Sa persévérance et sa confiance ont été récompensées.

French decal transfers, 1910s

French trade card, 1900s

French trade card, 1900s

Tennis: an introduction to tennis on trade cards

It was all about Borg & Connors, back then, in the age when this writer first acquired a tennis trade card, yet neither of those stars graced it. Later preferences would have had the precocious prodigy, John McEnroe, but no names from the men's game feature on the card.

It was a woman. In fact there were two cards, featuring the same woman. One card was made by Topps, in 1977; and the other was by Monty Gum, from 1979. The subject of the cards was better known as *The Million Dollar Man's* wife, rather than as a tennis player, yet the cards had her on a tennis court, and that was doubly attractive. Tennis was a personal favourite, among sports, in junior years.

Farrah Fawcett-Majors, née Fawcett, was the American wife of Lee Majors, the actor who played The Bionic Man, in *The Million Dollar Man*. Farrah was an actress in her own right. In 1977, she became known around the world for her role as Jill, in *Charlie's Angels*. Both trade cards featuring Jill playing tennis were from collections based on the TV show. Alas, they were swapped long ago for things of lesser value, like a collection of keyrings with miniature armaments (trendy toys, back then) and a set of pencil-top rubbers of *fruit-men figurines*.

It seemed a good deal at the time, gaining a lot of toys for a couple of cards. There is a lesson in that: don't trade qualitative merchandise for quantitative merchandise. The long-since lost collection of Hong Kong-made keyfobs, and a bunch of worn-down, long ago disposed of pencil erasers, is scant consolation for having let go of stereoscopic images of Farah pulling off a double forehand slam! Had the cards not been exchanged for trendy-at-the-time trash, they'd probably still be here. These days they are quite costly, especially the Monty Gum card.

Values for rare tennis cards of quality usually go one way: up! This is certainly the case with a Spanish card of Chris Evert, from 1974; and an Italian card of Billie Jean Moffitt, better known as Billie Jean King, from 1970. The former has been seen to sell for over £100 and the latter is seen for similar asking prices. Like most cards everyone seems to want, nowadays, the Farah Fawcett, Chris Evert and Billie Jean King cards were quite easy to acquire, in their day. Likewise, the Martina Navratilova sticker, by Americana München, which no one wanted in the 1970s, is now worth a small fortune, as are early cards featuring the rookie Nastase, a young Borg, the junior champion Henri Leconte. Tennis cards have long been collected but, until now, there was only one publication on the subject. Little more than a pamphlet consisting of long lists, the publication is called *Forty Love – Lawn Tennis Cigarette and Trade Cards, a Composite Listing*, by Derek Hurst. It includes none of the cards mentioned above, and it is scant in detail when it comes to non-tobacco trade cards; being comprehensive only in its coverage of British cigarette ephemera. However, it was a pioneering booklet and, nowadays, it's rare and fetches inordinate prices when and if it comes up for sale.

Since the middle of the 1990s the internet has disseminated images of rare tennis cards, though arguably less honestly in 2021 than in 2001. Two decades ago search results were sifted fairly, and openly shared by two dozen, or more, independent search engines, like Webcrawler and Altavista. Nowadays, bigger names have taken over and the results you see, when you ask for something, are skewed in someone else's favour. In 2001

Rookie card of Chris Evert Lloyd from Spain, 1974

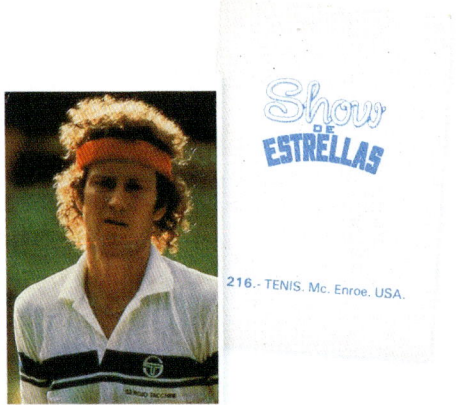
John McEnroe on a Spanish card by Maga, 1981

Billie Jean King on a Panini card, 1970

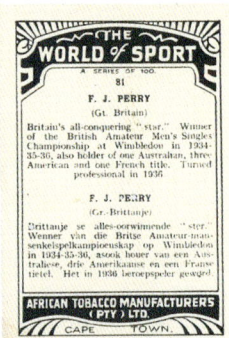
Fred Perry on a South African tobacco card, 1939

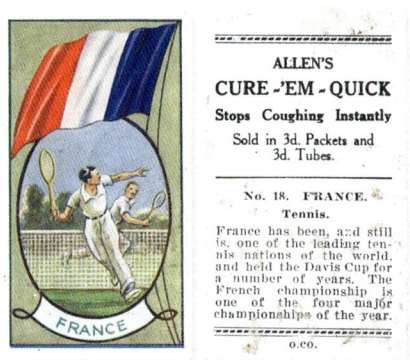
Australian pharmacy card by Allen's, 1936

Rookie Bjorn Borg by Panini, 1974

results of searches were neither manipulated in favour of corporate media, nor to the benefit of multinational interests, but they are in 2021. Since 2015 it has become harder to find antique and vintage images online. Such pictures are now harvested by digital photo libraries, as their own. However, buying the real thing, and acquiring very rare tennis cards, has become easier than ever, thanks largely to a batch of online auctions from around the globe. That said, there are more collectors now than there were previously, so rare tennis cards are more sought after and prices are upwards.

During 1954 the United Kingdom's first sports cards by A&BC showed up in shops. The collection was called *All Sports*. Its packaging was colourful yet the promising green-and-red wrappers contained but a single card. Dispensed by vending machines across the British Isles the waxy packets popped out of wall-mounted coin machines with a ball of chewing gum. A tiny window allowed a glimpse into the working apparatus, inside. It showed the cards stacked, ready for collecting. A second window revealed a mountain of gum balls, ready to chew. A sample card was displayed in a third aperture. There were various slots for coins, a handle, a gumball dispensing tray, and a locked drawer which opened all too rarely, to present wrapped, mint cards. Just one card was given, per halfpenny; one card from a series of 120 picture cards.

The A&BC Gum *All Sports* cards sported rather dull monotone photos, and the plain backs of the cards were a missed opportunity for potted biographies but it didn't seem to matter much. The cards became instant favourites with a new generation of collectors. These days, most of the *All Sports* cards are available for less than £5 but you will probably have to pay plenty for the collection's most sought-after stars. The four tennis cards included in the series do not feature all-time greats, so, unused cards of Tony Mottram, Greg Paish, Gordon Bailey and Bobby Riggs may still be found for less than £5 each. Many *All Sports* cards were glued into albums, or into scrapbooks. While a full set of cards glued down may be a pretty sight it is not worth half as much as a set of unused cards.

Abdulla's 1930s series, *Nationale & Internationale Sport-Recorde* [sic] includes a host of tennis stars. Card #195 shows the American tennis ace, William Tilden. The tennis cards from this edition will cost you far less than the baseball and golf cards of the same series, some of which exceed £1,000 each! That said, you'll still pay hundreds for Tilden. This is one of the most sought-after collections on the market.

Ace was a marque owned, indirectly, by British & American Tobacco (BAT). In 1977, Wiggins Teape (a firm owned by BAT) invited Ilie Nastase to sponsor a new game, called *Tennis Sporting Aces*. It was one of a number of Ace-branded sports card games which were the forerunners of Top Trumps, a cards craze that swept that nation in 1978. Card games of this genre are mostly based upon the pre-war game, Happy Families, which is known as Quartets in Continental European countries. *Tennis Sporting Aces* consists of 32 all-time great players, plus two cover cards. Values are around £2 for single cards, but the often elusive cards of great players may sell for much more. A boxed set of Ace

TENNIS: AN INTRODUCTION TO TENNIS ON TRADE CARDS

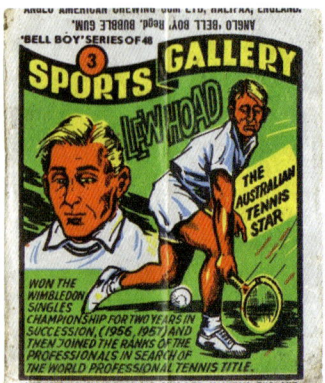

Lew Hoad on a Bell Boy gum insert, 1957

Bell Boy gum insert proof of Suzanne Lenglen, 1959

Sporting Aces, in near mint condition, may cost you £50.

In 1939, African Tobacco, of South Africa, issued a series of mixed-sports cards called *The World of Sport*. The cards are known in English and Dutch, and they were printed in two formats, the larger of which measure about 8x6cm. Suzanne Lenglen, Bill Tilden and Helen Jacobs feature among the various tennis players. Values for other tennis stars of the time start at £10 each card. Costs rise towards £100 for the aforenamed legends of the game, and for top condition Fred Perry cards.

Allen's of Australia issued a single tennis card in the *Sports & Flags of Nations* series. It is perhaps Allen's prettiest series of cards. The firm made many collections, mostly of cricketers and Australian-rules footballers. The firm's cards were given with medicinal formulas, like Irish Moss Gum Lube tablets, Steam Rollers soothing balms, and other snake-oil remedies, like Cure 'em Quick tinctures. No doubt the pretty cards did just as much to cure ailments as did the hoodoo-inspired potions they came with. Whatever, the most sought-after cards from this series tend to include the baseball card, which comes on a card representing USA; and the tennis card, which the issuer associated with France. You may have to pay over £20 to get the latter.

All Sports Illustrated Weekly was a journal which was published after World War One. It ran until about 1930. It would often issue free-gift souvenirs, typically in the format of paper supplements, a little like miniature posters. These days, the supplements are much rarer than the magazines. Tennis players were included in the series and they sell for between £50 and £100 each.

All Sports is also credited with a series of 12 large, coloured cards of sportsmen, which was issued around 1930. It includes the British tennis players Bunny Austin and Dorothy Round. Prices for these cards have exceeded £50 each.

Allen & Ginter included a foursome of tennis players in its 1889 collection of cards, *The World's Champions Second Series*. Each card may be found in two sizes. Expect to pay over £100 each, even for cards in grubby condition – if you can find them!

The American Tobacco Company, in USA, issued a series of *Chinese Girls* in 1900. One of them featured an oriental woman with a tennis racquet. Expect to pay three figures for her. Another tennis subject was issued on card #4 in the firm's 1913 *Bathing, Athletic & Dancing Girls* series. It's equally rare.

Americana München was created in the 1960s, in West Germany. It issued well over 100 series of stickers between 1964 and 1980. To this day its various collections of unbranded issues confound collectors, notably the *Soccer Parade* and the *WIP Parade* (the German acronym WIP translates to VIP, in English). The *Sport Parade* edition, from 1976, now sells for around £10 each sticker, if they remain unused, with their backing papers. However, two of the most sought-after stickers from the collection, those featuring the boxer Muhammad Ali and the young tennis star Martina Navratilova, will fetch ten times this price, for excellent condition examples.

Anglo-American Chewing Gum made Bell Boy gum, with which *Sports Gallery*, a series of 48 images printed on waxy paper, was issued in 1958. The gum inserts, for that's what they are known as, include Donald Budge, Lew Hoad,

British cigarette cards, 1935

British cigarette card, 1936

French trade card, 1920s

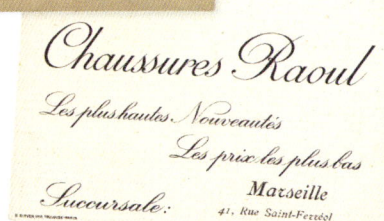

198 AN A TO Z OF **SPORTING COLLECTIBLES**

 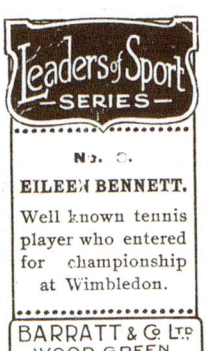

Barratt sweets cards, 1927

Maureen Connelly, Jack Kramer, Jaroslav Drobny, Althea Gibson, Suzanne Lenglen, etc. Values for gum inserts depend on the condition. It should be remembered that Bell Boy gum inserts were issued already folded and somewhat creased. Opening the packets, children often damaged the delicate paper which the inserts are made of. It's almost impossible to find top quality examples without some kind of damage. Prices start at around £25 each, rising to as much as £100 for the most sought-after stars.

The follow-up Bell Boy series was *Sports Parade*, which was issued sometime by 1960. It includes a further selection of tennis greats, including Suzanne Lenglen and Bill Tilden. Values for these inserts also start at around £25 each. Like the earlier series, almost all known examples are creased and damaged. However, some inserts from this series are known to be free of creases! They are called *proofs*. Prices for the proofs rise to over £200. They come with an attached wrapper, which is also free of creases. There is a fold but it runs through the paper between the wrapper and the insert, crossing neither part. Staple holes in the folded margin also date from the moment of issue. They were distributed in card folders – hence the staple holes and the single neat fold. They were given as redemption prizes but very few were issued and fewer still have turned up on the market since 1960. Examples of some of the proofs may be seen at www.footballsoccercards.com

A Pictorial History of the Sports and Pastimes of all Nations is the title of a series of colourful trade cards by Arbuckle, an American blend of instant coffee. Arbuckle's sports cards were given with coffee powder as far back as 1893. Arbuckle's images were also employed by European-based issuers, such as Thomas Holloway. It's not clear which brand issued the cards first. They feature a country and a handful of scenes stereotypically associated with it. The tennis image appears on the card devoted to France, just as a golf image appears on a card dedicated to Scotland, and so on. The rarest variations of these cards are probably those made by smaller producers in France (Chapu, Lorenz, Tapioca de l'Etoile, etc.) but the Arbuckle brand is the best known.

Ardath, a British tobacco merchant of the interwar years, published *Cricket, Tennis & Golf Celebrities*, in 1935. The series includes a dozen tennis players. Today, a cautious and patient buyer may find the cards for as little as £1 each. Even the most popular cards, like that of Helen Wills-Moody, are quite affordable if you wait. Likewise, with the firm's follow-up edition, *Sports*

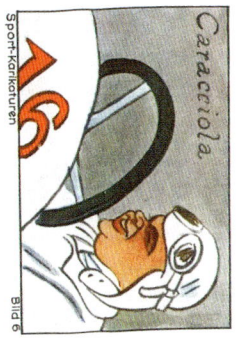   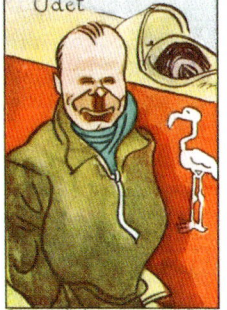 

Uncut sheet of sports caricatures by Haus Bergmann, Germany, 1930s

AN A TO Z OF **SPORTING COLLECTIBLES** 199

TENNIS: AN INTRODUCTION TO TENNIS ON TRADE CARDS

consists of many hundreds of cards, some of which show tennis players. These are some of the most sought-after tennis cards known. Suzanne Lenglen and Bill Tilden are found on card numbers #304 and #305, respectively. Values for Bunsen cards start at around £100 each but cards with very well-known names have been seen to top £1,000 each!

Cadet Sweets published a collection of transfers, or water-slide decals, called *All-Sports*. Issued soon after the summer Olympics, of 1956, the 48 sports stars included in the series are far rarer than the firm's later decals, such as the footballers of 1958. Prices paid for the tennis stars are over £50, but Althea Gibson and Lew Hoad have topped £100 each. Compared to the money paid for other items from this collection, such as golfer Ben Hogan, which has sold for over £500, Althea and Lew are relative bargains.

Carreras tobacco issued a *Personality Series* of cards with its Turf Cigarettes, in 1933. There are four tennis cards to be found in the series of 96 caricatures. Values are low. Most cards can be found easily, and for very little.

Carreras revolutionised the design of its cards, in 1935. An oval-shaped series of cards, called *Popular Personalities*, includes a selection of sporting stars one of whom shows Fred Perry. Prices remain very affordable for these little gems, and most cards from the set can be had for just £1.

After World War Two ended Carreras was one of the few tobacco merchants which continued to issue cigarette cards. However, post-war cards were different to pre-war cards. After 1946, many cigarette cards were printed as part of the cigarette box packaging. They were designed to be cut out. Cards like this are known as packet-issue cards. In the case of Carreras, the design was printed on the cigarette box slider, inside the hull of the packet, so that the buyer did not know which sports star he or she would find. Carreras understood the profit in making buyers buy the same thing twice, thrice or many more times over.

Carreras's 1949 *Sports Series* includes four tennis players. They are easily found and values are around £1 each. Prices are much higher for uncut sliders, being over £10 each in the case of the tennis cards – and even higher for other sports stars of note.

Cavanders cigarettes included a tennis court scene in its *Homeland Series*, of 1924. Such cards are known in a number of variations: monotone or colour; with different coloured backs; in different sizes, and so on. Most of the variations are available for very little, at around £1 each. Grouped together they make an attractive collection.

In 1934, *Champion* comic gave away strips of cards to cut and collect, called *Sportsmen of the World*. There are 32 sports cards, in all. An uncut strip of cards is worth over £50, whereas individual cut cards sell for around £2 each. An album was given in which to glue the cards. Complete albums are pretty but they are not as rare as uncut strips of cards. There are two tennis stars in the collection, one of whom is Fred Perry.

Churchman issued a series called *Lawn Tennis*, in 1928, a dozen of which, featuring the greats of the game, were reissued in a larger format, numbered from 1 to 12. The larger cards, which include Helen Wills-Moody, Bill Tilden, René Lacoste, etc., are rarer and more valuable than the smaller edition. Some sellers put the stars into plastic slabs and ask ten times the price but you can get the card for very little if you'll fore go the plastic – and who would not prefer less plastic, these days? Values for the smaller set, of 50 cards, range from £1 for lesser-known players to £5 each for the greats. Values for the larger cards may exceed £50 each. Churchman did a similar thing with an edition called *Men of the Moment in Sport*, also issued in 1928. The stars featured in the larger format (two of the nine

Rene Lacoste on a Swedish trade card, 1920s

US tennis player Ellsworth Vines on a French trade card, 1930s

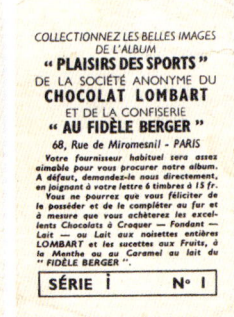

French trade card, 1930s

French trade card, 1910s

Decal transfers of Ashley Cooper & Althea Gibson, Cadet Sweets, 1956

British cigarette card, 1927

French trade card, 1920s

tennis players from the regular series) are worth much more than the smaller-size edition.

Sporting Celebrities, of 1931, includes eight tennis players among a series of 50 sports caricatures. The cards are more easily available than you would imagine. So, if you're watching internet auctions of perpetually unsold plastic-sealed cards, at starting prices over £50, you'll know why they don't sell. In reality these cards can be yours for around £5 each, singly, or an entire set for £100. Why buy a slabbed, single card for £50 when you can have all 50 cards for £100? If you only want a single card, sell the others on. You may even make money on the resale.

Churchman's Olympic Cigarettes came with *The World of Sport*, a rather late series of packet issues, in 1961. There are eight tennis cards to seek from this series of cut outs. Values are typically low, around £2 each, when the cards appear for sale but they rarely come to market. The cards are worth more if they remain uncut. Note: only packets of 10 came with tennis cards. There were none printed on packs of 20 cigarettes.

Clevedon Confectionery published cards called *International Sporting Stars*, in 1958, of which nine are tennis stars. The cards are worth around £5 each.

The *Sporting Memories* series, issued by Clevedon in 1962, includes a duo of famous tennis names: Jaroslav Drobny and Maureen Connelly. They are the rarest tennis cards issued by the firm, and may cost more than £25 each.

In 1925 Cope Brothers reissued a black-&-white series which had formerly been distributed with Couden's cigarettes. The earlier *Sports Alphabet cards*, from 1924, were given colour and a new edition title. As *Sports & Pastimes* the coloured Cope Brothers cards complement the monotone edition by Couden's. Examples of both types of card may be seen throughout this book. The earlier cards are a little duller but they are rarer and more valuable. Whereas the Cope cards may be found for less than £10 each, a Couden's card may sell for £50, depending on the subject illustrated. There is a tennis card in each of the collections.

Cope Brothers issued an edition called *Lawn Tennis Strokes*, between 1924 and 1925. Stars like Lenglen and Borotra will cost more than the other cards in the series but prices asked for certain cards, notably those put inside plastic slabs, are often quite ridiculous. Pay no more than £5 for regular cards and look to pay no more than £20 for the afore-mentioned big names.

Crescent Confectionery had produced sports trade cards from 1923 to 1925. By 1926, a different legal entity, called Crescent Confectionery (1926) Limited, had been founded by different owners. In 1927, the newly registered company launched a general interest series of trade cards, which included sports stars, but it was not until 1930 that tennis cards were issued. The pan-sports series which was released in that year is known as

Stanley Matthews's son on a British trade card, 1960

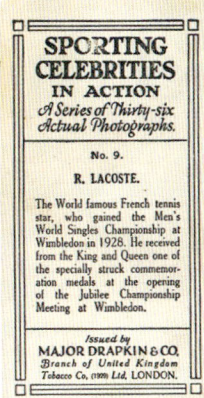

René Lacoste on a British cigarette card, 1930

AN A TO Z OF **SPORTING COLLECTIBLES** 205

Stadium

Articulo de Sport

Pida esta m

Anuncios PUBLICITAS

Merrysweets also issued a series of decals, issued in triples, which were called *Transpics*. They make far more sense than the trans-Plutonian structure of *Tracepiks*. The decals are enjoying a renaissance, nowadays. If you find uncut trios of decals expect to pay £50 for the ones with sports scenes. As for the scattered-disc designs of *Tracepiks*, they'll probably cost over £20 if they remain unused. Most surviving dot-to-dot cards have ink-pen lines. Defaced they are worth very little indeed.

Millhoff tobacco included a series called *In The Public Eye* with its De Reszke brand of cigarettes, in 1930. The one tennis star in the series is Betty Nuthall. She won't cost you much. This series of Millhoff cards is a good opportunity to see the wide range of prices being asked on internet auctions. It's not uncommon to see one example of a card at £50 and another, the very same card, at only £2. Don't pay more than £2 for Betty. There's plenty of her about. A million were made!

Mister Softee would cause rashes of inverted goose pimples at the sound of its cheap melodies. The nasty *plink plonk* off-key overtures which crackled from tin-pot loud speakers on the firm's ice cream trucks alerted children to the imminent arrival of cheaply made choc-ices and artificially coloured ice lollies. Mister Softee sold stodgy, low quality ices but kids loved them. Plastic-leaching toxins in creamy colloidal emulsion posing as real ice cream was sold by the bucket load, as the non-stop engine belched out fumes. The diesel-fumigated kerbsides of 1974 would see a queue of customers inhaling the filthy emissions while they waited to be served from the van. The street vendors of the time often gave out sports cards. Mister Softee's cards also featured pop stars. An edition of 20 *Famous Sports Trophies*, issued in 1974, includes a pair of tennis cards – The Queen's Cup and The Davis Cup. The attractive die-cut cards are shaped after the trophies. The cards are very scarce. A similar edition was issued by a competitor named Tonibel, which includes the same trophies on cards of a different cut. Cards from both collections usually cost around £20 each.

Mitchell cigarettes were sold with an edition called *A Series of 25 Sports*, in 1907. If condition is not everything then a canny buyer may find a card from this series for as little as £5. However, in top condition dealers tend to ask £20. It's a very attractive series of colour illustrations, though the tennis card looks more like a holiday camp attendant swatting at a fly than a tennis player serving a ball. Oddly, the ball seems to be levitating before the character's glazed-over gaze. The artist's exposure to tennis seems to have been rather limited.

Monopol, of Germany, produced tobacco cards during the Weimar years. In the last year before Hitler came to power, 1932, the firm issued *Sportphoto, serie A und B*, which consisted of over 1,000 different sporting cigarette cards. The collection contains over 20 tennis cards, including big-name players. Values are around £5 for unused cards, though stars such as Helen Wills-Moody will sell for closer to £50, if they are in top form.

As with Monopol, Muratti was a German firm. In 1936 it issued over 700 sports cards in *Brennpunkte des Deutschen Sports*. The cards of famous sports stars are typically worth a lot of money. Tennis cards with Crawford and Vines are worth around £20.

Nabisco is a name to torment people for whom school was purgatory. The bland, dry breakfasts forced down before leaving the house to trudge to the pit of despair, otherwise known as secondary school (high school), stifled creativity and invoked demons

> **Mister Softee would cause rashes of inverted goose pimples at the sound of its cheap melodies. The nasty *plink plonk* off-key overtures on the firm's ice cream trucks alerted children to the imminent arrival of cheaply made choc-ices and artificially coloured ice lollies.**

TENNIS: AN INTRODUCTION TO TENNIS ON TRADE CARDS

René Lacoste on a French trade card, 1920s

French trade card, 1910s

of depression. Nabisco was ingested to the sound of radio stations blurting out downbeat news and plastic pop. Mornings were TV-free in the 1970s (there simply was no daytime TV in Great Britain, let alone an internet, back then) and the sleepy gaze had little to look at other than Nabisco breakfast cereal boxes, and what was inside them. Aside from the dry stuff there was often a sports card, or another novelty, such as a free give-away toy. Though most Nabisco trade cards of the era relate to football, in 1980 tennis was included in a series of *Kevin Keegan Quiz Cards*. There were half a dozen cards, each of which consists of nine smaller cards, to tear apart. On one of the composite cards the smaller cards show tennis stars, including Virginia Wade, Bjorn Borg and Martina Navratilova. They don't cost a lot but finding them complete, and not torn to smaller cards, is the key.

A later series, from 1981, called *Kevin Keegan's Keep Fit With The Stars*, includes two cards of Sue Barker. The *road pizza*-coloured splatter patterns on the cards may upset more than just design expectations. A lad in school was sick after looking at the cards for too long. The unfortunate event led to the teacher banning trade cards in class for the rest of the term. Thanks Nabisco! The overly excited nature of the colouring on these cards is not as wild as the earlier football series but it does seem like a madman with too many felt-tip pens exorcised some demented kind of possession. Don't pay more than £1 per card. There are plenty of them out there.

North British Rubber trade cards are, perhaps, best known for the golfing subjects but the firm also included tennis, with a large-size card of Dan Maskell, in the 1952 *Sporting Personalities* collection. It's rare and like other cards by this firm you may have to pay over £30 for it.

Ogden's was a huge producer of tobacco and a prolific manufacturer of cards but tennis did not featured highly for the firm. Though it had started promisingly, in 1900, with Guinea Gold cigarettes, which included half a dozen tennis players in a collection of over 1,000 different cards, there was little afterwards. Aside from the 1902 *Series F General Interest* series, which features a few tennis players, there was little for over two decades, until the firm's *ABC of Sport* cards, in 1927. Though only one of these cards celebrates tennis it's a beauty, and well worth having. Its value is around £10.

Ogden inserted a pair of tennis stars cards into its *Champions of 1936*. The same cards were also issued by Hignett's tobacco, which will give you different backs – for a price! *Champions of*

Ice cream cards, 1974

Helen Wills-Moody on a French trade card, 1920s

French trade card, 1910s

Australian and US champions on a German tobacco card, 1930s

Jean Borotra on a French trade card, 1920s

Italian trade card, 1930s

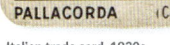

Various Italian trade cards by Nannina and VAV, 1947 to 1950

1936 may be found for about £1 each, though you'll see many greedy sellers asking more.

Panini, the Italian-based stickers giant, included tennis stars in its various, almost yearly *Campioni dello Sport* collections, of which there were six different editions between 1966 and 1973. Though the tennis stars are mostly Italians, there are notable exceptions, such as an early card of Billie Jean King, née Moffitt.

It was with *Sport Vedettes*, in 1974, that Panini captured the attention of international collectors of pan-sports cards. The publication was not only pan-sport in nature it was pan-European in its distribution. Amongst 17 tennis subjects are greats such as Borg, Nastase, Chris Evert and Billie Jean King. It's become quite a challenge to find unused stickers of these stars, not to mention pricey, at over £50 each subject for unused stickers with backing papers. A lot of Italian sellers offer these cards and stickers after being removed from albums. In that case they'll cost a mere £1 each. Look out for the word *recuperata*, which means it's been removed with acetone, or similar spirits. You won't get a new sticker, but you will get a cheap space-filler, until you are lucky enough to find the unadulterated article.

Panini included 25 tennis players in the *Sports Superstars Eurofootball 82* collection.

You'll find stickers of McEnroe, Martina Navratilova, Borg, Chris Evert, Connors, etc. They are quite easily available, in unused condition, for about £1 each.

Many tennis collectors will be familiar with Panini's tennis stickers from the 1987 *Supersport* series, and those from the following year's collection of the same name. Conversely, many collectors will not know that, in Spain, in 1988, Panini issued a totally different range of stickers for the Iberian edition of *Supersport*. The Spanish stickers are more elegant than the overly designed more usual fare, which was sold elsewhere. With the exception of the metallic pairs of stickers from the regular, pan-European editions (John McEnroe was paired with Chris Evert Lloyd, etc.), the sunny Spanish stickers are arguably more attractive than the garish stickers issued north of the Pyrenees. They come up for sale now and again and may be found for around £10 each, if unused. That's considerably more than the non-Iberian types but the Spanish variants are so much rarer.

Pattreiouex tobacco's *Celebrities in Sport*, of 1930; *Sporting Celebrities*, of 1934; and *Sporting Events & Stars*, of 1935, all feature tennis stars. The three collections are not hard to find, though prices asked by card slabbers are extraordinarily high. The secret is to buy sets, as and when they come up for sale by cards specialists & auction houses in the UK, not costly slabs from card flippers on the internet. With some patience most cards can be had inexpensively.

A fourth Pattreiouex collection to include tennis cards is the *Sports Trophies* series, of 1931, in which five tennis cups are to be found. If condition does not have to be of exceptional quality the cards may be bought for less than £5 each. They'll add glamour and glitter to any collection.

Phillips tobacco produced some of the earliest cigarette cards. Godfrey Phillips & Sons issued sports cards as long ago as the 1890s, though tennis only came to the fore in 1910, with the firm's *Sporting Series of Humourous Sketches*. The solitary tennis card in that series will probably cost you £20, though Phillips included the very same image on an updated card, in a reissued edition, in 1923. The cards look the same to the fronts but have different backs: the earlier ones have little detail, whereas the later issues have potted histories of each sport. The 1923 cards often seem as hard to find as the 1910 originals, so you may have to pay just as much for them.

Phillips issued *Sporting Champions*, in 1929. The edition includes seven tennis stars. The cards may seem pricey, at least with sales on

TENNIS: AN INTRODUCTION TO TENNIS ON TRADE CARDS

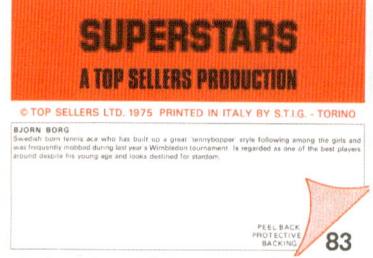

Panini-sponsored Top Sellers *Superstars* Bjorn Borg, 1975

John Newcombe & Arthur Ashe on Panini cards, 1969 and 1970

the internet, but patience usually rewards buyers with cards which cost as little as £5 each. There were certainly millions of them made. Sooner or later they'll appear in a British-based sports card auctioneer's sale and you'll get them for a bargain price.

Phillips dedicated a 25-card series to *Lawn Tennis*, in 1930. The cards demonstrate the correct strokes necessary for a good game. Lacking both stars and charm the set remains unpopular and may often be found for less than £25.

In 1932, the BDV brand, made by Phillips, came with sports stars printed on the box of cigarettes. The initials BDV stand for Boyd Dibrell Virginia. The various types of packet made by Phillips (cardboard as well as paper) and the fact this series was issued three times, with sports stars appearing over and over in different photos, with errors and variations makes it a fascinating series to collect. Cards that are cut tend to be worth less than uncut packets, or complete boxes. The general rule of thumb is this: the more card there is, the better; the wider the borders are, the higher the value climbs. However, the last of three series, issued in 1934, was short-lived and some of those cards are so rare that any kind of cut is valuable. There are 11 known tennis cards, two of which feature Helen Wills-Moody. One card shows her looking forwards, the other shows her glancing to the side. Both types will sell for £100 if they have, at the very least, a neat trim.

Phillips's *Who's Who in Australian Sport*, from 1933, includes a handful of tennis stars, each of whom is available in a variety of combinations. The cards were issued with pictures on both sides, so the same player may be backed by a racing greyhound, a jockey or a rower, and so on. The cards are not too costly and you can find all the variations of your favourite player, for about £5 each.

Phillips's *In The Public Eye* series, from 1935, includes five tennis players. Values for these cards are less than £5 each though many sellers try for much more money. The firm's 1937 series, *Spot The Winner*, is also easily available and there are three tennis players therein.

The final sports cards to include tennis, by Phillips, are some of the rarest of Phillips's post-war cards. Made in 1954, the *Sportsmen* cards comprise 25 packet issues, of which there are two tennis players: Tony Mottram and Geoff Paish. Cut-outs of these cards are worth up to £20 each but uncut card slides are worth £40 each. Entire boxes may sell for £75 each.

Player's cigarette cards are usually easy to find, for low prices. *Lawn Tennis*, a series of 50 cards, from 1928, is not in that bracket. Though the series is rather dull, consisting of monotone photos of players in action, it's popular and prices for many of the cards are higher than you would expect. The set includes all of the

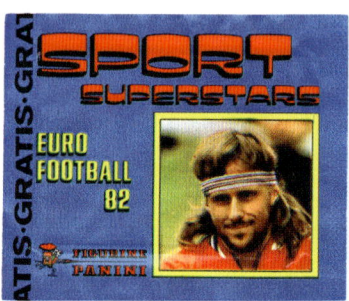

Unopened packet of Panini stickers, 1982

Tony Mottram & Geoff Paish, packet-issue tobacco cards, 1950s

Billie Jean King card and stickers from Spain and Italy, 1973 to 1974

Cards that are cut tend to be worth less than uncut packets, or complete boxes. The general rule of thumb is this: the more card there is, the better; the wider the borders are, the higher the value climbs.

Italian trade cards, 1930s

US Open winner Betty Nuthall, a packet-issue tobacco card, 1932

French trade card, 1930s

German trade card, 1900s

great stars from the time, like Helen Wills-Moody and Bill Tilden. The catalogues of old would have valued these cards at less than £5 each. It's fair to say – not for the first time – that the old price guides of last century undervalued many rare cards. This was so the publishers of such price guides could buy such cards cheaply. Then, they'd sell the same cards in auction, for much higher prices, to knowledgeable buyers. The original sellers were none the wiser. The practice was known as cards tumbling (card laundering does not sound right) but these days it's less subtle and the exponents are now known as flippers. Card flippers buy at £1, seal the card in a plastic slab, and try to re-sell it for £100 – because the card is now 'graded' (often by someone who knows less about the card than you do). What a flipping con! Player's *Tennis* cards, from 1936, are very easily available. The cards are not costly and a set of unused cards may cost you only £20. Albums with cards glued in are worth very little, indeed.

Quelcom, a Spanish firm, issued two sets of gum-cards. Both editions were released in 1979. They vary in size but not in their subjects. One edition is slightly smaller than the other. There are 31 international tennis stars in the edition, which consists of 256 cards. So, that's 62 tennis cards in all, for completists: two of every player. The cards are very colourful, and atypical for the genre of gum cards, not least because they are often with adhesion marks to the backs. The problem was caused by Quelcom issuing an album for its cards. Albums do not easily support 256 large, relatively heavy gum cards. Unwieldy albums have been broken apart, hence the amount of cards with gum residue. However, the cards are scarce. Tennis stars in top condition, with undamaged backs, sell for £10 to £100 each, bigger names hitting bigger prices.

Robinson's Barley Water was associated with Wimbledon tennis as long ago as the 1970s. The bottles of fruit drinks stood in the shade below the umpire's chair, their labels carefully turned to face the TV cameras. It was an early example of what now plagues sport: logos, advertising, product placement and big money. It's a wonder that Wimbledon has not yet been rebranded, as other sports events have been. Oddly, the tennis players of the 1970s would pour plain tap water into their plastic cups, instead of helping themselves to the fancy bottles of flavoursome liquid on show. Apocryphal tales told of unspoken rules: the players were not allowed to drink from them! Henri Leconte didn't give a damn. In the 1980s he broke the old rules, opened the holy of holies and quaffed a bottle of orange barley water, grinning to himself at his transgression. Robinson conspired to garner more business by offering a set of sports trade cards, in 1983. *Sporting Records* included three tennis cards. The entire series is easily available and you may acquire all 30 cards, and the plastic wallet in which they were collected, for as little as £10.

 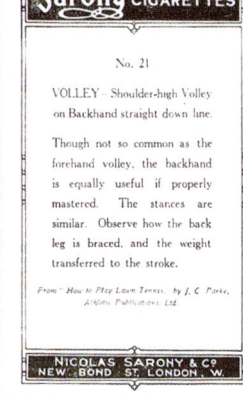

British cigarette card, 1923

AN A TO Z OF **SPORTING COLLECTIBLES** 215

TENNIS: AN INTRODUCTION TO TENNIS ON TRADE CARDS

French cheese card, 1930s

Jimmy Connors on a Japanese phonecard, 1990

Italian trade card, 1947

enamel badges and ephemera, such as trade cards. One of the most popular series of Spratt's trade cards was called the *Bonzo Series*. *Bonzo* was a cartoon dog. Two of the cards in the *Bonzo Series* show tennis accoutrements. They are not at all costly and may be found for as little as £5 each. Also made in the Spratt's buildings, in the 1990s, were the sports cards which went with Corinthian sporting figurines!

Sweetacres Champion Chewing Gum came with *Sports Champions* cards, around 1932. Among a host of legendary sports stars you'll find a handful of tennis players. The provenance of the cards is Australian. In 1932 the population of Australia was tiny, compared with today. Trade cards were not produced in great numbers. Most of the Sweetacres cards on the market are for cricket, though some, notably this series, feature tennis stars. Quality over quantity: the known cards feature mostly all-time greats, so you'll be facing some cost to acquire the handful of tennis stars in this edition. The collection includes Tilden, Wills-Moody, Vines and Crawford.

Top Sellers was a British publisher of erotica and horror, run by a firm called Thorpe & Porter Sales (the partnership's initials, T and P; and the S from Sales, had become the structural consonants in its trendier, trading name, Top Sellers). The firm had issued Panini cards in Great Britain, until 1977, being responsible for the import and distribution of the Italian firm's cards before the United Kingdom's membership of the EU trading block, which was known as the EEC in the 1970s. Best known for the Top Sellers football cards issued between 1972 and 1977 the firm imported and distributed Panini collections such as *Football Clubs*, in 1975, as well as the World Cup collections of 1970 and 1974.

In 1975, Top Sellers handled the British release of a large-format sticker collection called *Superstars*. The stickers were ostensibly printed by a firm called STIG, in Turin, but they are Panini-related issues. Most of the super-size *Superstars* stickers sell for about £5, nowadays, but some have exceeded £100. The collection includes two tennis players, Billie

Suzanne Lenglen and René Lacoste, Spanish chocolates cards, 1920s

Italian chocolates card, 1950

Jean King and Bjorn Borg. She's worth around £20 but the Borg sticker, being quite an early Borg relic has a much higher value.

Tiedemanns is a Norwegian brand. In the 1930s it issued the Cromwell marque of cigarettes. About a dozen tennis players are known to be included in the series. It is believed that each is available with either the Tiedermanns legend on the rear, or a Cromwell logo. Values start at around £25 for well-known, international players, and rise sharply. Less-well-known stars ought to cost little, just £5 each.

In 1974 Tonibel ice creams were sold with a collection of shaped, die-cut cards, called *Famous Sports Trophies*. The collection includes two tennis cards. It's similar to an edition issued by rival ice ream vendor, Mister Softee.

Tonibel also included tennis in a series of ten cards, from 1983, called *Junior Champs*. The card features the American champion, Chris Evert. It is scarce now but when it appears the price is usually low, at around £5.

Trebor Gold Medal Chewies, a type of British confectionery from 1969, came wrapped in packaging showing sports stars. One of the wrappers features the tennis champion, Maureen Connolly. It's very hard to find and may cost you £50.

Flik-Cards were issued by Venorlandus. Smaller than typical gum cards, *Flik-Cards* were considered very scarce, in the 1990s, but became much easier to acquire following the discovery of a trove of unsold stock, in a warehouse in Hackney, in London. The cards were first issued in 1978, being sponsored by a TV show called *World of Sport*. The edition includes a handful of tennis stars, for whom prices remain very low. A larger edition, a second series of super-size cards, is also known but there are no tennis players in it.

Weetabix included a picture card of Virginia Wade in its *World of Sport Quiz Pic* series, in 1981. The colourful series of cards also includes early examples of scratchcards. An unused card, with all silver boxes unscratched, would be worth £2.

Wills, a well-known firm based in Bristol, produced a beautiful series of sports cards in 1901. *Sports of All Nations* was issued with Capstan Navy Cut and also with the Westward-Ho brand of smokes. The 50 cards show sports and national flags. The set includes a card for *English Lawn Tennis*, which is shown alongside a pretty flag known as the Royal Standard of the United Kingdom. It's a beautiful card, a high-quality piece of ephemera. At around £10 it's a veritable bargain.

Sporting Girls, of 1917, is a very attractive series showing women and sports. The tennis card from this edition comes in two types. One variant has a plain back, while the other advertises Wills's Scissors cigarettes. The collector should expect to pay over £20 for each type.

Wills issued *Lawn Tennis* in 1931. The series of 25 cards includes many famous names of the day. It's still quite easily available as a complete set, for around £150, though single cards can be had for as little as £2 each! However, the bigger names in tennis will cost much more. The cards are some of the most attractive tennis cigarette cards known, being

Odd cards of tennis players would be included in general collections, such as *British Sporting Personalities* and *Homeland Events*, but, by the war, gone were editions devoted to the game.

TENNIS: AN INTRODUCTION TO TENNIS ON TRADE CARDS

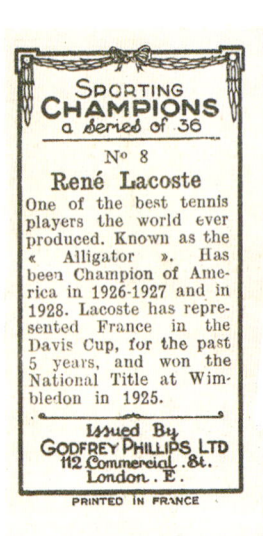

British cigarette cards, 1929 to 1931

Very stylish illustrations, echoing the lost epoch of *Brideshead Revisited* and golden era of *The Great Gatsby*.

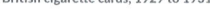

Sealed packet of tennis gaming cards, 1977

decorated with very stylish illustrations, echoing the lost epoch of *Brideshead Revisited* and golden era of *The Great Gatsby* (golden for the powerful few, that is). The cards are of a larger format than is usual for most tobacco cards.

After 1931, Wills issued little by way of tennis. Odd cards of tennis players would be included in general collections, such as *British Sporting Personalities* and *Homeland Events*, but, by the war, gone were editions devoted to the game. The general themes collections of the 1930s, which are made up of monotone photographs, are rather dull when contrasted with colourful, almost decadent, earlier editions such as *Lawn Tennis*. The later and duller cards cost very little, thankfully.

This brief introduction to tennis on trade cards, from Victorian times until the 1980s, serves out but one set in a five-set match. More tennis cards from France, Spain and Italy may be found on European-based auction websites. Further afield, the intrepid collector will be rewarded for his or her creativity in finding cards in Scandinavia. For Norwegian cards try Finn.no, and in using Tradera.com treasure troves in Sweden will come to light. Belgian and Dutch cards have their own eBay site, not to mention Catawiki auctions. Asian and South American auctions are also findable. For Latin America go to mercadolibre.com and for Asia try your luck with Trocadero.com, which includes many Asian sales in English. For many more rare tennis cards see under the tennis tab at: www.footballsoccercards.com

years, until 1973. In 1972, when the collection was not published, there were other collections to be bought, namely *Olympia* and *München 72*. All of the various series include plenty of winter sports cards, including such legends as Thorleif Haug, the Norsk cross-country skier. While celebrating glories of the distant past, recent triumphs like Sapporo's ice heroes from 1972 were included. *München 72* also looked forward, to the winter games in Denver, in 1976.

Though Panini had occasionally used paper in the 1960s, it was not until the 1970s that self-adhesive stickers became synonymous with the Italian firm. Before 1973, Panini used paper only for self-adhesive emblems.

During the first 12 years of Panini's reign, the Modena-based firm had preferred to use card, and most of its wares until 1972 were made of the more substantial material. They lasted better for it, too. Unused paper stickers from the 1970s are often far rarer than Panini's earlier cards!

In Italy, every so often a precocious challenger to Panini comes along. Guatteri dared take on the Modena giant in 1972, with *Tutto Sci Sport Invernali*. For winter sports *cognoscenti* the Guatteri collection is a must have, for the black-&-white chalkboard-style silhouettes on how to ski if for nothing else. The complete album will cost more than £200 but occasionally the colourful stickers of ski-bar frolics and glamorous stars come up for sale, inexpensively, on ebay.it

The winter sports stars of *Sports Vedettes*, from 1974, were among the last of the pan-sport *Campioni dello Sport* genre of stickers but Panini continued to issue ice sports stickers, firstly in its new Olympic Games collection,

Flight Without Wings

The sport of ski-ing.

SKI-ING as a sport started in Norway in 1860. For a period following the First World War British men and women skiers were supreme.

Ski-ing is a sport for which women have shown great aptitude, and in 1931 a sixteen-year-old English girl won the world's championship downhill race at Murren.

On a downhill racecourse any line can be taken so long as the skiers pass between the control flags which are placed to demark passage through dangerous hidden rocks, etc.

The world's record for downhill ski-ing is held by D. Netzell of Germany, who in 1950 did 95 m.p.h.

Ski-jumping is a particularly thrilling sport both to take part in and to watch and the sight of a skier flying through the air and alighting in a perfect landing leaves one breathless. Competition ski-jumping is of course a dangerous pastime, and the results of a bad landing can be grave.

The ski-jumper on impact with the ground has one ski well forward with the knees bent to relieve concussion, but he straightens up his body as soon as possible for the out-run.

In the 1948 Olympic Games results at St. Moritz the 18-km. Ski Race was won by Martin Lundström, of Sweden, in 1 hour 13 minutes 50 seconds, and the 50-km. race by N. Karlsson, also of Sweden, in 3 hours 47 minutes 48 seconds.

In the ski-jumping contest the highest points were scored by Petter Hugsted of Norway. Norwegians, Birger Rudd and T. Schjelderup, were the next in order.

In the thrilling Alpine Combination Event a woman, Trude Beiser of Austria, was top point-scorer. The international flavour in ski-ing is well proved by the nationalities in this event; next in order according to points scored were an American, another Austrian, an Italian, a Frenchman and a Swiss.

So much for championship-class ski-ing. Thousands of lucky British people take to skis in winter when visiting the famous Continental winter-sports resorts, some of them experts with many years of practice behind them, others gingerly taking the nursery slopes. There is quite serious ski-ing done in Scotland and the writer has had a lot of fun on an old pair of skis as far south as Suffolk.

Snow is imported specially every year so that ski-jumping can be demonstrated on Hampstead Heath.

called *Montreal 76*; and, latterly in a collection dedicated to winter sports, called *Ski 78*. The 1978 series not only includes ski jumpers and downhill skiers, it also features national ice hockey teams. Not surprisingly, with the cross over to hockey collecting, some of the stickers have become very valuable.

Panini's only ski output during 1979 was as part of a larger-than-usual collection, called *Super Stickers*. It includes a stunning sticker of Ingemar Stenmark, the Swedish all-time great, world champion and Olympic gold medal winner.

The Italian firm returned to winter sports three times during the 1980s, in a trio of pan-sport collections, one called *Sport Superstars* (1982), and two which bear the title *Supersport* (in 1987 and in 1988). Alas, even the Italian giant did not think to include a sticker of celebrated British legend, Michael Edwards, known to the world as Eddie The Eagle.

This is but the briefest introduction to the vast subject of winter sports on trade cards. Many more images may be seen at the winter sports cards gallery, under the relevant tab, at www.footballsoccercards.com

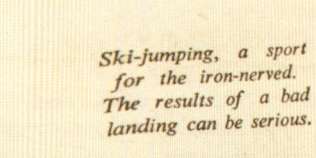

French gum card, 1937

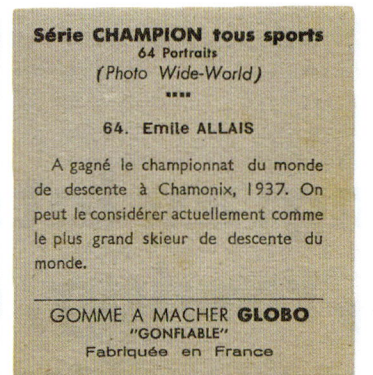

German tobacco cards, 1930s

Australian pharmacy cards, 1936

AN A TO Z OF **SPORTING COLLECTIBLES** 227

ZE OTHERS: AN INTRODUCTION TO OTHER SPORTS ON TRADE CARDS

Mountaineering on a French trade card, 1910s

Mountaineering on a French trade card, 1920s

Mountaineering on an Italian trade card, 1930s

Mountaineering on an Australian pharmacy card, 1936

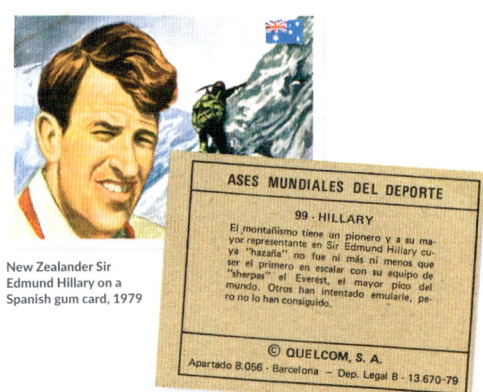
New Zealander Sir Edmund Hillary on a Spanish gum card, 1979

Fencing is a sport which Continental-based card manufacturers preferred to include, while British producers generally chose to ignore it. Fencing is an Olympic Games event, which producers like Panini made the most of by including fencers in many of its annual 1960s and 1970s pan-sport collections, from *I Campioni dello Sport* (the 1970 card of Antonella Ragno is something to behold) to *München 72* and *Sport Vedettes*. Baggioli and Mira, erstwhile competitors to the sticker giant from Modena, also included fencers in *Olimpiadi 1968* and *I Campionissimi*, respectively. These were by no means the earliest collections to feature foil, sabre and épée.

Italian confectioners of the 1920s, like La Felsinea caramels and Zaini chocolates, featured fencers on their cards. Biscuit makers, like Cevenini (1930s) and candy producers like VAV (1940s) also included fencing in mixed sports card collections. In 1953, the first Italian sticker producer, Lampo-Vecchi, included 3-D stickers of fencers – whose feints, parries and lunges only made visual sense to collectors wearing 3-D glasses – within the extra-dimensional and garish *Sport Magico* collection. Lampo's later *Enciclopedia Sportiva* offered more swordsmanship, thankfully without the need for special-effects spectacles.

More recently the Germanic-sounding Grünland, of Milan, issued circular cards of fencing which were included with an Italian cheese called Formaggino d'Oro.

Elsewhere, in Italy, Panini continued to include the sport in its all-sports collections of the 1980s, such as *Supersport*. There's also a fencing sticker in the over size series known as *Super Stickers*, from 1988.

As well as Italians, fencing found favour with French and Spanish producers, and many such cards are available from those countries. Useful websites for such treasure are to be found in Spain (www.todocoleccion.net) and in France (ebay.fr) but a gallery of available cards may easily be viewed under the fencing tab at www.footballsoccercards.com

Card games, especially poker, have featured on trade cards for over 130 years. Hess's *Poker Terms* cards are stunning. The Hess cards, which date from the 1890s, have been seen to sell for £250 each, though they are, in fact, worth even more money. A buyer known to this writer paid £250 each and then re-sold the cards in USA, to poker kings, for $1,000s each!

French cards issued during both Victorian and Edwardian epochs are known with poker and other cards games at play, and they often show women enjoying the thrill of the flush. The *fairer sex* oft' fared well on Gallic trade cards.

A series of 25 poker hands was illustrated for a set of cigarette cards issued by Cope Brothers in collaboration with Richard Lloyd tobacco, in 1936. The

Sir Edmund Hillary on an Irish gum insert, 1950s

A trio of target shooting & pistol duelling French trade cards, 1900s to 1910s

inexpensive collection can be found for as little as £1 a card, today. The attractive images illustrate poker hands such as a full house, a straight and so on. The set makes for a very frameable collection.

Poker cards may be seen under the relevant tab, under other sports, at www.footballsocccercards.com

British tobacco cards once came in the shape of dart flights! The cigarette card itself was designed to be folded and inserted into the metal tail of a dart, to be used in darts matches. Wills's Star brand cigarettes, Lambert & Butler's British Oak brand tobacco, and Carreras Black Cat brands are but three of the known types of dart flight cards available. They make for very practical collectibles but they are best left unused if you want their values to rise.

It seems strange that the game of darts does not feature highly on British-made cards because it was certainly a popular sport on Continental trade cards. One of the few Anglo-issue darts cards is to be found in a 1960s quiz-cards series issued by Dennis Productions, called *What's Wrong?* Also from the UK came the Tonibel and Mister Softee ice cream cards of sporting cups, of which one card from each series represents the England & Wales Darts Championship Trophy.

In the 1980s the television quiz show *Question of Sport* issued game cards on the strength of its brand, which featured notable darts players, such as Bobby George. Finding more British cards of darts is a challenge. Not so, abroad.

Au Bon Marché, in Paris, produced wonderful darts cards as long ago as the 1890s! A typical card shows three children, two girls and a boy, throwing darts at a board. Chocolate Carpentier, and its rival, Chocolate Guérin-Bouron, issued similar cards, around 1900, again showing youngsters with darts boards. Chocolate Debauve's card of the same genre goes one further – with four children. Van Lyden's *Jeux* series includes a more earnest darts match, played by adults.

Sports galore, myriad more, not featured here will reward the avid collector of cards. Greyhound racing is included in Ardath's Photocards, a series from the 1930s and croquet features on many colourful French trade cards. There's also a British croquet champ included in Gallaher's *British Champions of 1923*. Gaelic handball is included in the 1960 series called *Gaelic Sportstars*, by Liam Devlin, while sack racing is featured on German cigarette cards in the *Mokri Superb Der Weltkrieg* collection, by Lande. Netball can be found in *Plaisirs des Sport*, by Chocolat Lombart. Table tennis scenes are known on Turkish Trophies tobacco cards, by American Tobacco; on Cadet's transfers of sports stars from 1956. Lacrosse features widely amongst Canadian trade cards but also pops up in *Sporting Series*, the 1910 collection by Phillips (reissued in 1923) and in MacRobertson's *Sports*, of 1917. You'll find polo on cards by Liebig, and roller skating on French trade cards by Aux Deux Quartiers. Barrel rolling and tossing the caber are known on cards, too. In fact, just about all sports have been included on cards made somewhere, at some time. It's just a case of opening a search engine and mining them. Mining cards? A little like Bitcoin, rare cards of yore need a lot of work to find. They are great value-store assets because they are not easily available; they cannot be reprinted, like paper money and modern-day cards are. Antique and other rare cards need time and effort to mine but they will reward the hard work needed to find them.

For a gallery of rare cards of all sorts of sports see the other sports tab on the website: www.footballsoccercards.com

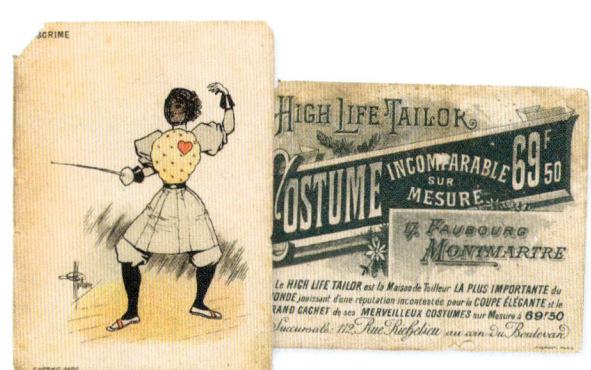
Fencing on a French trade card, 1900s

THE SOCCER CARDS RARITY SCALE

Cropan
1974 *Asi Juego al futbol Johan Cruyff* ★★☆☆☆
1975 football club emblems on glossy stickers ★★☆☆☆
1975 *Goool! Stickers within sticky frames*, intact stickers ★★★½☆
1975 *Goool! Stickers within sticky frames*, intact Cruyff ★★★★★

Crescent Confectionery
1923-25 *The Great Novelty House* footballers ★★★★★
(1926) Limited 1927 *General interest* cards, footballers ★★★★★
(1926) Limited 1930 *Sportsmen* ★★★★★

Crosse & Blackwell
1970 *World Cup Action* uncut cards ★★★☆☆

Cypal International
1977 Liverpool and Manchester United players ★★★☆☆

Daily Citizen
1913 *Football Teams* large paper supplements, free gifts ★★★★½

Daily Dispatch
1946 *Scott's Football Stars* cut outs ★★★★☆

Daily Express
1947 *Famous Footballers* cut outs, to be folded & glued ★★★☆☆
1955 *Full Report: Kick-off To Final Whistle* cards ★★★★½
1958 *Always On The Ball Sports Coverage* fold-out cards ★★★★½
1965 *Top Soccer News And Pictures* football teams ★★★★½

Daily Graphic Football Special (The Golden Penny)
1890s-1910s, intact issue ★★★★½

Daily Graphic
1948 *Football Stars* and *Goalkeeper Stars* cut out cards ★★★★½
1950 *Star Pictures Of Players* small cut-out cards ★★★★½

Daily Herald
1951 to 1953 *Sports Stars* ("Copyright SPORTFOTO") ★★☆☆☆
1951 to 1953 *Sports Stars* ("Copyright") ★½☆☆☆
1951 to 1953 *Sports Stars* ("Sportfoto") ★★★☆☆
1951 to 1953 large *Sports Stars* cards without legends ★★★★☆
1951 to 1953 paper folders with stapled large card inside ★★★★☆
1958 *Pencil Pics* cut-outs ★★☆☆☆

Daily Mail
1934 *Football Teams 1934-5* supplements ★★★★☆
1955 *Sports Parade by Eric Thompson* ★★★★☆
1970 *England's World Cup Footballers* ★★☆☆☆
1971 *Follow The...* [sic] uncut sheet of 22 stickers ★★★☆☆

Daily Mirror
1970 *Mirrorcards* small cards of teams ★☆☆☆☆
1970 *My Club* large cards of teams ★★½☆☆

Daily News Football Annual
1924 to 1927 fold-out *Football Supplements* ★★★★☆

Daily Sketch
1970 *World Cup Transfer* decals, uncut sheets ★★★☆☆
1970 *World Cup Transfer* decals, cut singles ★☆☆☆☆
1970 *World Cup Souvenirs* uncut strip of five cards with Pelé ★★★☆☆
1970 *World Cup Souvenirs* uncut strip of five cards ★★★½☆
1970 *World Cup Souvenirs* cut cards ★☆☆☆☆

Daily Star
1980 *Top British Teams* stickers ☆☆☆☆☆

Damm
1974 *Xibeca Sport* World Cup '74 stickers (folded) Johan Cruyff ★★★☆☆
1974 *Xibeca Sport* World Cup '74 stickers (folded) Scotland ★★★☆☆

Dandy Gum
1970 *Football Club Series* cards of club colours, British Isles clubs ★½☆☆☆

Danone
1982 *Daddies Football Greats* ★★☆☆☆

Davit
1930s footballers and teams, most ★★★☆☆
1930s footballers and teams, noted great players ★★★½☆

De Beukelaer
1932 *All Sports* players, most ★☆☆☆☆
1932 *All Sports* players, Gallagher [sic] ★★☆☆☆
1932 *All Sports* players, Dean ★★★☆☆

De Haas Van Brero
1949 to 1951 *Goal Voetbal Campioenen Leo Pagano*, British teams ★★★☆☆

De Jonge
1959 *Sportbilder*, players ★★★★½
1959 *Sportbilder*, Nottingham Forest ★★★★☆

Devlin
1952 *Famous Footballers New Series* untrimmed cards ★★★☆☆
1953 to 1955 *Famous Footballers A1, A2* and *A3* untrimmed cards ★★★½☆
1950s cards, as above, with trimmed sides ★★☆☆☆

Dickson Orde
1960 *Footballers*, set of 50 cards ★☆☆☆☆

Di Dasco
1950 to 1951 *Albosport* perforated stickers, most ★★★☆☆
1950 to 1951 *Albosport* perforated stickers, British stars ★★★★☆

Dipul
1971 *Campeões Europeus de Futebol 1970/71*, most ★★★☆☆
1971 *Campeões Europeus de Futebol 1970/71*, British players ★★★½☆

Doctor Storm's Winter Drops
1920s Bolton Wanderers players ★★★★☆

Dolcificio Lombardo (Perfetti)
1950s, b/w photo cards of footballers ★★★½☆

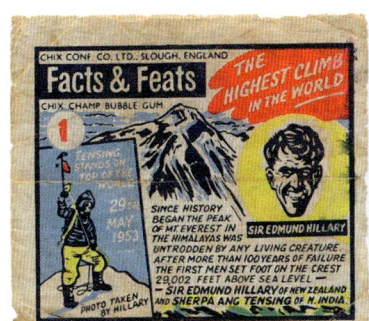
Sir Edmund Hillary on an Irish gum insert, 1950s

A trio of target shooting & pistol duelling French trade cards, 1900s to 1910s

inexpensive collection can be found for as little as £1 a card, today. The attractive images illustrate poker hands such as a full house, a straight and so on. The set makes for a very frameable collection.

Poker cards may be seen under the relevant tab, under other sports, at www.footballsocccercards.com

British tobacco cards once came in the shape of dart flights! The cigarette card itself was designed to be folded and inserted into the metal tail of a dart, to be used in darts matches. Wills's Star brand cigarettes, Lambert & Butler's British Oak brand tobacco, and Carreras Black Cat brands are but three of the known types of dart flight cards available. They make for very practical collectibles but they are best left unused if you want their values to rise.

It seems strange that the game of darts does not feature highly on British-made cards because it was certainly a popular sport on Continental trade cards. One of the few Anglo-issue darts cards is to be found in a 1960s quiz-cards series issued by Dennis Productions, called *What's Wrong?* Also from the UK came the Tonibel and Mister Softee ice cream cards of sporting cups, of which one card from each series represents the England & Wales Darts Championship Trophy.

In the 1980s the television quiz show *Question of Sport* issued game cards on the strength of its brand, which featured notable darts players, such as Bobby George. Finding more British cards of darts is a challenge. Not so, abroad.

Au Bon Marché, in Paris, produced wonderful darts cards as long ago as the 1890s! A typical card shows three children, two girls and a boy, throwing darts at a board. Chocolate Carpentier, and its rival, Chocolate Guérin-Bouron, issued similar cards, around 1900, again showing youngsters with darts boards. Chocolate Debauve's card of the same genre goes one further – with four children. Van Lyden's *Jeux* series includes a more earnest darts match, played by adults.

Sports galore, myriad more, not featured here will reward the avid collector of cards. Greyhound racing is included in Ardath's Photocards, a series from the 1930s and croquet features on many colourful French trade cards. There's also a British croquet champ included in Gallaher's *British Champions of 1923*. Gaelic handball is included in the 1960 series called *Gaelic Sportstars*, by Liam Devlin, while sack racing is featured on German cigarette cards in the *Mokri Superb Der Weltkrieg* collection, by Lande. Netball can be found in *Plaisirs des Sport*, by Chocolat Lombart. Table tennis scenes are known on Turkish Trophies tobacco cards, by American Tobacco; on Cadet's transfers of sports stars from 1956. Lacrosse features widely amongst Canadian trade cards but also pops up in *Sporting Series*, the 1910 collection by Phillips (reissued in 1923) and in MacRobertson's *Sports*, of 1917. You'll find polo on cards by Liebig, and roller skating on French trade cards by Aux Deux Quartiers. Barrel rolling and tossing the caber are known on cards, too. In fact, just about all sports have been included on cards made somewhere, at some time. It's just a case of opening a search engine and mining them. Mining cards? A little like Bitcoin, rare cards of yore need a lot of work to find. They are great value-store assets because they are not easily available; they cannot be reprinted, like paper money and modern-day cards are. Antique and other rare cards need time and effort to mine but they will reward the hard work needed to find them.

For a gallery of rare cards of all sorts of sports see the other sports tab on the website: www.footballsoccercards.com

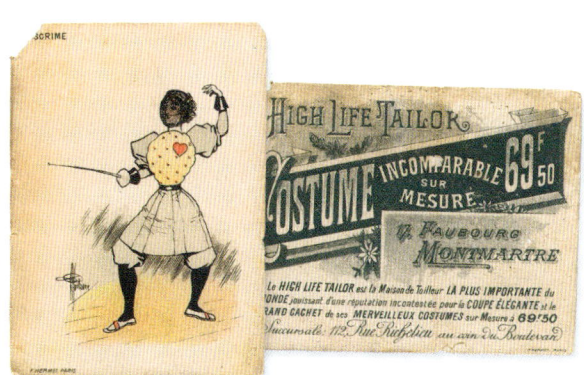
Fencing on a French trade card, 1900s

AN A TO Z OF **SPORTING COLLECTIBLES** 239

The Soccer Cards Rarity Scale

This rarity scale is for damage-free soccer cards and unused football stickers without glue residue, or other notable faults, from the 1880s to the 1980s.

Rarity grades are for pre-1960 cards and stickers in very good condition, and for post-1960 cards and stickers in excellent to near mint condition.

Stickers and cards with glue residue or damage are commoner than the same items without faults. Cards with wear and tear are less valuable than cards in very good, excellent or near mint condition. To find the rarity factor for damaged, faulty or otherwise worn cards, and for stickers with gum residue, downgrade the factors in the list, below, by 1 point for items from before 1960, and by 2 points for those from 1960 and later.

Most soccer cards made after the 1980s are not included because over 99% of them are very common.

Mint – truly mint – is almost impossible for cards from before 1980. Mint is not considered in this list.

Rarity scale points:

5 Stars: ★ ★ ★ ★ ★
Extremely rare – almost impossible to find; an asset that's a better value store than cash.

4 Stars: ★ ★ ★ ★ ☆
Very rare – very costly cards; you may never afford one if you don't find one & buy it now.

3 Stars: ★ ★ ★ ☆ ☆
Rare – these cards are ever harder to find, more expensive year on year; tomorrow's top cards.

2 Stars: ★ ★ ☆ ☆ ☆
Scarce to quite rare – now may be a good time to buy these cards; prices paid are starting to rise.

1 Stars: ★ ☆ ☆ ☆ ☆
Becoming scarce – values may rise yet future riches are unlikely; this card may always be available.

0 Stars: ☆ ☆ ☆ ☆ ☆
Very common – collect them for the love of collecting but not for profit; and pay very little for them.

Americana 1950

Balas Futebol Craques Mundial various collections 1950 to 1958, ★★★★⯪

A&BC Gum

1954 *All Sport* most cards ★☆☆☆☆
1954 *All Sport*, Puskás ★★☆☆☆
1954 *All Sport*, wrapper ★★★☆☆
1954 *All Sport*, empty album ★★☆☆☆
1954 *All Sport*, full album ★★⯪☆☆
1958 *Topstars* 1 to 46, players & Planet token, black ★☆☆☆☆
1958 *Topstars* 3 Robert Charlton & Planet token, black ★★☆☆☆
1958 *Topstars* 1 to 46, players, smaller photo, blue ★★⯪☆☆
1958 *Topstars* 3 Robert Charlton, smaller photo, blue ★★★⯪☆
1958 *Topstars* 1 to 46, players, larger photo, blue ★★⯪☆☆
1958 *Topstars* 3 Robert Charlton, larger photo, blue ★★★⯪☆
1958 *Topstars* 47 to 92, players & Planet token, black ★★☆☆☆
1958 *Topstars* 83 cartoon shows four players ★★★☆☆
1958 *Topstars* 84 cartoon shows padlocked pockets ★★★☆☆
1958 *Topstars* wrapper ★★★★☆
1959 *Footballer* 1 to 48, players, red ★☆☆☆☆
1959 *Footballer* 7 Jimmy Greaves ★★☆☆☆
1959 *Footballer* 49 Wolves checklist ★★☆☆☆
1959 *Footballer* 50 to 97, players, red ★★☆☆☆
1959 *Footballer* 98 Nottingham Forest checklist ★★★☆☆
1959 *Footballer* wrapper in blue ★★★☆☆
1960 *Footballer* 1 to 41, players, black ★☆☆☆☆
1960 *Footballer* 42 Wolves checklist ★★☆☆☆
1960 *Footballer* 43 to 83, players, black ★★☆☆☆
1960 *Footballer* 84 Blackpool checklist ★★★☆☆
1960 *Footballer* wrapper in green ★★★☆☆
1961 *Autographed Footballer* 1 to 64, players ★☆☆☆☆
1961 *Autographed Footballer* Topstars wrapper ★★★☆☆
1962 Scottish *Autographed Footballer* 1 to 40 players ★★☆☆☆
1962 Scottish *Autographed Footballer* 41 to 44 checklists ★★★☆☆
1962 Scottish *Autographed Footballer* Topstars wrapper ★★★☆☆
1962 Bazooka *Footballer* 1 to 40 players ★☆☆☆☆
1962 Bazooka *Footballer* 10 Bobby Moore ★★☆☆☆
1962 Bazooka *Footballer* 81 England checklist ★★☆☆☆
1962 Bazooka *Footballer* 82 Tottenham Hotspur checklist ★★☆☆☆
1962 Bazooka *Footballer* wrapper in orange & blue ★★★★☆
1963 *Footballer Make-a-Photo* 1 to 54 players ★☆☆☆☆
1963 *Footballer Make-a-Photo* 55 Manchester United checklist ★★☆☆☆
1963 *Footballer Make-a-Photo* 56 to 104 players ★☆☆☆☆
1963 *Footballer Make-a-Photo* 105 to 109 players ★★☆☆☆
1963 *Footballer Make-a-Photo* 105 Everton checklist ★★☆☆☆
1963 *Footballer Make-a-Photo* 110 Everton checklist ★★☆☆☆
1963 *Footballer Make-a-Photo* wrapper in red & yellow ★★★☆☆
1963 Scottish *Footballer Make-a-Photo* 1 to 40 players ★★☆☆☆
1963 Scottish *Footballer Make-a-Photo* 41 Rangers checklist ★★★☆☆
1963 Scottish *Footballer Make-a-Photo* 42 to 80, players ★★★☆☆
1963 Scottish *Footballer Make-a-Photo* 81 Hearts checklist ★★★☆☆
1963 Scottish *Footballer Make-a-Photo* wrapper in red & yellow ★★★☆☆
1964 *Footballer Quiz* 1 to 57 players, red ★☆☆☆☆
1964 *Footballer Quiz* 58 West Ham checklist ★★☆☆☆
1964 *Footballer Quiz* 59 to 102 players, red ★☆☆☆☆
1964 *Footballer Quiz* 103 Preston North End checklist ★★☆☆☆
1964 *Footballer Quiz* 103 to 148 players, red ★★☆☆☆

1964 *Footballer Quiz* 149 Liverpool checklist ★★★☆☆
1963 *Footballer Make-a-Photo* wrapper, in turquoise & brown ★★☆☆☆
1963 *Footballer Make-a-Photo* point-of-sale counter display box ★★★★☆
1964 Scottish *Footballer Quiz* 1 to 6 players, green ★★☆☆☆
1964 Scottish *Footballer Quiz* 7 Glasgow Rangers card ★★☆☆☆
1964 Scottish *Footballer Quiz* 8 to 43 players, green ★★☆☆☆
1964 Scottish *Footballer Quiz* 44 Glasgow Celtic checklist ★★★☆☆
1964 Scottish *Footballer Quiz* 45 to 80 players, green ★★★☆☆
1964 Scottish *Footballer Quiz* 81 Dundee checklist ★★★☆☆
1964 Scottish *Footballer Quiz* point-of-sale counter display box ★★★★☆
1965 *World Cup Football* stamps, portrait format ★★☆☆☆
1965 *World Cup Football* stamps, portrait format Pelé ★★★☆☆
1966 *World Cup Football* stamps, landscape format ★★☆☆☆
1966 *World Cup Football* stamps, landscape format Pelé ★★★☆☆
1966 *World Cup Football* stamps, landscape format Eusebio ★★★☆☆
1966 *World Cup Football* stamps, landscape format Yashin ★★★☆☆
1966 *World Cup Football* stamps wrapper ★★★★☆
1966 *World Cup Football* stamps point-of-sale counter display box ★★★★★
1966 *Footballers in Pairs* 1 to 102, player pairs ★★☆☆☆
1966 *Footballers in Pairs* 1 to 102, cut singles ★☆☆☆☆
1966 *Footballers in Pairs* 103 to 110 England checklists pairs ★★☆☆☆
1966 *Footballers in Pairs* 111 to 212 player pairs ★★★☆☆
1966 *Footballers in Pairs* 111 to 212, cut singles ★☆☆☆☆
1966 *Footballers in Pairs* 141 Charlie Cooke & 147 George Best ★★★☆☆
1966 *Footballers in Pairs* 213 to 220 West Germany checklist pairs ★★★☆☆
1967 Scottish *Footballers in Pairs* 1 to 42 player pairs ★★★☆☆
1967 Scottish *Footballers in Pairs* cut singles halved from pairs ★☆☆☆☆
1967 Scottish *Footballers in Pairs* 18 Alex Ferguson & player I ★★★☆☆
1967 Scottish *Footballers in Pairs* 18 Alex Ferguson & player II ★★★☆☆
1967 Scottish *Footballers in Pairs* 42 to 66 Celtic team cards ★★★★☆
1966 *Footballers in Pairs* wrapper in green and orange ★★★☆☆
1966 *Footballers in Pairs* point-of-sale counter display box ★★★★☆
1967 *Footballer Star Players* 1 to 55 players ★☆☆☆☆
1967 *Footballer Star Players* 13 George Best ★★☆☆☆
1967 *Footballer England's Stars Pin-Ups* [sic] posters ★★☆☆☆
1967 *Footballer (Star Players)* wrapper ★★★☆☆
1967 *Footballer* point-of-sale counter display box ★★★★☆
1968 *Footballer* 2 to 54, and 56 to 101 players, yellow ★☆☆☆☆
1968 *Footballer* 1 and 55 WBA and Man City checklists ★☆☆☆☆
1968 *Footballer Team* pennants ★★☆☆☆
1968 *Footballer Team Emblems* (metallic papers) ★★☆☆☆
1968 Scottish *Footballer* 2 to 44 players, yellow ★★★☆☆
1968 Scottish *Footballer* 23 Alex Ferguson ★★★☆☆
1968 Scottish *Footballer* 1 and 45 Celtic & Dunfermline checklists ★★★☆☆
1968 Scottish *Footballer* team pennants ★★★★☆
1968 *Footballer* wrapper (free team pennant) ★★★☆☆
1968 *Footballer* wrapper (free metalised team emblem) ★★★☆☆
1968 *Footballer* distribution bag for pennants ★★★★☆
1968 *Footballer* point-of-sale counter display box (emblems) ★★★★☆
1968 *Footballer* point-of-sale counter display box (pennants) ★★★★☆
1969 *Footballer* 1 to 117 (117 Woodfield) players, green ★☆☆☆☆
1969 *Footballer* 117 to 170 (117 Lawrence) players, green ★☆☆☆☆
1969 *Footballer* checklists with four-column lists ★★☆☆☆
1969 *Footballer* 29 Allan Clarke pair, with Leeds United variation ★★☆☆☆
1969 *Footballer* 54 Colin Suggett pair, with WBA variation ★★☆☆☆
1969 *Footballer* 125 David Sadler pair, with variation ★★☆☆☆
1969 *Footballer* 132 Frank McLintock pair, with variation ★★☆☆☆

AN A TO Z OF **SPORTING COLLECTIBLES** 243

THE SOCCER CARDS RARITY SCALE

1969 *Footballer* 145 Bobby Moncur pair, with variation	★★☆☆☆
1969 *Footballer* 151 John Sissons pair, with variation	★★☆☆☆
1969 *Footballer* checklist with five-column lists	★★☆☆☆
1969 *Footballer* deckled-edge card with facsimile autograph	★☆☆☆☆
1969 *Footballer* wrapper	★★☆☆☆
1969 *Footballer* wrapper (plus real photograph)	★★☆☆☆
1969 *Footballer* wrapper (real photograph new series)	★★★☆☆
1969 *Footballer* point-of-sale counter display box	★★★★☆
1969 *Footballer* point-of-sale counter display box (new series)	★★★★☆
1969 Scottish *Footballer* 1 to 75 players, blue	★★☆☆☆
1969 Scottish *Footballer* checklist cards	★★☆☆☆
1969 Scottish *Footballer* checklist error card (numbered to 77)	★★★☆☆
1969 Scottish *Footballer* deckled-edge card with facsimile autograph	☆☆☆☆☆
1969 *Footballer* World Cup Souvenir Card (cup in 3-D relief)	★★☆☆☆
1969 *Footballer* World Cup Souvenir Card (cup is not 3-D)	★★☆☆☆
1969 *Footballer* World Cup Giant Posters	★★★☆☆
1969 *Footballer* World Cup Giant Posters wrapper	★★★☆☆
1969 *Footballer* World Cup Giant Posters point-of-sale box	★★★★☆
1970 *Footballer* 1 to 83 players, orange	★☆☆☆☆
1970 *Footballer* 86 to 169 players, orange	★☆☆☆☆
1970 *Footballer* 171 to 255 players, orange	★★☆☆☆
1970 *Footballer* 84 to 85 & 170 (170 subject to change) checklists	★★☆☆☆
1970 *Footballer* 170 Series 3 checklist variety (numbered to 256)	★★☆☆☆
1970 *Footballer* 98 Brian O'Neil pair, with Burnley variation	★★☆☆☆
1970 *Footballer* 174 Jimmy Greenhoff pair, with Coventry variety	★★☆☆☆
1970 *Footballer* 174 John O'Rourke pair, with Stoke City variety	★★☆☆☆
1970 *Footballer* 242 Bobby Moore pair, with & without marque	★★☆☆☆
1970 *Footballer* Pin-Up Superstar poster	★☆☆☆☆
1970 *Footballer* Action Transfer (1st series)	★★☆☆☆
1970 *Footballer* New Action Transfer (2nd series)	★★★☆☆
1970 *Footballer* wrapper (plus pin-up poster)	★★☆☆☆
1970 *Footballer* wrapper (free action transfer)	★★☆☆☆
1970 *Footballer* wrapper (plus new action transfer)	★★★☆☆
1970 *Footballer* wrapper (plus new superstar poster)	★★★☆☆
1970 *Footballer* point-of-sale box	★★★☆☆
1970 Scottish *Footballer* 1 to 84, players	★☆☆☆☆
1970 Scottish *Footballer* 85 checklist card	★★☆☆☆
1970 Scottish *Footballer* 86 to 169, and 171 players	★★☆☆☆
1970 Scottish *Footballer* 170 checklist (numbered to 170)	★★☆☆☆
1970 Scottish *Footballer* 170 checklist (numbered to 171)	★★★☆☆
1970 Scottish *Footballer* Pin-Up Posters (1 to 14)	★★★☆☆
1970 Scottish *Footballer* New Superstars Posters (15 to 18)	★★★☆☆
1971 *Footballer* 1 to 109 players	★☆☆☆☆
1971 *Footballer* 110 to 219 players	★☆☆☆☆
1971 *Footballer* 220 to 290 players	★★☆☆☆
1971 *Footballer* with fancy, die-cut edges (like b/w cards issued in 1973)	★★★★☆
1971 *Footballer* with diamond-shape cuts from pinking shears (fakes)	☆☆☆☆☆
1971 *Footballer* checklists 57 and 170	★★☆☆☆
1971 *Footballer* checklist 277 (up to 290)	★★☆☆☆
1971 *Footballer* checklist 277 (up to 291)	★★★☆☆
1971 *Footballer* checklist 277 (up to 293)	★★☆☆☆
1971 *Footballer* 150 Neil Young standard front (blue shirt)	★☆☆☆☆
1971 *Footballer* 150 Neil Young variety (red-&-black shirt)	★★★☆☆
1971 *Footballer* 162 Mike Doyle standard front (red-&-black shirt)	★☆☆☆☆
1971 *Footballer* 162 Mike Doyle variety (blue shirt)	★★★★☆
1971 *Footballer* Club Crests	★☆☆☆☆
1971 *Footballer* Superstars	★★☆☆☆
1971 *Footballer* album for *Club Crests* and *Superstars*, empty	★★★☆☆
1971 *Footballer* album for *Club Crests* and *Superstars*, complete	★★★☆☆
1971 Scottish *Footballer* 1 to 73, players, purple	★☆☆☆☆
1971 Scottish *Footballer* 74 to 144, players, purple	★★☆☆☆
1971 Scottish *Footballer* 123 John Graham Hibs	★★☆☆☆
1971 Scottish *Footballer* 123 John Graham Ayr United	★★☆☆☆
1971 Scottish *Footballer* 57 and 115 checklists	★★☆☆☆
1971 Scottish *Footballer* club crests	★☆☆☆☆
1971 *Footballer* wrapper	★☆☆☆☆
1971 *Footballer* wrapper (free club crest)	★★☆☆☆
1971 *Footballer* wrapper (free superstars)	★★☆☆☆
1971 *Footballer* point-of-sale box	★★★★☆
1972 *Footballer* 1 to 109 players	★☆☆☆☆
1972 *Footballer* 110 to 219 players	★☆☆☆☆
1972 *Footballer* 179 Roger Morgan standard & variety pair of cards	★★☆☆☆
1972 *Footballer* 45 checklist	★★☆☆☆
1972 *Footballer* 154 checklist (to 218)	★★☆☆☆
1972 *Footballer* 154 revised checklist (to 219)	★★★☆☆
1972 *Footballer* playing card	☆☆☆☆☆
1972 *Footballer* wrapper	★★☆☆☆
1972 *Footballer* wrapper (plus free playing card)	★★★☆☆
1972 Scottish *Footballer* 1 to 89 players,	★★☆☆☆
1972 Scottish *Footballer* 90 to 179 players, vermilion red	★★☆☆☆
1972 Scottish *Footballer* 12 Wilson & Young variety pairs	★★☆☆☆
1972 Scottish *Footballer* 164 and 165 Stuart Rennie variety pair	★★☆☆☆
1972 Scottish *Footballer* 178 George Connelly pair, blue & red	★★☆☆☆
1972 Scottish *Footballer* Series 1 checklist, blue	★★☆☆☆
1972 Scottish *Footballer* Series 2 checklist (90 to 179), blue	★★☆☆☆
1972 Scottish *Footballer* Series 2 checklist (90 to 133), red	★★☆☆☆
1972 *Footballer* point-of-sale counter display box	★★★★☆
1973 *Footballer* 1 to 131, players, blue	★☆☆☆☆
1973 *Footballer* 132 to 263, players, blue	★★☆☆☆
1973 *Footballer* 241 John Toshack variety pair	★★☆☆☆
1973 *Footballer* 36 checklist	★☆☆☆☆
1973 *Footballer* 182 checklist, corrected (132 to 261)	★★☆☆☆
1973 *Footballer* 182 checklist, with unpublished cards (132 to 264)	★★☆☆☆
1973 *Footballer* cards with fancy, die-cut edges *Autograph Photo* cards	★☆☆☆☆
1973 *Footballer* the *Autograph Photo* cards with straight-cut edges	★★★☆☆
1973 Scottish *Footballer* 1 to 178, players, maroon	★★☆☆☆
1973 Scottish *Footballer* 53 and 171 checklists	★★★☆☆
1973 Scottish *Footballer* 155 Kenny Dalglish	★★☆☆☆
1973 *Footballer* wrapper	★★☆☆☆
1973 *Footballer* wrapper (free autograph photo)	★★★☆☆
1973 *Footballer* point-of-sale counter display box	★★★★☆
1973 *Giant Team Posters*	★★★☆☆
1973 *Giant Team Posters* wrapper	★★★☆☆
1973 *Giant Team Posters* point-of-sale counter display box	★★★★☆
1974 *Footballer* 1 to 132 players, vermilion red	★☆☆☆☆
1974 Scottish *Footballer* 1 to 132 players, green	★★☆☆☆
1974 *Footballer* wrapper	★★☆☆☆
1974 *Footballer* point-of-sale counter display box	★★★★☆
1974 Cup Winner Bag of Fun wrapper	★★★★☆
1974 Souvenir of the 1974 World Cup posters	☆☆☆☆☆
1974 Hobby Cards wrapper	★★★★☆
1950s to 1970s uncut, intact sheets of cards	★★★★★
1950s point-of-sale display posters	★★★★★
1960s point-of-sale display posters	★★★★½

Abdulla
1931 *Nationale & Internationale Sport-Recorde* players	★★★☆☆
1931 *Nationale & Internationale Sport-Recorde* Babe Ruth	★★★★☆
1931 *Nationale & Internationale Sport-Recorde* Bobby Jones	★★★★☆

Abissinia Cioccolato
1938 some with *La Portoghese Di Catania*, players	★★★☆☆
1936 as above, Meazza	★★★☆☆
1936 as above, Piola	★★★☆☆

Ace
1977 *Sporting Aces* complete boxed set	★★☆☆☆
1977 *Sporting Aces*, single card	★☆☆☆☆
1977 *Sporting Aces*, Dalglish	★★☆☆☆

Acropole
1978 *Mundial 78* players from Scotland	★★★☆☆

Adams Sports Virginia
1920s *Chesterfield FC* players	★★★★☆

Adkin & Sons
1914 *Sporting Cups & Trophies*	★★☆☆☆

Admiral & Major Sports
1974 *England's Soccer Stars*	★★★☆☆

Adolph see Subbuteo

Adventure
1921-22 English *Famous British Footballers Real Photographs*	★☆☆☆☆
1921-22 as above Max Woosnam	★★☆☆☆
1921-22 Scottish *Famous British Footballers Real Photographs*	★★★☆☆
1921/22 as above T. McInally, small "c"	★★★☆☆
1921/22 as above T. McInally, large "C"	★★★☆☆
1921/22 an English *Famous British Footballer* card & original comic	★★★☆☆
1921/22 a Scottish *Famous British Footballer* card & original comic	★★★★☆
1922 English series *Signed Real Photos*	★☆☆☆☆
1922 Scottish series *Signed Real Photos*	★★★☆☆
1922 an English *Signed Real Photo* with its original comic	★★★☆☆
1922 a Scottish *Signed Real Photo* with its original comic	★★★★☆
1923 metal coins: footballers and motor cars	★★★☆☆
1923 intact sheets of 9 *Famous Club Colours & Players*	★★★☆☆
1923 cut singles from sheets of *Famous Club Colours & Players*	★★☆☆☆
1923 *Famous Club Colours & Players* with its original comic	★★★★☆
1923 twin cards of *Coloured Photos of Star Footballers*, pairs	★★★☆☆
1923 as above, the pair with Hugh Gallacher, for Airdrie	★★★★☆
1923 cut singles from pairs of *Famous Club Colours & Players*	★☆☆☆☆
1924 intact pre-printed album *The 50 Star Players of 1924* 1st part	★★★☆☆
1924 intact pre-printed album *Star Footballers of 1924* 2nd part	★★★☆☆
1925 intact pre-printed album *Cup Fighters 1925*	★★★☆☆
1925 intact pre-printed album *Great Players of Today*	★★★☆☆
1925 intact pre-printed album *Star Footballers of 1925*	★★★☆☆
1925 single footballers cut from the above pre-printed albums	★☆☆☆☆

Adventure and Vanguard
1925 *Football Photos* cards	★★★☆☆
1925 *Football Photos* Dean, no full stop	★★★★½☆
1925 *Football Photos* Dean, with full stop	★★★★½☆

Adventure
1929 *Mysto Mind Reader Mystery* soccer clubs cards	★★☆☆☆
1930 *Footballers & Motor Cars* cards	★★☆☆☆
1931 twin cards, four *Football Towns and their Crests* and *Ships*, uncut pairs	★★★★☆
1931 *Football Towns and their Crests* card cut away from *Ships*, single card	★☆☆☆☆
1932 metal English *Footballers Cup-Tie Collection*	★★☆☆☆
1932 metal Scottish *Footballers Cup-Tie Collection*	★★★☆☆
1932 *Football Snapshots* cut single stickers	★★☆☆☆
1932 *Football Snapshots* uncut sheet of stickers	★★★★★
1932 *Football Snapshots* album, complete	★★★☆☆
1932 *Football Snapshots* album, empty	★★★☆☆
1933 strips of *Football Clubs* colours, single cut club	★☆☆☆☆
1933 *Football Clubs* colours, four in an uncut strip	★★★☆☆
1934 *Hunt The Cup* card	★★☆☆☆
1936 *Football Stamp Album* cut single stickers	★★☆☆☆
1936 *Football Stamp Album* uncut sheet of stickers	★★★★★
1932 *Football Snapshots* uncut sheet of stickers	★★★★★
1932 *Football Snapshots* album, complete	★★★☆☆
1932 *Football Snapshots* album, empty	★★★☆☆
1951 *Famous Footballers* package issue, blue or black cut-out players	★☆☆☆☆
1951 *Famous Footballers* uncut comic with players intact	★★★☆☆
1952 *Famous Goal-getters* cut-out famous player name tokens	★☆☆☆☆
1957 *Football Stars* cut single cards	★☆☆☆☆
1957 *Football Stars* strips of four cards	★★★☆☆
1957 *Football Stars* strips of four cards, with Duncan Edwards	★★★☆☆
1958 Pairs or triplets of *World Cup Footballers* uncut pair	★★☆☆☆
1958 *World Cup Footballers* uncut Jimmy Greaves trio	★★☆☆☆
1959 *World Footballers of Tomorrow* single, cut-out players	★★☆☆☆
1959 *World Footballers of Tomorrow* single, cut-out Denis Law	★★★☆☆
1959 *World Footballers of Tomorrow* single, cut-out Munich Man Utd	★★☆☆☆
1959 *World Footballers of Tomorrow* uncut sheet of stickers	★★★★☆
1959 *World Footballers of Tomorrow* album, complete	★★☆☆☆
1958 *Football Tips & Tricks by The Mystery Trainer* uncut pair	★★☆☆☆
1958 *Football Tips & Tricks by The Mystery Trainer* cut, single card	★☆☆☆☆
1961 *The ABC Chart of Football Colours* uncut sheet of stickers	★★★☆☆
1961 *The ABC Chart of Football Colours* cards with all stickers glued down	★★☆☆☆

African Tobacco Manufacturers
1939 *The World of Sport* Cowan large or small	★★★☆☆
1939 as above, Niewhenhuys, large or small	★★★☆☆
1939 as above, E. Drake large or small	★★★☆☆
1939 as above, Dean	★★★☆☆
1939 as above, Babe Ruth	★★★★☆

AG Éducatif
1970 *Etoiles du Football*, unused stickers	★★☆☆☆
1970 *Etoiles du Football*, complete album	★★☆☆☆
1971 *Football en Action*, unused stickers	★★☆☆☆
1971 *Football en Action*, complete album	★★★☆☆
1972 *Football en Match*, unused stickers	★★☆☆☆
1972 *Football en Match*, complete album	★★★☆☆
1973 *Football 1973/74*, unused stickers	★★☆☆☆

THE SOCCER CARDS RARITY SCALE

1973 *Football 1973/74*, complete album — ★★★☆☆
1973 *Football 1974/75*, unused stickers — ★★☆☆☆
1973 *Football 1974/75*, complete album — ★★★☆☆
1973 *Football 1974/75*, 289 Michel Platini used — ★★★☆☆
1973 *Football 1974/75*, 289 Michel Platini unused — ★★★★☆
1975 *Football 1975/76*, unused stickers — ★★☆☆☆
1975 *Football 1975/76*, complete album — ★★★☆☆
1976 *Football 1976/77*, unused stickers — ★★☆☆☆
1976 *Football 1976/77*, complete album — ★★★☆☆
1978 *Argentina 78*, unused stickers — ☆☆☆☆☆
1978 *Argentina 78*, complete album — ★★☆☆☆
1978 *Argentina 78 Jeux des Cartes*, complete boxed set of cards — ★★★☆☆
1978 *Argentina 78 Jeux des Cartes*, single cards — ★★☆☆☆

Agencia Portuguesa Revistas (APR)
1966 *Campeonato Mundial Futebol 1966*, stickers — ★★★☆☆
1966 as above, top internationals: Yashin, Pelé, Beckenbauer, etc. — ★★★★☆

Alba–Tortona
1959 *Lo Sport Italiano ATD82*, most cards — ★★☆☆☆
1959 *Lo Sport Italiano ATD82*, Charles — ★★★☆☆
1959 *Lo Sport Italiano ATD82*, Rivera — ★★★☆☆

Alifabolaget
1958 *VM-Spelare 1958*, most — ★★★☆☆
1958 *VM-Spelare 1958*, Brazil team — ★★★★☆
1958 *VM-Spelare 1958*, Pelé — ★★★★☆

Alifabolaget price note: in 2020 Pelé cards in excellent condition sold for US$43k, and US$75k, and near mint for US$292k.

Allen's of Australia
1926 *British Empire Sports Stars* soccer players — ★★★★☆

Allen, John
1978 *World Cup Legends* only three of each player made, most — ★★★★☆
1979 *World Cup Future Legends* only three of each player made, Maradona — ★★★★★
1981 *Allen's All Stars of Soccer* only three of each player made — ★★★★☆
1982 *London Legends* only three of each player made — ★★★★☆
1983 *Northern Nomads* only three of each player made — ★★★★☆
1995 *Broad's Braves* 25-exemplars of Preston NE stars, most — ★★★★☆
1995 *Broad's Braves* 25-exemplars of Preston NE stars, Beckham — ★★★★★
1996 *Underwood's Sportsmen* caricatures of sports stars, — ★★☆☆☆
1996 *Underwood's Sportsmen* caricatures of sports stars, full set — ★★★★☆

All Sports Illustrated Weekly
1919-1930 Sports souvenirs — ★★★☆☆

All Sports
1930 so-called *Grape Nuts* sports stars cards — ★★★☆☆

Althea
1962-66 *Cremifrutta Calciatori* die-cut players — ★★★☆☆

Amaika
1975 *Baraja Deportivo* playing card sports caricatures, most — ★★☆☆☆
1975 *Baraja Deportivo* playing card sports caricatures, Cruyff — ★★☆☆☆

Amalgamated Tobacco
1961 *Football Clubs and Badges* — ★☆☆☆☆

Amatller
1915 *Foot-ball* cards — ★★★☆☆
1915 as above, Plumstead — ★★★☆☆
1915 as above, Cardiff Corinthians — ★★★☆☆
1915 as above, Nomads — ★★★☆☆
1915 as above, New Crusaders — ★★★☆☆
1915 as above, English Amateur Team — ★★★☆☆
1915 as above, Percy Wallace Barcelona — ★★★★☆
1915 as above, Charles Wallace Barcelona — ★★★★☆
1920s soccer cards, various issues, regular players, clubs — ★★☆☆☆
1920s cards with P. Alcantara, J. Samitier, R. Zamora — ★★★☆☆

Americana München
1973 *Soccer Parade* cards — ★★★☆☆
1973 *Soccer Parade* complete album — ★★★☆☆
1976 *Sport Parade* unused stickers, regular sports stars — ★★★☆☆
1976 *Sport Parade* unused stickers, legendary stars — ★★★☆☆
1976 *Sport Parade* complete album — ★★★☆☆
1978 *Fussball Weltmeisterschaft Argentinien 1978* album — ★★☆☆☆
1978 as above, unused stickers (EAM/KPA) — ★★☆☆☆
1979 *Fussball 79* Paolo Rossi — ★★☆☆☆
1979 *Fussball 79* unused Liverpool stickers — ★★★☆☆

Anglo American Chewing Gum see Bell Boy

Anglo Confectionery
1969 *Football Quiz* George Best cards — ★★☆☆☆
1969 *Football Quiz* players — ★☆☆☆☆
1970 *Match Gum* wrappers with George Best — ★★★☆☆
1970 *National Team Colours* cards — ★★☆☆☆
1970 *World Cup 1970 & Learn The Game* Pelé — ★★☆☆☆
1970 *World Cup 1970 & Learn The Game* others — ★☆☆☆☆
1971 *World Famous Football Clubs* gum inserts — ★★★☆☆
1971 *World Famous Football Clubs* printed album, see also Bauer — ★★★☆☆
1972 *Football Hints* miniature booklets — ★★☆☆☆
1972 *Football Hints* wrapper — ★★★☆☆

Aquarela
1958 World Cup stickers with perforations Pelé, blue — ★★★★☆
1958 World Cup stickers with perforations Pelé, black — ★★★★☆
1958 World Cup album with all stickers glued down — ★★★★☆
1958 Uncut sheet of stickers — ★★★★☆
1959 2nd edition World Cup album with all stickers glued down — ★★★☆☆

Aral Petrol
1966 *Fussball WM* postcards of players, most — ★☆☆☆☆
1966 *Fussball WM* postcards of players, Eusebio and Pelé — ★★☆☆☆

Arbeshi
1972 *Caricatures of Footballers* players — ★★★☆☆
1972 *Caricatures of Footballers* players, checklist — ★★★☆☆

Ardath

1934 *Famous Footballers* players	★★☆☆☆
1934 *Famous Footballers* Stanley Matthews	★★☆☆☆
1934 *Sports Champions*	★★☆☆☆
1936 *Photocards* C, D and GS, and K series	★★☆☆☆
1936 *Photocards* as above with red overprints	★★★☆☆
1936 *Photocards* Series A to F and Z football teams	★★☆☆☆

Arga

1953 *Futbol* series 1, players, in sepia	★★★☆☆
1953 *Futbol* series 2, players, in sepia	★★★☆☆
1953 *Futbol* series 1 and 2 Gento, di Stefano and Kubala, each	★★★☆☆
1955 *Campeones del Futbol* players, in black & white, each	★★★☆☆
1955 *Campeones del Futbol* Gento, di Stefano and Kubala each	★★★☆☆

Ava Americana

Football Special 1977-1978 unused stickers	★★★☆☆
Football Special 1977-1978 album, complete	★★☆☆☆
Football Special 1977-1978 stickers with Cruyff & Best	★★★☆☆
Football Special '79 unused stickers	★☆☆☆☆
Football Special '79 album, complete	★☆☆☆☆

AVE (Italy)

1949 *Concorso Grandi Campioni, Il Vittorioso* cut-out British players	★★☆☆☆
1949 *Concorso Grandi Campioni, Il Vittorioso* complete comics	★★★☆☆

AVE Ltda (Brazil)

1958 *Colecao Titulares* complete album	★★★★☆
1958 *Colecao Titulares*, Pelé	★★★★☆

AVE 1958 price note: Pelé stickers 86 and 50 have been seen to sell for over £1,000 each.

AVE 1958 reproductions note: superb copies are in circulation which are hard to tell from originals.

BAB

1966-67 *Soccer Clubs* PVC shields (softer die-cut outline)	★★½☆☆
1967-68 *Soccer Clubs* PVC shields (softer die-cut outline)	★★½☆☆
1968-69 *Soccer Clubs* PVC shields (harder die-cut outline)	★½☆☆☆
1968-69 *Soccer Clubs* PVC shields with club nicknames	★★½☆☆
1969 *Soccer Clubs* PVC shields, named players (action figure, not a portrait)	★★☆☆☆
1969 *Soccer Clubs* PVC shields, named players (action figure, not a portrait), Best	★★☆☆☆
1969 *Soccer Clubs* PVC shields, named players (action figure, not a portrait), Pelé	★★☆☆☆
1969 *Soccer Clubs* PVC shields, named players (portrait)	★★★☆☆
1969 *Soccer Clubs* PVC shields, named players (portrait), Moore	★★★☆☆
1968-69 *Soccer Clubs* PVC shields with golden-coloured borders	★★☆☆☆
1970 *Soccer Clubs* PVC shield showing Brazil	★½☆☆☆
1970 *Football Badges* of league players, cartwheel-style stickers, matt finish	★★☆☆☆
1970 *Football Badges* point-of-sale display hanger	★★★★☆
1970 *World Cup Football Badges* cartwheel-style stickers, matt finish	★★☆☆☆
1970 *World Cup Football Badges* cartwheel-style stickers, matt finish, Riva	★★☆☆☆
1970 *World Cup Football Badges* cartwheel-style stickers, matt finish, Beckenbauer	★★☆☆☆
1970 *World Cup Football Badges* cartwheel-style stickers, Pelé (light)	★★½☆☆
1970 *World Cup Football Badges* cartwheel-style stickers, Pelé (red)	★★½☆☆
1970 *World Cup Football Badges* cartwheel-style stickers, Pelé (dark)	★★½☆☆
1971 *Century Series of Sticker Stamps: Soccer Favourites*, complete sheet	★★★☆☆
1971 *Century Series of Sticker Stamps: Soccer Favourites*, players & crests	★★☆☆☆
1971 *New Football Badges* of players, glossy cartwheel-style stickers	★★☆☆☆
1971 *New Football Badges* of players, glossy George Best	★★☆☆☆
1971 *Soccer Clubs* PVC shields (fancy) clubs	★★★☆☆
1971 *Soccer Clubs* PVC shields (fancy) Brazil 'World Cup Winners'	★★☆☆☆
1971-72 *Shooting Stars* first series	★★★☆☆
1972-73 *Shooting Stars* second series	★★★☆☆
1973 *Soccer Dip* shaped stickers: diminutive soccer balls, scarves, etc.	★★★☆☆
1974-75 *Football Club Rosettes*	★★★☆☆

Baggioli

1964 *Maghi Del Gol (Magicians of the Goal)* original cards	★★★☆☆
1965 *Calcio Italia Campionato 1965-66*, most players	★★★☆☆
1965 *Calcio Italia Campionato 1965-66*, Eusebio	★★★☆☆
1965 *Calcio Italia Campionato 1965-66*, Yashin	★★★☆☆
1965 *Calcio Italia Campionato 1965-66*, Pelé plain back/blue back	★★★☆☆
1965 *Calcio Italia Campionato 1965-66*, Baker	★★★☆☆
1965 *Calcio Italia Campionato 1965-66*, Springett	★★★☆☆
1965 *Calcio Italia Campionato 1965-66*, Law	★★★☆☆
1965 *Calcio Italia Campionato 1965-66*, Greaves	★★★☆☆
1965 *Calcio Italia Campionato 1965-66*, John Charles	★★★☆☆

Baines

1880s Club-&-triangle-shaped, sporting-arms back, sports teams & players	★★★★★
1880s Old-style shield-shaped cards, sporting-arms back, sports teams & players	★★★★★
1880s Sports stars on octagon-shaped cards	★★★★★
1880s Pears Soap descriptive advert back featuring rugby players or cricketers	★★★★★
1880s Pears Soap pictorial advert back featuring rugby players or cricketers	★★★★★
1880s Pears Soap pictorial advert back teams	★★★★★
1880s Sports shield-shape cards, sporting-arms back, teams & players	★★★★★
1880s Sports shield-shape cards (Cup Competition-1887) teams & players	★★★★½
1886 Arthur Wharton 1st soccer star & 1st black pro on a card, Darlington World Record	★★★★★
1890 Arthur Wharton for Rotherham, and others, older-style shield shape card	★★★★☆
1890s Arthur Wharton for Rotherham, and others, newer-style shield shape card	★★★★☆
1890s Various shapes, rugby soccer & cricket players for notable teams	★★★★☆
1880s Cricket ball-shape cards with a sporting-arms back, cricket teams	★★★★☆
1880s Sports fan-shape cards, with lion & unicorn crests teams & players	★★★☆☆
1890s Sports shield-shape cards, lion & unicorn backs teams & players	★★★☆☆
1890s Sports cards in other shapes with the lion & unicorn backs teams & players	★★★☆☆
1890s from circa 1896 to 1901: Smith, Bloomer, Meredith	★★★★½
1900s-1910s Sports shield-shape cards with North Parade address	★★★★☆
1910s cards with 'J. Baines Ltd', Oak Lane address	★★★☆☆
1910s-1920s Sports shields with 'J. Baines Ltd' Barnsley address	★★★☆☆
1916-1920s Sports ball-shape cards, golf-, rugby-, soccer-ball shapes	★★★☆☆
1916-1920s Sports shield-shape cards, Gillingham address	★★★★☆

THE SOCCER CARDS RARITY SCALE

Bainesesque
1880s Cards like those by Baines, printed by others with plain backs ★★★★★
1880s as above with bespoke advert backs ★★★★★

Balilla
1936 *Figurine Sportive* cards with black-borders, players ★★☆☆☆
1936 *Figurine Sportive* cards with black-borders, Meazza and Piola ★★★☆☆
1938 *Figurine Sportive* cards with flags, players ★★☆☆☆
1938 *Figurine Sportive* cards with flags, Meazza and Piola ★★★☆☆
1941 *Raccolta Nuove Figurine Squadre Calcio*, players ★★☆☆☆

Bailey's Agencies
c.1948 *Famous Football Internationals* in pairs ★★★☆☆
c.1948 *Famous Football Internationals* booklet of 16 ★★★★☆
c.1948 *Famous Football Internationals* stickers ★★★☆☆
c.1948 *Famous Football Internationals* sheet of 16 stickers ★★★★☆
c.1948 *Cigarette Card Transfer Series* single decal transfer ★★☆☆☆
c.1948 *Cigarette Card Transfer Series* sheet of 16 transfers ★★★★☆

Baker & Company
1902 *Cricketers* ★★★★☆

Bancroft Tiddlers
1960s are pages cut from miniature books – these are not cards

Barker of Ireland
1956 *Footballers* ★★★☆☆

Barna
1986 *Mexico 86*, most cards ★★☆☆☆
1986 *Mexico 86*, Alex Ferguson ★★★☆☆

Barratt
(no marque) 1923 Footballer cards, front, one line of text, plain back ★★★★☆
(no marque) 1923 Footballer cards, front, two lines of text, plain back ★★★☆☆
(other marques) 1923 Footballer cards with VCC, Watkins, etc ★★★★☆

Barratt note: the above cards do not show Barratt's logo but the generic type is typical of Barratt.

1924 matt cards, *Footballers* ★★★½☆
1925 matt cards, *Footballers* ★★★½☆
1926 matt cards, *Footballers* ★★★½☆
1927 matt cards, *Footballers* ★★★½☆
1924-27 matt cards of *Football Teams* ★★★★☆
1924-27 as above but varnished cards ★★★★☆
1927 *Leaders of Sport* ★★★½☆
1928 *Football "Stars"* [sic] caricatures of players ★★★☆☆
1930 *Football Greats*, coloured bodies with monotone photo heads ★★★☆☆
1931 *Football Teams 1st Division* ★★★☆☆
1932 *Football Teams*, English league clubs, folding cards ★★★☆☆
1933 *Football Teams*, English league clubs, folding cards ★★★☆☆
1934 *Football Teams*, English league clubs, folding cards ★★★½☆
1934 *Football Teams*, Stoke City with Matthews ★★★½☆
1934 *Football Teams*, Preston with Shankly ★★★½☆
1934 *Football Teams*, Scottish clubs, folding cards ★★★½☆
1934 *Football Teams*, Irish clubs, folding cards ★★★½☆

1935 *F.A. Cup Winners 1883 - 1935* ★★★½☆
1935 *Famous Footballers*, black ink, no numbers ★★★½☆
1935 *Famous Footballers*, black ink, no numbers, All Blacks ★★★½☆
1935 *Famous Footballers*, black ink, no numbers, Matthews ★★★★☆
1936 *Famous Footballers*, sepia ink, no numbers, ★★★★☆
1937 *Famous Footballers*, sepia ink, numbered to 110, most ★★★☆☆
1938 *Famous Footballers*, sepia ink, numbered to 20, most ★★★☆☆
1939 *Famous Footballers*, sepia ink, numbered to 112, most ★★★☆☆
1947 *Famous Footballers Series of 50*, sepia photos ★★★★☆
1947 *Famous Footballers Series of 50*, black photos, dark & sharp ★★★☆☆
1947 *Famous Footballers Series of 50*, black photos, dull & blurry ★★★☆☆
1948 *Famous Footballers Series of 50*, clear images with mixed tones ★★★☆☆
1949 *Famous Footballers Series of 50*, clear images with light backgrounds ★★☆☆☆

Barratt & WHC
1948 *Famous Footballers* decal transfers, cut singles ★★★☆☆
1948 *Famous Footballers* decal transfers, sheet of 20 ★★★★☆

Barratt & Napro
1949 *Famous Footballers* decal transfers, cut singles ★★★☆☆
1949 *Famous Footballers* decal transfers, sheet of 20 ★★★☆☆

Barratt
1950 *Famous Footballers New Series*, block lettering, most ★★☆☆☆
1950 *Famous Footballers New Series*, block lettering, rarer types ★★★☆☆
1951 *Famous Footballers New Series*, block lettering, different ★★☆☆☆
1951 *Famous Footballers New Series*, block lettering, rarer types ★★★☆☆
1952 *Famous Footballers New Series*, serif lettering ★★☆☆☆
1953 *Famous Footballers series*, A1 most ★★☆☆☆
1953 *Famous Footballers series*, rarer varieties ★★★☆☆
1954 *Famous Footballers series*, A2 most ★★☆☆☆
1954 *Famous Footballers series*, rarer varieties ★★★☆☆
1955 *Famous Footballers series A3*, most ★★☆☆☆
1955 *Famous Footballers series A3*, rarer varieties ★★★☆☆
1956 *Famous Footballers series A4*, most ★★☆☆☆
1956 *Famous Footballers series A4*, rarer varieties ★★★☆☆
1957 *Famous Footballers series A5*, most ★★☆☆☆
1957 *Famous Footballers series A5*, rarer varieties ★★★☆☆
1958 *Famous Footballers series A6*, most ★★☆☆☆
1958 *Famous Footballers series A6*, Greaves ★★★☆☆
1959 *Famous Footballers series A7*, most ★★☆☆☆
1959 *Famous Footballers series A7*, rarer varieties ★★★☆☆
1959 *Giants in Sport*, most ★★☆☆☆
1959 *Giants in Sport*, rarer varieties ★★★☆☆
1960 *Famous Footballers series A8*, most ★★☆☆☆
1960 *Famous Footballers series A8*, rarer varieties ★★★☆☆
1961 *Famous Footballers series A9*, most ★★☆☆☆
1961 *Famous Footballers series A9*, rarer varieties ★★★☆☆
1962 *Famous Footballers series A10*, most ★★☆☆☆
1962 *Famous Footballers series A10*, rarer varieties ★★★☆☆
1963 *Famous Footballers series A11*, most ★★☆☆☆
1963 *Famous Footballers series A11*, rarer varieties ★★★☆☆
1964 *Famous Footballers series A12*, most ★★☆☆☆
1964 *Famous Footballers series A12*, George Best ★★★☆☆
1965 *Famous Footballers series A13* ★★☆☆☆
1966 *Famous Footballers series A14*, most ★★☆☆☆
1966 *Famous Footballers series A14*, rarer varieties ★★★☆☆

1967 Famous Footballers series A15 ★☆☆☆☆
1970 Goldflake Famous Sportsmen, most ★★☆☆☆
1970 Goldflake Famous Sportsmen, rarer varieties ★★★☆☆
1970 Goldflake Famous Sportsmen, Pelé ★★★☆☆
1970 Goldflake Famous Sportsmen, Best ★★★☆☆
1971 Goldflake Famous Sportsmen, most ★★☆☆☆
1971 Goldflake Famous Sportsmenn, rarer varieties ★★★☆☆
1972 Soccer Stars ★★★☆☆
1973 Football Stars ★★★☆☆

Bassett
1974 Barratt Division Football Stars ★★☆☆☆
1974 World Cup Stars ★☆☆☆☆
1975 Football Stars 1975-6 [sic] ★★★☆☆
1976 Football Action (1976/77 season, no spacing between titles) ★★☆☆☆
1977 Football Action (1977/78 season, with spacing between titles) ★★☆☆☆
1978 Football 1978-79 ★☆☆☆☆
1979 Football 1979-80 ★☆☆☆☆
1980 onwards, most cards are ★½☆☆☆

Batger
1900 Well Known Football Clubs ★★★★★

Battock
1923 Football Club Colours, plain background ★★★★½
1924 Football Team Colouring Competition, monotone cards ★★★★☆
1925 Football & Cricket Clubs, full-colour cards ★★★★☆

Bauer
1970 Weltfussball 1970 / Football Mondial ★★★☆☆

Baytch Brothers (S&B Products)
1948 Torry Gillicks Internationals ★★★☆☆

Bazoka
[sic] 1950s Spanish football club emblems, stamps ★★☆☆☆

BEA (Buste ed Affini)
1949 Stadio football cards ★★★☆☆
1950 Gool! Premio Sport ★★★☆☆
1951 Campionato di Calcio ★★★☆☆
Norman Adcock, Bill Jordan and Paddy Sloan, each ★★★☆☆

Bell Boy
1958 Sports Gallery waxy paper gum inserts, issued creased, most ★★★☆☆
1958 Sports Gallery waxy paper gum inserts, issued creased, Jones ★★★½☆
1958 Sports Gallery waxy paper gum inserts, issued creased, Hagen ★★★☆☆
1958 Sports Gallery issued creased, soccer subjects, most ★★★☆☆
1958 Sports Gallery crease-free proofs of the above, all ★★★★★
1958 Soccer Hints ★★☆☆☆
1959 Sports Parade crease-free proof insert & wrapper, Tilden ★★★★☆
1959 Sports Parade crease-free proof insert & wrapper, Lenglen ★★★★☆
as above, crease-free proofs, Thorpe ★★★★☆
as above, crease-free proofs, Louis ★★★★☆
as above, crease-free proofs, Hogan ★★★★☆
as above, crease-free proofs, Matthews ★★★★☆
as above, crease-free proofs, other boxers ★★★★☆
as above, crease-free proofs, track athletes ★★★★☆
as above, crease-free proofs, others ★★★★☆
note: sales of proofs have made USD$500 each, regular inserts make only 25% of this figure.

1959 Sports Parade waxy paper gum inserts, regular items issued creased ★★★☆☆
1959 as above, album ★★★★☆
1961 Famous Soccer Clubs ★★★☆☆
1961 Famous Soccer Clubs, album ★★★★☆
1962 Noted Soccer Clubs ★★★☆☆
1962 Noted Soccer Clubs, album ★★★☆☆
1964 Coaching Secrets, most ★★★☆☆
1964 Coaching Secrets, Pelé ★★★★☆
1964 Coaching Secrets, Eusebio ★★★★☆

Bell
1902 Three Nuns Tobacco Three Bells footballers ★★★☆☆

Bergmann Haus
1930s Bunte Buch Sport-Karikaturen ★★★☆☆
1930s Bunte Buch Sport-Karikaturen, uncut sheets ★★★★☆

Bergmann Verlag
1961 European football teams ★★★☆☆
1966 Jules Rimet Cup England 1966 postcards ★★★☆☆
1970 World Cup Mexico 70 ★★☆☆☆

Bertcord
1982 Big League complete game with around 100 cards, box ★★☆☆☆

Bimbo
1967-69 Nuestro Mundos (three series) football stickers ★★★☆☆
1967-69 Nuestro Mundos (three series) football stickers, Pelé ★★★☆☆
1974 Futbol en Accion decal transfers, unused ★★★☆☆
1979 Historia del los Mundials Futbol transfers, unused ★★★☆☆

Binns
1924 Halifax Town Footballers by Hebble Cigarettes ★★★★★

Bird's Eye
1982 England World Cup Trail singles ★★☆☆☆
1982 England World Cup Trail, pairs ★★★☆☆

Birmingham Evening Gazette
1931 FA Cup Finalists 1930-1931 ★★★★☆
1935 FA Cup Finalists 1935 ★★★★☆
1945 These Are Soccer Stars, cut outs ★★★☆☆
1946 These Are Soccer Stars New Series ★★★☆☆
1940s cut, fold & glue escutcheons of footballers ★★★★☆

Blue Cap Cheese
1953 Sports Series, uncut pairs ★★★☆☆
1958 Flixies ★★☆☆☆

Bocnal
1938 Luminous Silhouettes ★☆☆☆☆

THE SOCCER CARDS RARITY SCALE

Bovalone Biscotti
[sic] 1950s *Calciatori*, most — ★★☆☆☆
[sic] 1950s *Calciatori*, Jeppson — ★★☆☆☆
[sic] 1950s *Calciatori*, Skoglund — ★★★☆☆

Bowater Scott
1969 *Scotties Famous Football Teams* postcards — ★★☆☆☆

Boxing, Racing & Football mag.
1928 *Personalities of British Sport* — ★★★★☆

Boys' Cinema
1931 football teams — ★★★☆☆

Boys' Friend
1908 *Football Teams 1908-9*, supplements — ★★★★☆
1911 *Picture Gallery*, uncut quad — ★★★★☆
1911 *Picture Gallery*, cut singles — ★★☆☆☆
1922 *Footballers*, in pairs — ★★☆☆☆
1922 *Footballers*, cut singles — ★☆☆☆☆
1923 *Special Photos (Hand-Coloured Real Glossy Photos)* — ★★☆☆☆
1922 *Teams Presented With The "Boys' Magazine"* [sic] — ★★★☆☆
1922 *Teams Presented With The "Boys' Magazine"* [sic] — ★★★☆☆
1922 *Art Photos of Famous Footballers* strips of three players — ★★★☆☆
1922 *Art Photos of Famous Footballers* strips cut to singles — ★☆☆☆☆
1922 *Football Teams / Football Series* team cards — ★☆☆☆☆
1922 *Coloured Studies of Famous Internationals* — ★☆☆☆☆
1923 *Famous Footballer Photos* sheets of four players — ★★★☆☆
1923 *Famous Footballer Photos* cut to singles — ★☆☆☆☆
1923-24 *Football Series 1923-'24* postcard-size teams — ★★★☆☆
1925-26 Dated teams, large paper supplements — ★★★☆☆
1925-26 as above. undated (Spurs, Man City & Cardiff C) — ★★★☆☆
1926 *The Cup-Final Teams (1925-26)* [sic] Man City. v Bolton — ★★★☆☆
1926 *Transfers of Big Heroes* sheet of six decals — ★★★★★
1926 *Transfers of Big Heroes* single, unused cut decals — ★★★★☆
1926 footballers, metal badges (discs, fold-over tabs) — ★★★★☆
1926 *Famous Footer Clubs*, die-cut, shaped cards — ★★★☆☆
1927/1928 *Transfer Photos of Famous Footballers* sheet of four — ★★★★☆
1927/1928 *Transfer Photos of Famous Footballers* unused cut singles — ★★★☆☆
1926/27 *Teams Presented free with Boys Magazine* [sic] — ★★★☆☆
1928 Teams, paper supplements (dated 1928) — ★★★☆☆
1929 black-and-white photographic cards of players — ★☆☆☆☆
1929 coloured *Football Teams* cards — ★★☆☆☆
1929 *The FA Cup Finalists 1929* (Bolton W. & Portsmouth) — ★★★☆☆
1930 Pairs of football teams and other sports, uncut pair — ★★★☆☆
1930 Pairs of football teams and other sports, cut single — ★☆☆☆☆
1931 *Gallery of Famous Footballers* sheets of four, uncut — ★★★☆☆
1931 *Gallery of Famous Footballers* cut singles — ★☆☆☆☆
1931 *Magic Transfers*, sheets of five decals, uncut — ★★★★★
1931 *Magic Transfers*, cut singles — ★★★★☆
1931 Pairs of teams (dated), uncut pair — ★★★☆☆
1931 Pairs of teams (dated), cut single — ★☆☆☆☆
1932 *Famous Footballers In Action*, uncut sheet of six stickers — ★★★★☆
1932 *Famous Footballers In Action*, cut singles — ★★☆☆☆
1932 *Famous Footballers In Action*, album, complete — ★★★☆☆
comics note: any of the above gifts with the original comic add 100% to value.

Boys' Own Paper
1890 to 1920 uncut pull-out soccer supplements — ★★★☆☆

Boy's Own
1910 chocolate cigarettes packet — ★★★★☆
1910 chocolate cigarettes sportsman card — ★★★☆☆

Boys' Realm
1900 to 1910 *Famous Football Grounds* — ★★★★☆
1920s *Famous Footballers Big Art Plates*, supplements — ★★★★☆
1922 *Famous Footballers* cards — ★☆☆☆☆
1923 *Football Trophies* metal cards — ★★★★☆
1927 *F.A. Cup Winners Medals* metal cards — ★★★★☆

Bremer Kaffee
1958 *Fussballbilder der Weltmeisterschaft 1958* any of seven different Pelé cards — ★★★★★
1958 *Fussballbilder der Weltmeisterschaft 1958* Yashin cards — ★★★★★
1958 *Fussballbilder der Weltmeisterschaft 1958* UK stars — ★★★★★
1958 *Fussballbilder der Weltmeisterschaft 1958* other players — ★★★★★

Bremer Kaffee price note: *in autumn 2020 a Bremer Pelé was offered on eBay for US$295k. The sale was ended one day later, for an undisclosed sum.*

Brigham
1912 *Pictures of The Reading Football Players* — ★★★★☆

British & American Tobacco (BAT)
1923 *Famous Footballers* — ★★☆☆☆
1924 *Famous Footballers* — ★★☆☆☆
1925 *Famous Footballers* — ★★☆☆☆
1926 *Who's Who in Sport 1926* teams — ★★☆☆☆

British Automatic
1954 *Sportsman Series Of 24* with printed backs — ★★☆☆☆
1954 *Sportsman Series Of 24* with plain backs — ★★★★☆

British Chewing Sweets Oh Boy Gum
1933 *Photos of Footballers* cards — ★★★☆☆
1933 *Photos of Footballers* wrapper — ★★★★★

Broadbent & Co
1880s *Will Eagland's Restaurant* shield-shaped cards of footballers — ★★★★★

Brooke Bond PG Tips
1972 *Place The Face Bingo* uncut trios — ★★★☆☆
1972 *Place The Face Bingo* singles — ★★☆☆☆

Bruciamonti & Figli
1930s *Comic Sporting Scenes* — ★★★★★

Bruguera El Gato Negro
1939 to 1940s paper stickers of footballers — ★★☆☆☆

Bruguera
1944 stand-up footballers — ★★★☆☆
1940s various series of football cards and stickers — ★★⯨☆☆
1950s various series of football cards and stickers — ★★⯨☆☆
1960s various series of football cards and stickers — ★★⯨☆☆

250 AN A TO Z OF **SPORTING COLLECTIBLES**

Bryant & May
1970s *Great British Achievements* matchboxes, uncut ★★★☆☆
1970s *Great British Achievements* matchboxes, cut ★★☆☆☆

Bucktrout
1928 Islanders-brand *Football Teams* ★★½☆☆

Bulgaria
1932 *Sport-Photos* ★★☆☆☆
1935 *Deutscher Sport Vorschau auf 1936* ★★☆☆☆

Bunsen Confectionery
1922-23 *Famous Figures Series*, black and sepia series ★★★★½

Buster & Jet
1970 *My Favourite Soccer Stars* uncut sheets of cards ★★★☆☆
1970 *My Favourite Soccer Stars* single cards ★☆☆☆☆

Cadbury's
1973 *Fantastic Football Badges* stickers of English footballers, unused ★★½☆☆
1973 *World Cup Badges* of Scottish footballers, unused ★★★☆☆

Cadet Sweets
1955 *Record Holders of the World* footballers and cricketers ★☆☆☆☆
1956 *All-Sports* decals, footballers and other sports stars ★★★★½
1957 *Footballers* transfer decals ★★★½☆
1957 *Footballers* number placed tightly below title to rear ★☆☆☆☆
1957 *Footballers* by Gee Products with plain backs ★★★☆☆
1958 *Footballers* upside-down backs ★★★☆☆
1958 *Footballers* upside-down backs, Greaves ★★★☆☆
1958 *Footballers* upside-down backs, Charlton ★★★☆☆
1959 *Footballers* small-script backs ★☆☆☆☆
1960 *Footballers* large-script backs ★☆☆☆☆

Cadet Sweets as CS Ltd.
1962 *Footballers and Club Colours* ★☆☆☆☆

Cadle
1904 *Footballers*, most ★★★☆☆
1904 *Footballers*, Smith ★★★☆☆
1904 *Footballers*, Bloomer ★★★☆☆

Caffa
1931 *Giocatori* small celluloid colour cards, most ★★★★☆
1931 *Giocatori* small celluloid colour cards, Ferrari ★★★★★
1931 *Giocatori* small celluloid colour cards, Meazza ★★★★★

Caffarel
1936 *Concorso Calcistico* football club emblems ★★★☆☆
1937 *Il Mondo del Calcio* footballer caricatures in colour by *Carlin* ★★★★☆

Cameron & Sizer
1893 *Occupations for Women*, Footballer ★★★★☆

Carsel Caramelos
1966 *Desfile Dos Famosos Futebolistas Mundiais* ★★★★☆

Caramelo Futbol
1920 *Caramelo Futbol* players from Spain on colourful small cards ★★★★☆
1920 *Caramelo Futbol* Zamora, Samitier, Alcántara each ★★★★½
1920 *Caramelo Futbol* uncut sheets of six of the above ★★★★★

Carreras
1934 *Footballers* with small titles (26mm) players ★☆☆☆☆
1934 *Footballers* with larger titles (27mm) players ★☆☆☆☆
1934 *Footballers* as above, Stanley Matthews, both types, each ★★☆☆☆
1935 *Famous Footballers* players ★☆☆☆☆
1935 *Famous Footballers* re-drawn players from 25 to 48 ★☆☆☆☆
1935 *Famous Footballers* Stanley Matthews ★★☆☆☆
1936 *Popular Footballers* players ★☆☆☆☆
1948 Turf cigarettes *Famous Footballers* packet sliders, cut card ☆☆☆☆☆
1948 Turf cigarettes *Famous Footballers* packet sliders, uncut single ★☆☆☆☆
1948 Turf cigarettes *Famous Footballers* packet sliders, uncut double ★★☆☆☆

Casera
1966 *Campeonao Mundial de Fùtbol* players ★★★☆☆
1966 *Campeonao Mundial de Fùtbol*, Pelé ★★★☆☆
1966 *Campeonao Mundial de Fùtbol*, Beckenbauer ★★★☆☆
1966 *Campeonao Mundial de Fùtbol*, Eusebio ★★★☆☆
1966 *Campeonao Mundial de Fùtbol*, Yashin ★★★☆☆
1966 *Campeonao Mundial de Fùtboll*, England footballers ★★★☆☆

Casket
1905-08 football fixtures cigarette cards, various teams ★★★★★

Casket & Critic Pattreiouex
1922 *Famous Footballers* F1 to F191 footballers ★★★☆☆
1922 *Football Teams* F192 to F241 teams ★★★★☆
1922 *Football Teams* F192 to F241 Man City (four variations) ★★★★½

Castello
1961 *Lo Sport* players ★★★★☆
1961 *Lo Sport* players, Baker ★★★★☆
1961 *Lo Sport* players, Law ★★★★☆
1961 *Lo Sport* players, Rivera ★★★★☆
1961 *Lo Sport* players, Charles ★★★★☆

Castoldi
1948 uncut sheet of cards, players, team and emblem ★★★★½
1948 uncut sheet of cards AC Milan, with Paddy Sloan ★★★★½
1948 uncut sheet of cards Juventus, with William Jordan ★★★★½
1948 single, cut cards ★★☆☆☆

Cedip
1961 *Campionato di Calcio* most ★★☆☆☆

CET
1967 *Forza Goal Figurine Discoidale* plastic pogs ★★★☆☆

Champion
1922 *Sporting Champions* English cards ★☆☆☆☆
1922 *Sporting Champions* Scottish cards ★★★☆☆
1922 *Famous Football Captains* ★☆☆☆☆
1923 *Famous Footballers* ★★☆☆☆

THE SOCCER CARDS RARITY SCALE

1923 *Famous British Record Breakers*	★★☆☆☆
1925 *English League (Div.1) Footer Captains*	★★☆☆☆
1920s-1930s *League Photo Albums*, uncut booklets	★★★☆☆
1920s-1930s *League Photo Albums*, cut outs of footballers	★☆☆☆☆
1930 *Glossy Photos of Famous Footballers* uncut sheet of stickers	★★★★★
1930 *The Champion Album Of Famous Footballers* album, complete	★★★☆☆
1933 *Record Breakers* single sticker stamps	★★★☆☆
1933 *Record Breakers* album, complete	★★★☆☆
1934 *Sportsmen of the World* strip of four cards, uncut	★★★☆☆
1934 *Sportsmen of the World* single, cut card	★☆☆☆☆
1934 *Sportsmen of the World* album, complete with cut cards	★★☆☆☆
1935 *Portfolio of Sport* complete with eight folders of pictures	★★★☆☆
1935 *Portfolio of Sport - Soccer's Wily Wizards*	★★☆☆☆
1935 *The Champion Sports Wallet - Football's Finest Goal-Getters*	★★☆☆☆
1935 *The Champion Sports Wallet - Wizards of the Football Field*	★★☆☆☆
1935 *The Champion Sports Wallet, Portfolio of Sport* single cut pictures	☆☆☆☆☆
1935 *Autographs* (red, white & blue cover) album, complete	★★★☆☆
1936 *Famous Footballers Autographs & Photographs*, album	★★★☆☆
1936 *Autographs* (cover in coloured quarters) full album	★★★☆☆
1936 as above, uncut sheets of stickers	★★★★☆
1936 as above, cut singles	★☆☆☆☆
1936 *Pilot Football Fame Series*, strips of four cards	★★★☆☆
1936 *Pilot Football Fame Series*, cut single cards	★☆☆☆☆
1936 *Pilot Football Fame Series* album, complete with cut cards	★★☆☆☆
1938 *Prominent Football Teams*, strips of three teams	★★★☆☆
1938 *Prominent Football Teams*, cut singles	★☆☆☆☆
1950 *Stars of the Sports World*, page of stickers to cut out	★★★☆☆
1950 *Stars of the Sports World*, page of stickers, cut	★☆☆☆☆
1950 *Stars of the Sports World* album, complete	★★★☆☆
1967 *Lion and Champion Album of Soccer Stars*, complete	★★☆☆☆
1967 *Lion and Champion Album of Soccer Stars* uncut sheet with Pelé & Best	★★★☆☆
1967 *Lion and Champion Album of Soccer Stars*, other uncut sheets	★★☆☆☆
1967 *Lion and Champion Album of Soccer Stars*, cut singles	★☆☆☆☆

price note: the above cards & the comic in which they came add 100% to value.

Charles Buchan

1960s postcards of teams & players (with a copyright number)	★★☆☆☆
1969 *World Stars*, sheets of 20 uncut sheet of stickers	★★★★☆
1969 *World Stars*, cut single sticker	★☆☆☆☆
1969 *World Stars*, album, complete	★★☆☆☆

Charlesworth & Austin

1902 *Cricketers*	★★★★☆
1902 *Cricketers*, Charles Burgess Fry	★★★★☆

Chix

1953 *Famous Scottish Footballers* (black & white)	★★★★½
1953-1958 *Famous Footballers*, series 1 to 3, most	★☆☆☆☆
1953-1958 *Famous Footballers*, series 1 to 3, rarer varieties	★★★☆☆
1953-1958 *Famous Footballers* albums, complete with cards	★★☆☆☆
1959 *Famous Footballers SFBL1*	★★☆☆☆
1960 *Facts & Feats* gum inserts	★★☆☆☆
1960 *Footballers* action and portraiture cards, b/w caricature back	★☆☆☆☆
1960 *Footballers* action and portraiture cards, b/w with pink caricature back	★★★☆☆
1960 *Footballers* action and portraiture cards, no caricature advert back	★★★☆☆
1961 *Buchan Publications Famous Footballers*	★☆☆☆☆

Chocolate Juncosa

1920s Spanish footballers, various series, players	★★½☆☆
1920s as above, Samitier	★★★☆☆
1920s as above, Zamora	★★★☆☆
1920s as above, Alcantara	★★★☆☆

Churchman

1907 *Football Club Colours*	★★☆☆☆
1914 *Footballers* (portraits in brown & white)	★★★☆☆
1914 *Footballers* (action scenes with oval portraits)	★★☆☆☆
1931 *Sporting Celebrities*	★★☆☆☆
1938 *Association Footballers*	★☆☆☆☆
1938 *Association Footballers*, 2nd series	★☆☆☆☆

Cibeles

1966 *Campeonato Mundial de Fútbol* players	★★☆☆☆
1966 *Campeonato Mundial de Fútbol*, Pelé	★★★½☆
1966 *Campeonato Mundial de Fútbol*, Beckenbauer	★★★☆☆
1966 *Campeonato Mundial de Fútbol*, Eusebio	★★★½☆
1966 *Campeonato Mundial de Fútbol*, Yashin	★★★½☆
1966 *Campeonato Mundial de Fútbol*, Yashin, England footballers	★★★½☆
1967 *Campeones y Estrellas* (*Seat Cars* advert), Moore	★★★☆☆
1967 *Campeones y Estrellas* (*Seat Cars* advert), Charlton	★★★☆☆
1967 *Campeones y Estrellas* (*Seat Cars* advert), Greaves	★★★☆☆
1970 *Mexico 70* Pelé and English players	★★½☆☆

Cicogna

1945 *Sportsmen* (cellulose cards, Italian coloured flanks)	★★★★☆
1946 *Footballers in Action* (black-&-white frames)	★★★☆☆
1947 *Footballers in Action* (black sides, large golden ball)	★★★☆☆
1948 *Tuttocalcio* (black-&-white chevrons, club colours shields)	★★★☆☆
1949 *Omnia Sports* (tri-colour chevrons)	★★★☆☆
1949 *Omnia Sports* as above, Ireland's Paddy Sloan	★★★☆☆
1949-50 *Tuttocalcio* (five Olympic rings)	★★★☆☆
1950 footballers in strips, perforated intact strip of four	★★★★☆
1950 footballers separated from strips, singles	★★☆☆☆
1950 footballer caricatures with illustrated action (on both sides)	★★☆☆☆
1950 footballer caricatures with illustrated action (on both sides), Piola	★★★☆☆

Cigarillos Londres

1920s Danckleman & Schrader silks, teams	★★★★☆

Cigarillos Plus Ultra

1920s Argentine & Uruguayan footballers	★★★★½

City Bakeries

1950 *Soccards* shield-shaped cards	★★★★☆
1952 *British football teams* shield-shaped cards	★★★☆☆
1952 *British football teams* shield-shaped cards	★★★★½
1978 *World Cup All-Time Greats*	★★★☆☆

Clark's Toffees

1925 *Footballers*	★★★★★

Clarke, Nicholls & Coombs (Clarnico)
1922 *Footballers* ★★★⯨☆

Clarke's
1901 *Football Series*, most ★★★⯨☆
1901 *Football Series*, Smith ★★★★☆
1901 *Football Series*, Bloomer ★★★★☆
1901 *Football Series*, Meredith ★★★★☆
1901 *Cricketer Series*, most ★★★⯨☆
1901 *Cricketer Series*, Fry ★★★★☆

Clevedon Confectionary
1959 *Football Club Managers*, blue or violet ★★★⯨☆
1960 *Hints on Association Football* ★★☆☆☆
1960 *International Sporting Stars* ★★⯨☆☆
1960 *Famous Football Clubs* ★★☆☆☆
1961 *Famous Footballers* ★★⯨☆☆
1962 *Sporting Memories* ★★★⯨☆

Clifford Series
1950 *First Edition Footballers*, cards ★★★☆☆
1950 *First Edition Footballers*, booklet of nine cards ★★★★★

Cloetta
1934 *Sportsmen* ★★⯨☆☆

Clube do Cromo
1974 *Futebol Campeonato Mundial Munique 74* Scots players ★★★⯨☆

Coffer
1970 football postcards ★★⯨☆☆

Cohen Weenen
1897 *Circus Girl Heroes of Sport*, most players ★★★⯨☆
1897 *Circus Girl Heroes of Sportt*, Devey ★★★★☆
1897 *Circus Girl Heroes of Sport*, Smith ★★★★☆
1897 *Circus Girl Heroes of Sport*, Spikesley ★★★★☆
1900 *Sweetcrop Celebrities* ★★★☆☆
1900 *Sweetcrop Celebrities*, Fry ★★★☆☆
1900 *Sweetcrop Celebrities*, Smith ★★★☆☆
1905 *Actresses, Footballers & Jockeys* ★★★★☆
1906 *Owners, Jockeys, Footballers, Cricketers, series 2*, most ★★☆☆☆
1907 *Owners, Jockeys, Footballers, Cricketers, series 3*, most ★★☆☆☆
1908 *Football Captains 1907-8*, most ★★★☆☆
1908 *Football Captains 1907-8*, noted players ★★★☆☆

Colgate Palmolive
1970 *Mexico 70* packet issue footballers, England stars ★★★★☆

Colinville
1958 *International Footer Photos* footballers, most ★★★☆☆
1958 *International Footer Photos* footballers, Greaves ★★★★☆
1958 *International Footer Photos* footballers, Bobby Charlton ★★★★☆
1958 *International Footer Photos*, wrapper ★★★★☆
1958 *International Footer Photoss*, album, complete ★★★★☆

Comet Sweets
1960 *Olympic Achievements* ★☆☆☆☆

Comic Life
1922 *Sports Champions*, paired cards ★★☆☆☆
1922 *Sports Champions*, cut single cards ★☆☆☆☆

Compton's Gravy Salts
1923 *Football Clubs Series A* ★★★☆☆
1923 *Football Clubs Series B* ★★★☆☆
1924 *Football Clubs Series C* ★★★★☆
1924 *Football Clubs Series D* ★★★★☆
1925 *Football Clubs Series E* ★★★☆☆
1926 *Football Clubs Series F* ★★★☆☆
1927 *Football Clubs A* ★★★☆☆
1927 *Football Clubs B* (with 'see other side') ★★★☆☆
1927 *Football Clubs B* ★★★☆☆
1927 *Football Clubs B* (blue ink-stamped back) ★★★☆☆

Co-op (Co-operative Society)
1982 *España 82* uncut strips of cards ★★☆☆☆

Copcards
1980s police force football cards ★⯨☆☆☆

Cope Brothers
1908 *Solace Noted Footballers* ★★★★☆
1908 *Solace Noted Footballers* Meredith ★★★★⯨
1909 *Clips Noted Footballers* (120) ★★★★⯨
1909 *Robert Crompton* insert ★★★★☆
1909 *Robert Crompton* medallion ★★★★⯨
1909 *Football Teams* (postcard-size pictures) ★★★★★
1910 *Clips Noted Footballers* (282) ★★★★⯨
1911 *Clips Noted Footballers* (501) ★★★★⯨
1910 *Clips Noted Footballers* (282) 125 Meredith ★★★★☆
1910 *Clips Noted Footballers* (282) 279 Bloomer ★★★★☆
1910 *Clips Noted Footballers* (500) 125 Meredith ★★★★☆
1910 *Clips Noted Footballers* (500) 279 Bloomer ★★★★☆

Corriera dei Piccoli
1960s Cut-out, stand-up teams of footballers, uncut sheets ★★☆☆☆

Courage
1980s *Know Your Team*, *Sporting Heroes*, *World Cup 82* beer mats ★☆☆☆☆

Crack
1978 *Album de Figuritas El Libro De Los Mundiales Supercoleccion* most ★★★☆☆
1978 *Argentina 78* Diego Maradona ★★★★☆
1979 *Super Futbol*, most ★★★☆☆
1979 *Super Futbol*, Maradona ★★★★☆

Credit cards
1990s bank-issued payment cards with football teams and club badges ★★★⯨☆

THE SOCCER CARDS RARITY SCALE

Cropan
1974 *Asi Juego al futbol Johan Cruyff* ★★☆☆☆
1975 football club emblems on glossy stickers ★★☆☆☆
1975 *Goool! Stickers within sticky frames*, intact stickers ★★★⯨☆
1975 *Goool! Stickers within sticky frames*, intact Cruyff ★★★★★

Crescent Confectionery
1923-25 *The Great Novelty House* footballers ★★★★★
(1926) Limited 1927 *General interest* cards, footballers ★★★★★
(1926) Limited 1930 *Sportsmen* ★★★★★

Crosse & Blackwell
1970 *World Cup Action* uncut cards ★★★☆☆

Cypal International
1977 Liverpool and Manchester United players ★★★☆☆

Daily Citizen
1913 *Football Teams* large paper supplements, free gifts ★★★★⯨

Daily Dispatch
1946 *Scott's Football Stars* cut outs ★★★★☆

Daily Express
1947 *Famous Footballers* cut outs, to be folded & glued ★★★☆☆
1955 *Full Report: Kick-off To Final Whistle* cards ★★★⯨☆
1958 *Always On The Ball Sports Coverage* fold-out cards ★★★⯨☆
1965 *Top Soccer News And Pictures* football teams ★★★⯨☆

Daily Graphic Football Special (The Golden Penny)
1890s-1910s, intact issue ★★★★⯨

Daily Graphic
1948 *Football Stars* and *Goalkeeper Stars* cut out cards ★★★⯨☆
1950 *Star Pictures Of Players* small cut-out cards ★★★⯨☆

Daily Herald
1951 to 1953 *Sports Stars* ("Copyright SPORTFOTO") ★★☆☆☆
1951 to 1953 *Sports Stars* ("Copyright") ★⯨☆☆☆
1951 to 1953 *Sports Stars* ("Sportfoto") ★★★☆☆
1951 to 1953 large *Sports Stars* cards without legends ★★★★☆
1951 to 1953 paper folders with stapled large card inside ★★★★☆
1958 *Pencil Pics* cut-outs ★★☆☆☆

Daily Mail
1934 *Football Teams 1934-5* supplements ★★★★☆
1955 *Sports Parade by Eric Thompson* ★★★★☆
1970 *England's World Cup Footballers* ★★☆☆☆
1971 *Follow The...* [sic] uncut sheet of 22 stickers ★★★☆☆

Daily Mirror
1970 *Mirrorcards* small cards of teams ★☆☆☆☆
1970 *My Club* large cards of teams ★★⯨☆☆

Daily News Football Annual
1924 to 1927 fold-out *Football Supplements* ★★★★☆

Daily Sketch
1970 *World Cup Transfer* decals, uncut sheets ★★★☆☆
1970 *World Cup Transfer* decals, cut singles ★☆☆☆☆
1970 *World Cup Souvenirs* uncut strip of five cards with Pelé ★★★☆☆
1970 *World Cup Souvenirs* uncut strip of five cards ★★⯨☆☆
1970 *World Cup Souvenirs* cut cards ★☆☆☆☆

Daily Star
1980 *Top British Teams* stickers ☆☆☆☆☆

Damm
1974 *Xibeca Sport* World Cup '74 stickers (folded) Johan Cruyff ★★★☆☆
1974 *Xibeca Sport* World Cup '74 stickers (folded) Scotland ★★★☆☆

Dandy Gum
1970 *Football Club Series* cards of club colours, British Isles clubs ★⯨☆☆☆

Danone
1982 *Daddies Football Greats* ★★☆☆☆

Davit
1930s footballers and teams, most ★★★☆☆
1930s footballers and teams, noted great players ★★★⯨☆

De Beukelaer
1932 *All Sports* players, most ★☆☆☆☆
1932 *All Sports* players, Gallagher [sic] ★★☆☆☆
1932 *All Sports* players, Dean ★★★☆☆

De Haas Van Brero
1949 to 1951 *Goal Voetbal Campioenen Leo Pagano*, British teams ★★★☆☆

De Jonge
1959 *Sportbilder*, players ★★★⯨☆
1959 *Sportbilder*, Nottingham Forest ★★★★☆

Devlin
1952 *Famous Footballers New Series* untrimmed cards ★★★☆☆
1953 to 1955 *Famous Footballers A1, A2 and A3* untrimmed cards ★★⯨☆☆
1950s cards, as above, with trimmed sides ★★☆☆☆

Dickson Orde
1960 *Footballers*, set of 50 cards ★☆☆☆☆

Di Dasco
1950 to 1951 *Albosport* perforated stickers, most ★★★☆☆
1950 to 1951 *Albosport* perforated stickers, British stars ★★★★☆

Dipul
1971 *Campeóes Europeus de Futebol 1970/71*, most ★★★☆☆
1971 *Campeóes Europeus de Futebol 1970/71*, British players ★★★⯨☆

Doctor Storm's Winter Drops
1920s Bolton Wanderers players ★★★★☆

Dolcificio Lombardo (Perfetti)
1950s, b/w photo cards of footballers ★★★⯨☆

1967 *Pop, film & sports*, most	★★★☆☆
1967 *Pop, film & sports*, British players	★★★☆☆
1967 as above, Pelé	★★★☆☆
1967 as above, Beckenbauer	★★★☆☆
1967 as above, Eusebio	★★★☆☆

Domani d'Italia

1931 *Campionato Foot-Ball 1931-1932*, most	★★★★☆
1931 *Campionato Foot-Ball 1931-1932*, Meazza	★★★★½
1932 *Campionato Foot-Ball 1931-1932*, most	★★★★☆
1932 *Campionato Foot-Ball 1931-1932*, Meazza	★★★★½

Domus

1937 *Giocatori* caricatures by *Carlin & Unica*	★★★★☆

Donald

1966 *Campeonato Mundial 1966*, England football stadia, pairs	★★★★★
1966 *Campeonato Mundial 1966*, England football stars	★★★★★
1966 *Campeonato Mundial 1966*, complete album	★★★★★

Donaldson

1946 *Sports Favourites*, large heads I on waste or Xmas cards	★★★★☆
1946 *Sports Favourites*, large heads II no name/address to back	★★★☆☆
1947 *Sports Favourites*, large heads III name/address but no copyright	★★★☆☆
1947 *Sports Favourites*, large heads IV name/address and copyright	★★★☆☆
1948 *Sports Favourites*, small heads types I & II no copyright	★★★☆☆
1949 *Sports Favourites*, small heads types III thru XI copyright	★★★☆☆
1949 *Sports Favourites*, postcards	★★★★☆
1950 *Sports Favourites*, small heads, numbers over 502	★★★★½
1950 *Sports Favourites*, *Golden Series* numbers 1 to 32	★★★★☆
1951 *Sports Favourites*, *Golden Series* numbers 33 to 64	★★★★½
1954 *Gold Cups* die-cut cup-shaped cards	★★★★½

Donaldson Rogue cards

1947 (actually Kiddy's Favourites *1st Series*)	★★★★☆

Donaldson

1967 *Celtic European Cup Winners* uncut sheet	★★★★½
1968 *Unissued Card drawn by John Barr by R.T. Muat*: Hurst, Law, Charlton, etc.	★★★★☆
1980s Art cards of rare Donaldsons by R.T. Muat, b/w	★★★☆☆
1980s Art cards of rare Donaldsons by R.T. Muat, coloured by the artist	★★★★☆

Dubreq

1977 Top Trumps boxed gaming cards, set	★★☆☆☆
1977 Top Trumps boxed gaming cards, team sets with badge	★★★☆☆
1980 Top Trumps boxed gaming cards, team sets with badge, updated	★★★☆☆

Dunkin

1969 *¿Cual es su nombre?* waxy paper gum inserts	★★★★☆
1969 *¿Cual es su nombre?* waxy paper gum inserts, Pelé	★★★★★
1969 *¿Cual es su nombre?* waxy paper gum inserts, Di Stefano, Kubala, Ali, each	★★★★☆
1973 *Kubala te Enseña a Jugar*, most	★★½☆☆
1973 *Kubala te Enseña a Jugar*, Moore, Charlton, Cruyff, Eusebio all	★★★☆☆

Dura

1968 *Deportes* stickers, most	★★★☆☆
1968 *Deportes* stickers, unused Bobby Charlton	★★★★☆

Eagle Swift

1963 *Eagle Swift Soccer Stars*, uncut strips of four	★★★☆☆
1963 *Eagle Swift Soccer Stars*, cut singles	★☆☆☆☆

EDI

1962 *Calciocampioni*, plain back	★★★☆☆
1962 *Calciocampioni*, Greaves	★★★★☆
1962 *Calciocampioni*, Law	★★★★☆
1962 *Calciocampioni*, Pelé	★★★★☆
1962 *Calciocampioni* logo & title to back,	★★★★☆
1962 *Calciocampioni* logo & title to back, Sivori	★★★★☆
1962 *Calciocampioni* logo & title to back, Rivera	★★★★☆
1962 *Calciocampioni* logo & title to back, Pelé	★★★★☆
1962 *Calciocampioni* logo & title to back, Baker	★★★★☆
1962 *Calciocampioni* logo & title to back, Charles	★★★★☆
1962 *Calciocampioni* biography back with a large red spot, as above, all	★★★★☆
1962 *Calciocampioni* biography back without a large red spot, as above, all	★★★★☆

Edições 7 Cores

1974 reprints of Aquarela, uncut sheet of Aquarela 1958 stickers	★★★★☆
1974 reprints of Aquarela, Pelé	★★★★☆
1974 reprints of Aquarela, album of Aquarela reprints	★★★★☆

Ediguia

1974 *Munique 74*, most cards	★★★☆☆
1974 *Munique 74*, Law	★★★★☆
1974 *Munique 74*, Dalglish	★★★☆☆

Ediraf

1974 *Calcio 74*, most	★★☆☆☆
1974 *Calcio 74*, Pelé	★★★☆☆
1974 *Calcio 74*, Cruyff	★★★☆☆
1974 *Calcio 74*, Beckenbauer	★★★☆☆
1974 *Calcio 74*, Scottish players	★★★☆☆
1974 *Calcio 74*, club and country emblems in self-adhesive silk	★★★★☆

Edis

1969 *Calciatori 1969/70 - Mexico 70*, Eusebio	★★★★☆
1969 *Calciatori 1969/70 - Mexico 70*, Pelé	★★★★☆
1969 *Calciatori 1969/70 - Mexico 70*, Best	★★★★☆

1969 *Calciatori 1969/70* note: modern-day copies of the above cards exist, and have been slabbed!

Edito Service

1978 *Sportscaster* archive cards in English	★☆☆☆☆
1978 *Sportscaster* archive cards in French	★★☆☆☆
1978 *Sportscaster* archive cards in Italian	★★★☆☆
1978 *Sportscaster* archive cards in Nordic languages	★★★★☆
1978 *Sportscaster* archive cards in Serbo-Croat language	★★★☆☆

THE SOCCER CARDS RARITY SCALE

1975 *Euro-Soccer*, complete album	★☆☆☆☆
1975 *Euro-Soccer*, postally used postcards from 1975 with soccer-themed cancels to stamps	★★★★½
1975 *Euro-Soccer*, unopened packet	★★★☆☆
1975 *Euro-Soccer*, open packet	★★☆☆☆
1975 team postcards from Spain, France & Benelux (British teams, different backs in each country)	★★★☆☆
1976 *Soccer Stars '76'77*, unused stickers	★★☆☆☆
1976 *Soccer Stars '76'77*, complete album	★★☆☆☆
1976 *Soccer Stars '76'77*, unused Dalglish (twin sticker)	★★★☆☆
1977 *Soccer Stars '76'77*, unused stickers	★★½☆☆
1977 *Soccer Stars '76'77*, unused Cruyff	★★★☆☆
1977 *Soccer Stars '76'77*, complete album	★★★☆☆
1977 *Soccer Stars* (cards game, boxed) backs with football, blue	★★☆☆☆
1977 *Soccer Stars Series One* (cards game, boxed)	★★☆☆☆
1977 *Soccer Stars Series Two* (cards game, boxed)	★★☆☆☆
1978 *Soccer Stars 1977-78*, unused stickers	★☆☆☆☆
1978 *Soccer Stars 1977-78*, complete album	★★☆☆☆
1978 *Argentina 78*, unused stickers	★½☆☆☆
1978 *Argentina 78*, empty packet	★★☆☆☆
1978 *Argentina 78*, sealed packet	★★★☆☆
1978 *Argentina 78*, complete album	★☆☆☆☆

1978 Argentina 78 note: stickers from Argentina, Portugal & Germany have differences & are rarer. ★★★☆☆

1978 *Soccer Stars 78-79 Golden Collection*, unused stickers	★★½☆☆
1978 *Soccer Stars 78-79 Golden Collection*, empty packet	★★☆☆☆
1978 *Soccer Stars 78-79 Golden Collection*, sealed packet	★★★☆☆
1978 *Soccer Stars 78-79 Golden Collection*, complete album	★★½☆☆
1978 *Football League 1st Division 1978-79*, metal coins	★★★★☆
1979 *Soccer Stars 80*, unused stickers	★★★☆☆
1979 *Soccer Stars 80*, empty packet	★★★☆☆
1979 *Soccer Stars 80*, sealed packet	★★★★☆
1979 *Soccer Stars 80*, full album	★★★☆☆
1980 *Soccer 81*, unused stickers	★★★☆☆

note: glue fails with time, backing papers come off.

1980 *Soccer 81*, American Major League Soccer unused stickers Best, Cruyff, etc.	★★★☆☆
1981 *World Cup Special*, unused stickers	★★★☆☆

note: glue fails with time, papers come off.

1981 as above, Maradona	★★★☆☆
1981 *World Cup Special*, empty packet	★★☆☆☆
1981 *World Cup Special*, sealed packet	★★★☆☆
1981 *World Cup Special*, full album	★★★☆☆
1981 *Soccer 82*, unused stickers	★★★☆☆

note: glue fails with time, backing papers come off.

1981 *Soccer 82*, full album	★★★☆☆
1982 *Soccer 82*, unused stickers	★★★☆☆

note: glue fails with time, backing papers come off.

1982 as above, Maradona	★★★☆☆
1982 as above, empty packet	★★☆☆☆
1982 as above, sealed packet	★★★☆☆
1982 as above, full album	★★★☆☆

note: the Spanish *Spain 82*, by Fher, had cards not paper stickers.

1982 Spanish, as above, unused	★★★☆☆
1982 Spanish, as above, unused Maradona	★★★★☆
as Quadriga 1983 *Laws Of Soccer*, stickers	★★★☆☆
as Quadriga 1983 *Laws Of Soccer*, complete album	★★★★☆
as Quadriga 1983 *Soccer Stars 83-84*, unused stickers	★★★☆☆
as Quadriga 1983 *Laws Of Soccer*, complete album	★★★★☆

Flash (Lampo)

1977 *Calcio Lampo 1977-1978*, most unused stickers	★★★☆☆
1977 *Calcio Lampo 1977-1978*, Rossi	★★★☆☆
1977 *Calcio Lampo 1977-1978*, Zoff	★★★☆☆
1978 *Mondiali Argentina 78*, most	★★☆☆☆
1978 *Mondiali Argentina 78*, unused Scots players	★★☆☆☆
1978 *Mondiali Argentina 78*, unused Dalglish	★★★☆☆
1979 *Calcio Internazionale 79*, most	★☆☆☆☆
1979 *Calcio Internazionale 79*, unused Liverpool players	★★★☆☆
1980s stickers of British and Irish players, various series	★★½☆☆
1980s stickers, various collections: 1982 Maradona	★★★☆☆
1980s stickers, various collections: 1986 Maradona	★★☆☆☆

Fleetway

1959 *Tiger Football Teams 1958/59*, uncut sheet four teams	★★★☆☆
1959 *Tiger Football Teams 1958/59*, uncut pair	★★☆☆☆
1959 *Tiger Football Teams 1958/59*, singles	★☆☆☆☆
1959 *Tiger Football Teams 1959/60*, uncut sheet four teams	★★★☆☆
1959 *Tiger Football Teams 1959/60*, uncut pair	★★☆☆☆
1959 *Tiger Football Teams 1959/60*, singles	★☆☆☆☆
1925 FA Cup Final postcards (West Ham, Bolton Wanderers)	★★★☆☆

FM Brand Foods

1926 *Welsh Sportsmen*, rugby players	★★★★½
1926 *Welsh Sportsmen*, soccer players	★★★★☆

Folgore (Fol-Bo)

1970 *Mexico 70 - Sempre Forza Italia*, unused stickers	★★★☆☆
1970 *Mexico 70 - Sempre Forza Italia*, unused metallic stickers	★★★★½

Football & Sports Favourite (Sports Fun)

1922 *Photo Stamps*, small stickers	★★★☆☆
1922 *Photo Stamps*, large stickers	★★★☆☆
1922 *Photo Stamps*, large stickers, Woosnam	★★★☆☆
1922 *Photo Stamps*, sheets of 12 small stickers	★★★★½
1922 *Photo Stamps*, uncut triples of three large stickers	★★★★☆

Football & Sports Favourite

1924 *Football Moves & Transfers*	★★★☆☆
1927 *Straight From The Stars*	★★★☆☆

Football Favourite

1910 *Players in Their Club Colours* (a.k.a. Liverpool Weekly Courier)	★★★★½
1923 *Football Favourite & Football Special Our Football Boys* postcards	★★★☆☆

Football Favourites

1950s *Art Plates Grand Pictures Your Favourite Soccer Stars*, uncut sheet	★★★★☆
1950s *Art Plates Grand Pictures Your Favourite Soccer Stars*, cut singles	★★☆☆☆

Football Pictorial & Football Supporter
1969 to 1974 *Super Strikers*, uncut page	★★☆☆☆
1969 to 1974 *Pennants*, uncut pennant	★★☆☆☆
1969 to 1974 *Team Set*, uncut page	★★☆☆☆

Football Post
1904 *Our Series of Popular Footballers*	★★★★★

Football Snaps (unknown issuer)
1948 *Football Snaps*, paper stickers (numbers 1-24)	★★★☆☆
1948 *Football Snaps*, paper stickers (numbers 1-24), packet	★★★☆☆
1948 *Football Snaps*, paper stickers (numbers 25-48)	★★★⯪☆

Football Star
1973 *All-Britain Team*, stand-up cards, uncut sheet of six	★★★⯪☆
1973 *All-Britain Team*, stand-up cards, magazine	★★★⯪☆
1973 *All-Britain Team*, stand-up cards, single cut card and stand	★★☆☆☆
1973 *Super Strikers*, hexagonal cut-out stickers,	★★★☆☆

Football Supporter
1969 *Portraits by Rex Benlow*	★★☆☆☆

Formaggino Mio Locatelli
1965 *Serie Campioni di Calcio 1965-66*, card with a pair of players	★★☆☆☆

Foto Calcio
1965 *Calciatori 1965-1966*, most	★★☆☆☆
1965 *Calciatori 1965-1966*, Gerry Hitchens	★★☆☆☆

Fotopropaganda
1950 *Rotalfoto*	★★★★☆

Frame
1948 *Sport Stars*, cards	★★★★☆
1948 *Sport Stars*, booklet of cards	★★★★★
1950 *Sport Aces*, cards	★★★★☆
1948 Sport Stars, booklet of cards	★★★★★
1951 *Smashers Sport Photos*, cards	★★☆☆☆
1951 *Smashers Sport Photos*, reissued cards (different text matrix)	★★☆☆☆

Franklyn & Davey
1906 *Loadstone Football Club Colours*, most	★★☆☆☆
1906 *Loadstone Football Club Colours*, Bloomer	★★☆☆☆

Freeman Manikin Cigars
1969 *£10,000 Football Challenge*, uncut trios	★★★☆☆
1969 *£10,000 Football Challenge*, singles	★☆☆☆☆

Fullers
1974 *Scottish World Cup Squad Munich 1974*, transfer decals	★★★★⯪

Fun Products
1982 *England's World Cup Squad*, stickers (bronze plaque nameplates)	★★☆☆☆

Gabardine Detrás De La Universidad
1950 *Mundial 50*, World Cup teams	★★★★⯪

Gabriel
1902 *Cricketers*, most	★★★☆☆
1902 *Cricketers*, Fry	★★★★⯪

Gaceta del Norte
1974 *Mundiales 74*, teams	★★★☆☆

Galbani
1965 *Gli Eroi Della Domenica*, card	★★★☆☆
1965 *Gli Eroi Della Domenica*, Greaves	★★★☆☆
1965 *Gli Eroi Della Domenica*, Law	★★★☆☆
1965 *Gli Eroi Della Domenica*, Baker	★★★☆☆
1965 *Gli Eroi Della Domenica*, Eusebio	★★★☆☆
1965 *Gli Eroi Della Domenica*, Yashin	★★★☆☆
1965 *Gli Eroi Della Domenica*, Pelé	★★★☆☆

Gallaher
1910 *Association Football Club Colours*	★⯪☆☆☆
1924 *British Champions of 1923*, soccer cards	★☆☆☆☆
1925 *Famous Footballers*, with green backs	★☆☆☆☆
1926 *Famous Footballers*, with brown backs	★☆☆☆☆
1927 *Footballers In Action*, with blue backs	★☆☆☆☆
1928 *Footballers*, with red backs	★☆☆☆☆

Gallaher images on Teasdale cards (see Teasdale)
	★★★☆☆
1934 *Park Drive Champions*, soccer players with names to the front	★☆☆☆☆
1934 *Park Drive Champions*, soccer players without names to the front	★☆☆☆☆
1936 *Sporting Personalities*, footballers	★☆☆☆☆

Gallina Blanca
1940s teams and players in uncut pairs	★★★☆☆

Garbaty
1931 *Kurmark Sportwappen – Fussball 645*, unused cards	★★★☆☆
1931 *Kurmark Sportwappen – Fussball 645*, full album	★★★☆☆

Gartman
1930s *Sportbilder sportserien 1-15*	★★☆☆☆

Gazzetta dello Sport
1934 postcard-style trade cards players, most	★★★☆☆
1934 postcard-style trade cards players, Ferrari	★★★★☆
1934 postcard-style trade cards players, Meazza	★★★★☆
1978 *Argentina 78 Copa Mundial*, uncut sheet	★★⯪☆☆
1978 *Argentina 78 Copa Mundial*, Scottish stars	★★☆☆☆

Gem
1922 *Special Action Photos*, most	★☆☆☆☆
1922 *Special Action Photos*, Max Woosnam	★⯪☆☆☆
1922 *Footballers*, uncut pairs	★★☆☆☆
1922 *Footballers*, cut singles	⯪☆☆☆☆
1922 *Autographed Real Action Photo Series*	★☆☆☆☆
1926 *Footer Puzzle*, uncut sheet with 16 players	★★★★⯪
1933 *The Year's Sport*, full album	★★★★☆
1933 *The Year's Sport*, uncut sheet	★★★★★
1933 *The Year's Sport*, cut singles	★★★☆☆
1933 *The Year's Sport*, Dean	★★★★⯪

THE SOCCER CARDS RARITY SCALE

Gente
1970 *Mexico 70*, cut singles — ★⯪☆☆☆
1970 *Mexico 70*, England stars — ★★☆☆☆
1970 *Mexico 70*, uncut sheet — ★★☆☆☆

Gilda
1978 Mintina *World Championship* stickers, most — ★★⯪☆☆
1978 Mintina *World Championship* stickers, Cruyff — ★★★☆☆

Gines Hellin Abelian
1946 *Album Chicote* — ★★☆☆☆
1946 *Gainza* — ★★★☆☆

Giornalino
1970s to 1990s cards, cut singles — ★★☆☆☆
1970s to 1990s cards, uncut sheets — ★★★☆☆

Glasgow Weekly Mail
1913 *Famous Footballers*, sheet of nine players — ★★★★★
1913 *Famous Footballers*, cut singles — ★★★☆☆
1910s colour supplements of footballers — ★★★★★

Globo Gum
1937 *Les As du Football*, most — ★★★☆☆
1937 *Les As du Football*, Hiden — ★★★⯪☆
1937 *Les As du Football*, Diagne — ★★★★☆
1938 *Champions Tous Sports*, most — ★★★☆☆
1938 *Champions Tous Sports*, Joe Louis — ★★★★☆
1939 *Footballers*, in a postcard format, most — ★★★☆☆
1951 *Equipes Et Scenes Du Foot* — ★★★☆☆
1952 *Footballers* — ★★★☆☆

Goal Crisps
1971 *Steve Heighway All Star Series* — ★★★☆☆

Goal Magazine
1969 *Goal Gallery of World Stars* — ★★⯪☆☆

Golden Wonder
1978 *Soccer World Cup All Stars*, most — ⯪☆☆☆☆
1978 *Soccer World Cup All Stars*, unopened in plastic wrapper — ★★☆☆☆
1978 *Soccer All Stars*, most — ⯪☆☆☆☆
1978 *Soccer All Stars*, unopened in plastic wrapper — ★★☆☆☆
1979 *Sporting All Stars*, most — ⯪☆☆☆☆
1979 *Sporting All Stars*, unopened in plastic wrapper — ★★☆☆☆

Goodies
1974 World Cup 2 to 3, uncut sheet — ★★★★☆

Green Shield
1934 footballers on shield-shaped cards (similar to Baines) — ★★★★⯪

Greiling
1926 *Fussballsport* and *Fussballmomente* British Isles soccer stars & teams — ★★★★⯪

Grimsby Evening Telegraph
1952 *Town Stars* — ★★★☆☆

Groothoff
1933 *Voetbal Techniek en Tactiek*, British-related scenes and players — ★★☆☆☆

Guardian Journal
1969 *Two In Gear* — ★★★☆☆

Guara
1950s *Cartela Campeoes Mundiais Futebol*, complete team of discs on uncut folder — ★★★★★
1950s *Cartela Campeoes Mundiais Futebol*, single cut discs of Brazil's stars — ★★★★☆
1950s *Cartela Campeoes Mundiais Futebol*, single cut discs, Pelé — ★★★★⯪

Heijn
1972 *Sport en Spel*, uncut with to-cut borders, most — ★★★⯪☆
1972 *Sport en Spel*, uncut with to-cut borders, uncut with borders Cruyff — ★★★★☆

Heinerle & Keystone
1960 *Die Kleine Regelecke*, Brazil team, Puskás, di Stefano, Vava, each — ★★★☆☆
1960 *Die Kleine Regelecke*, Stevens, Wright, Man Utd team, each — ★★☆☆☆
1960 *Die Kleine Regelecke*, Yashin — ★★★⯪☆
1960 *Die Kleine Regelecke*, Pelé — ★★★⯪☆

Heinerle & Carl Schütt
1959/60 *Beliebte Sportler* (two weightlifters back) Brazil and Man Utd, each — ★★★⯪☆
1959/60 as above, England, Puskás, di Stefano, Wolves each — ★★★★☆
1959/60 as above, Didi mistaken for Pelé (*wündersturmer*) — ★★★⯪☆

Heinerle
1961 *Footballers & Teams* (3/4 figures on back) Pelé — ★★★☆☆
1961 *Footballers & Teams* (3/4 figures on back) British subjects — ★★★☆☆
1961 *Footballers & Teams* (3/4 figures on back) Kubala — ★★★☆☆
1961 as above, Gento, Suarez, Didi mistaken for Pelé (*göttliche*), Puskás, each — ★★★☆☆

Heinerle & Lutter
1962 Football cards (3/4 figures *Weltklassespieler*, etc. on rear) Pelé — ★★★★☆
1962, as above, Gento, di Stefano, Suarez, Barcelona each — ★★★★⯪

Heinerle
1962 *International Footballers & teams*, Pelé — ★★⯪☆☆
1962 *International Footballers & teams*, British Isles players each — ★★⯪☆☆

Helvetia
1920s *Cioccolato Sport-Regalo*, most — ★★★★⯪
1920s *Cioccolato Sport-Regalo*, footballers — ★★★★★

Hignett
1933 *A.F.C. Nicknames* — ★★⯪☆☆
1935 *Football Caricatures* — ★★☆☆☆
1936 *Football Club Captains* — ★★☆☆☆

Hill
1906 *Football Captains Series* — ★★★★☆
1912 Nyasa-brand, *Famous Footballers* — ★★⯪☆☆

1912 Nyasa-brand, *Famous Footballers*, Meredith	★★★☆☆
1923 Sunripe-brand, *Famous Footballers*	★★☆☆☆
1934 *Sports* (*Sports* back) football subjects	★⯪☆☆☆
1934 *Sports* (*Sports Series* back) football subjects	★★⯪☆☆
1934 *Sports* (untitled back) football subjects	★★⯪☆☆
1935 Gold Flake Honeydew Navy Cut-brands, *Popular Footballers*, most	★⯪☆☆☆
1935 Gold Flake Honeydew Navy Cut-brands, Matthews	★★☆☆☆
1938 *Famous Footballers*, numbers 1 to 50 (*Shoreditch* back) most	★☆☆☆☆
1938 *Famous Footballers*, numbers 1 to 50 (*Shoreditch* back) Matthews	★★☆☆☆
1938 *Famous Footballers*, numbers 1 to 50 (*Hy.Archer* back) most	★★☆☆☆
1938 *Famous Footballers*, numbers 1 to 50 (*Hy.Archer* back) Matthews	★★★☆☆
1939 *Famous Footballers*, numbers 51 to 75	★★☆☆☆
1939 *Celebrities of Sport* (*Hill London E1* back) most	★⯪☆☆☆
1939 *Celebrities of Sport* (*Hill London E1* back) Matthews	★★☆☆☆
1939 *Celebrities of Sport* (*Gold Flake* back) most	★★☆☆☆
1939 *Celebrities of Sport* (*Gold Flake* back) Perry	★★☆☆☆
1939 *Celebrities of Sport* (*Gold Flake* back) Cullis	★★☆☆☆
1939 *Celebrities of Sport* (*Gold Flake* back) Matthews	★★★☆☆

Hitschler

1970 *Mexico 70*, most £10, world stars and England players	★★★⯪☆
Holy Head Football Rock 1920s *Football Teams*	★★★★★

Holmar

1950s *Sportsmen*	★★★☆☆

Hunter Tobacco

1900 *Footballers*	★★★★★

Hurricane

1960s *Footballers of 1964*, stickers, intact sheet	★★★☆☆
1960s *Footballers of 1964*, stickers, single stickers	★☆☆☆☆

Hobbies of Dereham

1956 *Hobbies & Handicrafts Sportsmen*, decals, uncut sheet	★★★★⯪
1956 *Hobbies & Handicrafts Sportsmen*, decals, single	★★★☆☆

Hornet

1964 *International Cup Teams*, uncut sheet of four cards	★★★☆☆
1964 *International Cup Teams*, cut singles	★☆☆☆☆
1965 *Top Players*, uncut intact	★★☆☆☆
1965 *Top Players*, cut singles	★☆☆☆☆
1965 *Teams of Today and Yesterday*, folded colour supplements, uncut	★★⯪☆☆
1965 *Teams of Today and Yesterday*, folded colour supplements, cut singles	★☆☆☆☆
1966 *Top Cup Teams*, uncut sheets of four cards	★★★☆☆
1966 *Top Cup Teams*, cut singles	⯪☆☆☆☆
1967 *Gallery Of Sport*, folding supplements, uncut intact	★★★☆☆
1967 *Gallery Of Sport*, folding supplements, cut singles	⯪☆☆☆☆
1968 *Bernard Briggs Football 68 stickers*, full album	★⯪☆☆☆
1968 *Bernard Briggs Football 68 stickers*, uncut sheet	★★★☆☆
1968 *Bernard Briggs Football 68 stickers*, cut singles	⯪☆☆☆☆

Hornet & Hotspur

1970 *World Cup Stars*, uncut sheets of eight or ten cards	★★⯪☆☆

Hornet

1972 *The All-Star Ring*, plastic ring & stickers, uncut sheet of stickers	★★★★★
1972 The All-Star Ring plastic ring & stickers, cut singles	★★★☆☆

Horsley's

1960s *Football Clubs and Badges*	★★☆☆☆

Hotspur

1965 *Stand-up Footballers*, uncut sheets of five	★★★⯪☆
1965 *Stand-up Footballers*, cut singles with name cards	★★☆☆☆
1975 *Super Stand-up Stoppers and Strikers*, uncut sheets of 12	★★★☆☆
1975 *Super Stand-up Stoppers and Strikers*, singles	★⯪☆☆☆

Idamar

1962 *Coisas Nossas No.1*, Football stickers of Pelé (two different) and Brazil players	★★★★☆

Ideas magazine

1908 to 1910 football teams postcards	★★★★☆

Ilsa

1930s *Album Sportovců* (three collections known) legendary sports stars	★★★⯪☆
1930s *Album Sportovců*, as above, Dixie Dean	★★★★☆

1930s note: fake, modern copies of the cards are known, some have been slabbed!

Imeson's Boots

1890s *The Boot People Of The North*, football cards	★★★★★

Imperia Caramelle

1933 *Sport*, most	★★★★⯪
1933 *Sport*, bigger names in all sports	★★★★★
1934 *Sport 2*, most	★★★★⯪
1934 *Sport 2*, bigger names in all sports	★★★★★

Imperia

Calcio 1963-64, most	★★★⯪☆
Calcio 1963-64, Pelé	★★★★☆

Indiana-Sport

1930s sports stars by Dupont, most	★★★⯪☆
1930s sports stars by Dupont, all-time greats	★★★★☆

Ivlas

1936 *Raccolta Premio*, most	★★★★☆
1936 *Raccolta Premio*, Ferrari	★★★★⯪
1936 *Raccolta Premio*, Meazza	★★★★⯪
1937 *Concorso dell'Avvenire*, most	★★★★☆
1937 *Concorso dell'Avvenire*, Ferrari	★★★★⯪
1937 *Concorso dell'Avvenire*, Meazza	★★★★⯪

Jackdaw

1969 to 1971 monotone cards of famous footballers	★☆☆☆☆
1969 to 1971 a complete portfolio with cards and ephemera	★★★☆☆

Jag

1968 *Soccer'68 All The Club Colours*, paper fold-out	★★⯪☆☆
1968 to 1969 packet-issue cut-out cards, uncut comics	★★★★☆
1968 to 1969 packet-issue cut-out cards, cut singles	★★★☆☆

THE SOCCER CARDS RARITY SCALE

Jardinière Chicory	
1930s famous sportsmen	★★★½☆
Jay Dees	
1979 to 1983 *The Cornish Match Company*, football clubs	★☆☆☆☆
Jean's Fussball by Ali Erzeugnisse	
1976 to 1978 *Wappen*, silk stickers of club emblems	★★½☆☆
J♦B	
1934 footballers	★★★★½
Junior Pastimes	
1950 *Popular English Players*, most	★★☆☆☆
1950 *Popular English Players*, with variations in card or design	★★★½☆
1951 *Popular Players*, most	★★☆☆☆
1951 *Popular Players*, rarer types & variations in card or design	★★★½☆
Junior Pastimes cards with overprints by a rival brand, Kiddy's	★★★★☆
Jugoslavija	
Yugoslavian issues of the 1950s and 1960s British players	★★★★½
Yugoslavian issues of the 1950s and 1960s, Didi as Pelé	★★★½☆
Juwo-Vereinigung	
1962 *Fussball–Football–1962*, most	★★★☆☆
1962 *Fussball–Football–1962*, Fontaine & di Stefano	★★★★☆
1962 *Fussball–Football–1962*, Pelé	★★★★☆
Kane Products	
1956 *Football Clubs and Colours*	★☆☆☆☆
Kauvit	
1954 *Deutsche Nationalfussball & WM'54*, most	★★½☆☆
1954 *Deutsche Nationalfussball & WM'54*, Puskás	★☆☆☆☆
Keisa	
1970s *Campeones Del Deporte Mundial*, most	★★½☆☆
1970s *Campeones Del Deporte Mundial*, Chris Evert	★★★★☆
1970s *Campeones Del Deporte Mundial*, Cruyff	★★★½☆
Kellogg's	
1961 *International Soccer Stars*, most	★½☆☆☆
1961 *International Soccer Stars*, Charlton	★★☆☆☆
1961 *International Soccer Stars*, complete folder	★★★☆☆
1973 *International Soccer Tips*	★½☆☆☆
Kenner	
1989 *Sportstars*, cards	★★★☆☆
1989 *Sportstars*, cards, mint & boxed toys with cards	★★★½☆
Kentalong	
1978 *Football Card Game*, most cards, each	★½☆☆☆
1978 *Football Card Game*, boxed game as new	★★☆☆☆
Kiddy	
1954 Fussball Weltmeisterschaft 1954 Finney, Matthews, Wright, Puskás	★★★★☆

Kiddy's Favourites	
1947 unbranded (a.k.a. *rogue Donaldson*) *Sports Favourites* 1 to 52	★★★★☆
1948 unbranded Football Stars (black stars) #53 to #120	★★★★½
1948 unbranded Football Stars (red stars) #53 to #120	★★★★☆
1948 *Popular Footballers*, 1st edition, on thick, glossy white card	★★★★☆
1948 *Popular Footballers*, 2nd edition on thin, grey card	★☆☆☆☆
1948 *Popular Footballers*, with reverse b/w images to rear	★★★★★
1948 *Popular Players* (with shamrocks) most	★★☆☆☆
1948 *Popular Players* (with shamrocks) card #44	★★★☆☆
1949 *Popular Players* (red hearts)	★★☆☆☆
1949 miniature unbranded *Popular Players* (red hearts)	★★★★½
1951 Junior Pastimes football cards overprinted by Kiddy's Favourites	★★★★☆
KHA	
1955 cards may be fakes, with an applied rubber stamp legend to the rear. *Caveat emptor!*	
King Chewing Gum	
1955 *Footballers*	★★★☆☆
1957 Football Teams	★★★☆☆
1960s postcard-size football player cards	★★★☆☆
Knorr	
1954 *Siege Rekorde Sensationen*, Joe Louis	★★★☆☆
1954 *Siege Rekorde Sensationen*, British footballers	★★☆☆☆
1966 World Cup cards, most	★½☆☆☆
1966 World Cup cards, Franz Beckenbauer	★★☆☆☆
Kunold	
1962 *Fussballsterren*, postcard-size cards, plain back, b/w photos & colour borders, most	★★★☆☆
962 *Fussballsterren*, postcard-size cards, plain back, b/w photos & colour borders, Pelé	★★★★☆
1966 FussballWM 1966, b/w postcards with red stripe atop, England players	★★★☆☆
1966 FussballWM 1966, b/w postcards with red stripe atop, Pelé	★★★☆☆
1966 FussballWM 1966, b/w postcards with red stripe atop, Yashin	★★★☆☆
1966 *Fussball Weltmeisterschaft 1966*, cards, most	★★★½☆
1966 *Fussball Weltmeisterschaft 1966*, cards, England	★★★☆☆
1966 *Fussball Weltmeisterschaft 1966*, cards, Eusebio	★★★☆☆
1966 *Fussball Weltmeisterschaft 1966*, cards, Pelé	★★★☆☆
Lacey's Chewing Wax	
1924 to 1925 footballers	★★★★½
Lacey's Chewing Wax & Gum	
1925 to 1926 footballers	★★★★½
Lacey's, as above, Syd Puddefoot variety	★★★★★
Lacey's, as above, Jack Swann variety	★★★★★
Lacey's, as above, Charles Buchan variety	★★★★★
Ladbroke	
1975 Panama *Spot-Ball* folding cards with two parts, pairs	★★★☆☆
1975 Panama *Spot-Ball* folding cards with two parts, singles	★★★☆☆

Lambert & Butler

1927 *Who's Who in Sport (1926)*, most	★☆☆☆☆
1927 *Who's Who in Sport (1926)*, football teams	★★☆☆☆
1927 *Who's Who in Sport (1926)*, unbranded cards by BAT, most	★☆☆☆☆
1927 *Who's Who in Sport (1926)*, unbranded cards by BAT, football	★★☆☆☆
1931 *Footballers 1930-1*	★⯨☆☆☆

Lamberts of Norwich

1958 *Football Clubs and Badges*	★☆☆☆☆

Lampo as Vecchi

1953 *Sport Magico*, 3-D stickers	★★★☆☆
1953 *Sport Magico*, 3-D booklet-cards	★★★☆☆

Lampo

1958 *Calciatori*, Tony Marchi	★★★☆☆
1958 *Calciatori*, John Charles	★★★☆☆
1961 *Albo Figurine del Campionato di Calcio*, Charles	★★★☆☆
1961 *Albo Figurine del Campionato di Calcio*, Law	★★★☆☆
1961 *Albo Figurine del Campionato di Calcio*, Baker	★★★☆☆
1961 *Albo Figurine del Campionato di Calcio*, Pelé	★★★★☆
1961 *Albo Figurine del Campionato di Calcio*, di Stefano	★★☆☆☆
1961 *Albo Figurine del Campionato di Calcio*, Puskás	★★☆☆☆
1961 *Albo Figurine del Campionato di Calcio*, Kubala	★★☆☆☆
1961 *Albo Figurine del Campionato di Calcio*, Fontaine	★★☆☆☆
1961 *Albo Figurine del Campionato di Calcio*, McIlroy	★★★☆☆
1961 *Albo Figurine del Campionato di Calcio*, Bentley	★★★☆☆
1961 *Albo Figurine del Campionato di Calcio*, Greaves	★★★⯨☆
1962 *Calcio Mondiale 1962*, cards of footballers and teams, most	★★☆☆☆
1962 *Calcio Mondiale 1962*, cards of footballers and teams, England players	★★☆☆☆
1962 *Calcio Mondiale 1962*, cards of footballers and teams, Gento	★★☆☆☆
1962, as above, team cards	★★⯨☆☆
1962, as above, Brazil winners cards	★★⯨☆☆
1962, as above, Pelé	★★★☆☆
1962, as above, Yashin	★★☆☆☆
1962, as above, Suarez	★★☆☆☆

Lampo Verbania

1965 footballer stamps, most	★★⯨☆☆
1965 footballer stamps, Pelé	★★★☆☆
1966 *Coppa Rimet 1966*, grey-cardstock cards	★★⯨☆☆
1966 *Coppa Rimet 1966*, white paper stickers	★★★☆☆
1966 *Coppa Rimet 1966*, white paper stickers, Greaves	★★★☆☆
1966 *Coppa Rimet 1966*, white paper stickers, Beckenbauer	★★★☆☆

Lampo Moderna

1970 *Mexicorama*, most	★★⯨☆☆
1970 *Mexicorama*, England	★★★☆☆
1970 *Mexicorama*, Pelé	★★★☆☆
1970 *Mexicorama*, Beckenbauer	★★★☆☆

La Pie Qui Chante

1930 *Hollywood Sports*, most	★★⯨☆☆
1930 *Hollywood Sports*, Fred Kennedy	★★★☆☆
1930 *Hollywood Sports*, Diagne	★★★☆☆
1950s *KikLac Football*	★★⯨☆☆

La Vache Qui Rit (Laughing Cow)

1931 *Sports Vedettes*	★★★☆☆
1982 *Nouvelle Collection Football World Cup*, triple cards	★★☆☆☆

Leaf Gum

1961 *Soccer Internationals*, b/w football photos and/or caricatures	★☆☆☆☆

Lees Tobacco

1912 *Northampton Town Football Club*, most	★★★★⯨
1912 *Northampton Town Football Club*, Walter Tull	★★★★☆

Letraset

1981 *Kevin Keegan's Action Replay*, action transfer folders, if unused	★★★☆☆
1981 *Kevin Keegan's Action Replay*, action transfer folders, used	★☆☆☆☆

Lewis's Hollywood Scale

1937 Merseyside footballers	★★★★★

Liebig

1966 *Campeonato Mondiali di Calcio*, most	★☆☆☆☆
1966 *Campeonato Mondiali di Calcio*, Pelé	★★☆☆☆

Lincolnshire Boot Stores

1900 shield-shaped cards of teams	★★★★★

Lion

1950s *Sports Stars In Action*, booklet, uncut & intact	★★☆☆☆
1950s *Sports Stars In Action*, booklet, cut images	☆☆☆☆☆
1959 *Famous Football Teams 1958-59*, uncut quads	★★★☆☆
1959 *Famous Football Teams 1958-59*, uncut pairs	★★☆☆☆
1959 *Famous Football Teams 1958-59*, cut singles	⯨☆☆☆☆
1959 *Famous Football Teams 1959-60*, uncut quads	★★★☆☆
1959 *Famous Football Teams 1959-60*, uncut pairs	★★☆☆☆
1959 *Famous Football Teams 1959-60*, cut singles	⯨☆☆☆☆
1961 *Famous Football Trophies*, 26 cups, on uncut sheets	★★★★☆
1961 *Famous Football Trophies*, 26 cups, single cups	★☆☆☆☆
1967 *The Lion Album of Soccer Stars*, red-framed stickers, uncut sheets	★★☆☆☆
1967 *The Lion Album of Soccer Stars*, red-framed stickers, singles	⯨☆☆☆☆

Lion and Thunder

1970 *My Favourite Soccer Stars*, uncut sheets of eight cards	★★☆☆☆
1970 *My Favourite Soccer Stars*, singles	⯨☆☆☆☆

Lipton Tea

1979 *New England Tea-men*	★★★☆☆
1982 World Cup footballers (English language)	★⯨☆☆☆
1982 World Cup footballers (Arabic language)	★★★☆☆

Liverpool Daily Post

1974 *Goals That Led To Wembley*	★★★⯨☆

London Daily Chronicle

1904 circular-shaped teams and players	★★★★★

London Daily Chronicle

1905 rectangular football team cards dated thus: 1904-5	★★★★⯨

THE SOCCER CARDS RARITY SCALE

London Evening News
1967 *Stars In Action*, footballers ★★☆☆☆

Lord Neilson
1971 *1st Div. League Club Badges*, hexagonal cards ★★★⯪☆

Lovell's
1909 *Football Series* ★★★★⯪
1927 *Toffee Rex. Photos of Football Stars* ★★★☆☆

Lot-O-Fun
1922 *Sports Champions*, uncut pairs ★★☆☆☆
1922 *Sports Champions*, cut singles ⯪☆☆☆☆
1922 *Sports Champions*, Meredith pair ★★☆☆☆

Luratti
1929 *Raccolta di 80 Stars*, footballer cards, most ★★★☆☆
1929 *Raccolta di 80 Stars*, footballer cards, Meazza ★★★★☆

Lutter (by Heinerle)
1962 Football cards (3/4 figures rear *Weltklassespieler*, etc.), most ★★★⯪☆
1962 Football cards (3/4 figures rear *Weltklassespieler*, etc.), Pelé ★★★★☆
1962, as above, Gento ★★★★☆
1962, as above, di Stefano ★★★★☆
1962, as above, Suarez ★★★★☆
1962, as above, Barcelona ★★★★☆

Lyons Maid
1971 *Soccer Stars*, with tokens ★★☆☆☆
1971 *Soccer Stars*, without token ★☆☆☆☆
1972 *International Footballers*, with tokens ★★☆☆☆
1972 *International Footballers*, without token ★☆☆☆☆

Mabilgrafica
1982 *Caricaturas e Fotos Mundial de Futebol Espanha-82*, British players ★★★☆☆
1986 *Mundial de Futebol Mexico 86*, British Isles players ★★★☆☆

MacDonald
1900 *Winning Team & Tontine*, cricket teams ★★★★★
1900 *Winning Team & Tontine*, football teams ★★★★★

Maclure & MacDonald
1900s Scottish football teams postcards ★★★★⯪

Maga
1962 *Olimán*, comic cut-out stickers of footballers, cut singles ★★☆☆☆
1962 *Olimán*, comic cut-out stickers of footballers, uncut comic ★★★☆☆
1975 *Futbol*, die-cut stickers, unused & intact with frame ★★★☆☆

Magnet Library
1922 *Real Photos of Famous Footballers*, uncut pairs ★★☆☆☆
1922 *Real Photos of Famous Footballers*, cut singles ⯪☆☆☆☆
1922 *Football Teams* ★☆☆☆☆

Major Drapkin
1930 *Sporting Celebrities in Action*, most ★★⯪☆☆
1930 *Sporting Celebrities in Action*, Jones ★★★☆☆
1930 *Sporting Celebrities in Action*, Wills ★★★☆☆
1930 *Sporting Celebrities in Action*, soccer players ★★⯪☆☆
1930 *Sporting Snap*, footballers ★☆☆☆☆

Manchester Evening News
1973 *Footballer caricatures*, stickers (*Fasprint* back), uncut strip ★★★☆☆
1973 *Footballer caricatures*, stickers (*Fasprint* back), cut singles ★☆☆☆☆
1974 *Footballers*, photo stickers, uncut sheets ★★★☆☆
1974 *Footballers*, photo stickers, singles ★★☆☆☆
1970s *Pink Final Legends*, uncut sheets ★★☆☆☆
1970s *Pink Final Legends*, cut singles ★☆☆☆☆

Mandelbaum
1890 *Types of People*, Sporting Girl ★★★★⯪

Manil
1986 *Mundial Mexico 86*, most ★★⯪☆☆
1986 *Mundial Mexico 86*, Maradona ★★★☆☆
1986 *Mundial Mexico 86*, British Isles players ★★★☆☆
1988 *Euros 88*, most ★★⯪☆☆
1988 *Euros 88*, bigger-name players ★★★☆☆
1990 *Italia 90*, most ★★☆☆☆
1990 *Italia 90*, legends of the game ★★⯪☆☆
1990 *Italia 90*, British Isles players ★★⯪☆☆
1993 *USA 94*, most ★★☆☆☆
1993 *USA 94*, legends of the game ★★⯪☆☆
1993 *USA 94*, British Isles teams & players ★★⯪☆☆

Maple Leaf & Genescambi
1951 *Voetbal 1ste Klasse 1951-1952*, most ★★★☆☆
1951 *Voetbal 1ste Klasse 1951-1952*, complete album ★★★★☆

Maple Leaf
1950s Dutch sportsmen on playing cards, the set of cards ★★★★☆
1950s Dutch sportsmen on playing cards, single cards ★★★☆☆
1960 *International Football Teams*, British teams ★★☆☆☆
1960 *International Football Teams*, Brazil with Pelé ★★★☆☆

Marcus
1890s football club colours & footballers ★★★★☆
1890s as above but rubber stamped in purple (*Kinnear*) ★★★★☆

264 AN A TO Z OF **SPORTING COLLECTIBLES**

Marshall Cavendish
1971 *Book of Football Top Teams*, cut-out stickers — ★⯨☆☆☆
1971 *Book of Football Top Teams*, uncut sheets — ★★⯨☆☆
1971 *Book of Football Top Teams*, cut-out Keegan — ★★★☆☆
1971 *Book of Football Top Teams*, uncut sheet with Keegan — ★★★★☆

Mas
1982 *Ases Mundial Espanha 82*, circular stickers (like Reyauca but smaller) — ★★⯨☆☆
1982 *Ases Mundial Espanha 82*, circular stickers, Maradona — ★★★☆☆

Masters Winners Matches
1980 *Winners Against The Odds*, uncut boxes — ★★★☆☆
1980 *Winners Against The Odds*, cut singles — ★★☆☆☆
1981 *Footballing Winners*, uncut boxes — ★★★☆☆
1981 *Footballing Winners*, cut singles — ★★☆☆☆

Master Vending
1958 *Cardmaster Football Tips*, most — ★☆☆☆☆
1958 *Cardmaster Football Tips*, Charlton (three variations are known) — ★★☆☆☆
1959 *Did You Know?* — ★☆☆☆☆
1959 *Cardmaster – Sport*, most — ★★★⯨☆
1959 *Cardmaster – Sport*, Charles — ★★★★☆
1959 *Cardmaster – Sport*, Pelé — ★★★★☆

Match Magazine
1995 stickers, most — ★☆☆☆☆
1995 stickers, uncut sheets — ★⯨☆☆☆
1995 stickers, uncut sheets including the David Beckham rookie — ★★★★☆

Mateu
1954 cut-out, stand-up footballers, most — ★★★☆☆
1954 cut-out, stand-up footballers, di Stefano — ★★★☆☆
1954 cut-out, stand-up footballers, uncut sheet with di Stefano — ★★★⯨☆

May Gum
1970 *Emblems, Equipamentos e Bandeiras*, British clubs — ★★★★☆

Maynard's Confectionery
1933 Club colours and histories — ★★★☆☆

McVitie's
1980 *Know Your Superstars*, footballers, — ★⯨☆☆☆
1980 *Know Your Superstars*, footballers uncut sheet of cards — ★★☆☆☆

Melrose Tea
1986 *World Cup Promotions*, most — ★★☆☆☆
1986 *World Cup Promotions*, Alex Ferguson — ★★★☆☆

Mera & Longhi
1930 *Gli Assi dello Sport*, sepia cards — ★★★☆☆
1937 *Gli Assi dello Sport*, colour cards, most — ★★★☆☆
1937 *Gli Assi dello Sport*, colour cards, Allemandi (Roma) — ★★★★☆

Merlin
1996 Euro 96 withdrawn collection of stickers showing full-length photos — ★★☆☆☆
1997 Premier Gold card of David Beckham #92 [500,000 examples made] — ★☆☆☆☆

Mercurycard
1990 presentation packets — ★★★⯨☆
1990 presentation packets, used cards — ★★☆☆☆
1990 presentation packets, overprinted cards — ★★★☆☆

Midjy
1948 *Midjy Photo Outfit*, intact kit — ★★★★☆
1948 *Midjy Photo Outfit*, single player cards — ★★★☆☆

Millhoff De Reszke
1933 *In The Public Eye*, most — ★☆☆☆☆
1933 *In The Public Eye*, Dean — ★⯨☆☆☆

Mira
1962 *Mondiali di Calcio 1962*, most — ★★★⯨☆
1962 *Mondiali di Calcio 1962*, England players — ★★★★⯨
1962 *Mondiali di Calcio 1962*, Yashin — ★★★★☆
1962 *Mondiali di Calcio 1962*, Pelé — ★★★★⯨
1962 as above, proofs missing design elements, England — ★★★★★
1962 as above, proofs missing design elements, Yashin — ★★★★★
1962 as above, proofs missing design elements, Pelé — ★★★★★
1964 *Tutti I Calciatori*, green/black backs, most — ★★☆☆☆
1964 *Tutti I Calciatori*, green/black backs, Hitchens — ★★☆☆☆
1964 *Tutti I Calciatori*, green/black backs, Riva — ★★☆☆☆
1964 *Tutti I Calciatori*, green/black backs, Zoff — ★★☆☆☆
1964 *Tutti I Calciatori*, as above with Regalo backs — ★★★☆☆
1964 *Tutti I Calciatori*, as above with Regalo backs, Hitchens — ★★★☆☆
1964 *Tutti I Calciatori*, as above with Regalo backs, Riva — ★★★⯨☆
1964 *Tutti I Calciatori*, as above with Regalo backs, Zoff — ★★★⯨☆
1965 *Il Pallone 1965 1966*, blank backs, most — ★★☆☆☆
1965 *Il Pallone 1965 1966*, blank backs, Rivera — ★★☆☆☆
1965 *Il Pallone 1965 1966*, blank backs, Riva — ★★☆☆☆
1965 *Il Pallone 1965 1966*, blank backs, Zoff — ★★☆☆☆
1967 *Tutti I Calciatori* — ★★☆☆☆
1967 *Tutti I Calciatori*, British subjects — ★★☆☆☆
1967 *Tutti I Calciatori*, Beckenbauer — ★★☆☆☆
1967 *Tutti I Calciatori*, Yashin — ★★☆☆☆
1967 *Tutti I Calciatori*, Pelé — ★★☆☆☆
1967 *Tutti I Calciatori*, with Regalo backs, British subjects — ★★★⯨☆
1967 *Tutti I Calciatori*, with Regalo backs, Beckenbauer — ★★★☆☆
1967 *Tutti I Calciatori*, with Regalo backs, Yashin — ★★★☆☆
1967 *Tutti I Calciatori*, with Regalo backs, Pelé — ★★★☆☆
1967 *Tutti I Calciatori*, metallic stickers with original backing papers — ★★★★⯨

Mira & Tuttosport
1968 *I Campionissimi*, most — ★★☆☆☆
1968 *I Campionissimi*, British — ★★☆☆☆
1968 *I Campionissimi*, Beckenbauer — ★★☆☆☆
1968 *I Campionissimi*, Pelé — ★★☆☆☆
1968 *I Campionissimi*, with Regalo backs — ★★★⯨☆
1968 *I Campionissimi*, with Regalo backs, Beckenbauer — ★★★☆☆
1968 *I Campionissimi*, with Regalo backs, Pelé — ★★★☆☆
1968 *I Campionissimi*, metallic stickers & original backing papers — ★★★⯨☆

THE SOCCER CARDS RARITY SCALE

Mira
1968 *Calciatori 1968-69*, most ★★☆☆☆
1968 *Calciatori 1968-69*, British ★★☆☆☆
1968 *Calciatori 1968-69*, Pelé ★★☆☆☆
1968 *Calciatori 1968-69*, metallic stickers with papers ★★★☆☆

Miroir-Sprint
1958 to 1959 b/w postcards with deckled edges, most ★★★☆☆
1958 to 1959 b/w postcards with deckled edges, Pelé portrait ★★★★☆
1958 to 1959 b/w postcards with deckled edges, Pelé action ★★★★☆
1959 to 1960 Colour postcards of footballers ★★☆☆☆
1959 to 1960 Colour postcards of footballers, Fontaine ★★⯪☆☆
1960 *Sport Gum*, cards, most ★★★☆☆
1960 *Sport Gum*, cards, Puskás ★★★☆☆
1960 *Sport Gum*, cards, Gento ★★★☆☆
1960 *Sport Gum*, cards, Fontaine ★★★☆☆
1960 *Sport Gum*, cards, Pelé ★★★☆☆
1960 cards in strips of three, most ★★★☆☆
1960 cards in strips of three, strips with international players ★★★⯪☆
1960 footballers & teams playing cards ★★☆☆☆
1960 footballers & teams playing cards, Puskás ★★⯪☆☆
1960 footballers & teams playing cards, Fontaine ★★⯪☆☆
1960 footballers & teams playing cards, Pelé ★★⯪☆☆
1961 footballers large postcard-size trade cards, designs on both sides ★★☆☆☆

Miss Blanche
1930s Dutch sports cards by Vittoria Egyptian cigarettes, full albums ★★★☆☆

Mister Softee
1972 *1st Division Football League Badges* ★⯪☆☆☆

Mitcham Foods
1956 *Footballers*, a full set of 25 cards ★☆☆☆☆

Mitchell
1934 *Scottish Footballers* ★☆☆☆☆
1935 *Gallery of 1934* ★☆☆☆☆
1935 *Scottish Football Snaps* ★☆☆☆☆
1936 *Gallery of 1935* ★☆☆☆☆

Mobil Oil
1983 *Football Club Badges* ★☆☆☆☆

Mohr
1952 *Fussball, Das Spiel Der Welt* ★★⯪☆☆

Moncar
1975 football team emblems on silk stickers, sealed packets ★★★☆☆
1975 football team emblems on silk stickers, singles ★★☆☆☆

Monello
1972 *i Divi della Domenica*, most ★⯪☆☆☆
1972 *i Divi della Domenica*, Greaves ★★☆☆☆
1972 *i Divi della Domenica*, Law ★★☆☆☆
1972 *i Divi della Domenica*, uncut magazine ★★⯪☆☆

Monopol
1932 *Sportphoto, serie A und B*, most ★⯪☆☆☆
1932 *Sportphoto, serie A und B*, Pym ★☆☆☆☆
1932 *Sportphoto, serie A und B*, Goodall ★☆☆☆☆

Monty
1959 *Caricatures of International footballers playing cards*, most ★★★☆☆
1959 *Caricatures of International footballers playing cards*, Pelé Santos (two types) ★★★⯪☆
1960 *Caricatures of British Isles footballers playing cards*, most ★★⯪☆☆
1961 *Football Teams*, black-and-white images ★★★★☆
1968 *Football Teams*, orange borders ★★☆☆☆
1969 *Football Teams*, jigsaw picture puzzle to back ★★☆☆☆
1972 *Fussball Football Voetbal Club*, circular & pennant-shaped stickers, most ★★⯪☆☆
1972 as above, British ★★★☆☆
1974 *World Cup '74*, stickers, most ★★☆☆☆
1974 *World Cup '74*, stickers, Scottish ★★⯪☆☆
1974 *World Cup '74*, stickers, Cruyff ★★★☆☆
1976 *Football* (footballs top & bottom corners) ★☆☆☆☆
1978 *Hannah's World Cup*, cards (larger cards with world-cup legend) ★☆☆☆☆
1980 *Football Parade*, most ★★⯪☆☆
1980 *Football Parade*, British teams ★★★⯪☆
1982 *World Cup Football*, cards (smaller cards without world-cup legend) ★★☆☆☆
1984 *Euro Cup*, most ★★☆☆☆
1984 *Euro Cup*, all-time-great players ★★⯪☆☆
1986 *Mexico 86*, cards ★★☆☆☆
1988 *Euro Cup 88*, most ★★☆☆☆
1988 *Euro Cup 88*, all-time-great players ★★⯪☆☆

Motta & Edis
1974 *Monaco '74 Coppa dei Campioni*, circular cards, most ★★★⯪☆
1974 *Monaco '74 Coppa dei Campioni*, circular cards, Scots ★★★★☆
1974 *Monaco '74 Coppa dei Campioni*, circular cards, Beckenbauer ★★★★☆
1975 *Coppa dei Campioni*, Italian league players, most ★★★☆☆
1975 *Coppa dei Campioni*, Italian league players, Zoff ★★★★☆

Muratti
1936 *Brennpunkte des Deutschen Sports* ★★★⯪☆

Murray's
1908 Maple cigarettes, *Football Colours*, flag-shaped cards ★★★★⯪
1911 *Football Rules* ★★★☆☆
1912 & 1913 *Footballers series H & J*, most ★★★☆☆
1912 & 1913 *Footballers series H & J*, Bloomer ★★★★☆
1912 & 1913 *Footballers series H & J*, Meredith ★★★★☆

Nabisco
1961 Shredded Wheat *Champions of Sport*, with tokens ★★⯪☆☆
1961 Shredded Wheat *Champions of Sport*, cut & without tokens ★☆☆☆☆
1969 *Footballers* (gum-card format) ★★☆☆☆
1969 *Footballers* (gum-card format), George Best ★★☆☆☆
1969 *Footballers*, large colour photo cards, in folders with facsimile autographs ★★★★☆
1971 *Cup Winners Badges*, stickers, in pairs ★★⯪☆☆
1971 *Cup Winners Badges*, stickers, cut single stickers ★☆☆☆☆
1972 League table of 11, team stickers ★★☆☆☆

266 AN A TO Z OF **SPORTING COLLECTIBLES**

1972 League table of 11, a set & the cereal-packet league ladder	★★★☆☆
1973 Iron-on transfer silks of footballers	★★★☆☆
1973 *Champions of Europe*, a trio of stickers	★★★☆☆
1973 as aboves, uncut trio with Cruyff & Eusebio	★★★⯨☆
1975 *Coached By Johan Cruyff*, oval-shaped stickers	★★☆☆☆
1975 *Johan Cruyff Demonstrates*, lenticular 3-D cards	★☆☆☆☆
1977 *Kevin Keegan's Play'n'Score*	⯨☆☆☆☆
1978 *English Soccer Star Tactics*	⯨☆☆☆☆
1980 *Keegan's Skill Scratchcards*, unused	★☆☆☆☆
1980 *Keegan's Skill Scratchcards*, used	☆☆☆☆☆
1980 *Superstar Ace sticker*, of Kevin Keegan	★☆☆☆☆
1981 *Waddington's Kevin Keegan's Quiz Card Game*, complete, with all nine sections	★★☆☆☆
1984 Henry Cooper's Champions	★☆☆☆☆
1978 *Scotland World Cup Argentina 1978*, stickers	★★★☆☆
1978 *Scotland World Cup Argentina 1978*, complete album	★★★⯨☆

Nannina

1946 *Figurine Tecni-Color*, uncut, complete folder of cards	★★★★★
1946 *Figurine Tecni-Color*, cut-out cards, legend to front, most	★★★☆☆
1946 *Figurine Tecni-Color*, cut-out cards, legend to front, Puskás	★★★★☆
1947 *Figurine Tecni-Color*, uncut, complete folder	★★★★★
1947 *Figurine Tecni-Color*, cut-out card, legend to back	★★★☆☆
1948 *Figurine Tecni-Color*, uncut, complete folder	★★★★★
1948 *Figurine Tecni-Color*, cut-out card, legend to back, most	★★★☆☆
1949 *Figurine Tecni-Color*, uncut, complete folder	★★★★★
1949 *Figurine Tecni-Color*, cut-out card, legend to front, most	★★★☆☆
1949 *Calciotavolo*, folded card & two teams of 11 cards, pairs of teams	★★★★⯨
1949 *Calciotavolo*, folded card & two teams of 11 cards, cut singles	★★★☆☆

Nannina & Wamar

1950 Footballers like the 1949 *Figurine Tecni-Color*, most	★★★☆☆

Nannina

1950 *Calciovaluta*	★★★⯨☆

Nannina & Bovolone

1950s footballers	★★☆☆☆

Naninna

1952 b/w footballer cards with plain backs	★★☆☆☆
1950s matchbox cut-out cards, two per box, uncut box	★★★★☆
1950s matchbox cut-out cards, cut card	★★☆☆☆
1954 *Calciatori 1954-55*, unnumbered: red, green, yellow or blue borders	★★★☆☆
1955 *Calciatori 1955-56*, numbered top left, with yellow borders	★★★☆☆
1956 *Calciatori 1956-57*, numbered top left, again with yellow borders	★★★☆☆
1956 *Campioni dell Sport*, numbered, white borders, paper, all sports,	★★★☆☆
1957 *Calciatori 1957-58*, numbered top left, again with yellow borders	★★★☆☆
1958 *Calciatori 1958-59*, numbered top left, with yellow or blue borders	★★★☆☆
1958 *Campionato del Mondo*, footballers of the final, most	★★★★⯨
1958 *Campionato del Mondo*, footballers of the final, Pelé	★★★★★
1959 *Gol 1959-1960*, most	★★☆☆☆
1959 *Gol 1959-1960*, John Charles	★★★☆☆
1959 *Gol Gigante 1959-1960*, most	★★⯨☆☆
1959 *Gol Gigante 1959-1960*, John Charles	★★★☆☆
1960 *Gol 1960-1961*, most	★★☆☆☆
1960 *Gol 1960-1961*, John Charles	★★★☆☆
1960 *Gol 1960-1961*, Denis Law	★★★☆☆
1960 *Gol Gigante 1960-1961*, most	★★☆☆☆
1960 *Gol Gigante 1960-1961*, John Charles	★★★☆☆
1960 *Gol Gigante 1960-1961*, Denis Law	★★★☆☆

note: 1961 Nannina's *Gol Gigante 1960-1961* cards were relaunched in 1961 by Panini.

Nannina through Panini *Gol Gigante 1960-1961*, as above, red overprints (Valida)	★★★⯨☆
1961 footballers & teams (gum-card size), most	★★★☆☆
1961 footballers & teams (gum-card size), Law	★★★⯨☆
1961 footballers & teams (gum-card size), Charles	★★★⯨☆
1962 *Cile Mondial 62*, most	★★☆☆☆
1962 *Cile Mondial 62*, Springett	★★⯨☆☆
1962 *Cile Mondial 62*, Flowers	★★⯨☆☆
1962 *Cile Mondial 62*, Charlton	★★★☆☆
1962 *Cile Mondial 62*, Armfield	★★★☆☆
1962 *Cile Mondial 62*, Pelé – there are two cards of Pelé, each	★★★★☆
1962 as above, Yashin	★★★☆☆
1962 as above, Didi	★★★☆☆
1962 as above, Garrincha	★★★☆☆
1963 *Calciatori in Azione*, stickers, most	★★★★☆
1963 *Calciatori in Azione*, stickers, Pelé	★★★★☆
1963 *Calciatori in Azionee*, stickers, Armfield	★★★★☆

note: colour Xerox copies of the Nannina 1963 plain-back stickers are known, originals are less glossy.

1963 *Campioni Del Goal*, postcard-size cards, most	★★★☆☆
1963 *Campioni Del Goal*, postcard-size cards, Pelé	★★★⯨☆
1963 *Campioni Del Goal*, metal discs of club emblems,	★★☆☆☆

note: the album for the above postcards and tokens was titled *Squadre E Campioni 1963/64*.

National Spastics Society

1959 *Famous Footballers*	★☆☆☆☆

Nelson Lee

1921 *Photo Plates of Noted Players*, English Stars, issued in England	★★⯨☆☆
1921 *Photo Plates of Noted Players*, Scottish stars, issued in Scotland	★★★★☆

Nelson Lee Library

1922 Photographs of Famous Footballers, uncut pairs	★★☆☆☆
1922 Photographs of Famous Footballers, cut singles	⯨☆☆☆☆

Nettuno

1935 *Cine–Sport*, most	★★★⯨☆
1935 *Cine–Sport*, bigger name-stars of world football	★★★★☆

Newham Recorder

1968 uncut pairs of footballer stars	★★★☆☆

News Chronicle (Hulton's Daily Dispatch)

1923 Footballers	★★★★★

News Chronicle

1955 *Famous Soccer Teams*	★★★★☆
1956 *Pocket Portrait Footballers* most cards	★★⯨☆☆

note: some cards were over produced, prices and values vary massively, some examples:

THE SOCCER CARDS RARITY SCALE

1956 *Pocket Portrait Footballers*, Everton players	★☆☆☆☆
1956 *Pocket Portrait Footballers*, Newcastle	★☆☆☆☆
1956 *Pocket Portrait Footballers*, Man City	★☆☆☆☆
1956 *Pocket Portrait Footballers*, Dundee players	★★★☆☆
1956 *Pocket Portrait Footballers*, Birmingham	★★★☆☆
1956 *Pocket Portrait Footballers*, Sheff Utd	★★★☆☆
1956 *Pocket Portrait Footballers*, Liverpool players	★★★★☆
1956 *Pocket Portrait Footballers*, Wolves players	★★★★☆
1956 *Pocket Portrait Footballers*, Hibs	★★★⯨☆
1956 *Pocket Portrait Footballers*, Hearts	★★★⯨☆
1956 *Pocket Portrait Footballers*, Celtic	★★★★⯨
1956 *Pocket Portrait Footballers*, Manchester Utd, most	★★★☆☆
1956 *Pocket Portrait Footballers*, Manchester Utd, Edwards	★★★★☆

Nimbus

1970s *Vedettes du Football / Fussball Spieler in Aktion 72/73*, full album	★★★★☆

No brand name, no year, no title, no logo?
see: www.footballsoccercards.com

Nora

1959 *Balas Bombons*, World Cup Winners stickers, most	★★★★⯨
1959 *Balas Bombons*, World Cup Winners stickers, Pelé	★★★★★

note: very good copies are known! Buyer beware.
even some experts can't tell them apart.

1962 *Idolos de Ouro*, play money, most	★★★★☆
1962 *Idolos de Ouro*, play money, two different Pelé banknotes	★★★★⯨

Northern Trancessories

1960s shield-shaped stickers of players and teams	★★★★⯨

Nuzzi (Cedip)

1962 *Giocatori di Serie A Campionato 1962/63*, most	★★☆☆☆
1963 *Campioni dello Sport Stagione 1963-64*, most	★★☆☆☆
1963 *Campioni dello Sport Stagione 1963-64*, Pelé folded card	★★★☆☆

Odhams Press

1950s Sports Stars redemption trade cards, styled as postcards	★★★☆☆

Ogden's

1895 *Sporting Girls*, cricket & football women cigarette cards	★★★★★
1898 *Sporting Girls*, postcard-sized cards of sporting women	★★★★★
1898 *Cricketers & Sportsmen*	★★★★⯨
1899 *Guinea Gold*, untitled footballers (150 footballers, rugby & soccer)	★★★★⯨
1899 *Guinea Gold*, untitled sports & sportsmen (33 rugby & soccer)	★★★★⯨
1900 Untitled General Interest cards (56 footballers)	★★★★⯨
1901 Cards with cartouche, numberless series of 100 (some football)	★★★★⯨
1901 Cards with cartouche, numberless series of 300 (25 football)	★★★☆☆
1901 Cards with cartouche, numbered series of 420, many, various types	★★★★⯨
1901 *Our Leading Footballers*	★★★☆☆
1902 *Tabs General Interest, A series*, footballers	★★★⯨☆
1902 *Tabs General Interest B Series*, footballers	★★★⯨☆
1902 *Tabs General Interest B Series*, Charles Burgess Fry for Southampton	★★★☆☆
1902 *Tabs General Interest C Series*, footballers	★★⯨☆☆
1902 *Tabs General Interest C Series*, most	★★⯨☆☆
1902 *Tabs General Interest C Series*, Fry	★★★☆☆

1902 *Tabs General Interest C Series*, Smith	★★★☆☆
1902 *Tabs General Interest D Series*, most	★★★⯨☆
1902 *Tabs General Interest F Series*, most	★★★⯨☆
1906 *Football Club Colours*, most	★☆☆☆☆
1906 *Football Club Colours*, Bloomer	★★⯨☆☆
1908 *Famous Footballers*	★★⯨☆☆
1910 *Club Colours Badges*, shaped cards with rugby & soccer club colours	★★★★⯨
1926 *Captains of Association Football Clubs & Colours*	★☆☆☆☆
1933 *AFC Nicknames*	★☆☆☆☆
1935 *Football Caricatures*	★☆☆☆☆
1936 *Football Club Captains*	★☆☆☆☆
1937 *Champions of 1936*	★☆☆☆☆

Oh Boy Gum (British Chewing Sweets)

1933 *Footballers of the Principle Teams*	★★★★☆
1933 *Footballers of the Principle Teams*, wrapper	★★★★★

Olympiad Gum

1950s b/w football teams	★★★☆☆
1954 colour postcard-size football team cards	★★★☆☆
1950s *Collection Chewing-Gum Olympiad*, b/w	★★★☆☆
1950s *Collection Chewing-Gum Olympiad*, colour	★★★☆☆
1950s trade cards as playing cards with footballers in action	★★★☆☆

Onze

1979 *Les 100 Ecussons des Plus Grands Clubs du Monde*, most	★★☆☆☆
1979 *Les 100 Ecussons des Plus Grands Clubs du Monde*, full album	★★★☆☆

Opera Mundi

1967 football mascots stickers and postcards	★★★☆☆

Ormerod Brothers

1880s oval- and shield-shaped cards of footballers	★★★★★

Or.ve.do (VAV)

1962 to 1966 *Campionato Nazionale di Calcio*, most	★★★⯨☆
1962 to 1966 *Campionato Nazionale di Calcio*, most	★★☆☆☆
1962 to 1966 *Campionato Nazionale di Calcio*, Hitchens Aston Villa colours	★★★☆☆
1962 to 1966 *Campionato Nazionale di Calcio*, most	★★☆☆☆
1962 to 1966 *Campionato Nazionale di Calcio*, Charles	★★★☆☆
1962 to 1966 *Campionato Nazionale di Calcio*, Hitchens Torino	★★☆☆☆
1962 to 1966 bank notes, so-called play money	★★★☆☆

P for Panini, etc.

note: this book's scope is focussed on 1880 to 1980, with a few later issues included in passing, so Panini and other issuers' material from after 1990 is not included. except for one or two notable examples.

Packer

1909 Footballers given with Packer's Chocolates, issued with glue marks to rear, monotone	★★★★★
1909 Footballers given with Packer's Chocolates, issued with glue marks to rear, colour	★★★★★

Pagliarini

1974 *Forza Italia*, most	★★★★⯨
1974 *Forza Italia*, Riva	★★★★★

1974 *Forza Italia*, Rivera ★★★★☆
1974 *Forza Italia*, Zoff ★★★★☆
1974 *Arbitro Vince! (Monster Football)* ★★★★☆

Palirex
1968 *Campeoeos Europeus de Futebol*, most ★★★★½☆
1968 *Campeoeos Europeus de Futebol*, Cruyff ★★★★½☆
1968 *Campeoeos Europeus de Futebol*, McNeil ★★★☆☆
1968 *Campeoeos Europeus de Futebol*, Best ★★★★½☆
1968 *Campeoeos Europeus de Futebol*, large team stickers, Celtic ★★★★☆
1968 *Campeoeos Europeus de Futebol*, large team stickers, Man Utd ★★★★☆
1968 *Campeoeos Europeus de Futebol*, large team stickers, Man City ★★★★☆
1968 *Campeoeos Europeus de Futebol*, large team stickers, Glentoran ★★★★☆
1970 *Ases do IX Mundial de Futebol*, England players ★★★★½☆
1970 *Ases do IX Mundial de Futebol*, Pelé ★★★★½☆
1970 *Ases do IX Mundial de Futebol*, Beckenbauer ★★★★½☆

Palitoy
1978 *Top Team*, complete games, depending on the team ★★½☆☆

Palmera
1945 *Los Clubs de 1° Division de la Liga* (white on blue lettering), most ★★★★½☆
1945 *Los Clubs de 1° Division de la Liga* (white on blue lettering), Gainza ★★★★★½
1948 *Los Clubs de 1° Division de la Liga* collection (light blue lettering), most ★★★★½☆
1948 *Los Clubs de 1° Division de la Liga* collection (light blue lettering), Zarra ★★★★★
1949 *Los Clubs de 1° Division de la Liga* (white lettering on red), most ★★★★½☆
1949 *Los Clubs de 1° Division de la Liga* (white lettering on red), Ben Barek ★★★★★

Palmin-werke
1920s *Moderne Sport* ★★★☆☆
1920s *Palmin Post* ★★★☆☆

Pals
1922 *Famous Footballers Fine Art Supplements* ★☆☆☆☆
1922 *Football Series* (aka *Footballer Series*) team cards ★☆☆☆☆
1923 *Football Series 1923-'24*, postcard-size pictures of footy teams ★★★☆☆
1923 *New Football Series*, teams, with rugby & race horses, uncut doubles ★★★☆☆
1923 *New Football Series*, teams, with rugby & race horses, cut singles ★☆☆☆☆

Panini (by Nannina)
1961 *Gol Gigante 1960-61*, rarity status as per Nannina cards, most ★★☆☆☆
1961 *Gol Gigante 1960-61*, cards with red overprints (Valida) ★★★★½☆
1961 *Gol Gigante 1960-61*, original wrapper fold-in seal, empty wrapper ★★★★★
note: fake wrappers, from the 1970s, 80s, 90s & 2000s are in circulation. Crimp-sealed 1961s are fakes.

Panini
1961 *Calciatori 1961-62*, most ★★★☆☆
1961 *Calciatori 1961-62*, less well-distributed, rarer cards ★★★★☆
1961 *Calciatori 1961-62*, red-&-blue *Valida* back ★★★★☆
1961 as above, Charles ★★★☆☆
1961 as above, Law ★★★☆☆
1961 as above, Baker ★★★☆☆
1961 as above, Rivera ★★★★☆
1961 as above, Mazzola ★★★☆☆
1961 as above, Hitchens ★★★☆☆
1961 as above, each with *Valida* ★★★★☆
1961 *Calciatori 1961-62*, wrapper ★★★★☆
note: packets were not glued so a 'sealed' packet is unlikely.

1962 *Calciatori 1962-63* ★★½☆☆
1962 *Calciatori 1962-63*, paper differences and other variations ★★★½☆
1962 *Calciatori 1962-63*, club & national emblems, new with backing paper ★★★★☆
1962 *Calciatori 1962-63*, club & national emblems, used ★★☆☆☆
1962 *Calciatori 1962-63*, cards have Premio add 100% to values for these prize-offer backs ★★★★☆
1962 *Calciatori 1962-63*, empty packet ★★★★½☆
1962 *Calciatori 1962-63*, sealed packet ★★★★★
note: fakes are on the market!

1963 *Calciatori 1963-64*, most ★★☆☆☆
1963 *Calciatori 1963-64*, Eusebio yellow ★★★★☆
1963 *Calciatori 1963-64*, Eusebio blue ★★☆☆☆
1963 *Calciatori 1963-64*, Eusebio blue *Valida* ★★★☆☆
1963 *Calciatori 1963-64*, empty wrapper ★★★☆☆
1963 *Calciatori 1963-64*, sealed packet ★★★★★
note: with omaggio add 100% to values.

1963 *Calciatori 1963-64*, club & other emblems, as new with backing paper ★★★★☆
1963 *Calciatori 1963-64*, club & other emblems, used ★★☆☆☆
1964 *Calciatori 1964-65*, most ★½☆☆☆
1964 *Calciatori 1964-65*, Pelé ★★★☆☆
note: with *Valida* to back add 100% to values.

1964 *Calciatori 1964-65*, club & other emblems, as new with backing paper ★★★☆☆
1964 *Calciatori 1964-65*, club & other emblems, used ★☆☆☆☆
1964 *Calciatori 1964-65*, empty wrapper ★★★☆☆
1964 *Calciatori 1964-65*, sealed packet ★★★★½
note: with omaggio add 100% to values.

1964 *Bandiere Nazionali e Sportive*, plastic flags & flagpoles of football teams ★★★★½☆
1965 *Calciatori 1965-66*, most ★★☆☆☆
1965 *Calciatori 1965-66*, Salvori ★★★☆☆
1965 *Calciatori 1965-66*, Pelé ★★★☆☆
1965 *Calciatori 1965-66*, emblem with backing paper ★★★☆☆
note: the above cards with *Valida* backs add 100% to values.

1966 *Campioni dello Sport*, most ★★½☆☆
1966 *Campioni dello Sport*, Cassius Clay ★★★☆☆
1966 *Campioni dello Sport*, Pelé ★★★☆☆
1966 *Campioni dello Sport*, Puskás ★★☆☆☆
1966 *Campioni dello Sport*, Eusebio ★★☆☆☆
1966 *Campioni dello Sport*, Bruce McLaren ★★★☆☆
1966 *Campioni dello Sport*, Jackie Stewart ★★★☆☆
1966 *Campioni dello Sport*, Sonny Liston (two different colours) ★★★☆☆
1966 *Campioni dello Sport*, Moore ★★★☆☆
1966 *Campioni dello Sport*, Beckenbauer ★★★☆☆
1966 *Calciatori 1966-67*, cards ★★☆☆☆
1966 *Calciatori 1966-67*, cards, foil emblems with backing papers ★★★★½☆
1966 *Calciatori 1966-67*, Stiles ★★★½☆
1966 *Calciatori 1966-67*, Hunt ★★★½☆
1966 *Calciatori 1966-67*, Charlton ★★☆☆☆
1966 *Calciatori 1966-67*, Moore ★★☆☆☆
1966 *Calciatori 1966-67*, England ★★☆☆☆
1966 *Calciatori 1966-67*, Man Utd ★★☆☆☆
1967 *Campioni dello Sport 1967-68*, most ★★☆☆☆
1967 *Campioni dello Sport 1967-68*, unused foil emblems ★★½☆☆

THE SOCCER CARDS RARITY SCALE

1967 *Campioni dello Sport 1967-68*, Cassius Clay ★★⯨☆☆
1967 *Calciatori 1967-68*, most ★★⯨☆☆
1967 *Calciatori 1967-68*, unused foil emblems ★★★☆☆
1967 *Calciatori 1967-68*, George Best ★★★⯨☆
1967 *Calciatori 1967-68*, Hunt ★★☆☆☆
1967 *Calciatori 1967-68*, McNeil ★★☆☆☆
1967 *Calciatori 1967-68*, Pelé ★★☆☆☆
1967 *Calciatori 1967-68*, Beckenbauer ★★☆☆☆
1967 *Calciatori 1967-68*, Eusebio ★★☆☆☆
1967 *Uomini Illustri*, most ★★☆☆☆
1967 *Uomini Illustri*, Stanley Matthews ★★★☆☆
1968 *Campioni dello Sport 1968-69*, most ★★☆☆☆
1968 *Campioni dello Sport 1968-69*, unused emblem stickers ★★★☆☆
1968 *Calciatori 1968-69*, most ★★☆☆☆
1968 *Calciatori 1968-69*, intact transfer decals of team emblems ★★★★☆
1968 *Calciatori 1968-69*, unused decals of: Celtic ★★★★☆
1968 *Calciatori 1968-69*, unused decals of: Man Utd ★★★★⯨
1968 *Calciatori 1968-69*, unused decals of: Leeds ★★★★☆
1968 *Calciatori 1968-69*, unused decals of: Spurs ★★★★☆
1968 *Calciatori 1968-69*, unused decals of: West Ham ★★★★☆
1969 *Campioni dello Sport 1969-70*, most ★★☆☆☆
1969 *Campioni dello Sport 1969-70*, unused self-adhesive stickers ★★★☆☆
1969 *Campioni dello Sport 1969-70* 'buono' promotional coupons with attached cards ★★★★⯨
1969 *Calciatori 1969-70*, most ★⯨☆☆☆
1969 *Calciatori 1969-70*, unused self-adhesive badges ★★★☆☆
1970 *Mexico 70*, Italian green & black cards, most ★★☆☆☆
1970 *Mexico 70*, Italian green & black cards, unused stickers ★★★★★
1970 *Mexico 70*, Italian green & black cards, Pelé ★★★⯨☆
1970 *Mexico 70*, Italian blue & red cards ★★★★⯨
1970 *Mexico 70*, Italian blue & red cards, uncut 'buono' sheet with cards ★★★★★
1970 *Mexico 70*, International black & red, most ★★☆☆☆
1970 *Mexico 70*, International black & red, unused stickers ★★★★★
1970 *Mexico 70*, International black & red, Pelé ★★⯨☆☆
note: all above *Mexico 70* types cards with *Valida* backs add 100% to values.

1970 *Campioni dello Sport 1970-71*, most ★★☆☆☆
1970 *Campioni dello Sport 1970-71*, legendary players ★★⯨☆☆
1970 *Campioni dello Sport 1970-71*, 'buono' coupons & cards ★★★★☆
1970 *Calciatori 1970-71*, most ★★☆☆☆
1970 *Calciatori 1970-71*, Arsenal and Man City cards ★★☆☆☆
1970 *Calciatori 1970-71*, unused emblem stickers in pairs ★★★☆☆
1970 *Calciatori 1971-72*, most ★★☆☆☆
1970 *Calciatori 1971-72*, Celtic ★★☆☆☆
1970 *Calciatori 1971-72*, Linfield ★★☆☆☆
1970 *Calciatori 1971-72*, Distillery ★★☆☆☆
1970 *Calciatori 1971-72*, Liverpool ★★☆☆☆
1970 *Calciatori 1971-72*, Chelsea ★★☆☆☆

Panini & Williams
1970 *Fotboll 1971*, most ★★☆☆☆
1970 *Fotboll 1971*, Arsenal ★★⯨☆☆
1970 *Fotboll 1971*, Leeds ★★⯨☆☆
1970 *Fotboll 1971*, Leeds uncut sheet & magazine ★★★★★

Panini Top Sellers
1971 *Football 72*, most ★★☆☆☆
1971 *Football 72*, sheet of six uncut cards ★★★★☆
1971 *Football 72*, wrapper ★★★☆☆
1971 *Football 72*, full album ★★★★☆

Panini
1971 *Olympia (1896-1972)*, most cards ★★☆☆☆
1971 *Olympia (1896-1972)*, Cassius Clay card ★★☆☆☆
1971 *Olympia (1896-1972)*, Cassius Clay *Valida* card ★★★☆☆
1972 *München 72*, most card ★★☆☆☆
1972 *München 72*, unused self-adhesive stickers ★★★☆☆
Top Sellers 1972 *Football 73*, most ★★☆☆☆
Top Sellers 1972 *Football 73*, wrapper ★★★☆☆
Top Sellers 1972 *Football 73*, full album ★★★★☆
1972 *Calciatori 1972-73*, most ★⯨☆☆☆
1972 as above, intact quartets ★★★☆☆
1972 as above, with Derby ★★★☆☆
1972 as above, Celtic ★★★☆☆
1972 as above, Leeds ★★★☆☆
1972 as above, Liverpool ★★★☆☆
1972 as above, Spurs ★★★☆☆
1972 *Football 1972-73*, Benelux issue, most ★★⯨☆☆
1972 *Football 1972-73*, Benelux issue, Best ★★★☆☆
1972 *Football 1972-73*, Benelux issue, Charlton ★★★☆☆
1972 *Football 1972-73*, Benelux issue, Moore ★★☆☆☆

Panini Top Sellers
1973 *Football 74*, most ★★☆☆☆
1973 *Football 74*, the first card in the collection ★★★☆☆
1973 *Football 74*, wrapper ★★★☆☆
1973 *Football 74*, full album ★★★★☆

Panini
1973 *OK VIP*, most ★★⯨☆☆
1973 *OK VIP*, Best ★★★☆☆
1973 *OK VIP*, Yashin ★★★☆☆
1973 *OK VIP*, Eusebio ★★☆☆☆
1973 *OK VIP*, Pelé ★★☆☆☆
1973 *OK VIP*, Moore ★★☆☆☆
1973 *OK VIP*, Charlton ★★☆☆☆
1973 *OK VIP*, empty wrapper ★⯨☆☆☆
1973 *OK VIP*, sealed packet ★★★☆☆
1973 *OK VIP*, promo poster ★★★★☆
1973 *OK VIP*, full album ★★★☆☆
1973 *Campioni dello Sport 1973-74*, most unused stickers ★★★☆☆
1973 *Campioni dello Sport 1973-74*, Pelé ★★★☆☆
1973 *Campioni dello Sport 1973-74*, Cruyff ★★★☆☆
1973 *Campioni dello Sport 1973-74*, Eusebio ★★★☆☆
1973 *Campioni dello Sport 1973-74*, Moore ★★☆☆☆
1973 *Calciatori 1973-74*, most ★★★☆☆
1973 *Calciatori 1973-74*, full album ★★★☆☆
1974 *München 74*, International edition, most stickers ★★☆☆☆
1974 *München 74*, International edition, Dalglish ★★★☆☆
1974 *München 74*, International edition, full album ★★★☆☆
1974 *Minhen 74*, Serbo-Croat edition, full album ★★★★☆

Panini Top Sellers

1974 *Football 75*, most	★★☆☆☆
1974 *Football 75*, 2nd puzzle cards, each	★★★☆☆
1974 *Football 75*, wrapper	★★★☆☆
1974 *Football 75*, full album	★★★★☆

Panini

1974 *Sport Vedettes*, unused stickers most	★★★⯪☆
1974 *Sport Vedettes*, Sheene	★★★★☆
1974 *Sport Vedettes*, Borg	★★★★⯪
1974 *Sport Vedettes*, Lauda	★★★⯪☆
1975 *Football Clubs*, unused stickers most	★★★☆☆
1975 *Football Clubs*, intact metallic emblems	★★★⯪☆
1975 *Football Clubs*, Serbo-Croat edition, full album	★★★★⯪
Top Sellers STIG 1975 *Superstars*, unused, most	★★⯪☆☆
Top Sellers STIG 1975 *Superstars*, unused, football subjects	★★★☆☆
Top Sellers STIG 1975 *Superstars*, unused, Ali	★★★⯪☆
Top Sellers STIG 1975 *Superstars*, unused, Frasier	★★★⯪☆
Top Sellers 1975 *Football 76*, most	★★☆☆☆
Top Sellers 1975 *Football 76*, card #350	★★★☆☆
Top Sellers 1975 *Football 76*, full album	★★★⯪☆
1976 *Football 76*, French edition, most	★★★☆☆
1976 *Football 76*, French edition, Bremner	★★★★☆
1976 *Football 76*, French edition, Cruyff	★★★★☆
1976 *Football 76*, French edition, full album	★★⯪☆☆

Panini Top Sellers

1976 *Football 77*, most	★★☆☆☆
1976 *Football 77*, full album	★★★⯪☆

Panini

1977 *Euro Football*, most unused stickers	★⯪☆☆☆
1977 *Euro Football*, full album	★⯪☆☆☆
1977 *Euro Football*, uncut printer's sheet	★★★★★
1978 *Football 78*, most	★⯪☆☆☆
1978 *Football 78*, intact metallic emblems	★★⯪☆☆
1978 *Euro Football 78*, blue backs or black backs: most	★★☆☆☆
1978 *Euro Football 78*, blue backs or black backs: uncut pairs	★★★☆☆
1978 *Euro Football 78*, blue backs or black backs: uncut pairs, puzzle stickers	★★★☆☆
1978 *World Cup 78*, unused stickers most	★★☆☆☆
1978 *World Cup 78*, full album	★⯪☆☆☆
1979 *Football 79*, most	★⯪☆☆☆
1979 *Football 79*, unused satin-fabric stickers of club emblems	★★★☆☆
1979 *Euro Football 79*, most	★★☆☆☆
1979 *Euro Football 79*, intact club emblems	★★⯪☆☆

Panini Bergmann

1979 *Fussball Bundesliga 79*, most	★★☆☆☆
1979 *Fussball Bundesliga 79*, Liverpool stickers	★★★☆☆

Panini

1980 *Europa 80*, most	★⯪☆☆☆
1980 *Europa 80*, intact metallic emblems	★★★☆☆
1980 *Europa 80*, intact metallic emblems with San Carlo backs	★★★★☆
1980 *Europa 80* and *Football 81* most unused stickers	★⯪☆☆☆

note: Panini collections from after 1980 are generally outside the scope of this vintage cards listing.

1982 *Sport Superstars Euro Football 82*, most	★☆☆☆☆
1982 *Sport Superstars Euro Football 82*, Maradona	★★☆☆☆
1981 and 1984 *Football Superstars*, International versions, most	★⯪☆☆☆
1981 and 1984 *Football Superstars*, Italian versions, most	★★☆☆☆
1987 *Supersport*, International version, most	★☆☆☆☆
1987 *Supersport*, International version, #98 Higgins	★★☆☆☆
1987 *Supersport*, International version, #105 Higgins & Davis pair	★⯪☆☆☆
1987 as above, #153 Tyson	★★☆☆☆
1987 as above, #109 Tyson & Hagler	★★★☆☆
1987 *Supersport*, Italian version, most	★⯪☆☆☆
1987 *Supersport*, Italian version, different stickers to international version	★★☆☆☆
1988 *Supersport*, International version, most	★☆☆☆☆
1988 *Supersport*, International version, Tyson	★★☆☆☆
1988 *Supersport*, Spanish version (yellow borders) most	★★☆☆☆

Pattreiouex

1922 *Famous Footballers*, numbered F1 to F191, most	★★⯪☆☆
1922 *Football Teams*, F192 to F241, most	★★★⯪☆
1922 *Football Teams*, F192 to F241, Liverpool	★★★⯪☆
1922 *Football Teams*, F192 to F241, Arsenal	★★★★☆
1922 *Football Teams*, F192 to F241, Man Utd	★★★★☆
1922 as above, Man City variations basic pair	★★★★⯪
1922 as above, Dick Kerr Ladies	★★★★☆
1923 *Footballers*, FA series,	★★☆☆☆
1923 *Footballers*, FB series,	★★☆☆☆
1924 *Footballers*, FC series,	★★☆☆☆
1927 *Football Series*, brown lettering	★★☆☆☆
1927 *Football Series*, brown lettering, Dean	★★★☆☆
1927 *Football Series*, blue lettering	★★☆☆☆
1928 *Photos Of Football Stars*, most	★★★⯪☆
1928 *Photos Of Football Stars*, Dean	★★★★☆
1930 *Celebrities In Sport*, most	★⯪☆☆☆
1930 *Celebrities In Sport*, Dean	★★⯪☆☆
1931 *Sports Trophies*	★★☆☆☆
1934 *Footballers in Action*, most	★⯪☆☆☆
1934 *Footballers in Action*, card #37 varieties	★⯪☆☆☆
1935 *Sporting Celebrities*	★★☆☆☆
1936 *Sporting Events and Stars*, most	★☆☆☆☆
1936 *Sporting Events and Stars*, Joe Louis	★★☆☆☆
1936 *Sporting Events and Stars*, Bobby Jones	★★☆☆☆

Paulton

1923 Wolverhampton Wanderers players, various issues, most	★★★⯪☆

People's Journal

1914 *Gallery of Famous Footballers*	★★★★★

Pepys Castell

1930s *It's A Goal!*, each card	★⯪☆☆☆
1930s *It's A Goal!*, complete boxed games	★★⯪☆☆
1940s *International Football Whist*, each card	★⯪☆☆☆
1940s *International Football Whist*, complete boxed games	★★☆☆☆
1950s and 1960s *It's A Goal!*, various reissues, each card	★☆☆☆☆
1950s and 1960s *It's A Goal!*, complete boxed games	★⯪☆☆☆

THE SOCCER CARDS RARITY SCALE

Pequeno Artista
1920s Football club colours cards to paint, unused card ★★★★★
1920s Football club colours cards to paint, painted card ★★★★½

Perfetti
1967 *Stars of Sports, Film & Music*, most ★★½☆☆
1967 *Stars of Sports, Film & Music*, Pelé ★★★☆☆
1967 *Stars of Sports, Film & Music*, Eusebio ★★★☆☆
1967 *Stars of Sports, Film & Music*, Beckenbauer ★★★☆☆
1967 as above, Law ★★½☆☆
1967 as above, Charlton ★★☆☆☆
1967 as above, Moore ★★☆☆☆
1967 as above, Greaves ★★½☆☆
1967 as above, Mazzola and Inter cards, each ★★★☆☆
1970s *Football Teams*, gum wrappers ★★★★½
1980s *Forza Goal!*, most ★★½☆☆
1980s *Forza Goal!*, British players ★★★☆☆

Perry Books
1949 *Footballers & Cricketers*, cut-out cards ★★★★☆
1949 *Footballers & Cricketers*, cut-out cards, uncut folded sheet of cards ★★★★½
1949 *Footballers & Cricketers*, cut-out cards, book with sheet of cards ★★★★★
note: the above are known in paper and of card. Later copies, made of paper, are also known.

Perry Books
1950 *Footballers*, by Kerr, large paper cards (trimmed cut outs) about gum-card size. ★★☆☆☆

Phillips
1896 *Footballers* ★★★½☆
1910 *Sporting series* ★★★☆☆
1923 *Sports* ★★★☆☆
1914 *League Colours* (no brand) ★★★★☆
1920 *League Colours* BDV, small, each ★½☆☆☆
1920 *League Colours* BDV, large ★½☆☆☆
note: backing papers add 100% to value. ★☆☆☆☆

1919 to 1920 *Footballers*, small, brown oval, most ★★★☆☆
1919 to 1920 *Footballers*, small, brown oval, rarer varieties ★★★★☆
note: the above series (brown ovals) contains more rookies than most other series of sports cards.

1920 *Footballers*, small, black oval ★★½☆☆
1920 *Footballers*, small, black oval, varieties ★★★½☆
1920 *Footballers*, small, black oval, Meredith ★★★☆☆
1921 to 1922 *Footballers*, small, double frame lines, most ★★★☆☆
1921 to 1922 *Footballers*, small, double frame lines, varieties ★★★½☆
1922 *Footballers*, small, single frame lines with the word 'photo', most ★★½☆☆
1922 as above, varieties ★★★½☆
1922 to 1923 *Footballers*, small, double frame lines with 'Pinnace', most ★★★☆☆
1922 to 1923 Hugh Gallacher small cards ★★★★☆
1920 to 1921 *Footballers*, medium (gum-card size) oval back, most ★★½☆☆
1920 to 1921 as above, varieties ★★★☆☆
1922 to 1923 *Footballers*, medium (gum-card size) frame-lines back ★★★★☆
1922 to 1923 Hugh Gallacher medium card, frameless ★★★★☆
1922 to 1923 *Footballers*, large (postcard-size card) blank back ★★★★½

1922 to 1923 Hugh Gallacher postcard-size card ★★★★★
1922 to 1923 *Football Teams*, extra-large card, blank back ★★★★★
1932 to 1934 BDV *Sportsmen*, packet-issues, paper and card ★★☆☆☆
1932 to 1934 BDV *Sportsmen*, packet-issues, rarer varieties ★★★★½☆
1932 to 1934 BDV packet-issue *Sportsmen*, uncut packets ★★★★½
1935 *In The Public Eye* ★☆☆☆☆
1935 *In The Public Eye*, Dean ★☆☆☆☆
1935 *Famous Footballers*, most ★☆☆☆☆
1936 *International Caps*, most ★☆☆☆☆
1936 *Spot The Winner*, unused, without colour blotches ★★☆☆☆
1936 *Spot The Winner*, used with colour blotches ★☆☆☆☆
1948 *Footballers*, packet issues, paper cut-out cards ★★★½☆
1948 *Footballers*, packet issues, uncut packets ★★★★☆
1949 *Sportsmen & footballers*, packet issues, paper cut-outs ★★★½☆
1949 *Sportsmen & footballers*, packet issues, uncut packets ★★★★☆
1950 *Footballers*, on paper and on card, cut-outs ★★★½☆
1950 *Footballers*, on paper and on card, uncut packets ★★★★☆
1951 *Footballers*, on paper and on card, cut-outs ★★★½☆
1951 *Footballers*, on paper and on card, uncut packets ★★★★☆
1952 *Footballers*, (name above team's name) on paper and on card, cut-outs ★★★½☆
1952 *Footballers* (name above team's name) on paper and on card, uncut packets ★★★★☆
1954 *Sportsmen* (name above firm's name) on card, cut-outs ★★★★½☆
1954 *Sportsmen* (name above firm's name) on card, uncut packets ★★★★½

Philmar
1946 *Footballers*, decal transfers, cut singles ★★★★☆
1946 *Footballers*, decal transfers, uncut sheet ★★★★★

Phoskitos
1976 *Footballers* on folding cards, various series, each card ★★½☆☆
1976 *Footballers* on folding cards, various series, Platini ★★★☆☆
1979 *Liga 79-80 Juego De Fichas*, cards with push-out circular discs ★★★☆☆

Piazza
1930 *Album Fotografie* ★★★★☆

Pinguin
1964 *Spieler des Deutsche Fussball-Bundes* ★★½☆☆
1964 *Spieler des Deutsche Fussball-Bundes*, Morlock ★★★☆☆

Pini by Carlo Pini
1930s *Foot-ball Pirelli*, small monotone cards of football stars ★★★★½

PK Gum
1983 *Football Facts* ★★☆☆☆

Planta
1952 *Olympische Spielen* ★★☆☆☆

Platin
1953 *Seleccione Campeones*, blue, most ★★★☆☆
1953 *Seleccione Campeones*, blue, Kubala ★★★½☆
1953 *Seleccione Campeones*, blue, Di Stefano ★★★★☆
1953 *Seleccione Campeones*, red, most ★★★☆☆
1953 *Seleccione Campeones*, red, Kubala ★★★½☆
1953 *Seleccione Campeones*, red, Di Stefano ★★★★☆

Player
1926 *Footballers Caricatures by RIP*	★☆☆☆☆
1927 *Football Caricatures by MAC*, each	★☆☆☆☆
1927 *Football Caricatures by MAC*, Dean	★☆☆☆☆
1928 *Footballers 1928*, each	★☆☆☆☆
1929 *Footballers 1928-29 2nd Series*, each	★☆☆☆☆
1929 *Footballers 1928-29 2nd Series*, Dean	★☆☆☆☆
1930 *Association Cup Winners*	★☆☆☆☆

Pluck
1922 *Famous Football Teams*, Scottish clubs issued only in Scotland	★★★☆☆
1922 Blackburn, Barnsley, Oldham, Darlington, Swansea, Leicester, Hudd (Scottish versions)	★★★☆☆
1922 *Famous Football Teams*, English clubs issued in England, English versions	★☆☆☆☆

Poly
1970 *Grosse Stars Des Runden Leders*, most	★★☆☆☆
1970 *Grosse Stars Des Runden Leders*, Best	★★⯨☆☆
1970 *Grosse Stars Des Runden Leders*, Pelé	★★⯨☆☆
1970 *Grosse Stars Des Runden Leders*, Cruyff	★★★☆☆
1971 *Goldene Tore*, most	★★☆☆☆
1971 *Goldene Tore*, Pelé	★★⯨☆☆

Poolette Sphinx Products
1938 *The Great Football Pool Card Game*, red back cards	★★☆☆☆
1938 *The Great Football Pool Card Game*, red back cards, boxed set	★★★☆☆
1946 *The Great Football Pool Card Game*, blue back	★★☆☆☆
1946 *The Great Football Pool Card Game*, blue back, boxed set	★★★☆☆

Poppleton
1920s *Footballer*, cards overprinted with a Poppleton rubber stamp	★★★★⯨

Popular
1930 *Pop Cards Famous Footballers*, folded paper cut-out cards	★★★★☆

Poulain
1980s *3615 Poulain sports stars*, most	★⯨☆☆☆
1980s *3615 Poulain sports stars*, Pelé	★★☆☆☆

Prescott Pickup Chewing Gum
1974 *Famous Football Club Flags*	★★⯨☆☆
1974 *Famous Football Club Flags*, packet	★★★★☆
1975 *Famous Football Club Pennants*	★★⯨☆☆
1975 *Famous Football Club Pennants*, packet	★★★★☆

Prescott Pickup
1979 *Sigma Sports Silhouettes*	★☆☆☆☆

Primrose Confectionery
1961 *Famous Footballers FBS1*, cards	★☆☆☆☆
1972 *Cup Tie Quiz*, cards	★⯨☆☆☆

Principe
1932 *Cine-Sport*	★★★★☆

Progresso Foods
1978 *Meet The Cosmos*, cut singles	★★★☆☆
1978 *Meet The Cosmos*, uncut strips	★★★★☆
1978 *Meet The Cosmos*, Pelé	★★★★⯨

PS (Provincial Sports Publications)
1948 *Soccer Stars*, journal gift cards, uncut cards	★★★★☆
1948 *Soccer Stars*, journal gift cards, cut singles	★☆☆☆☆
1949 *Wolves and Leicester City FA Cup card*	★★★★☆

Pulgarcito
1940s & 1950s footballers and teams, most	★★★☆☆
1940s & 1950s footballers and teams, Kubala	★★★★⯨
1940s & 1950s footballers and teams, Ben Barek	★★★★☆

Quadriga
1982 *English Football Tips 82/83* (Scandinavian) stickers	★★★☆☆
1982 *English Football Tips 82/83* (Scandinavian) wrapper	★★★☆☆
1982 *English Football Tips 82/83* (Scandinavian) full album	★★★★☆
1983 *The Laws Of Soccer*, most stickers	★★★☆☆
1983 *The Laws Of Soccer*, wrapper	★★★★☆
1983 *The Laws Of Soccer*, full album	★★★★☆
1983 *Soccer 83-84*, most stickers	★★★☆☆
1983 *Soccer 83-84*, wrapper	★★★★☆
1983 *Soccer 83-84*, full album	★★★★☆
1984 *Snooker Kings*, most	★★⯨☆☆
1984 *Snooker Kings*, Alex Higgins	★★★☆☆
1984 *Snooker Kings*, Jimmy White	★★★☆☆
1984 *Snooker Kings*, full album	★★★☆☆
1984 *English Football Tips 83/84* (Scandinavian)	★★★☆☆
1984 *English Football Tips 83/84* (Scandinavian), wrapper	★★★☆☆
1984 *English Football Tips 83/84* (Scandinavian), full album	★★★★☆

Quaker Oats
1959 *Stars of Sport Picture Cards*	★★⯨☆☆
1960 *Great Moments in Sport*	★★☆☆☆
1964 *Phiz-quiz*, cards, most	★★☆☆☆
1964 *Phiz-quiz*, cards, Joe Louis	★★★☆☆
1962 *Photos of World Cup Football Stars*, redemption cards, most	★★★☆☆
1962 *Photos of World Cup Football Stars*, redemption cards, Bobby Moore	★★★★☆

Question of Sport
1986, 1992, 1996 quiz cards	★☆☆☆☆

Radio Corriera
1970 *Coppa Rimet Mexico 70*, cut singles	★★☆☆☆
1970 *Coppa Rimet Mexico 70*, uncut sheets	★★★★☆
1970 *Coppa Rimet Mexico 70*, England singles	★★☆☆☆
1974 *Mondiali Monaco 74*, most cut singles	★★☆☆☆
1974 *Mondiali Monaco 74*, uncut sheets	★★★★☆
1974 *Mondiali Monaco 74*, Scotland singles	★★★☆☆

Record
1954 *Goal!* most	★★⯨☆☆

Record Cigarette Co. by Dubrico
1934 *Talkie Cigarette Card*, footballers	★★★★☆

THE SOCCER CARDS RARITY SCALE

Red Star
1933 *Footballer*, transfer decals, most	★★★★½☆
1933 *Footballer*, transfer decals, uncut sheet	★★★★½
1933 *Footballer*, transfer decals, Stanley Matthews	★★★★☆

Reddish Maid
1965 *International Footballers of Today*	★★½☆☆
1965 *International Footballers of Today*, Moore	★★★☆☆
1965 *International Footballers of Today*, Best	★★★½☆
1965 *International Footballers of Today*, Pelé	★★★☆☆

Regina Chocolates
1930 *Rebucados Azes do Football*	★★★★☆

Rekord
1950s & 1960s *Sportsmen*, cut singles	★★☆☆☆
1950s & 1960s *Sportsmen*, cut doubles	★★½☆☆
1950s & 1960s *Sportsmen*, Yashin pair	★★★★☆
1950s & 1960s *Sportsmen*, Pelé pair	★★★★☆

note: un-cut Rekord front covers with intact pairs adds 50%; entire magazines add 100% to values.

Reunion
1928 *Fussball Und Ander Sportarten*	★★★☆☆

Reyauca
1982 *Ases Mundial 82 circular stickers* (larger than similar Mas), most	★½☆☆☆
1982 *Ases Mundial 82 circular stickers* (larger than similar Mas), Maradona	★★☆☆☆
1982 *España 82*, rectangular stickers, most	★★★☆☆
1982 *España 82*, rectangular stickers, unused Maradona & Ardiles	★★★★☆
1986 *Futbol Mundial*	★★☆☆☆

Ripley Brothers
1920s *Football Club Colours*	★★★★★

Ritchie & Company
1990s *Footballers 1994-1995*	★½☆☆☆

Rizla Chewing Gum
1974 *World Cup*, cards	★★★★☆

Roche Rising Sun
1927 *Rising Sun Famous Footballers*, most	★★☆☆☆
1927 *Rising Sun Famous Footballers*, card #21 Kelly	★★★☆☆
1927 *Rising Sun Famous Footballers*, #32 Dean	★★★☆☆

Rollan
1985 *Super Futbol 85*, most	★★½☆☆
1985 *Super Futbol 85*, Archibald	★★★☆☆

Rotalfoto
1950 *Fotopropaganda*, cards	★★★★½

Rotopress
1958 *Prärie-Serier & Vilder Västerns Samlarserie*, with tokens, most	★★★★½
1958 *Prärie-Serier & Vilder Västerns Samlarserie*, with tokens, Brazil	★★★★☆

Rover
1922 to 1923 *Real Photos*, pairs of footballers, English issue, uncut pairs	★★☆☆☆
1922 to 1923 *Real Photos*, pairs of footballers, English issue, cut singles	★½☆☆☆
1922 to 1923 *Real Photos*, pairs of footballers, Scottish issue, uncut pairs	★★★★☆
1922 to 1923 *Real Photos*, pairs of footballers, Scottish issue, cut singles	★★☆☆☆
1923 *Dandy Stand-up Footballers All Star XI Team*	★★★☆☆
1924 *Football Transfers in Brilliant Colours*, sheets of four players	★★★★½
1924 *Football Transfers in Brilliant Colours*, cut single decals	★★★☆☆
1925 *100 Best Players*, booklet, uncut booklet	★★★☆☆
1925 *100 Best Players*, booklet, cut singles	★½☆☆☆
1923 to 1927 *Team Flags*, uncut page from comic of 22 flags & a league ladder	★★★★☆
1923 to 1927 *Team Flags*, cut singles	★★☆☆☆

note: as with all comic cut-outs (which were intended to be cut) complete comics add 100% value.

1927 *This Year's Top Form Footballers*, uncut sheets of four	★★★★☆
1927 *This Year's Top Form Footballers*, cut cards	★☆☆☆☆
1927 *This Year's Top Form Footballers*, Dean	★★☆☆☆
1927 *The A.B.C. of Famous Football Clubs*, booklet	★★★☆☆
1927 *The A.B.C. of Famous Football Clubs*, cut outs	★½☆☆☆
1937 *Big Badges [of] Famous Teams*, sheet of stickers	★★★★☆
1937 *Big Badges [of] Famous Teams*, cut singles	★☆☆☆☆
1948 *Football Club Colours*, to cut out, uncut comics	★★★☆☆
1948 *Football Club Colours*, to cut out, cut single badges	★½☆☆☆
1950 *Football Club Badges*, to cut out, uncut comics	★★★☆☆
1950 *Football Club Badges*, to cut out, cut single badges	★½☆☆☆
1951 *Famous Footballers*, to cut out, blue or b/w pictures, uncut comics	★★★☆☆
1951 *Famous Footballers*, to cut out, blue or b/w pictures, cut singles	★☆☆☆☆
1953 to 1956 *Famous Footballers*, intact comics	★★★☆☆
1953 to 1956 *Famous Footballers*, single cut outs	★☆☆☆☆
1958 *Stars of Sport & Entertainment*, uncut quads	★★★☆☆
1958 *Stars of Sport & Entertainment*, cut single cards	★½☆☆☆
1958 as above, Joe Baker, uncut quad	★★★☆☆
1958 as above, Joe Baker, single	★☆☆☆☆
1958 as above, Charlton, uncut quad	★★★★☆
1958 as above, Charlton, single	★★☆☆☆
1960 *Football Teams of Northern Ireland*, uncut paired teams	★★★★☆
1960 *Football Teams of Northern Ireland*, cut singles	★★☆☆☆
1961 *ABC Chart of Football Colours*, unused set of four cards & 4 sheets of stickers	★★★☆☆
1963 *Ace Album of Football Stars*, uncut trios	★★★★☆
1963 *Ace Album of Football Stars*, cut singles	★★☆☆☆
1963 *Ace Album of Football Stars*, cut single Moore	★★½☆☆

Rover and Wizard
1968 to 1970 *Famous Football Stars*, cut-outs, comics with sheets of cards	★★★☆☆
1968 to 1970 as above, cut singles with bases	★★☆☆☆
1968 to 1970 as above, Kenny Dalglish, cut	★★☆☆☆
1968 to 1970 as above, Dalglish on an uncut sheet	★★★☆☆

RuiRomer

1962 *Campeonatos Futbol 1962 & Copa de Europa*, most	★★⯨☆☆
1962 *Campeonatos Futbol 1962 & Copa de Europa*, Wolves pair	★★★☆☆
1966 *Futbol Torneos Continentales 1967*, most	★★⯨☆☆
1966 *Futbol Torneos Continentales 1967*, Chelsea	★★★☆☆
1966 *Futbol Torneos Continentales 1967*, Man Utd	★★★☆☆
1966 *Futbol Torneos Continentales 1967*, Rangers	★★★☆☆
1973 *Campeonatos Nacionales Liga 1973*, most	★★☆☆☆
1973 *Campeonatos Nacionales Liga 1973*, Chelsea	★★⯨☆☆
1973 *Campeonatos Nacionales Liga 1973*, Newcastle	★★★☆☆
1973 *Campeonatos Nacionales Liga 1973*, Saints	★★★☆☆
1973 *Campeonatos Nacionales Liga 1973*, Spurs	★★★☆☆
1973 as above, Celtic	★★★☆☆
1973 as above, Leicester	★★⯨☆☆
1973 as above, Liverpool	★★★☆☆
1973 as above, Man City	★★★☆☆
1973 as above, Man Utd	★★★☆☆
1973 as above, Hibs	★★★☆☆
1974 *Campeonatos Mundiales Munich 74*, most	★★☆☆☆
1974 *Campeonatos Mundiales Munich 74*, Scottish players	★★⯨☆☆
1977 *Historia y Tecnica del Futbol*, most	★☆☆☆☆
1977 *Historia y Tecnica del Futbol*, portraits of British & world greats	★★☆☆☆
1978 *Argentina 1978*, most	★⯨☆☆☆
1978 *Argentina 1978*, Scottish players	★★☆☆☆

Rutherford

1898 *Footballers*	★★★★★

Saint Petersburg

1900 *Footballers*	★★★★★

Sartori Laporta

1950s *Spurs Sports Favourites*, a booklet of stapled cards	★★★★★
1950s *Spurs Sports Favourites*, single cards	★★⯨☆☆

S&B Products

1948 *Torry Gillick's Internationals*, booklet of eight cards	★★★☆☆
1948 *Torry Gillick's Internationals*, single cards	★⯨☆☆☆

SAIM

1961 to 1962 *Campionati Nazionali & Campionati Mondiali di Calcio*, on thin paper, most	★★☆☆☆
1961 to 1962 as above, on thin paper, Pelé	★★★☆☆
1961 to 1962 as above, on thin paper, Mel Hopkins (*Blankflowers*)	★★★☆☆
1961 to 1962 as above, on thin paper, Puskás	★★★☆☆
1961 to 1962 as above, on thin paper, Brazil	★★★☆☆
1961 to 1962 *Campionati Nazionali & Campionati Mondiali di Calcio*, on card, most	★★☆☆☆
1961 to 1962 as above, on card, Pelé	★★⯨☆☆
1961 to 1962 as above, on card, Mel Hopkins	★★★☆☆
1961 to 1962 as above, on card, Puskás	★★☆☆☆
1961 to 1962 as above, on card, Brazil	★★☆☆☆
1961 to 1962 as above, on card, di Stefano	★★☆☆☆
1961 to 1962 *Campionati Nazionali & Campionati Mondiali di Calcio*, plastic, most	★★★☆☆
1961 to 1962 as above, on plastic, Pelé	★★★☆☆
1961 to 1962 as above, on plastic, Mel Hopkins	★★★☆☆
1961 to 1962 as above, on plastic, Puskás	★★⯨☆☆
1961 to 1962 as above, on plastic, Brazil	★★☆☆☆
1961 to 1962 as above, on plastic, Hitchens	★★☆☆☆

Sada

1958 *Girandola di Successi*, most	★★☆☆☆
1958 *Girandola di Successi*, Rocky Marciano	★★★☆☆

Salem

1935 *Deutscher Sport Vorschau Auf 1936*, most	★⯨☆☆☆

San Giorgio

1962 *Le Più Forti Squadre Partecipanti ai 1962 Campionati Mondiali Cile*, most	★★★⯨☆
1962 as above, Pelé #10	★★★☆☆
1962 as above, Pelé #175	★★★☆☆
1962 as above, England stars	★★★⯨☆
1962 as above, Moore	★★★★☆

Sanella

1920s *Handbuch des Sports*	★★☆☆☆

Santi Salvatore

1966 toy banknotes with footballers	★★★⯨☆
1966 toy banknotes with footballers, Rivera	★★★⯨☆

Scerri

1936 *International Footballers*, most	★★★⯨☆
1936 *International Footballers*, Dean	★★★⯨☆
1936 *International Footballers*, Matthews	★★★★☆

Scoop

1979 *Soccer Superstars*, circular stickers, uncut sheet	★★★☆☆
1979 *Soccer Superstars*, circular stickers, cut singles	★⯨☆☆☆

THE SOCCER CARDS RARITY SCALE

Scorcher & Score
1970 *My Favourite Soccer Stars*, uncut sheets of cards ★★☆☆☆
1970 *My Favourite Soccer Stars*, cut singles ★☆☆☆☆

Scottish Daily Express
1956 *Super Sports Postcards* ★★☆☆☆
1960s *Souvenir Photographs 1962/63* ★★★☆☆
1972 *Scotcards* ★☆☆☆☆

SEIP
1954 *Figurine Sportive* ★★★☆☆

Seix & Barral
1924 self-standing *Footballer* cards, most ★★★☆☆
1924 self-standing *Footballer* cards, Samitier ★★★★☆
1924 self-standing *Footballer* cards, Zamora ★★★★☆

Semic Press
1970 *Fotboll VM 70*, most ★★☆☆☆
1970 *Fotboll VM 70*, England players ★★☆☆☆
1970 *Fotboll VM 70*, Beckenbaur ★★☆☆☆
1970 *Fotboll VM 70*, Pelé ★★☆☆☆

Seveso Dolciaria
1930s *Footballer* cards ★★★★☆

Seymour Juesbury
1900 *Football Series Puzzle* cards ★★★★★

Sharpe
1890s *Play Up Football Cards*, smaller teams ★★★★☆
1890s *Play Up Football Cards*, bigger names ★★★★★

Sheffield Telegraph
1920s *Football Guide*, cards of players and teams ★★★★☆

Shell Petrol
1970 *Top Voetbal*, coins, most ★★☆☆☆
1970 *Top Voetbal*, coins Beckenbauer ★★★☆☆
1970 *Top Voetbal*, coins Cruyff ★★★☆☆
1970 *Top Voetbal*, coins, Cruyff, coin in sealed packet ★★★★☆

Sherman's Pools
1937 *Searchlight on Famous Players* ★☆☆☆☆
1938 *Searchlight on Famous Teams* ★☆☆☆☆

Shoot!
1969 self-standing soccer player cards, with bases ★★★☆☆
1969 self-standing soccer player cards, without bases ★☆☆☆☆

Shredded Wheat
1958 *Football Tips from Tom Finney* ★★★★☆
1972 *Bob Wilson's Soccer Action*, uncut trios ★★★☆☆
1972 *Bob Wilson's Soccer Action*, cut singles ★☆☆☆☆
1976 *World Super Stars and Sporting Trophies*, most ★☆☆☆☆
1976 *World Super Stars and Sporting Trophies*, unfolded Pelé ★★☆☆☆
1976 *World Super Stars and Sporting Trophies*, folded Pelé ★☆☆☆☆

Shurey's
1910s football postcards ★★★★★

Sicker
1964 *Die Besten Fussballspieler... 1964/1965*, most ★★☆☆☆
1964 *Die Besten Fussballspieler... 1964/1965*, Greaves ★★☆☆☆
1964 *Die Besten Fussballspieler... 1964/1965*, Pelé ★★★☆☆
1964 *Die Besten Fussballspieler... 1964/1965*, Eusebio ★★☆☆☆
1965 *Die Fussball-Saison 1965/66*, most ★★☆☆☆
1965 *Die Fussball-Saison 1965/66*, Pelé ★★☆☆☆
1965 *Die Fussball-Saison 1965/66*, Beckenbauer ★★★☆☆
1965 *Die Fussball-Saison 1965/66*, Liverpool players ★★☆☆☆
1965 *Die Fussball-Saison 1965/66*, as above, uncut sheets of nine stamps ★★★★★
1966 *Die Weltmeisterschaft 1966 im England*, most ★★☆☆☆
1966 *Die Weltmeisterschaft 1966 im England*, players ★★★☆☆
1966 *Die Weltmeisterschaft 1966 im England*, Pelé ★★☆☆☆
1967 *Die Fussball-Saison 1967/68*, as above, uncut sheets of eight stamps ★★★★★

Sidam
1959 *Il Calcio Italiano 1959-60*, most ★★☆☆☆
1959 *Il Calcio Italiano 1959-60*, Rivera ★★★☆☆
1959 *Il Calcio Italiano 1959-60*, Charles ★★☆☆☆

Sidea
1933 *Calciatori* ★★★★☆

Sidol
1938 *Lodis medaglioni*, footballers ★★★★☆

Sifta Sam by Palmer Mann
1955 packet-issue *Famous Footballers*, cut-out cards ★★★★☆
1955 packet-issue *Famous Footballers*, entire boxes ★★★★★

Simon Chocolates
1964 *Album 3 Anos De Vida Mundial*, most ★★☆☆☆
1964 *Album 3 Anos De Vida Mundial*, di Stefano ★★★☆☆

Sinclair (John Sinclair)
1906 *Football Favourites* ★★★★☆
1935 *English & Scottish Football Stars* ★☆☆☆☆
1937 *Well Known Footballers, North Eastern Counties* ★☆☆☆☆
1938 *Well Known Scottish Footballers* ★☆☆☆☆

Sinclair (Robert Sinclair)
1898 mauve or b/w *Footballers* ★★★★★

Singleton & Cole
1905 *Footballers* ★★★★☆

Skipper
1931 *Football Towns and their Crests & Famous Ships*, uncut with ship ★★★★★
1931 *Football Towns and their Crests & Famous Ships*, cut ★☆☆☆☆
1933 *Football Clubs*, uncut strips of four cards ★★★★☆
1933 *Football Clubs*, cut singles ★☆☆☆☆
1934 *Winner Football Flags*, uncut sheets of 21 flags ★★★★★
1934 *Winner Football Flags*, full album ★★★☆☆
1934 *Winner Football Flags*, flags ★★★☆☆

1939 *Football Tricky Tips*, stickers, uncut sheet	★★★★⯨
1939 *Football Tricky Tips*, stickers, most stickers	★★★☆☆
1939 *Football Tricky Tips*, stickers, Matthews	★★★⯨☆

Smashers by Sport Photos
1950 booklet of cards	★★★★☆
1950 single cards	★★⯨☆☆

Smith
1902 *Champions of Sport*, blue backs and red backs, footballers	★★★★☆
1901 *Cup Tie* footballers (brown backs)	★★★⯨☆
1909 *Cup Tie* footballers (blue backs)	★★★☆☆
1909 *Cup Tie* footballers (blue backs), Meredith	★★★☆☆
1912 *Footballers* (series of 150)	★⯨☆☆☆
1912 *Footballers* (series of 150), Meredith	★★⯨☆☆
1917 *Football Club Records*, most	★★⯨☆☆
1917 *Football Club Records*, Meredith	★★★☆☆
1922 *Football Club Records*, most	★⯨☆☆☆

Smith's Crisps
1971 *George Best Picture Card* black backs & blue backs, uncut pairs	★★★⯨☆
1971 *George Best Picture Card* black backs & blue backs, cut	★☆☆☆☆

Soccer Bubblegum by Merry Sweets
1957 *Soccer No.1 Series*	★☆☆☆☆
1958 *Soccer No.2 Series*	★☆☆☆☆

Soirée Cigarettes by Alan Ramsey
1958 *Famous Footballers*, packet issues to cut out, most	★★★★☆
as above, uncut players with packaging	★★★★★
as above, cut Jimmy Greaves	★★★★☆
as above, cut Bobby Charlton	★★★★☆
as above, uncut Jimmy Greaves	★★★★★
as above, uncut Bobby Charlton	★★★★★

Speranza & Carità
1975 *Goal!*, uncut strips of six	★★⯨☆☆
1975 *Goal!*, cut single stickers	★⯨☆☆☆

Somportex
1972 *Football Club Badges with Sweets*, plastic shield-shape emblems	★⯨☆☆☆
1972 *Football Club Badges with Sweets*, wrapper	★★☆☆☆

Sorcacius
1982 *XII Campeonato do Mundo de Futebol*, most	★★☆☆☆
1982 *XII Campeonato do Mundo de Futebol*, British Isles players	★★⯨☆☆
1982 *XII Campeonato do Mundo de Futebol*, Maradona	★★★☆☆

Sorcacius
1984 *Campeonato da Europa de Futebol*, most	★★☆☆☆
1984 *Campeonato da Europa de Futebol*, British Isles players	★★⯨☆☆

Sports Budget
1927 *Who's Who of Famous Footballers*, uncut booklet	★★⯨☆☆
1927 *Who's Who of Famous Footballers*, cut-out players	⯨☆☆☆☆

Spiro's Mixture by Spiro & Valleri
1906 *Noted Footballers*	★★★★⯨

Sport & Bilder by Dreyer
1980s *Lagserien*, football teams	★★☆☆☆

Sport
1949 *Wonderful Team Portraits Presented by Sport* (colour), booklet of cards	★★☆☆☆
1949 *Wonderful Team Portraits Presented by Sport* (colour), single card	★☆☆☆☆
1951 *Wonderful Team Portraits Presented by Sport* (monotone) card	★★★☆☆

Sport & Adventure
1922 *Famous Footballers*, English, uncut trios	★★★☆☆
1922 *Famous Footballers*, English, uncut pairs	★★⯨☆☆
1922 *Famous Footballers*, English, cut singles	★☆☆☆☆
1922 *Famous Footballers*, Scottish, uncut trios	★★★★☆
1922 *Famous Footballers*, Scottish, uncut pairs	★★★⯨☆
1922 *Famous Footballers*, Scottish, cut singles	★★☆☆☆

Sport Pictures
1921 & 1922 supplements of sports stars dated 1921-22 or 1922-23, most	★★★★☆

Sportfoto
1952 large cards stapled into paper folders (*Famous Footballers Series No.1*)	★★★★☆
1952 large cards, different to above, card shows player's name above team name	★★★★☆
1953 small cards with "*Sportfoto*", most	★★☆☆☆
1953 small cards with "*SPORTFOTO*", most	★★★☆☆
1954 small cards with "*Daily Herald Copyright SPORTFOTO*", most	★★⯨☆☆
1954 small cards with "*Daily Herald Copyright*", most	★☆☆☆☆

Sporting Mirror
1948 fold-out series of concertina-like cards with envelope, uncut complete	★★★☆☆

Sport-Pics
1950s footballers, b/w photographic heads on illustrated bodies, uncut sheet	★★★⯨☆

Stenval
1975 *Pink Panther j'Aime ...* sports stickers, most	★★⯨☆☆
1978 World Cup sticker cards (a sticker *and* a card in one) intact, most	★★★☆☆

THE SOCCER CARDS RARITY SCALE

Stella
1961 *Raccolta Figurine Calcio*, most ★★☆☆☆
1961 *Raccolta Figurine Calcio*, Pelé (with blue, yellow or white frames) ★★½☆☆
1962 *Raccolta Figurine Calcio*, small Pelé card with a strange shape behind Pelé's head ★★☆☆☆
1962 *Raccolta Figurine Calcio*, small Pelé card without the strange shape behind Pelé's head ★★★☆☆
1962 *Raccolta Figurine Calcio*, large square card of Pelé ★★★☆☆
1963 *Raccolta Figurine Calcio*, large rectangular cards, most ★★½☆☆
1963 *Raccolta Figurine Calcio*, large rectangular cards, Pelé ★★☆☆☆

Stockhaus
1974 *Fussball WM74*, most ★★☆☆☆

Suchard
1968 *A La Decouverte Du Sport, Champions, Techniques*, most ★★☆☆☆
1968 *A La Decouverte Du Sport, Champions, Techniques*, Pelé ★★★☆☆
1968 *A La Decouverte Du Sport, Champions, Techniques*, England ★★★☆☆

Subbuteo by P. A. Adolph
1947 to 1964 *Soccer Market* cards, single cards ★★½☆☆
1947 to 1964 *Soccer Market* cards, complete boxed sets ★★★★☆
1953 *Famous Footballers Series of 50*, most ★★★★½
1953 *Famous Footballers Series of 50*, Bury & Notts County cards ★★★★☆
1954 *Famous Footballers Series of 24 cards*, two diverse series, most ★☆☆☆☆

Sugosa
1964 *Famous Footballers* ★★½☆☆

Sultana y Americano
1920s *Football scenes* ★★☆☆☆
1920s *Football scenes* cards with Dundee & Notts County ★★★½☆

Sun
1969 *Football Strips of the 1st Division 1969-70*, uncut strips ★★★☆☆
1969 *Football Strips of the 1st Division 1969-70*, singles ★★★☆☆
1970 *World Cup Souvenir Wall Chart*, uncut strips ★★★☆☆
1970 *World Cup Souvenir Wall Chart*, Pelé ★★☆☆☆
1970 *World Cup Souvenir Wall Chart*, Eusebio ★★☆☆☆
1970 *World Cup Souvenir Wall Chart*, Beckenbauer ★★☆☆☆
1970 *Soccer Calendar*, stickers, uncut strips ★★★☆☆
1970 *Soccer Calendar*, stickers, singles ★★☆☆☆
1970 to 1971 *Scrapbook Encyclopædia 1971*, most ★☆☆☆☆
1971 *Swap Cards* ★☆☆☆☆
1971 *Football Encyclopædia Soccer Stamp Album 1971-70*, most ½☆☆☆☆
1971 *Football Encyclopædia Soccer Stamp Album 1971-70*, Matthews ★☆☆☆☆
1971 *Football Encyclopædia Soccer Stamp Album 1971-70*, Best ★½☆☆☆
1972 *Football Encyclopædia and 3D Album 1972-73* lenticular 3-D cards, small & large ★☆☆☆☆
1979 *Soccercards*, full set ★☆☆☆☆
1979 *Soccercards*, single cards ☆☆☆☆☆

Sunday Chronicle
1906 supplements of *Football Teams* ★★★★½

Sunday Dispatch
1948 packet-issue *Football League Stars* to cut out ★★★☆☆

Sunday Empire News
1953 *Famous Footballers of Today (Mickey Durling)*, booklets ★★★☆☆
1953 *Famous Footballers of Today (Mickey Durling)*, single cards ★½☆☆☆

Sunday Express
1950s *Play Soccer The Matthews Way*, postcard-size cards ★★½☆☆

Sunday Mail
1950 *Junior Sports Club Scottish Footballers*, facsimile autographs in white ★★½☆☆
1951 *Scottish Footballers* ★★½☆☆

Sunday Post
1933-34 *Football Teams 1933-1934*, large, b/w cards with two ribbon holes ★★★☆☆

Sunnyvale
1947 *Famous Football Internationals*, players, in pairs ★★★☆☆
1947 *Famous Football Internationals*, players, single cut cards ★½☆☆☆
1947 as above, *Cigarette Card Book*, the above pairs, in a booklet of 16 players ★★★★½
1948 *Famous Footballers*, sheet of 16 transfers, intact ★★★★½
1948 *Famous Footballers*, sheet of 16 transfers, a cut single ★★★☆☆

Sweetule
1958 *Sports Quiz* ★☆☆☆☆
1959 *Junior Service Quiz* ★☆☆☆☆
1959 *Football Club Nicknames* ★☆☆☆☆
1962 *International Footballers*, packet-issue series, uncut packets ★★½☆☆
1962 *International Footballers*, packet-issue series, cut cards ★☆☆☆☆

Swettenhams
1936 *Popular Stoke & Port Vale Football Players*, most ★★★☆☆
1936 *Popular Stoke & Port Vale Football Players*, Matthews ★★★½☆

Tabay Gum
1948 *Deportivo Reportages Photograficos*, most ★★☆☆☆
1948 *Deportivo Reportages Photograficos*, golf and football cards ★★½☆☆

Taddy
1907 *Prominent Footballers*, Grapnel or Imperial (no footnote) London clubs ★★☆☆☆
1907 *Prominent Footballers*, Grapnel or Imperial (no footnote) other clubs ★★★☆☆
1908 *Prominent Footballers*, Grapnel or Imperial (Myrtle Grove) London clubs ★★☆☆☆
1908 as above, other clubs ★★★½☆
1908 as above, some ★★★★☆
1914 *Prominent Footballers*, London Mixture, players from London clubs ★★½☆☆
1914 *Prominent Footballers*, London Mixture, players from other clubs, most ★★★★☆
194 as above, some ★★★★½

Tavermatic
1961 *Calciatori*, most ★★☆☆
1961 *Calciatori*, Rivera ★★½☆
1961 *Calciatori*, Charles ★★½☆
1961 *Calciatori*, Hitchens ★★½☆

Teasdale
1929 *Footballers and Action* (like the 1928 Gallaher series with red backs) ★★★½☆
1930 *Jigsaw Footballers* ★★★★★

Tempo

1966 *Campeonato del Mondo di Calcio*	★☆☆☆☆
1966 *Campeonato del Mondo di Calcio*, Pelé	★★☆☆☆
1966 *Campeonato del Mondo di Calcio*, England	★⯨☆☆☆
1966 *Campeonato del Mondo di Calcio*, Eusebio	★★☆☆☆
1966 *Campeonato del Mondo di Calcio*, Beckenbauer	★★☆☆☆
1966 *Campeonato del Mondo di Calcio*, uncut sheets	★★★☆☆
1966 *Campeonato del Mondo di Calcio*, sheet with Pelé	★★★☆☆
1966 *Campeonato del Mondo di Calcio*, sheet with Beckenbauer	★★★☆☆
1966 as above, uncut sheets with England stars	★★⯨☆☆
1966 as above, uncut sheet with Eusebio	★★★☆☆
1966 as above, uncut sheet with Yashin	★★★☆☆
1966 as above, flipped images facing the other way, yellow borders: Greaves	★★★☆☆
1966 as above, flipped images facing the other way, yellow borders: Pelé	★★★☆☆

Tennent

1974 *Are You Ready?* Beermats,	★★☆☆☆
1974 *Are You Ready?* Dalglish	★★★☆☆
1978 *Argentina 1978*, glass-shaped beermats	★⯨☆☆☆

Tex

1961 *Navajo Striscia Calciatori*, cut-out footballers	★★★☆☆
1961 *Navajo Striscia Calciatori*, uncut intact comics with card	★★★⯨☆
1961 as above, intact comics with cut-out, Greaves	★★★★☆
1961 as above, intact comics with cut-out, with Baker	★★★⯨☆
1961 as above, intact comics with cut-out, with Denis Law	★★★⯨☆

Texaco

1969 *Famous Footballers*, coins	★☆☆☆☆
1971 *Soccer Map of Teams*, unused sticker	★★⯨☆☆
1971 *Soccer Map of Teams*, cut-out used sticker	★☆☆☆☆
1972 *Soccer Match*, fold-out game, a pair of matched halves	★★☆☆☆
1972 *Soccer Match*, fold-out game, single halves	★☆☆☆☆
1970s Club colours rosette stickers	★★★☆☆

Thomson ephemera are listed under publication names:
Adventure, Rover, Skipper, Vanguard, Wizard, etc.

Tiger

1959 *Famous Football Teams 1958–59*, uncut quads	★★★☆☆
1959 *Famous Football Teams 1958–59*, uncut pairs	★★☆☆☆
1959 Famous Football Teams 1958–59, cut singles	⯨☆☆☆☆
1959 *Famous Football Teams 1959–60*, uncut quads	★★★☆☆
1959 *Famous Football Teams 1959–60*, uncut pairs	★★☆☆☆
1959 *Famous Football Teams 1959–60*, cut singles	⯨☆☆☆☆
1963 *Star Footballers of 1963*, uncut sheet	★★⯨☆☆
1963 *Star Footballers of 1963*, single cut stickers	★☆☆☆☆

Tiger & Hurricane

1967 *Roy Race's Album of Football Club Badges*, uncut sheets	★★⯨☆☆
1967 RoRoy Race's Album of Football Club Badges, cut sticker	⯨☆☆☆☆
1970 & 1971 *My Favourite Soccer Stars*, uncut sheets	★★⯨☆☆
1970 & 1971 *My Favourite Soccer Stars*, cut single cards	★☆☆☆☆

Tiger & Jag

1973 *Stars of British Sport*, intact wheel of footballers	★★⯨☆☆
1973 *I'm A Fan*, rosette with sticky letters, unused set	★★★★☆

Tiger

1982 *World Cup Soccer Cards*, sheet of eight cards and original comic	★★☆☆☆
1982 *World Cup Soccer Cards*, cut single cards	⯨☆☆☆☆

Tiket (Amatller)

1914 *Foot-ball*, cards	★★★⯨☆
1914 *Foot-ball*, cards, Wallace Brothers	★★★★☆
1914 *Foot-ball*, cards, Kinké Armet	★★★☆☆
1914 *Foot-ball*, cards, Roma Forns	★★★☆☆
1914 *Foot-ball*, Gilbert, Gibson, Burnett, Allack and Hodge cards, each	★★★⯨☆

Tinghalls

1950 *VM World Cup 1950* cards	★★★⯨☆

Tip Top (Xuereb) Malta

1950s cards showing classic football matches of the pre-war era	★★☆☆☆

Toblerone

1938 to 1939 Famous Footballers with or without manufacturer's name to front	★★★★☆

Tom Broad & John Allen

1995 *Broad's Braves*, Preston NE stars (25-exemplars), most	★★★★☆
1995 *Broad's Braves*, Preston NE stars (25-exemplars), Beckham	★★★★★

Tonibell

1970 *England's Soccer Stars*	★⯨☆☆☆
1971 *Team of All Time*	★☆☆☆☆
1972 *1st Division Football League Club Badges*	⯨☆☆☆☆

Top Flight

1960 *Top Flight Stars*	★☆☆☆☆

Topical Times

1930 *Football Teams* on metal cards	★⯨☆☆☆
1927 *Footballer*, coloured paper supplements	★★★⯨☆
1927 *Footballer*, coloured paper supplements, Gallacher	★★★⯨☆
1927 *Footballer*, coloured paper supplements, Dean	★★★★☆
1929 *Real glossy photos of footballers*, in pairs, uncut pairs	★★★☆☆
1929 *Real glossy photos of footballers*, cut singles	★☆☆☆☆
1930 *100 Football Stars of 1930*, miniature magazines, intact	★★★☆☆
1930 *100 Football Stars of 1930*, miniature magazines, cut singles	⯨☆☆☆☆
1934 *Special Issues*, large coloured portraits of footballers, English	★☆☆☆☆
1934 *Special Issues*, large coloured portraits of footballers, Scottish	★★⯨☆☆
1934 *Special Issues*, large coloured portraits of footballers, Walker	★★★☆☆
1936 large single panel portraits in colour, English	★☆☆☆☆
1936 large single panel portraits in colour, Scottish	★★⯨☆☆
1937 *Three-in-One Panel Portraits*, English uncut triples	★☆☆☆☆
1937 *Three-in-One Panel Portraits*, Scottish uncut triples	★★★★☆
1932 to 1939 large single panel portraits b/w English issues	★☆☆☆☆
1932 to 1939 large single panel portraits b/w Irish issues	★★★⯨☆
1932 to 1939 large single panel portraits b/w Scottish issues	★★⯨☆☆
1932 to 1939 note: any card with an original magazine whence it came adds 100% to value.	
1937 *Miniature Panel Portraits*, Scottish issue	★★☆☆☆
1937 *Miniature Panel Portraits*, English issue	★☆☆☆☆

THE SOCCER CARDS RARITY SCALE

1937 *Stars of Today* (like *Miniature Panel Portraits*) Scottish issue ★★☆☆☆
1937 *Stars of Today* (like *Miniature Panel Portraits*) English issue ★☆☆☆☆
1938 *Great Players* (gum-card format) Scottish issue ★★☆☆☆
1938 *Great Players* (gum-card format) English issue ★☆☆☆☆

Topps
1975 *Footballer*, gum cards with red & black backs, English ★☆☆☆☆
1975 *Footballer*, gum cards with blue & black backs, Scottish ★★☆☆☆
1975 wrapper (green with rainbow) ★★★☆☆
1975 counter display box ★★★★½
1976 *Footballer*, gum cards with blue & black backs, English ★½☆☆☆
1976 *Footballer*, gum cards with red & black backs, Scottish ★★☆☆☆
1976 wrapper (yellow, player in red) ★★★☆☆
1976 counter display box (Liverpool & Man City) ★★★★½
1977 *Footballer*, gum cards with red & black backs, English ★½☆☆☆
1977 *Footballer*, gum cards with yellow & black backs, Scottish ★★½☆☆
1977 wrapper (red, player in blue & yellow) ★★★☆☆
1977 box (with Sheffield United, Chelsea, West Ham, Newcastle United & Birmingham City) ★★★★☆
1978 *Footballer*, gum cards with orange & brown backs, English ★½☆☆☆
1978 *Footballer*, gum cards with green & black backs, Scottish ★★½☆☆
1978 wrapper (light blue, figure in red) ★★★☆☆
1978 box ★★★★☆
1979 *Footballer*, gum cards with blue & white backs, English ★½☆☆☆
1979 *Footballer*, gum cards with red & brown backs, Scottish ★★½☆☆
1979 *Footballer*, gum cards sheet of six English cards given with *Victor* comic ★★★☆☆
1979 wrapper (two players, one in a Wolves shirt) ★★★☆☆
1979 box (Wolves v Villa 1977) ★★★★☆
1979 *NASL Soccer Stickers* ★☆☆☆☆
1979 *NASL Soccer Stickers*, wrapper ★☆☆☆☆
1979 *NASL Soccer Stickers* box ★★☆☆☆
1981 *Footballer '81*, gum cards with pink backs, uncut trios ★☆☆☆☆
1981 *Footballer '81*, gum cards with pink backs, cut singles ☆☆☆☆☆
1981 *Football Posters*, miniature, folded posters ★☆☆☆☆
1981 wrapper ★☆☆☆☆
1981 display box ★★☆☆☆
1982 *Footballer*, gum cards with blue backs, uncut trios ★☆☆☆☆
1982 *Footballer*, gum cards with blue backs, cut singles ☆☆☆☆☆
1982 wrapper (yellow & blue) ★☆☆☆☆
1982 display box ★★☆☆☆

Topps & Jolly Press
1982 *Topps Spotlights*, English cards ★½☆☆☆
1982 *Topps Spotlights*, French-issue & German-issue cards ★★★☆☆

Top Sellers – see Panini

Tower Press
1966 *Famous Football Clubs 1st series*, transfer decals, uncut sheet ★★★☆☆
1966 *Famous Football Clubs 1st series*, transfer decals, singles ★½☆☆☆
1967 *Famous Football Clubs 2nd series*, transfer decals, uncut sheet ★★★☆☆
1967 *Famous Football Clubs 2nd series*, transfer decals, singles ★½☆☆☆

Transfers
1931 a series of 36 numbered *Famous Footballers* colour decals by an unknown issuer ★★★★☆

Transimage
1979 *Football 79/80*, uncut pairs ★☆☆☆☆
1979 *Football 79/80*, cut singles ☆☆☆☆☆

Trebor
1974 *All Stars Pop & Soccer Ring*, sheet of stickers ★★★★☆
1974 *All Stars Pop & Soccer Ring*, single soccer sticker ★★☆☆☆
1982 *Squad 82*, uncut wrappers ★★☆☆☆
1982 *Squad 82*, stickers cut from wrappers ★☆☆☆☆

Triumph
1926 *English League (Div1) Footer Captains*, set ★★½☆☆
1926 *English League (Div1) Footer Captains*, single cards ★½☆☆☆
1926 *Famous Footer Internationals*, set ★★½☆☆
1926 *Famous Footer Internationals*, single cards ★½☆☆☆
1930 *Transfers of Footballers, Historic Events, Peoples & Transport*, uncut sheets ★★★★½

Troman
1900 *Football Team Colours & Rules*, cards ★★★★☆

Tuckett
1928 *Photos of Football Stars* ★★★½☆
1928 *Photos of Football Stars*, Dean ★★★½☆

Tudor Crisps
1970s *Soccer Fans League*, football club rosettes ★★★☆☆

Tupinamba
1960 *Quigol*, unused stickers ★★★½☆
1960 *Quigol*, unused stickers, Garrincha ★★★★☆
1960 *Quigol*, unused stickers, Pelé ★★★★☆

Turnwright Toffee
1967 *Your Favourite Player's History* ★★☆☆☆

Typhoo Tea
1963 *Famous Football Clubs*, b/w packet issues, on box of tea ★★★☆☆
1963 *Famous Football Clubs*, b/w packet issues, cut-out card ★½☆☆☆
1963 *Premium Football Clubs*, large colour cards ★★★☆☆
1963 *Football Club Rosettes*, cloth rosette & a card, paired ★★★☆☆
1965 *Famous Football Clubs (2nd Series)*, b/w packet issues, box ★★★☆☆
1965 *Famous Football Clubs (2nd Series)*, b/w packet issues, cut-out card ★½☆☆☆
1965 *Premium Football Clubs*, large colour cards ★★★☆☆
1967 *International Football Stars*, b/w packet issues, box ★★★☆☆
1967 *International Football Stars*, b/w packet issues, cut-out card ★½☆☆☆
1967 *Premium International Football Stars*, most ★☆☆☆☆
1967 *Premium International Football Stars*, as above, Derek Dougan for Leicester City ★★★★☆
1969 *International Football Stars (2nd series)*, b/w packet issues, box ★★★☆☆
1969 *International Football Stars (2nd series)*, b/w packet issues, cut card ★½☆☆☆
1967 *Premium International Football Stars (2nd series)*, most ★☆☆☆☆
1967 *Premium International Football Stars (2nd series)*, Ian Ure variation ★½☆☆☆
1971 *Football Club Plaques*, packet-issue cut-out card tokens, uncut box ★★★☆☆
1971 *Football Club Plaques*, packet-issue cut-out card tokens, cut card ★☆☆☆☆
1971 *Football Club Plaques*, large plastic badges ★★½☆☆
1973 *New Series of Football Stars*, packet-issue cut-out cards, box ★★★½☆
1973 *New Series of Football Stars*, packet-issue cut-out cards, cut card ★½☆☆☆
1973 *New Series of Football Stars* – premium redemption cards, most ★½☆☆☆
1973 *New Series of Football Stars* – premium redemption cards, Best ★★☆☆☆

Unela Pam-Pam
1958 *World Cup '58*, gum wrappers, most	★★★½☆
1958 *World Cup '58*, gum wrappers, Fontaine	★★★½☆
1958 *World Cup '58*, gum wrappers, Charlton	★★★★☆
1958 *World Cup '58*, gum wrappers, Pelé	★★★★½

Union
1938 *König Fussball*, by Ramona, Solo, Nile Princess & Turmac tobacco, most	★★½☆☆
1938 as above Drake, Bastin, Hapgood, Dean, Walker all	★★½☆☆
1938 as above, Doherty	★★★☆☆

United Services
1935 *Interesting Personalities*, most	★½☆☆☆
1935 *Interesting Personalities*, footballers	★★☆☆☆
1937 *Popular Footballers*, most	★½☆☆☆
1937 *Popular Footballers*, Dean	★★☆☆☆

Unknown issuer
1922 *Footballers*, by Albert Wilkes and Sport & General, most	★★★☆☆
1923 *Sportsmen in pairs*, uncut pairs	★★★☆☆
1923 *Sportsmen in pairs*, cut single cards	★½☆☆☆
1936 *Football Teams & Footballers*, on tri-colour, shield-shaped cards	★★★½☆

Urodonal
1922 *Campeones Regionales 1922-23*, most	★★★☆☆

Val Gum by Klene
1938 *Val Footer Gum footballers*, blank backs, most	★★½☆☆
1938 as above, Matt Busby	★★★☆☆
1938 as above, Matthews	★★★☆☆
1938 as above, Ancell	★★★★☆
1938 as above, McKay	★★★★½

1938 Val Footer Gum footballers note: advertising backs add 100% to value.

Valentine & Sons
1910s *Football Club Colours* and *Football Stadia* postcards	★★★☆☆

Vanguard
1924 *Magic Photos*, of footballers	★★★★½
1924 *Footballers*, with gold borders	★★☆☆☆

Vanguard & Adventure
1925 to 1926 *Football Photos*, most	★★½☆☆
1925 to 1926 *Football Photos*, Fred Kennedy	★★★☆☆
1925 to 1926 *Football Photos*, Dean	★★★½☆

VAV
1946 *Campioni dello Sport*, small cards with inset circular portraits atop, footballers	★★½☆☆
1947 *Footballers*, on circular cards	★★★½☆
1948 *Footballers in groups or a footballer with a crest*, on rectangular cards	★★★☆☆
1949 *Playing Cards with Footballers*	★★★½☆
1950 *Calcio 1950*, most	★★☆☆☆
1951 *Serie Campioni* (inset circular portrait on quartered card) most	★★☆☆☆
1954 *Serie Campioni* (shield-shape colour portraits & emblems on white cards)	★★★☆☆
1955 *Squadre Calcio e Scudetti in Metallo*, cards, mostly	★★☆☆☆
1955 *Squadre Calcio e Scudetti in Metallo*, cards, metal discs	★½☆☆☆
1956 *Sport e Ciclismo*, most	★★★☆☆
1957 *Figurine Calcio con Dischi Metallici*, cards & discs; cards	★★★☆☆
1957 *Figurine Calcio con Dischi Metallici*, cards & discs; discs	★★☆☆☆
1957 *Figurine Calcio con Dischi Metallici*, cards & discs; Charles	★★★☆☆
1958 *Figurine Calcio con Dischi Metallici*, cards & discs; cards	★★★☆☆
1958 *Figurine Calcio con Dischi Metallici*, cards & discs; discs	★★☆☆☆
1958 *Figurine Calcio con Dischi Metallici*, cards & discs; Charles	★★★½☆
1958 as above, Brazil World Cup Winners cards, most	★★★☆☆
1958 as above, Brazil World Cup Winners cards, Pelé & Vava paired on a card	★★★½☆
1959 *Figurine Calcio con Dischi Metallici*, cards	★★★☆☆
1959 *Figurine Calcio con Dischi Metallici*, cards, discs	★★☆☆☆
1959 *Figurine Calcio con Dischi Metallici*, cards, Charles	★★★½☆
1959 *Figurine Calcio con Dischi Metallici*, cards, Rivera	★★★☆☆
1960 *Figurine Calcio*, cards & discs, cards	★★★☆☆
1960 *Figurine Calcio*, cards & discs, discs	★★☆☆☆
1960 *Figurine Calcio*, cards & discs, Charles	★★★½☆
1960 *Figurine Calcio*, cards & discs, Rivera	★★★½☆
1961 *Squadre Calcio* (pairs of players)	★★★½☆
1961 *Squadre Calcio* (pairs of players), Charles	★★★½☆
1961 *Squadre Calcio* (pairs of players), Rivera	★★★½☆
1961 *Squadre Calcio* (pairs of players), Baker	★★★½☆
1961 *Squadre Calcio* (pairs of players), Law	★★★½☆

VCC
1922 to 1923 *Cricketers and Footballers*	★★★★☆

Vecchi (Italy)
1934 *Assi del Ciclismo e del Calcio*	★★½☆☆
1934 *Assi del Ciclismo e del Calcio*, Meazza	★★★☆☆
1934 *Assi del Ciclismo e del Calcio*, Piola	★★★☆☆

Vecchi (Brazil)
1962 *Futebol Mundial 1962*, stickers, most	★★★☆☆
1962 *Futebol Mundial 1962*, stickers, England players	★★★½☆
1962 *Futebol Mundial 1962*, stickers, Pelé	★★★½☆

Venlico
1982 *Los Ases del Mundial*, most	★★☆☆☆
1982 *Los Ases del Mundial*, British stars	★★½☆☆
1982 *Los Ases del Mundial*, Roger Milla	★★½☆☆

Venorlandus
1978 *World of Sport Flik-Cards*, small cards	½☆☆☆☆
1978 *World of Sport*, very large cards	★★☆☆☆

Verbania – see Lampo

Victor
1961 *Star Teams of 1961*, uncut sheets of four or six teams	★★★☆☆
1961 *Star Teams of 1961*, cut single cards	½☆☆☆☆
1965 *Footballers*, self-standing cards with name cards, intact sheets	★★★½☆
1965 *Footballers*, self-standing cards with name cards, singles	★½☆☆☆
1968 *Footballers*, self-standing cards, uncut sheets	★★★½☆
1968 *Footballers*, self-standing cards, single players	★½☆☆☆
1969 *Football Challenge*, cards, uncut sheet	★★☆☆☆
1969 *Football Challenge*, cards, single cut cards	★☆☆☆☆
1970 *Football Favourite*, uncut	★★☆☆☆
1970 *Football Favourite*, cut images	½☆☆☆☆
1972 *Super Stars of 72*, sheet of small cards	★★½☆☆
1972 *Super Stars of 72*, pairs of larger cards	★★☆☆☆
1972 *Super Stars of 72*, cut singles	½☆☆☆☆

THE SOCCER CARDS RARITY SCALE

Victoria Vedetien Chocolates
1968 *Sport*, most with glue as issued — ★☆☆☆☆
1968 *Sport*, most with glue as issued, Charlton — ★★☆☆☆
1968 *Sport*, most with glue as issued, Pelé — ★★☆☆☆
1968 *Sport*, most with glue as issued, Eusebio — ★★☆☆☆

Vidall
1958 *Calciatori & Premi*, most — ★★★★½☆
1958 *Calciatori & Premi*, British players — ★★★★☆

Vittoria Egyptien
1932 *Competitie Wedstryden 1932-33 Spelfotos (Miss Blanche)*, most — ★★☆☆☆

Vittorioso
1949 *Concorso Grandi Campioni*, uncut comics — ★★★☆☆
1949 *Concorso Grandi Campioni*, cut singles — ★½☆☆☆
1949 *Concorso Grandi Campioni*, British players — ★½☆☆☆

Vulcano & Panini
1974 *Munich 1974*, most — ★★☆☆☆
1974 *Munich 1974*, Dalglish — ★★★☆☆
1974 *Munich 1974*, wrapper — ★★★★☆
1975 *Futbol 75/76*, most — ★★☆☆☆
1975 *Futbol 75/76*, Cruyff — ★★★☆☆
1975 *Futbol 75/76*, British football team emblems — ★★½☆☆
1975 *Futbol 75/76*, wrapper — ★★★★☆
1976 *Futbol 76/77*, most — ★★☆☆☆
1976 *Futbol 76/77*, Cruyff — ★★★☆☆
1976 *Futbol 76/77*, wrapper — ★★★★☆

Walker's Tobacco
1920s *London Footballers* — ★★★★★

Wayfarer
1937 *Wayfarer Raincoats Football Scenes*, large cards — ★★★★½☆

Webcosa
1960 *Dubble-Bubble Footballer* caricatures, gum inserts — ★★★★½
1960 *Dubble-Bubble Footballer* caricatures, full album — ★★★★★
1962 *Football Bingo*, gum inserts — ★★★★½
1962 *Football Bingo*, gum inserts, unmarked Bingo cards — ★★☆☆☆

Wilkes
1930s *Footballer*, postcard-size photo cards — ★★★★½
1940s and 1950s *Football Team*, postcard-size photo cards — ★★★☆☆

Wilkinson
1956 *Popular Footballers*, plain backs — ★★★★☆
1956 *Popular Footballers*, printed backs — ★★★☆☆

Williams Forlag
1971 *Fotboll 1971*, most — ★★☆☆☆
1972 *Fotboll 1972*, most — ★★☆☆☆
1972 *Foldbold 72/73*, most — ★★★☆☆
1974 *Fodbold VM74*, most — ★★★☆☆
1974 *Fodbold VM74*, Best — ★★★☆☆
1974 *Fodbold VM74*, Charles — ★★★☆☆
1974 *Fodbold VM74*, all silk stickers — ★★★★☆

Williamson Tickets of Ashton
1880s *Footballers*, shield-shaped cards — ★★★★★

Wills
1896 *Cricketers*, most — ★★½☆☆
1896 *Cricketers*, Fry — ★★★☆☆
1902 *Vanity Fair*, most — ★½☆☆☆
1902 *Vanity Fair*, Fry — ★★½☆☆
1902 *Football Series*, violet, most — ★★☆☆☆
1902 *Football Series*, violet, Needham, Smith, Bloomer and Meredith, each — ★★★☆☆
1902 *Football Series*, black, most — ★½☆☆☆
1902 *Football Series*, black, Needham, Smith, Bloomer and Meredith, each — ★★½☆☆
1902 *Football Series*, Foulkes with a wide name caption, black — ★★☆☆☆
1902 *Football Series*, Foulkes with a wide name caption, violet — ★★½☆☆
1902 *Football Series*, Foulkes with a narrow name caption not touching frame, black — ★★★☆☆
1902 *Football Series*, Foulkes with a narrow name caption not touching frame, violet — ★★★½☆
1907 *Football Club Colours* — ★½☆☆☆
1910 *International Footballers Season 1909-1910*, Scissors brand — ★★☆☆☆
1910 as above, Meredith — ★★½☆☆
1910 *International Footballers Season 1909-1910*, United Services brand — ★★★☆☆
1910 as above, Meredith — ★★★½☆
1910 *International Footballers Season 1909-1910*, Flag brand — ★★★½☆
1910 as above, Meredith — ★★★★☆
1914 *Famous Footballers*, Scissors brand most — ★★½☆☆
1914 as above, Meredith — ★★☆☆☆
1914 *Famous Footballers*, Star brand most — ★★½☆☆
1914 as above, Meredith — ★★★☆☆
1932 *Homeland Events*, West Brom versus Birmingham City — ★½☆☆☆
1935 *Association Footballers*, without full frame on back, most — ★½☆☆☆
1935 *Association Footballers*, without full frame on back, Matthews — ★☆☆☆☆
1935 *Association Footballers*, with full frame on back, most — ★½☆☆☆
1935 *Association Footballers*, with full frame on back, Matthews — ★☆☆☆☆
1936 *Irish Sportsmen* — ★★☆☆☆
1937 *British Sporting Personalities* — ★☆☆☆☆
1939 *Association Footballers* — ★½☆☆☆
1939 *Association Footballers*, Matthews — ★☆☆☆☆

Winston
1948 *Sporties Internationals*, most — ★★★☆☆
1948 *Sporties Internationals*, Matthews — ★★★½☆
1948 *Sporties Internationals*, Billy Liddell — ★★★½☆

Wizard
1922 *British Team of Footballers Our Greatest Players* — ★☆☆☆☆
1922 *Footballers (with the editor's compliments)* — ★☆☆☆☆
1929 *Secret Signs & Footballers*, metal amulets — ★★★½☆
1932 *A.B.C Chart of Football Colours*, uncut sheet — ★★★★☆
1932 *A.B.C Chart of Football Colours*, set of four cards and all stickers — ★★★★½
1955 *Famous Footballers*, monotone cards with red backs, uncut quads — ★★½☆☆
1955 *Famous Footballers*, monotone cards with red backs, single cards — ★½☆☆☆
1955 *Famous Footballers*, colour cards with magenta backs, uncut fives — ★★½☆☆
1955 *Famous Footballers*, colour cards with magenta backs, single cards — ★½☆☆☆
1959 *Football Stars of 1959*, uncut octets — ★★½☆☆
1959 *Football Stars of 1959*, uncut dozen — ★★½☆☆
1959 *Football Stars of 1959*, single cut card — ★½☆☆☆

1970 *Great Captains*, uncut sheet of cards ★★☆☆☆
1970 *Great Captains*, cut single card ★½☆☆☆
1970 *Great Stars of Football*, uncut octets ★★☆☆☆
1970 *Great Stars of Football*, single cut cards ★½☆☆☆
1970 *Great Stars of Football*, Best ★☆☆☆☆
1970 *Famous Footballers*, iron-on transfers, uncut quad ★★★★★
1970 *Famous Footballers*, iron-on transfers, cut single ★★★★☆
1971 *Super Photos of Famous Footballers* (green, gummed paper), uncut sheet ★★★½☆
1971 as above, cut single ★★☆☆☆
1973 *All-Star Sports Ring*, with a sheet of stickers, uncut sheet ★★★★½
1973 *All-Star Sports Ring*, with a sheet of stickers, cut singles ★★☆☆☆

Wood Brothers
1900 *Famous Football Clubs* ★★★★★

WS Verlag
1950 *Fussball Weltmeisterschaft* ★★½☆☆
1952 *Sportbilder*, postcards white borders ★★☆☆☆
1952 *Sportbilder*, postcards golden borders ★★½☆☆
1954 *Fussball Weltmeisterschaft*, most ★½☆☆☆
1954 *Fussball Weltmeisterschaft*, Puskás stickers ★★½☆☆
1958 *Fussball Weltmeisterschaft*, most ★½☆☆☆
1958 *Fussball Weltmeisterschaft*, British players ★★☆☆☆
1958 *Fussball Weltmeisterschaft*, Pelé celebration ★★★☆☆
1958 *Fussball Weltmeisterschaft*, Pelé action ★★★★☆
1962 *Fussball Weltmeisterschaft*, most ★½☆☆☆
1962 *Fussball Weltmeisterschaft*, Greaves (Hitchens) ★★★☆☆
1962 *Fussball Weltmeisterschaft*, various Pelé cards ★★★☆☆

Xuereb
1966 Maltese variations of A&BC Gum WC66 stamps, British players, di Stefano, Suarez, each ★★★★☆
1966 as above, Lev Yashin (different design), Pelé (with and without blue rays), each ★★★★★

Yanky Bubblegum
1948 *Popular Footballers (Buy Yanky Gum)* ★★★★☆

Zaini
1928 *Cioccolata Cine-Foto-Sport* ("*cioccolata*" b/w cards, names but no numbers at top) most ★★★½☆
1928 as above, Meazza action cards, the earliest-known Meazza rookie cards ★★★★☆
1929 *Cioccolata Sport* ("*cioccolata*" b/w cards, numbers and names at top), most ★★★☆☆
1929 as above, Meazza with number atop ★★★½☆
1934 *footballers* (purple-monotone cards) most ★★★☆☆
1934 *footballers*, World Cup greats ★★★½☆
1936 *Da Roma Imperiale a Roma Fascista* (*cioccolato* b/w name at base) most ★★½☆☆
1937 *Cioccolato Cine-Sport* (*cioccolato* colour cards) most ★★★★½
1938 *Cioccolato Cine-Foto-Sport* (*cioccolato* colour cards) most ★★★½☆

Zuban
1928 *Torwart* ★★★☆☆

Zucconi
1924 *Sporting Heroes* ★★★★☆

In 2020, two Pelé cards, both rookie cards from 1958, sold for over $250,000 each! They sold in public auctions held in USA. In 2019 the cards would have cost less than $5,000 each. In 1999 the cards would have cost less than $50 each. That's quite a rise in value. It's a better return on investment than housing, gold or the best-performing paper on the stock market. The cards are set to break the $million barrier before the 2026 World Cup. Their halo effect draws other Pelé cards higher, and in turn, all other rare soccer cards.

Also, in 2020, the world's biggest collector of football memorabilia liquidated his enormous collection of rare soccer cards. This gave a momentary blip to the market. Month after month, auction after auction, it had seemed like old material was in ready supply again, for the first time in decades. The collector took a lifetime to assemble his collection. It was exhausted in little over a year. Vintage material will never again be so readily available.

Prices for rare soccer cards are rising at such a pace that ascribing values to cards, today, will mean obsolescence tomorrow, hence, this list evaluates rarity rather than giving today's prices. Unlike stickers and cards made since the 1990s, rarity remains more or less constant for older cards. Whereas 'newly discovered' stashes of newer cards deluge the market intermittently, when dealers offload stocks of *hors commerce* and *ex-series* material, vintage and antique cards from before 1970 are relatively safe and stable, not to mention rarer.

Whether it's a $250,000 Pelé rookie by Bremer Kaffee Fachring or Alifa, or a £250 rookie Tom Finney by Barratt & Co. it's going up in value! While top rarities like Bremer Kaffee Fachring cards of Pelé and Yashin escalate in price (there are but a handful of Bremer cards known, worldwide) yesterday's easy-to-find cards, like Barratt & Co. cards, are becoming difficult to acquire. Sets of soccer cards are almost impossible to complete because rookie card hunters have done what end-number card collectors once did: broken sets for ever.

There will come a day when sets of cards, which include such rarities, may generate more money than single, rare rookie cards. Is there a complete set, anywhere in the world, of the 1922 Pattreiouex Casket Cigarettes F-number football teams, with all varieties of the Manchester City cards? It's rarer than a complete set of Bremer Kaffee Fachring cards, and that's saying something! When and if one shows up it will garner a fortune, as will the first soccer player to be shown on a card, Arthur Wharton, from 1886.

Rare cards are up!

Appendix 1:
Rookie Cards versus Rare Cards: tips for good choices

A line from a Mario Puzo novel, a book which was made into a well-known movie, goes like this: *"It's not personal, it's business."* The refrain could have been dedicated to certain sellers in the graded sports cards market.

You don't need to break the bank to own rare cards. Rare cards rise in value, so it's probably wise to collect them. On the other hand, if you are buying rookie cards you can go bust if you are not immensely careful. The rookie cards market is talked up by those with a lot of rookies to sell and much to gain. Rookie-card prices are often inflated by shill bidders. Then there are customs & excise officers imposing taxes on valuable rookie card shipments outside USA – even on packets containing your own cards sent back from a grader. Such tax tariffs can be enormous! You've paid to have your card slabbed; you paid to send it, and now you are paying hundreds or thousands in import taxes, which are imposed on its insured value, just to get it back! The pumped-up market for rookie cards suits some dealers and certain businesses – those which have cornered the market in a particular card. It is big money and shill bidders massage their sales just as acolytes serve devils.

Dealers corner markets. They do this, firstly, by targeting a card they want. They will endlessly talk down the card. Talking badly about a card usually helps keep prices low. Dismissing cards before owning them improves profits after buying. Secondly, dealers buy as many of the targeted cards as they can find. Thirdly, once they have acquired them they talk up the cards. Hyping-up sales results in soaring prices. With an ever-ready supply of the now pricier cards there are profits in the bank and tequilas on the beach, not to mention the sunset of a card's availability to everyone else. That's the idea, anyway. It works for some, not for others. It works if you are in USA, not so much in Europe, or in GB.

Some businesses and individuals have been hoarding crates of new stickers and cards. These people are sitting on millions of unopened packets, many of which contain the rookies of the last 30 or 40 years. It's not like that with cards from before 1980. With cards made in the last three or four decades it's more about markets and manipulation of profits than it is about collecting.

As with end-number card hunting, a cards obsession which predated today's trend for finding the first-made card of a sports star, rookie card hunting does not have to be about the rarest card. Though there are instances where the twain meet, where the rarest card is also the rookie card. One such example is from a noted series of exceedingly rare football cards which were manufactured in Bremen, in the newly formed country of West Germany. There are 60 soccer cards in the series. They were made by Bremer Kaffee. The cards were not given with Bremer Kaffee but were redeemed for tokens, from the coffee packets, which is part of the reason they are so rare. The other reason is distribution. The newly formed country was only six years old at the time of the 1958 World Cup. It had been created from the British, American and French post-war military zones of the old Germany. The Bremer cards were only distributed in the British zone, around the city of Bremen, in the far north. The series includes eight cards which feature Pelé. The octet is among the rarest Pelé collections in the world. In poker terms, having such a sub-set of seven is a little like making a *straight flush*.

In August 2020, one of the cards was sold on eBay. The seller had advertised it at $100,000. He accepted an offer. The offer price exceeded the previously held record price for a Pelé card. The previous record-breaking sale was for an almost-as-rare Alifabolaget card. In fact, two Alifabolaget cards had sold, in spring 2020, the first for $43,000 and a second for $75,000! So, the Bremer Pelé card set the new record – for a few weeks, at least.

Records are there to be broken. Before 2020 was over, just six months after the $43,000 and $75,000 sales, a further example of the same Alifabolaget card sold for $290,200! No doubt, at this rate and sooner than later, both Bremer and Alifabolaget cards will break into the seven-figures price range.

For any given sports star from the past, say from the 1880s to the 1910s, there are usually less than a handful of available exemplars of any extant card. As such, a sport star's rarest cards will quickly become exhausted, especially with new collectors arriving on the scene almost daily. It only takes a couple of new buyers to seek the same card of a given sports star of yesteryear and the few available cards soon become impossible to find. Most such cards are not rookie cards yet they may be far rarer than the priciest of easier-to-find rookies.

Canny collectors have been quietly sourcing cards of generally uncollected heroes of soccer, and sport, for some time. One such collector has put together the world's best collection of cards featuring the legendary Willie Woodburn. Woodburn was a great player for both Glasgow Rangers and Scotland. The American collector has created a veritable tabernacle of Woodburn's images on cards on his website at www.mybrokensite.com. Other collectors have been

The rarest Bruce McClaren Italian card, 1968

Caitlyn Jenner when she was Bruce Jenner, a gold-medal decathlete, 1976

quietly buying cards of Gerry Hitchens, the Aston Villa player for whom Italian Serie A football became an irresistible draw. Others seek cards of the post-war Welsh Wizard, John Charles. Some collectors pride themselves in finding Jimmy Greaves cards, and the other British players for whom the lure of foreign football was irresistible, such as Denis Law and Joe Baker. The latter's brother, Gerry Baker, was an international player for USA, and his cards are now being collected due to that honour. A wide range of Nordic and Germanic players, from Nacka Skoglund to Helmut Haller, both of whom played in the Serie A Italian league during the 1950s and 1960s, are collected by buyers from Spitzbergen to Stuttgart. Similarly, international players of more recent times, for whom success came whilst playing in countries other than their birth, such as Liam Brady, Gordon Cowans and Steve Archibald are now being collected by buyers as from as far afield as Australia to South Africa!

Generally, collectors of rare cards collect for collecting, with an eye on making a good investment for the distant future, whereas rookie cards collectors generally buy to invest, flip and quickly make profits on their cards. It seems that rare cards collectors often do better, in the long run. This is because rookie cards are risky. Players of today lose value quickly, tomorrow. One rookie-card collector known to this writer went bankrupt. He possessed a million cards of players from ten to twenty years ago, but no cash. He was flooded out of his own market by bigger dealers with the same, modern cards; many more! He was overpriced and he sold fewer and fewer stickers as the others undercut his prices. He ended up liquidating his stock, to those by whom he was bankrupted, all in order to pay off debts. He is now unemployed and broke. The risk of this happening with rare cards of antiquity is almost nil. Rare cards from 120 years ago go up in value more gently than rookie stickers of the last 30 years but they don't crash back down.

A rookie-card seller known to this writer, Christopher, cares not for one player in particular nor for a football team in general. He simply wants as many rookies as he can squeeze into his house. Christopher's home is now insulated with retail boxes and wholesale cartons of Panini stickers and cards by other manufacturers. He can no longer see the interior walls of his home. Where pictures once hung – and may still hang – there are crates and containers full of cards. Were you to take down the storage crates you'd probably find the wallpaper has not been sun bleached, and the domestic décor is as fresh as it was in 1997. Plastic storage towers are built high, all the way up to the ceilings. Each stackable casket is crammed full of every kind of football card, not to mention other sports. It's not just British stuff. Christopher has cards from most European countries. If Panini made a card in the last 25 years, and distributed it in Western Europe, Christopher has it. His kitchen cupboards don't have cornflakes, they have *Euro 96*. His bathroom cupboards have stickers where you would find sanitary products in other homes – not that he uses stickers! It's just that his cupboards are precious storage space for *rookie mining*.

Christopher explained his reasons for insulating his home with cartons full of cards, floor to ceiling, saying, *"You see, it's worth buying a carton or two of everything they make because you never know! Most cases have a dozen counter-display retail boxes, each of which contain 50 or 100 packets of stickers. In the future, when a truly great player emerges, then I've got very valuable*

Barry Sheene on an Italian-only Panini sticker, 1970

Joe Louis on a French gum card, 1937

APPENDIX 1: ROOKIE CARDS VERSUS RARE CARDS: TIPS FOR GOOD CHOICES

Murad tobacco cards from USA, 1910

Belgian gum card, 1940s

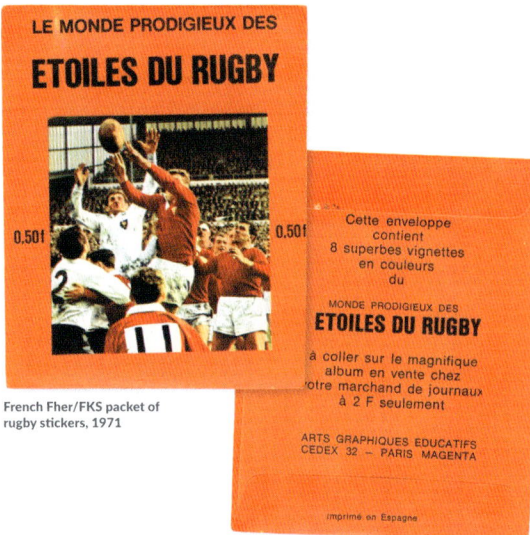

French Fher/FKS packet of rugby stickers, 1971

French trade card, 1930s

stickers which can be worth thousands each. *You just need to open the packets to find them.*" On how often he buys and how much he spends, Christopher commented, "*Every month there's an order coming in from some country or other, money going out to distributors in Belgium or Portugal, even USA these days, so I spend thousands. But I don't spend a penny on house insulation and fuel bills are low in such an insulated property, so it balances out.*"

Christopher's walls of boxes of stickers also serve as noise-reduction barriers to the eternal rumble from the main road, nearby. A home like Christopher's dominion, though not to everyone's taste, is indeed very well insulated. Though industrial-grade cladding may have cost him a lot less than a billion stickers, his thermal-reflecting wall of cards is a value store in itself. He spends thousands every year buying them, to mine rookies which may be worth tens of thousands each, one day. It may make a profit, eventually, but it seems like a lot of work and it needs a lot of financial outlay. He has spent well over £125,000 since the year 2000. His once spacious home now feels more like a maisonette; the car is on the street (the garage is full of cards) and his wife left him when he bribed his children to move out so he could utilise their bedrooms. "*I don't have to work, it's great, I get up when I want, I go on the computer and see what's happening with the values of stickers; I make an order for some more and, then, after breakfast I go mining for Mbappe. I bought some French stickers from 2017 and they are here somewhere. There's an Mbappe in every box and they are worth £500 each!*" So says Christopher. Whether they are, or not, remains to be seen.

Modern-day stickers may be a very risky bet. With a few thousand unused Mbappe stickers out there maybe Christopher ought to get rid of his quickly. Let's assume there are two Mbappe stickers in every counter-display sales box made. If so, it would mean Panini may have produced 500,000 examples of the 2017 Mbappe sticker, in France. The figure may even be as high as one million! The print run for Zidane's rookie was less – in 1992 France had not yet won the World Cup and French soccer stickers were a little less popular than they are nowadays. Let's say there were at least half a million of the Cannes #43 Zidane 1992 rookie distributed across France. That's quite a lot of availability. Does Chris know something, or are people like Chris spending big money on the tip of an iceberg which, when it melts as it surely will, may flood away his market?

A rookie card from 1919 is not dangerous to your fortune, or to your mental health. A rookie card from 1999 may be both. A rookie card made since 2010 is almost certainly more common than people want to believe. Be careful of anything made since 1990, but especially since 2000, whether it's a rookie card or not. There are many more exemplars of the same thing out there than you would want to believe.

Now, aside from rookie cards what about card *populations*? Such things are tables drawn up by graders in USA. North American collectors are familiar with such things but none of the French collectors known to this writer send away their stickers to a US grader to be added to card population tables in USA. Neither do Italian collectors nor Spanish collectors, and most Brits are unfamiliar with slabbing and grading, let alone card population tables. Outside USA, in 99% of cases, such things mean little to most people who own cards or stickers. By extension, most cards and stickers around the world are not known to the slabbers, whose population tables for soccer cards are woefully under-populated, especially

The world's earliest golf card, 1880s

Italian trade card, 1920s

for cards made since 1960. However, there is no country on the planet where sports cards are made and collected in the numbers enjoyed in USA. Thus, cards made elsewhere are made in much lower numbers than American-made cards, therefore, non-US cards are mostly rarer than cards made in USA. To estimate card production numbers it's useful to use historical population tables for different countries. West Germany in the 1950s had a much smaller population then the reunified Germany has now. Cards made in West Germany, back then, were made in much smaller numbers than cards made in today's Germany. Cards made in Malta are far rarer than cards made in Portugal, and Portuguese cards are rarer than those made in Great Britain, just as cards made in Uruguay are rarer than cards made in Brazil. No matter how rare Brazilian stickers from 1958 may seem to be, because Brazil has had a huge population since many decades ago, it has produced many more cards and stickers than countries like West Germany. Millions more! More people mean a bigger market; bigger markets mean higher numbers of cards are made. So, West German cards of Pelé from 1958 are often, if not always, rarer than Brazil-issues of the Pelé.

Very rare cards are not available in mammoth quantities anywhere but, these days, there are two types of rare: rare cards from the past and modern cards and stickers which are manufactured to be rare. The latter are contrived rarities. They are not rare because of the accidents of history and the ravages of age but because a multinational conglomerate created a conceit which is designed to extract value: your money in exchange for their contrived card, a product which cost them almost nothing to make. The betting is that firms which make these *rarities* will have *hors commerce* and *ex-series* versions of the same cards. They may come to flood markets one day. Most of today's publishers of rare ephemera and rare books do the same. It's a legal loophole and "... *it's not personal, it's business.*"

Really rare vintage stickers and antique cards may be very hard to acquire, and they may be costly, but they won't easily let you down. The risk of buying rare antiquities is minimal. No one can unleash a stash of vintage stickers or antique cards to flood the market. There are not enough of such rarities left to provide all of the prospective buyers with one each. Wherever you go, notwithstanding the amount of money you have to spend, you probably won't be able to find the very rarest cards of antiquity, not for love nor for money. If the card comes to market there are so many buyers seeking it that the card is bound to sell for more, much more money than the vendor had paid in the first place. So, if you have them, they are a good value-store asset to hold. They are a good long-term bet and will probably be highly lucrative investments. On the other hand, if you collect rookie cards, and money matters to you, the safest bets are the oldest ones. Older cards are where the future profits lie. Over 90% of the rookies from 1885 to 1955 have not yet been mined. They are out there, waiting for you.

Slabbing has worked wonders for US graders, and many buyers and sellers have benefitted too. However, European and British Isles readers will have problems with this market. Valuable rookie cards need insurance in the mail. The moment you insure an expedited packet for thousands your mail will be intercepted by customs agents in the US, or other countries. Excise duty may be as high as 30%. That's a lot of money on a card insured for £10,000. Do you risk sending a valuable Pelé rookie uninsured? If so you risk total loss. Also, if the packet is opened by customs agents making an irregular check, you risk having undeclared goods of value impounded, at least you do if you live in countries which have no trading unions or trade deals. Such strange lands are a customs agent's paradise.

If you send your cards to USA, to have them graded and returned to you in slabs, if your valuable card gets past US import controls (let alone if it gets to the grader in the first place, and if the grader sends it back to you) when it finally arrives back at your house, some weeks or months later, the chances are about 100% likely that it will be accompanied by a tax bill from HM Customs & Excise, if you live in the UK. Will you be able to pay the 30% tariff on a card valued at £10,000 or more? You may argue that it was your card in the first place but try proving that to beyond-appeal British customs & excise officials seeking an import quota. If you don't pay they impound your cards. You can appeal but it'll take a year and you may need a lawyer. You'll almost certainly lose the case and the cards because customs agents are above the law and they always win.

The truth is neither rookie nor rare cards need slabbing, so neither need sending anywhere for grading. Rare stamps are not slabbed, and they can be worth millions. Rare postcards are not slabbed. Rare antiques are not slabbed. Paintings by Renaissance masters are not slabbed but "*It's business ...*"

Appendix 2:
Rookie Card Alchemy: how to create your own rookie cards

Alchemy is the ancient and occult art of turning cheap, base metals into precious gold. Rookie card dealers have been using a form of alchemy with baseball cards for some decades and with soccer cards more recently. They never run out of rookies because they simply create more by acquiring cards of different players. Cards are bought inexpensively, repackaged and sold by potting the briefest biography and slabbing the card. It makes for easy profits. If and when rookie cards of one player run dry another source of rookie cards is divined. It's not ceremonial magic it's a basic form of sorcery called money magic. It has been used throughout the ages, and every reader can do the same; after a little time learning the basics the magic of alchemy in cards may begin.

A few years ago it was possible to buy 1923 Pinnace cards of Hughie Gallacher, the young Airdrieonians star, for between £5 and £10 for the smallest sized cards (the cards came in three sizes). *Pinnace* cards, made by Godfrey Phillips, were ubiquitous in their day and a million or more *Pinnace* cards may still be in circulation, yet two of the smallest-sized cards of Gallacher – the easiest to find of the three dimensions the card was produced in – recently sold for over £600 and for over £1,000 each! The cards are presently on their way to be slabbed after which, it's mooted, they will be returning to the market for around £5,000 each. These cards went from £5 to £5,000 due to rookie-card alchemy.

The card alchemist buys targeted cards. Each time a purchase is made it's the same card or cards acquired, over and again. He may have to spend a little more at each purchase but he successfully removes more and more cards from circulation, and in the process he frustrates various collectors: set makers, team loyalists and rookie-card buyers, not to mention other, generalist collectors. Each time he outbids other prospective buyers it makes them more likely to spend more money next time. He goes as far as he can and spends as much as he can afford, then he brings the cards back to the market, entombed in plastic with a dainty sing-song sales spiel sticker on top. Remarkably, collectors will buy at the inflated price. Once the first collector buys the next collector will pay more, usually, and so the price goes up for successive sales. It may have cost just £5 but the card flipper re-sold it for £5,000! It's rookie-card alchemy.

Some rookie-card dealers do not have the interests of rookie-card collectors at heart. They will talk down rare cards of great players. Some have been heard to utter such soccer blasphemy as, *"Apart from Dean, British footballers from before Bobby Charlton weren't known to anyone outside GB."* The self-assured idiot making this ignorant pronouncement deserved to be haunted by the internationally capped ghosts of England's Vivian Woodward, Wales's Grenville Morris and Scotland's Bobby Walker, to name but three of the greatest British internationals of yore. He was not heard of, again, after pronouncing his vapid judgement so, it seems, the ghosts of olde laid their boots into him. The first internationals in the world were matches played by British teams. Early British players played in Europe well over 100 years ago. Further back in time, British league clubs toured South America (as early as the 1900s).

Internet-framed history from the last 20 years, with Champions League or Premier league bias, seems to assume the world started in the middle of the 1990s when those monied leagues were created. Superficial *facts* taken from the internet are skimmed over by sellers with even less knowledge, and the diluted results show up in the form of so-called *Greatest* lists and omission-rich *Best-ever* lists which fail to include almost all of the greatest footballers from the past, the likes of whom, war survivors aplenty, would walk over many of today's spoiled and coddled stars.

Narrow-interest, internet-generated listings are great for sellers of stickers made since 2000 but really rare cards and stickers, those from before the 1970s, are quietly being bought and processed by the next generation of rookie-card alchemists and rare-card wizards. Each year that passes sees yet more rare cards disappear from sale. Just a couple of years ago, the three series of Cadet *Footballer* cards from 1958 to 1960 were available for next to no cost. In fact, they were being refused by British auctioneers due to their commonplace low value. Now, just one of those cards may sell for £200 and the sales of low-priced sets have dried up. Chix cards too. Such series were once considered common. These days they have been mined, bought up cheaply, by the rookie-card dealers of tomorrow for re-sale in the future, at profit.

So, how do you get ahead of them? Well, rookie-card dealers don't want you buying rookie cards they cannot yet offer for sale, therefore, you should seriously consider buying such cards. Don't compete with costly, trendier rookie cards in slabs, find your own!

Some sellers source as many cards as possible before marketing a single one of them. Until they

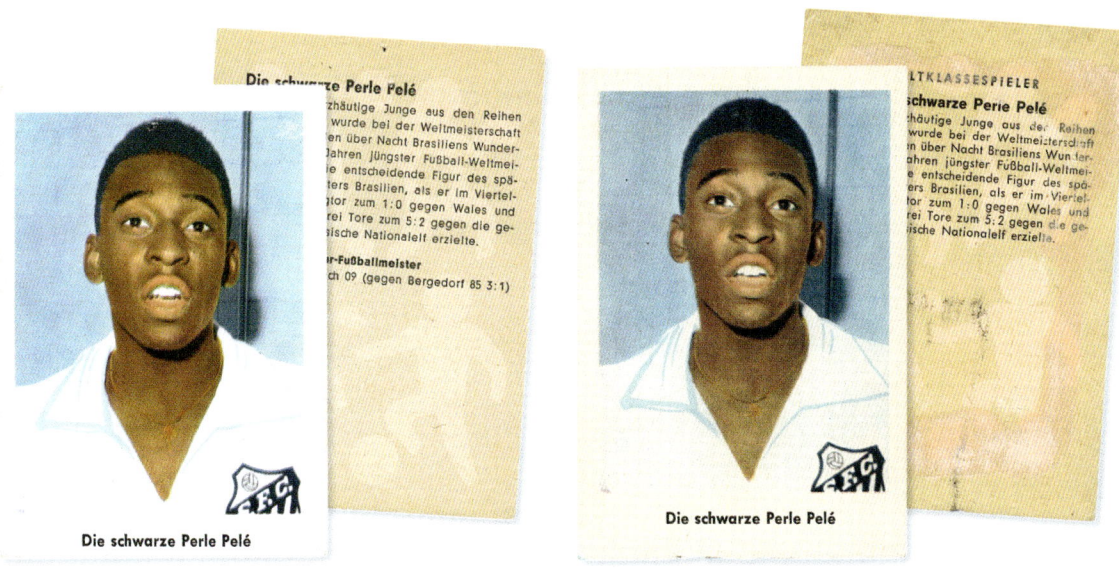

Left: by Heinerle, sold in packets in 1961, for inserting into an album of plastic pouches. Right: printed by Muller & Son for Heinrich Lutter, known as the Lutter-Heinerle variation, sold singly with vended gum, 1962, to be glued into a classic album

have enough they won't mention a particular player let alone sell any. Such card cornering involves the buying of as many rookie cards, of the same player, for as little as possible. Some dealers will even talk down the player they are quietly buying, or otherwise talk collectors out of buying the same. Then, when enough cards of that player have been accumulated, the reselling begins, whether as rookies or as new additions to a seller's range of all-time greats. The inflated prices and profits which follow are a result of rookie-card alchemy. Anyone can do it. It's not a science. It's an art and anyone can learn it.

Readers can work their own rookie-card alchemy, not just with players already inducted into the historic Halls of Fame but not overtly collected, but with any player whose earliest cards you can find. There's still time to work your own rookie-card alchemy and there are plenty of names to evoke and transform.

To mention just a handful of the hundreds of noted soccer players of the past, from the British Isles, whose cards ought to be sought a good starting point would be Joe Bache, the goal-scoring star of Aston Villa. Bache was the England international by whom the forward's back pass to a teammate, to run on to and to shoot for goal, was perfected. It's a move taken for granted these days but it was unseen until Bache's flourishing performances. Another great of yesteryear is Sam Hardy, also of Aston Villa, and Liverpool as well as Nottingham Forest. He was considered the greatest goalkeeper since Arthur Wharton. By the 1930s racist writers had airbrushed the latter, the first British goalkeeping legend, out of history but Wharton, the Gold Coast goalie for *The Old Invincibles* (Preston North End), a native of modern-day Ghana, has now been fittingly reinstated as a legend of the game. Another one to look out for is Bill McCracken, of Newcastle United and Belfast Distillery, a star known in his day as *the Offside King*. He was a master tactician by whom players on opposing teams were confounded into technical errors due to McCracken's understanding of the more sophisticated laws of the game. Another legend, ahead of his time, was Sam Chedgzoy of Everton and England, the corner-kick king responsible for a change in the rules of soccer. *The Football Who's Who* of 1935 lists two dozen more all-time greats including Bob Kelly the goal scoring doyen of Burnley; Sheffield United's Ernest Needham, the *Prince of Half Backs*; and William 'Fatty' Foulkes the chubby goalkeeper, not to mention thousands more stars from the inter-war years all of whom are listed with potted biographies. The rarest cards featuring such players are numbered in single figures. Get them whilst they remain affordable!

It's not just British soccer from the 1890s to the 1930s. There are the greats of the Spanish game, like Samitier, Zamora and Alcantara, to name but three; the early Italians, Germans and Czechs, etc. Study your soccer history and look at Halls of Fame created by sports clubs rather than top-100 lists created by commercial organisations for their own profits. Many so-called *official* top-100 lists of players are skewed towards looking after the interests of advertisers and promoters, just as many of today's commercially coddled footballers would be knocked off the ball by war-surviving heroes of yore, baby faces of today may fade in the presence of the great players of the past. Not many of yesteryear's superstars make money for today's multinationals, which may be why the greats of yore fail to make slick lists of the *greatest*. Notwithstanding corporate interests and modern-day business bias towards recent players, the sports heroes of times gone may well become very lucrative for ordinary collectors. Start researching names and dates today!

What about slabbing? Why risk sending away your rookie soccer cards to USA for slabs and grades from baseball card specialists? Aside from mistakes made by some graders (many soccer cards have been wrongly classified or mislabelled) there's the risk of import and export duties and customs tariffs. The likelihood of excise seizures of cards at borders is higher than ever, thanks to crackdowns on imports from USA, and to Brexit-imposed customs duties on imported goods from Europe, as well as on British exports worldwide. Why risk loss or sky-high charges when you can buy your own slabs and grade your own cards at home? It's relatively easy. You can buy high-grade security labels, to print, and slabs are inexpensive. It's a lot less costly than grading cards in USA and paying customs duties to import your own cards back to GB or Europe. Blank labels and slabs can be bought online. So, grade your own cards and avoid the risks. Then, if you sell to a foreign buyer it's a safer, one-way trip for the card, which you can export by insured mail. The buyer has to deal with customs, not you. There is no risky or costly return needed as there is with getting your own cards back from a foreign grader.

Rookie-card alchemy – it's easy!

Appendix 3:
Real and Unreal: rookie card reality – the actual Beckham rookies

The definitive David Beckham rookie card, from early 1995. Images courtesy of Jane Allen

The *actual* Beckham rookie cards of 1995 may not be the cards you think you know. Further, the *actual* Beckham rookie cards do not include the spurious card by Raven.

Long-standing mistakes made by card slabbers can be quite hard to rectify in a post-truth era, in a time when facts seem to matter less than greenbacks or *group think*. Wanting to believe something is genuine because you bought it, and you know other buyers bought the same, is understandable but it does not mean it's genuine. Much time-consuming study and serious research have exposed the Beckham Raven card as a mistake, at best, or a fraudulent *con* card at worst. Seeing how many of the Raven cards keep appearing from the same source, it may well be the latter!

The *actual* David Beckham rookies are stickers and cards, from 1995, which have been blinded from sight by the glitzy sale of the spurious Raven card. While those in the know have been cornering the market in the real thing, they've also been earning a fortune selling the 2001-made Raven cards as so-called rookie cards – stating wrongly that the cards were made seven years earlier! Well, the attention of collectors need no longer be distracted by this con card, because it's a fraudster amongst cards; a *Frankenstein* card put together with old images, erroneous information and disingenuous intent. It's caused a lot of people to lose a lot of money. Some buyers have paid many thousands but they may be able to get their money back. It's a consumer protection matter, if not a police matter. Most countries have such legislation and one of the key tenets goes something like this: if goods you buy are not what they are described as you can get your money back.

The card was ostensibly made by a firm named Raven SA, which is seemingly a Spanish firm (not South African *RSA* as some commentators have wrongly surmised). The manufacturer may not have known what he or she made when creating the card. The marque's logo bears the initials S and A. In Spain, these initials stand for *Sociedad Anónima*. The letters are often seen on Spanish lorries and on Spanish produce. However, the Raven card is not Spanish. The anonymous cover brand-name was, perhaps, a useful ploy to mislead licence investigators for the misuse of copyrighted images, the unauthorised use of logos and trademarks, and the failure to get Premier League permission to make the cards in the first place.

The card was made in the years after the millennium yet card graders seem to have conspired to grade the card wrongly, as if the card was from 1995. It seems to be hard for graders to admit their mistake. No admissions have been forthcoming but it has been noted that an enormous stock of the Beckham Raven cards were sold off, in the latter months of 2020, after this writer exposed the fraudulent card. A certain card grader and its favourite auctioneer divested themselves of the troublesome stock, selling many cards on eBay, and making a fortune selling it. Many examples of the card, slabbed and graded as a 1995 original, were sold for $1,000s each! It's probably worth less than $100.

Anyone who was around at the time when Fergie's Fledglings first flew would know something was fishy about the Raven Manchester United cards. In 1995, Beckham was known to very few people outside of Preston North End FC and Manchester United FC. When a certain MSM overly well-paid pundit made an infamous miss-by-a-mile prediction for United, by quipping that such a team of 'kids' would win nothing, Beckham was still unknown to the general public. By the time the young Manchester United team had made the BBC talking head eat his words, by winning the Premier League, nine months later, Beckham had become known to a wider audience but he was still half a year away from an England cap, which he first won in September 1996. The Raven card states that he was capped by England in 1995, which is utter rubbish but useful in proving the card is not from 1995. It seems the card's makers knew as little about Beckham as today's card graders know about the card itself.

Beckham's first goal at Wembley, in the 1996 Charity Shield, was followed a week later by a strike which was celebrated by a now defunct rag called *News of the World* as, "the greatest goal ever". The sex-

Spanish detergent cards of Alfredo di Stefano & László Kubala, 1953

Uncut double card with rookie of Hughie Gallacher

and-scandal paper published the aforementioned headline on Sunday, 18 August 1996. Beckham's goal, from the day before, had been scored from 55-yards out; from inside his own half of the field. Even Pelé had failed to score such a goal! Due to this miracle goal, scored against Wimbledon, Beckham became a household name in England in August 1996.

A year earlier, in 1995, no one would have celebrated Beckham, let alone Fergie's Fledgling, with a new-fangled series of costly state-of-the-art, foil-stamped deluxe soccer cards. Moreover, such a quality card finish, with foil-stamping, was about two years away from actual production. It only came to British shops between 1997 and 1998, thanks to firms like Futera and Merlin. Such an expensive series of cards would have been very costly to make, and were it possible in 1995, had anyone had the technology back then, why make a series of cards for a team of kids which had, until then, won nothing? They had just been vanquished, in the 1995 FA Cup Final, to boot.

The Raven card itself demonstrates it is not from 1995. The incorrect facts on the rear of the card prove the card is not 1995 by the mention of Beckham's first cap. His first cap came in September 1996. That makes 1997 the earliest possible date but for the fact that the card first appeared in 2001.

Few people, other than this writer, have called out the goof. Further, bringing the misgrading of the card to the attention of the grader and to prospective buyers was not welcomed in some quarters. Some sellers were keen to polish this bit of fool's gold, and they have kept pushing the card, which they are selling, as genuine.

In the UK selling this card as a 1995-made card is illegal. If you bought one from a UK seller you stand a good chance of getting your money back. Its sale breaches both the Sale of Goods Act (1979) and the Consumer Rights Act (2015) in that the card is not as described: it's not from 1995. Making a claim in the British Small Claims Court is easy. So is making a report to the police. Claim fees are relatively low. Here's a link for British buyers who've been defrauded: www.gov.uk/make-court-claim-for-money/court-fees

While sales of the spurious Beckham rookie were in full flow, the cannier buyer was busy collecting the actual 1995 rookies of Beckham, of which seven different types are known: two cards and five stickers Their gradual disappearance from the market has gone mostly unnoticed.

The earliest Beckham rookie card, by some way, was a limited edition card made by a pair of football ephemera and merchandise dealers, Tom Broad and John Allen, around the time of Easter in 1995. Tom Broad was a Preston North End fanatic. He was also one of only three football-card dealers in the UK, in 1995. John Allen and a trader in Brigg, in Humberside, UK, were the other two. Tom Broad and John Allen were good friends. Both of them were known personally to this writer. During the 1980s and 1990s they made limited editions of soccer cards. One such edition was a series dedicated to Preston North End footballers. The set consists of 25 numbered and embossed cards. The series is titled, *Broad's Braves*, and it includes the definitive David Beckham rookie card – the earliest David Beckham card! Beckham is shown on both sides of the card, wearing Preston's mostly white-coloured kit. Each card bears a circular, embossed seal with the maker's name and a number.

Then, there was a trading card made by One Touch Publishing in a series called *Premier Striker*. The series was issued in two formats, in late 1995. The Beckham card is not believed to be among the few cards included in the promotional launch, which consisted of a handful of cards with different designs to the later release, made on thick cardstock. He's certainly in the later release, on the thinner cardstock, which are relatively easy to acquire, having been made in the hundreds of thousands and distributed nationally across England and Wales.

Cards aside, there are five known Beckham rookie stickers from 1995. Four were made by *Match* magazine, the earliest of which was issued in August 1995; and a fifth was made by Merlin in tandem with *Shoot* magazine, in autumn 1995. Three of the four *Match* stickers are small, numberless items with yellow frames. The fourth type is slightly larger, with a blue-&-yellow side panel, and it is numbered.

The three yellow-frame stickers show photos of a very young Beckham wearing a red-coloured sweat shirt. One nameless sticker shows Beckham holding a Manchester United scarf above his head. The sticker has a MATCH logo in red, upper-case letters. Another sticker shows Beckham leaning on a wall, with his name in white upper-case letters plus a MATCH logo in white, with a red outline. A third, similar *Match* sticker shows Beckham looking towards his left. These three constitute 60% of the David Beckham rookies from 1995. Note: these stickers are also available in non-sticky format on printed sheets which came as the backing paper for the stickers. So, you can find both a sticky sticker and a printed picture with a plain, waxy-paper back. The images were not aligned with each other, so the backing papers do not sit against the stickers of the same players, so Beckham's stickers will be on backing papers showing other players, and vice versa.

The fourth Beckham rookie by *Match* was issued in a collection called *Footy Mad*. Collections like this were released annually by *Match*. The earliest *Footy Mad* series to feature Beckham dates from autumn 1995. It shows a head-and-shoulders portrait of a very young-looking Beckham wearing Manchester United kit. The sticker is numbered 71 (the digits are in white, in a red circle which is

APPENDIX 3: REAL AND UNREAL: ROOKIE CARD REALITY – THE ACTUAL BECKHAM ROOKIES

Pelé, Mel Charles & Jack Kelsey, by WS Verlag, 1958

A&BC Gum card and kit car packet 1970

The Ayrton Senna rookie cards, 1984

mounted on a black square). A sticker of similar design, showing Beckham in a grey baseball cap, numbered 44 (digits are white on an orange diamond) is not a 1995 rookie. The baseball cap sticker is from a similar, later collection which was issued in November 1996 for the *Match & Sported Sticker Album*. Yet another, similar-looking sticker shows Beckham in a white top with tramlines on the sleeve. It's numbered 9 (digit is white on an orange oval). This was issued in 1997.

The fifth Beckham rookie sticker happens to be the first Merlin sticker of David Beckham. For Merlin completists this is an almost impossible sticker to find. It's smaller than the much better known series of Premier League stickers from 1996. It has a green frame and shows a young Beckham in a white T-shirt, with his chin in hand. He's wearing a gold watch strap around one wrist, and he's shown gazing downwards, towards the camera lens. The sticker appeared on a sheet with about 50 other stickers, called *Stick With Shoot*. The sheet of stickers includes a Merlin Collections sticker and, at the bottom, it states that it was produced by the FA Premier League and Merlin Publishing. The sheet of stickers was given with *Shoot* magazine sometime in 1995. It includes David Ginola, a new recruit at Newcastle United, which dates the sheet to no earlier than late summer 1995, even though Ashley Cole is shown as a Newcastle player – with a machine gun – in a photo taken by the Tyne Bridge during January 1994.

Incidentally, the next Beckham sticker by Merlin was not the regular *Premier League 96* sticker. It was the advance, promotional Shreddies breakfast cereal version of the same. The Merlin *Premier Gold* card, with Beckham celebrating the wonder goal, came out for 1997.

Some collectors are now seeing through rookie-card deceptions and are refusing to follow blindly the rookie-card King Johns of yesterday. In Disney's Robin Hood an avaricious lion represented bad King John, a medieval monarch in England. Readers may remember the movie. Greedy King John hoarded all the coins in his kingdom. He passed his nights counting the money he'd extracted from others. In a way, the same thing happens with rookie cards. Someone amasses all the examples of a certain card, and in doing so he corners a market for the card, and in creating rarity, lack and want follow. Then he cranks into action his money-making machine.

Some of the King Johns of the rookie-card world work in tandem with auctioneers. Between them they may take control of a chunk of the market and make millions! In addition to taking money for disingenuously graded cards they also advise collectors not to take possession of the cards after buying them. This may sound odd but it happens. Some sellers suggest that collectors leave cards with them, after the sale, for safe keeping! Amazingly some collectors do this. A national government will step in to cover some of your bank savings, in the event of a crash, but if you try claiming your rookie Pelé card, which was lost in a vault theft or fraud, from government funds or from insurance you stand at about zero chance of succeeding. Cards vaults are lock-ups in storage facilities. That's all. Vaults are no guarantee against natural disasters or crime. Anything can happen to your cards in someone else's lock-up store and if it befalls you you'll lose everything.

On to another issue, it has been noted that graders are refusing to add some cards to 'master set' lists. Baseball card graders in the US, the likes of whom still dominate the soccer cards grading world, say things like *"we won't include that soccer card because a rookie soccer card needs to show the name of the player"*, or *"it needs to be vertical in portrait format, not horizontal in landscape format"*, or *"it needs to show only the player, not a teammate"*, or *"it's black & white"*, and even, *"we don't know that card!"* A well-known grader often grades a landscape-format Italian card of Pelé. The card is in its 'master set' list. It's made by VAV. The VAV card features two players. It neither names Pelé nor the other player. It shows black-&-white photos. It has no logo, no marque and no mention of what's shown on the card. It has no biography and the card is not in portrait format, it is of landscape dimension. So much for 'master sets' and their rules!

Moreover, a certain grader's 'master set' list for Pelé cards is based on partly erroneous information on an out-of-date web page, which was put together by a collector in 2014! The collector's collection was only ever partially complete when he gave up and sold his cards. So, is 'master set' the card-collecting world's misnomer of all time? So-called 'master sets' are often little more than cobbled together lists of errors and omissions which suit one group's interests while failing to include cards which a grader does not have knowledge of. So-called 'master set' lists are used by graders because it suits them. They know little about vintage and antique soccer cards and they don't want to admit to mistakes. Imagine a postage stamp cataloguer doing the same. Say, for example, that a Penny Black variation was discovered but not in time for inclusion in a printed catalogue (a 'master set'). Would Stanley Gibbons say *"it's not part of our catalogue so it doesn't exist, and we will never mention it"*? No, surely Stanley Gibbons would never do such a

Sheet of nine stamps by Sicker, with a rookie Franz Beckenbauer, 1965

Sheets of four stamps by Verbania, with Eusebio and Pelé, 1964-65

Joe Wright & a Zenith, world speed record holder, 1930

thing. The firm is respectable. It would update the next catalogue to include the newly discovered rare stamp. Yet, a certain card grader stated, *"We won't ever change our 'master-set' list because it's our own heritage; it's our 'founding father' sets; it's a vestige of our own history, and it dates from 2014!"* Yes, and it was based on an erroneous list of cards in the first place!

Collectors would be right to feel astounded by a grader refusing to include or grade rare cards simply because they themselves had none, or knew no better, yet it happens. Collectors must remember that grading is about cash. Grading is a money-driven business. Graders grade not for a collector's interest but for their own. Between a willing grader and an unscrupulous auctioneer many errors, altered cards and con rookies may be foisted on collectors.

Slabbed cards which cost hundreds of dollars to grade – yes, graders do charge $100s per slab for valuable cards – ought to be at least made of silver, not cheap plastic, with tempered glass front and back. There's a reason a slab is plastic: it's cheap. It costs graders almost nothing. As most slabbed cards are graded in less than 20 seconds the entire process of grading costs almost nothing but they charge a fortune. If you want your $2,500 card slabbed, by express grading, a certain grader asks for $200 to do it, so they are raking in a fortune. Just imagine how many cards they grade in one day. It's hundreds if not thousands. Big money is involved. For more on scandals which include well-known graders read *The Card* (see bibliography for details). It's a must-read book and an eye-opening tale that's stranger than fiction. Anyone and everyone in cards should read it. It's priceless.

Collectors do not need graders, collectors need cards. Only graders need graded cards.

Appendix 4:
Reliable & Recommended: how to sell your cards & from whom to buy

Please inform the author of this book, Carl Wilkes, about rare sports cards or soccer card collections you intend to sell. Carl buys rare soccer and sports cards for himself. As a collector, and as a retail buyer, he can offer you the highest possible price and the best deal, so please contact him first if you are selling sports cards. Whether collections or single rare cards; whether you have one card or 10,000 sports cards; whether it's old or recent, rare or rookie, singles or boxes full of soccer cards, for the highest offer, the best price or a referral to a trusty third party, contact Carl:

Email: cards@rarecards.co.uk
Website: www.footballsoccercards.com

Tim Davidson Auctions. Tim's internet, postal and public auctions are held most months. With Tim you can buy and sell cigarette cards, trade cards, postcards and other collectibles and rarities such as vinyl records, cinema posters, matchboxes, beer bottle labels, photographs and so on. Tim and his delightful staff, Julie, Lorna and Rachel, run their public auctions at select venues in Nottingham. They are based at New Market House, Meadow Lane, Nottingham, NG2 3GY. Call the girls on **0115 986 8550**. Please mention Carl's book when contacting the auctioneer:

Email: timdavidsonauctions@hotmail.co.uk
Website: www.timdavidsonauctions.co.uk

Loddon Auctions. This is a superlative auction for rare cards. Based in Arborfield, Berkshire, the firm is a long-established specialist in the sale of cigarette & trade cards, and all other forms of collectibles from coins and stamps to football programmes and match tickets, and much more besides. Loddon holds bi-monthly sales of around 1,200 lots. Entries are always invited and this auction enjoys competitive commission rates. All sales are featured live on the internet. Contact the auctioneer & chief valuer, Gary Arkell, on **0118 976 1355**. Please mention Carl's book when writing to Gary:

Email: info@loddonauctions.co.uk
Website: www.loddonauctions.co.uk

Martin Horton is a thoroughly nice chap and a trusty buyer and seller of cigarette cards on all subjects. Martin sells thousands of rare cards yearly through his eBay account: *rarecigarettecards*. His eBay shop is *the* place to go for all and sundry subjects on cards. For trade cards of the best value, and cigarette cards of the rarest calibre, Martin offers a very wide range indeed. You are assured of relaxed, pleasant transactions, the fairest of treatment and quality cards. On eBay you will be able to see his auctions and fixed-price sales of sporting and non-sports cards. His amazing stock will be attractive to all collectors, young or old; whether you are a beginner, a specialist or an advanced collector, a buyer or a seller. Do remember that Martin buys cards and collections too; all subjects, nothing is too large for Martin to consider. Ask him:

Email: martinjohnhorton@gmail.com
eShop: www.ebay.co.uk/str/rarecigarettecards

Alan Jenkins does not sell cards but he has all of the information collectors need and he's kindly shared it all with the world! He runs the Football Cartophilic Info Exchange. Back in the 1990s Alan's first outings were published in Carl Wilkes's soccer cards journal, *Football Card Collector Magazine*. Since those early days his Exchange has developed into an incredible website – one you'll probably never leave! Please mention Carl's book when writing to him:

Email: alanjenkins1899@gmail.com
Website: www.cartophilic-info-exch.blogspot.com

James Cotton is a charming gentleman and a superlative scholar of soccer history. He runs one of the greatest resources for tracking down details about the players of yesteryear. He also sells modern football memorabilia to celebrate them. His is a must-visit website where you will learn much about myriad soccer stars of yore:

Website: www.vintagefootballers.com

Roger Pashby has created many fine websites, blogs and channels about football cards from the past, ranging from Pinnace cards to Cope Brothers cards, and much more besides. You can track all of Roger's sites from his fascinating homage to cards of the jazz age, at:

Website: www.1920sheaven.wordpress.com

Buying? Seeking rare football-soccer cards, and other rare sports cards? For the greatest selection on offer, for very rare antique & vintage soccer cards; and for thousands of soccer cards for sale, from rookies to rarities, with many more cards to be listed over the next few years, there is only one place to go:

Website: www.footballsoccercards.com

N. 1   Lire 30

FIGURINE TECNI COLOR

ATTENZIONE: esclusivamente per voi piccoli tifosi è stato creato l'albo più nuovo e interessante. Tutti i giocatori delle principali **squadre di calcio** partecipanti al campionato 1946-47, i campioni del **ciclismo**, dell'**automobilismo**, del **pugilato** e di ogni sport sono raccolti per voi in questo meraviglioso albo

SOMMARIO:

83 FIGURINE

LA FORMAZIONE DEL
TORINO F. C.
e
INTERNAZIONALE

I più noti Campioni del:
**PUGILATO
CICLISMO
IPPICA
AUTOMOBILE
TENNIS
NUOTO
ATLETICA**

I più noti Divi del:
CINEMA

RUBRICHE
**INDISCREZIONI SPORTIVE
AVVENTURA LAMPO**

CONCORSO A PREMIO
1 Figurina TABÙ
del valore di Lire
50.000

 Pautasso Fernanda
Camp. Ital. Tuffi

 Emanuel Manuela
Camp. Ital. 200 m. rana

 Katharine Hepburn

 Mercuri Pericle

 Caprioli Paolo

 Ortelli Vito

 Frosio Elia
Camp. mond. Dietro motori

 Ingrid Bergman

 Peire Egisto

 Bisterzo Bruno

 Nuvolari Tazio

 Trossi Gian Felice

 Merle Oberon

 Bossi Annalisa
Camp. Ital. Doppio Misto

 Vigorelli Costanza
Camp. Ital. Pattinaggio Artistico

Non è uno dei soliti giornaletti: è la novità che aspettavate. Nuove fotografie ritagliabili vi daranno la possibilità di costituire una interessante e completa raccolta di figurine con tutti i campioni dello sport.

Select Bibliography and Social Media
Books and magazines about cards and collectin:

The Card: Collectors, Con Men and the True Story of History's Most Desired Baseball Card, by Michael O'Keeffe and Teri Thompson. Published by It Books, 2008.

This is a must-read book. It's not to be missed! It's for all and any card collectors, buyers, sellers and dealers. Apocryphal in its exposure of secrets you need to know. Don't believe the few bad reviews about this book, for they are almost surely written by the people exposed in the book. It reveals dodgy dealings in the multi-million card slabbing and grading business, and tells a tall tale of *The Card*, a sports card which came to sell for over $3 million in 2016. Don't be put off by the subject of baseball, if it's not your sport, for this book could be about a soccer cigarette card, or any sports tobacco card. It's entertaining, eye-opening and a warning. It's also inexpensive. You can pick up a copy on Amazon marketplace or ebay for a couple of pounds. Entertainment and education are guaranteed.

Cromos Para Recordar, by Juan Ral. Published in Spain, in 2007 by Graf.

Though not about football cards, this is a most elegant book of cards. The focus is on Spanish trade cards from Edwardian times until World War Two.

Deutsche Cards und Tütenbilder, band 1 und 2, by Gerd Päsler. Published in Germany, in 2014, by Fodito Verlag.

For the most reliable information on German trade cards these books are not only the standard reference guides they are biblical in scale and epic in scope.

Köberich's Reklame und Sammelbilder Katalog, 1946–2001. Published in Germany, in 2002, by Lumdatel.

A price guide for post-war German cards. The same publisher also issued a book, with an earlier frame of reference, about pre-war tobacco cards.

Kaufmannsbilder-Katalog 2011 mit Bewertung, by Nick Bolton

A vintage cards catalogue in German by a British researcher and collector.

The Card Scene, a magazine edited by John Devaney, issued quarterly. Write for details to: John Devaney, 10 Yelverton Road, Whitley, Reading, RG2 7SU.

The Card Scene magazine emerged after the demise of *Card Times*. It is Great Britain's only printed card-collecting journal.

Cricket cards
Cricket Cigarette and Trade Cards, an Extended Listing, by Derek Deadman, published in 1985.

The book is about as hard to digest as a medieval book on conjuring spirits. Illustrations are curiously scattered to the four winds so they don't relate to the text at hand. Incomplete listings and dead ends may send baffled readers to Umberto Eco's *The Name of the Rose* for a solvable mystery. Nevertheless, esoteric knowledge is bestowed – at a cost. This pioneering work is well worth having for devil-in-the-detail cricket card disciples.

Cricket Cigarette and Trade Cards, a Further Listing, by Alan Harris and Geoff Seymour, published in 1993.

It's a book with a diabolical layout and an abysmal design. Half of all the sides are blank, and it's in spiral ring-bound format. The helter-skelter binding, the miniscule print and the blanks make reading it a chore yet it's worth having because it includes cards missed by Deadman. Don't lose your soul in its pages which are born of unstill shadows in the darkest reaches of a ghostly cricket pavilion. This grimoire's arcane scrawl is for cricket card addicts only.

Golf cards
A Century of Golf Cards, a Pictorial History of the Game, by Bruce Berdock and Michael Baier. Privately published in Canada, in 1993.

A little dated now, but this was a stunner in 1993! It's still a must-have book for collectors of golf cards. It's become a very rare tome and it's usually very expensive if and when it comes to market.

The Price Guide to Golf Cards, parts I and II, by Philip Smedley and Bruce Berdock, privately published in Canada, in 1994.

The values ascribed are long since outdated but the information and pictures will help any golf card collector. The books are very rare and may prove to be costly.

Tennis cards
Forty Love: Lawn Tennis Cigarette and Trade Cards, a Composite Listing, privately published by Derek Hurst, in 1993.

This is an invaluable guide for collectors of tennis cards. It has become very rare and ever more costly to buy when and if it appears on the market.

North American sports cards
American Tobacco Cards – Price Guide & Checklist, by Robert Forbes and Terence Mitchell, published by Tuff Stuff Books, 1999.

The Standard Catalogue of Baseball Cards, by Bob Lemke, published annually by Krause.

Beckett also publishes a yearly guide to baseball cards.

The Photographic Baseball Cards of Goodwin & Company 1886–1890, by Jay Miller, Joe Gonsowski and Richard Masson, privately published, reissued in 2008.

Soccer cards

An A to Z of Football Collectibles, Priceless Cigarette Cards and Sought-after Soccer Stickers, by Carl Wilkes, published by Pitch Publishing, in 2019.

The market-leading book on soccer cards from 1880 until modern times. If you are serious about vintage football cards, from around the world, this deluxe hardback book of 300 pages has 2000 colour pictures of the rarest cards, their stories and their values. The book was shortlisted for the Best British Sports Book 2020 award.

The Football Who's Who, by The Leader (Frank Johnston), published by Associated Sporting Press, in 1935.

A gold mine of a resource! There are potted biographies for thousands of players and select treatment for football's greats of yesteryear, not just for Billy Meredith and Steve Bloomer! The same publisher's earlier book, *The Football Encyclopædia*, from 1934 is worth finding. Together, the pair of books will give any rookie cards researcher much scarce information on footballers of yore.

England's Oldest Football Clubs, 1815–1889, privately published by Martin Westby in 2020.

This is a notable book on the history of England's oldest soccer clubs. It helps make sense of the earliest sports cards.

Half-Time, by David Thompson. Published in Great Britain by Murray's, 1987.

In its day this was the best book on soccer cigarette cards. Though it's now dated it's still useful. Alas, it does not include post-war cards, like Phillips Sports packet issues, nor cigar cards of the 1960s and 1970s, and neither are foreign-issue cards included but the book does list many of the better known cigarette cards and it includes checklists too, though many lists are far from complete. Alas, the book lists absolutely no non-tobacco trade cards or trading cards, so it's Capstan all the way; for Navy Cut lovers only. Old fashioned, hard on the eyes, frustrating and incomplete but a respected pioneer from times of yore.

The First Black Footballer, Arthur Wharton 1865 to 1930, written by Phil Vasili. Published by Frank Cass, in 1998.

Every soccer card collector needs to read this book. It's about the first soccer star ever to be celebrated on a sports card, Arthur Wharton. He was the fastest and the most creative player of his day. He occasionally played outfield, from where he often scored goals, but he was best known for his goalkeeping with the Old Invincibles, the undefeated Preston North End team; and for his spells with Darlington CFC and Rotherham Town. Wharton was considered for England. His African background may have been the factor which kept him out of the national squad. Between the 1900s and the 1930s he was completely written out of soccer history. This was certainly because of his colour. In recent decades he's been reinstated as one of the greats, a legend of the game. This was not done in a nod to the fashionably woke rewriting of history. Wharton was the first soccer star on a card; the very first in the world! That happened for a reason. It's because he was already a legend, way back then, in 1886 when they put him there.

A book that's tangential to cards but which helps explain why some cards are worth *more* than cash
Four Horsemen, The Survival Manual, Understand How The World Really Works, by Mark Braund & Ross Ashcroft, published by Motherlode, in 2012.

How was it possible that sports cards came to be more valuable than cash, outperforming gold and the stock market? It's a must-read book on how things really work, and where it is all going. You'll have a better idea about the why and wherewithal after reading it. You'll be getting out of fiat folding money and deeper into cards.

A brief note on the price guides published in Great Britain, last century.

In the twentieth century certain books proclaimed themselves to be price guides for cards. Some of those tomes were cleverly contrived cons which served as buying-in price guides for the publishers themselves. At least, that's what wise twentieth century collectors knew them as. The books were nothing more than a publisher's means of acquiring rare cards for relatively little money. Publishers would quote prices printed in their own guides as a reason for paying out very little to sellers of rare cards. The same publisher would then sell the newly acquired cards in private auctions, often for a lot of money. These days some of the books are defunct – not before time – while others struggle to survive under new ownership. What future they have is anyone's guess. With internet channels and web pages devoted to cards such old fashioned resources seem to be, like their prices, obsolete.

Selling cards? Buying? Information?
This writer will buy single cards and collections. His Facebook, Twitter and other social media channels have thousands of pictures, stories and articles on rare cards, going back 10 years:

Facebook soccer cards news channel:
www.facebook.com/rarecards

Twitter soccer cards news channel:
www.twitter.com/rarecards_fcc

Much information is also shown on the website:
www.footballsoccercards.com

Contact?
Email: **cards@rarecards.co.uk**
Write to: **Carl Wilkes, BM:** *A to Z Football Cards Book***, London WC1N 3XX**.

Remember, this writer collects so he is able to pay higher prices than card flippers and resellers will offer.

AFTERWORD

Afterword

The first association footballer on a card, 1886

It is fair to say prices are on the rise for all rare sports cards yet it is still possible to afford to buy a card which has a global *population* of only one or two exemplars.

Seeing prices paid, lately, such as the $2 million paid for a 2003 Upper Deck 1-of-23 *limited edition* card, it may surprise readers to know that even now, in the 2020s, collectors can still acquire one of the rarest sports cards in the world for less than $200! This needs emphasising: readers may still be able to buy a card with a worldwide count of just one or two, for little more than £100 sterling!

So which cards exist in numbers of only one, two or three exemplars globally but cost as little as £100, or less than $200? Key names to remember are Baines, Sharpe and Richardson. Also, there are cards by Brigg, William Toole, Williamson of Ashton and Ormerod Brothers. Cards made by these Victorian-era firms, and especially by John Baines Litho in Manningham, later known as both J. Baines and J. Baines Ltd, are way undervalued and can be had, at the time of writing, for as little as £100. This situation won't last long and prices will rise.

The way things are going such cards will, one day soon, become unaffordable to most buyers. As more collectors discover them prices for the few which remain available will rise. The earliest Baines cards illustrate world-famous cricketers, nationally known rugby-football players and they show the first soccer stars, like the legendary Arthur Wharton, a world-record athlete, an infamous goalkeeper and an outfield goal scoring footballer, to boot. Wharton was not only the first professional black soccer player in the world; he was the very first soccer star to appear on a sports card! His earliest card dates from 1886, on which he is shown with the colours and name of Darlington CFC. Upon the same card his 1885-set world record run, 100 yards in 10 seconds, is also duly celebrated.

The handful of well-known and very costly sports cards which have recently sold for prices in the millions, such as those by Piedmont Cigarettes, Topps and Upper Deck, are nowhere near as rare as cards by Baines, Sharpe and Richardson. For example, there are over 50 known Honus Wagner Piedmont Cigarette cards in circulation – that's the infamous $3 million baseball cigarette card from 1910. Further, there are 1,000 exemplars known of the 1952 gum card of Mickey Mantle which sold for $3 million, in 2018. Thus, the costliest cards are not necessarily the rarest cards. In contrast, the extant examples of Baines cards in circulation, most of which exist in quantities of less than a handful each, can still be yours for as little as £100 per card.

Baseball, though it does not enjoy the largest of worldwide collector markets, enjoys a very highly developed collecting scene. It remains some decades ahead of soccer cards collecting due to American guide books having been published since the end of the 1980s, 30 years earlier than the first books on soccer cards. When compared to soccer, baseball has a relatively small fan base. Soccer has an absolutely huge global reach, yet its card-collecting market has only been coming of age since 2010. It has a way to go to match the sophistication of the baseball cards market but it will catch up, one day – sooner rather than later. Soccer cards will certainly spike in value and collectability in the run up to the North American World Cup, in 2026.

In October 2020, $292,200 was paid for a soccer card of Pelé. An auction hammer price of $240,000 accrued sales commission and sales taxes of almost $50,000 so the seller paid a gross total of almost $300,000 for his Pelé card, which dates from 1958. When such halo-effect soccer cards arrive at the $million mark imagine the satisfaction you will feel for having bought one or two Baines *Gold Medal Football Cards* or Sharpe's *Play Up Football Cards*, before 2026 when they

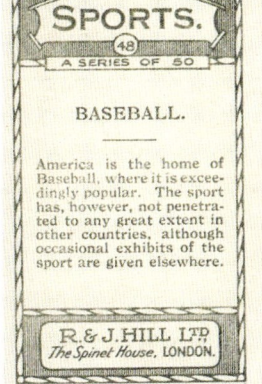

Tris Speaker on a rare British tobacco card by Hill, 1934

were still affordable. Remember, soccer and rugger are of the same root. The earliest known football cards, which date from 1879 to 1885, were rugby-football cards. The first soccer card is the Arthur Wharton Darlington CFC card from 1886.

Cards collectors are, in a way, quietly talented investors in alternative assets. They prefer value-store assets of beauty. Such assets have been more stable than cash for some decades. The leading collectors are sure that cards are likely to further increase in value. *Fiat* currencies – money that is simply printed out of the air, for free by central bankers, and pegged to nothing of real value – such as pounds sterling, dollars and euros, tend to perform in the opposite way to rare collectibles: they all devalue. Due to endless *fiat* money printing, which they euphemistically term quantitative easing, as if it's something grand and helpful, cash is becoming worth less and less on a daily basis. Unlike cash, rare, vintage and antique cards are not reprinted. Cards are value-store assets just as a .999-silver coin is, and just like a gold ring is. If you know what you are doing cards can be incredible investments (but be wary of modern cards and stickers). In three decades this writer has never known a collector of rare, vintage and antique cards to sell at a loss. In the last decades cards have only acquired more worth. When collections of rare cards do come to market it is usually though bereavements and rarely out of a wish to liquidate cards to get back into cash.

Value is in the expression of the possessor. Cards lovers love cards just as vintage and classic car drivers love old cars; just like model die-cast vehicle collectors love miniature vehicles. Hobbies and interests, especially those that demand a certain application of mind, patience and wit, may be as good as medicines. People who pursue interests like collecting often live longer and healthier lives than those without hobbies. Younger people who start collections early often end up with assets of enormous worth by the time they are ready to retire. Collecting makes most collectors feel good. In a stress-inducing world healthy states of mind are priceless. A collection of rare cards is a little gallery of magical images which glows with value, just as it reflects history. It's also good for you.

This book has illustrated and detailed sports cards which are, for the most part, findable and affordable. Two decades ago, rare soccer cards were where most of the general sports cards in this book are today: available and inexpensive. Most of the cards featured in this book are valued at around about where soccer cards were in the years after the millennium, yet the rarity for general sports cards is similar to soccer cards, so prices for sports cards in general may follow where soccer cards have gone. All it takes is a few new collectors in each sport and the handful of available cards will disappear from the market. When that happens, cards become scarce and values rise.

Rare cards are up!

A visionary Baines design, made circa 1890